THE CONCISE GUIDE TO
WINE
AND
BLIND TASTING

*O thou invisible spirit of wine, if
thou hast no name to be known by,
let us call thee devil!*

—Shakespeare: Othello: Act 2, Sc. iii

THE CONCISE GUIDE TO
WINE
AND
BLIND
TASTING

Neel Burton
James Flewellen

Acheron Press

Flectere si nequeo superos
Acheronta movebo

© Acheron Press 2014

Published by Acheron Press

A CIP catalogue record for this book is available from the British Library.

ISBN 978 0 9560353 9 4

Typeset by Phoenix Photosetting, Chatham, Kent, United Kingdom

Printed and bound by SRP Limited, Exeter, Devon, United Kingdom

About the authors

Neel Burton is a psychiatrist, philosopher, writer, and wine-lover who lives and teaches in Oxford.

James Flewellen is a biophysicist at Oxford University. While still a student, he led the university's blind tasting team to victory in several competitions, most notably the Sciences Po International Tasting (SPIT) and the Varsity Match against Cambridge University. Reporting on the 58th Varsity Match in the Financial Times, Master of Wine Jancis Robinson described him as 'the most impressive taster of the lot'.

Neel and James are the founders of the Oxford Wine Academy, which runs bespoke courses and events on the appreciation of fine wine.

Acknowledgments

The authors would like to single out Dr Hanneke Wilson, the Oxford University blind tasting coach, for all her help throughout the years, including with this manuscript. *Terminat hora diem; terminat auctor opus.*

Preface

*Chi più conosce
più ama,
più amando
più gusta.**
—Santa Caterina da Siena

When you uncork a bottle of mature fine wine, what you are drinking is the product of a particular culture and tradition, a particular soil, a particular climate, the weather in that year, and the love and labour of people who may since have died.

The wine is still changing, still evolving, so much so that no two bottles can ever be quite the same. By now, the stuff has become incredibly complex, almost ethereal. Without seeking to blaspheme, it has become something like the smell and taste of God.

Do you drink it alone? Never. The better a bottle, the more you want to share it with others ... and that is the other incredible thing about wine, that it brings people together, makes them share with one another, laugh with one another, fall in love with one another and with the world around them.

Welcome to our book, welcome to our passion!

Neel Burton
James Flewellen

*Who knows more, loves more, and, loving more, tastes/enjoys more.

Contents

Contents

PART I

Chapter 1

The Beginnings of Wine

Early foragers and farmers made wine from wild grapes or other fruits. According to archaeological evidence, by 6000BC grape wine was being made in the Caucasus, and by 3200BC domesticated grapes had become abundant in the entire Near East. In Mesopotamia, wine was imported from the cooler northern regions, and so came to be known as 'liquor of the mountains'. In Egypt as in Mesopotamia, wine was for nobles and priests, and mostly reserved for religious or medicinal purposes. The Egyptians fermented grape juice in amphorae that they covered with cloth or leather lids and then sealed up with mud from the Nile. By biblical times, wine had acquired some less dignified uses. According to the Old Testament, Noah planted a vineyard, and 'drank of the wine, and was drunken; and he was uncovered within his tent' (Genesis 9:21). Skip to the New Testament and here is Jesus employed as a wine consultant: 'And no man putteth new wine into old wineskins: else the wine bursts the skins, and the wine is lost as well as the skins: but new wine must be put into new skins' (Mark 2:22).

Many of the grape varieties planted in Greece are similar or identical to those planted there in ancient times. Wine played a central role in Ancient Greek culture, and the vine—which, as in the Near East, had been domesticated by the Early Bronze Age—was widely cultivated. The Minoans, who flourished on the island of Crete from c.2700 to c.1450BC, imported and exported different wines, which they used not only for recreational but also for religious and ritual purposes. Wine played a similarly important role for the later

Mycenaeans, who flourished on mainland Greece from c.1600 to 1100BC. In fact, wine was so important to the Greeks as to be personified by a major deity, Dionysus or Bacchus, and honoured with a number of annual festivals. One such festival was the Anthesteria, which, held in February each year, celebrated the opening of wine jars to test the new wine. Active in the 8th century BC, the poet Homer often sang of wine, famously alluding to the Aegean as the 'wine dark sea'. In the *Odyssey*, he says that 'wine can of their wits the wise beguile/ Make the sage frolic, and the serious smile'. In the *Works and Days*, the poet Hesiod, who lived in the 7th or 8th century BC, speaks of pruning and even of drying the grapes prior to fermentation. The Greeks plainly understood that no two wines are the same, and held the wines of Thassos, Lesbos, Chios, and Mende in especially high regard; Theophrastus, a contemporary and close friend of Aristotle, even demonstrated some clear notions of terroir.

In Ancient Greece, vines were supported on forked props or trained up trees. In his *Natural History*, the 1st century naturalist Pliny the Elder describes the Ancient Greek practice of using partly dehydrated gypsum prior to fermentation, and some type of lime after fermentation, to remove acidity—but this was no doubt a relatively recent or infrequent practice. The wine was neither racked nor fined, and it was not uncommon for the drinker to pass it through a sieve or strainer. Aromatic herbs, spice, honey, or a small measure of seawater were often added to improve and preserve the wine, which could also be concentrated by boiling. Finished wine was stored in amphorae lined with resin or pitch, both substances that imparted some additional and characteristic flavour. Generally speaking, the wine was sweeter than it is today, reflecting not only prevalent tastes, but also the ripeness of the grapes, the use of natural yeasts in fermentation, and the lack of temperature control during fermentation (see Chapter 3). However, wine did come in a wide variety of styles, some of which were markedly dry and austere. To drink undiluted wine was considered a bad and barbarian practice—almost as bad as drinking beer like those Babylonian or Egyptian peasants. Wine was diluted with two or three parts of water to produce a beverage with an alcoholic strength of around 3-5%. The comedian Hermippus, who flourished in the golden age of Athens, described the best aged wines as having a nose of violets, roses, and hyacinths.

Together with the sea-faring Phoenicians, the Ancient Greeks disseminated the vine throughout the Mediterranean, and even named southern Italy *Oenotria* or 'Land of [Staked] Vines'. If wine was important to the Greeks, it was even more so to the Romans, who considered it a daily necessity and democratized its drinking. They established a great number of Western Europe's major wine producing regions, not only to provide steady supplies for their soldiers and colonists, but also to trade with native tribes and convert them to the Roman cause. In particular, the trade of Hispanic wines surpassed that even of Italian wines, with Hispanic amphorae having been unearthed as far as Britain and the *limes Germanicus* (German frontier). In his *Geographica* (7BC), Strabo states that the vineyards of Hispania Beatica, which roughly corresponds to modern Andalucia, were famous for their great beauty. The area of Pompeii produced a great deal of wine, much of it destined for the city of Rome, and the eruption of Mount Vesuvius in 79AD led to a dramatic penury. The people of Rome panicked, uprooting food crops to plant vineyards. This in turn led to a wine glut and food shortage, which in 92AD compelled the emperor Domitian to issue an edict banning the planting of vineyards in Rome.

The Romans left behind a number of agricultural treatises that provide a wealth of information on Roman viticulture and winemaking. In particular, Cato the Elder's *De Agri Cultura* (c.160BC) served as the Roman textbook of winemaking for several centuries. In *De Re Rustica*, Columella surveyed the main grape varieties, which he divided into three main groups: noble varieties for great Italian wines, high yielding varieties that can nonetheless produce age-worthy wines, and prolific varieties for ordinary table wine. Pliny, who also surveyed the main grape varieties, claimed that 'classic wines can only be produced from vines grown on trees', and it is true that the greatest wines of Campania, such as Caecuban or Falernian, nearly all came from vines trained on trees—often elms or poplars. Both Caecuban and Falernian were sweet white wines, although there also existed a dry style of Falernian. Undiluted Falernian contained a high degree of alcohol; so high that a candle flame could set it alight. It was deemed best to drink Falernian at about 15-20 years, and another classed growth called Surrentine at 25 years or more. The Opimian vintage of 121BC, named after the consul in that year, Lucius Opimius, acquired legendary fame, with some examples still being drunk more than a hundred years later.

The best wines were made from the highly prized free-run juice obtained from the initial treading of the grapes. At the other end of the spectrum were *posca*, a mixture of water and sour wine that had not yet turned to vinegar, and *lora*, a thin drink or *piquette* produced from a third pressing of grape skins. Following the Greek invention of the screw, screw presses became common on Roman villas. Grape juice was fermented in large clay vessels called *dolia*, which were often partially sunk into the ground. The wine was then racked into amphorae for storing and shipping. Barrels invented by the Gauls and, later still, glass bottles invented by the Syrians, vied as alternatives to amphorae. As in Ancient Greece, additives were common: chalk or marble to neutralize excess acid; and boiled must, herbs, spice, honey, resin, or seawater to improve and preserve thin offerings. Maderization was common and sought after; even so, rooms destined for wine storage were sometimes built so as to face north and away from the sun. Following the decline and fall of the Western Roman Empire, the Church perpetuated the knowledge of viticulture and winemaking, first and foremost to furnish the blood of Christ for the celebration of Mass.

NB: Histories of the various wine regions are subsumed under their chapters.

Chapter 2

Principles of Viticulture

L ong gone is the era in which wine was flavoured with herbs and spices, or diluted with fresh or salt water. For our purposes, wine is made from grapes and from grapes only: though wine may be described in terms of fruits, flowers, and so on, for the most part these aroma and flavour compounds derive from the grapes themselves. Other aromas and flavours arise from processes in winemaking and maturation, including maturation vessels and especially oak barrels.

Vines

Most wines are made from the fruit of the Eurasian grape vine *Vitis vinifera*. Over thousands of years, man domesticated the dioecious forest creeper *V. vinifera silvestris* into the hermaphroditic crop-bearing *V. vinifera sativa*, the source of almost all wine. Its success stems from a number of factors including adaptability, ability and readiness to self-propagate, and, of course, a heavy crop of flavoursome fruit with high levels of sugar that can readily be fermented into alcohol. Today, there are over one thousand identifiable varieties of *V. vinifera* cultivated to make wine on a commercial scale. Some of these varieties are ancient, others much more recent—often the products of modern cultivation and crossing techniques, although not (yet) of genetic modification. A single variety can have several clones, which, though closely related to one another, are genetically distinct, each with different properties such as deeper colour, higher yield, earlier ripening, better disease resistance, or a more complex flavour profile. Whether a plant is a clone or a separate variety can be a matter of heated debate, especially among us blind tasters!

Other species of *Vitis* include *V. labrusca*, *V. berlandieri*, *V. riparia*, and *V. rupestris*, which are native to North America, and *V. amurensis*, native to the Far East. Early settlers to North America cultivated *V. labrusca*, and *labrusca* varieties such as Concord are still planted on the Eastern Seaboard of the United States. Hybrid crosses of *vinifera* and non-*vinifera* vines such as Seyval Blanc, Vidal Blanc, and De Chaunac are more commonly found in North America than in Europe, not least because the European Union (EU) forbids their use in quality wine. By far the most important contribution of non-*vinifera* vines to modern viticulture has been to provide phylloxera- and nematode-resistant rootstocks on which to graft *vinifera* scions (see later).

Grapes

You can make bad wine from good grapes, but you can't make good wine from bad grapes. A balanced wine can only be made from balanced grapes. As they ripen, grapes concentrate sugars that can be partly or wholly fermented into alcohol. The amount of sugar in the grapes, or 'sugar ripeness', corresponds to the potential alcohol of the wine. 'Phenolic ripeness' on the other hand refers to the maturity of flavour in the grapes, as determined by examining and sampling the grapes. With increasing phenolic ripeness, the grape skin, pips, and stems change colour, the grape skin and pulp texture become softer, and the tannins in the grape skin and pips become less bitter. Although sugar ripeness and phenolic ripeness are related, they do not necessarily occur at the same rate. In overly hot conditions, grapes can reach sugar ripeness before phenolic ripeness. The grower is then caught between a rock and a hard place: either pick early to make a wine with astringent tannins and a green streak; or wait to make a full-bodied, alcoholic wine that is flat and flabby and lacking in acidity. Conversely, in overly cool conditions, grapes can struggle to accumulate sugars, and turn into wines that are unpleasantly thin and acidic.

Grape ripening is related to sunlight and heat, which can vary markedly from one region to another—even from one vineyard to the next. One of the challenges for the grower is to arrive at ripe-tasting fruit with optimal levels of sugars and acids. This sometimes delicate balancing act requires an intimate understanding of the vine's dynamic interaction with elements of climate, topography, geology, pedology (soil science), hydrology, botany, and zoology, for example, the life cycles of local plants and insects and the feeding patterns of birds, bats, and boars, among many others. These all are aspects of terroir, a French concept that denotes the entire ecosystem of a vine and vineyard. At its broadest, terroir also encompasses local customs and traditions honed over centuries, including methods of planting, training, harvesting, and even winemaking and ageing.

Climate and geography

A vine with an ample supply of water and nutrients tends to expend its energy on foliage rather than fruit. For the reverse to be true, it must come under sufficient stress that it feels the need to propagate its genetic material. The quality of fruit produced depends to a large extent on the climate, which in turn depends on a number of geographical factors such as latitude, altitude, proximity to the sea or ocean, and exposure to prevailing winds.

Whereas 'weather' refers to short-term or exceptional events such as rains, frosts, hailstorms, flooding, and drought, 'climate' refers to long-term underlying patterns measured in terms of sunshine hours, mean temperature, diurnal temperature range, rainfall, humidity, and such like. Broadly speaking, macroclimate describes the climate of a particular region, mesoclimate the climate of a particular sub-region or vineyard site, and microclimate the specific conditions in a small part of the vineyard or even within the canopy of an individual vine. Grapes require a certain amount of warmth and sunshine to arrive at sugar and phenolic ripeness. However, just as too much heat can impede ripeness, so too much sunshine can burn the grapes. The best results are obtained in temperate climates with a growing season that extends over 180+ consecutive frost-free days with mean temperatures of 16-21°C

(61-70°F) and more than 1,250 sunshine hours. Outside the growing season, vines are able to tolerate freezing conditions, but sustained double-digit negative temperatures can lead to damage and even death. The judicious exploitation of mesoclimates, varieties, rootstocks, canopy management techniques, trellising methods, irrigation, and harvest times and methods can mitigate adverse or borderline macroclimatic conditions.

Broadly speaking, the world's most successful wine regions lie within latitudes 30-50° North and South. Within these diverse temperate zones, some grape varieties such as Riesling, Pinot Noir, and Sauvignon Blanc do best in cooler, more marginal climates. Others, such as Grenache, Nero d'Avola, and Touriga Nacional need hotter conditions. Cabernet Sauvignon insists on a moderate but still sunny climate, whereas Chardonnay is less demanding, yielding lean and mineral wines in cool Chablis but blousy and buttery wines in hot parts of South Australia. Generally speaking, white grape varieties need less heat than black grape varieties, and so predominate in the coolest, most marginal regions. Even so, they may be softened or made more palatable by double fermentation, arrested fermentation (to retain residual sugar), the addition of sugar, or ageing on the lees. The geographical distribution of a grape variety is not determined solely by climate, but also by cultural, economic, and even legal factors: although Airén is the most planted of all white grape varieties, it is almost entirely confined to the Spanish region of La Mancha.

Regions that are in the interior of a large landmass or sheltered from the sea by mountains (or both as, for example, Alsace) are described as continental, with cold winters and hot, relatively dry summers. In contrast, coastal regions such as Bordeaux with direct exposure to the sea are described as maritime, with warmer winters and milder, wetter summers. Some regions such as Châteauneuf-du-Pape and Chianti are best described as mediterranean, with mild winters and very warm and dry summers. A similar climate can also be found in parts of California, Western and South Australia, central coastal Chile, and the Western Cape in South Africa.

Altitude can make it possible to produce quality wine in hotter regions such as the Duero/Douro Valley in Iberia, Mount Etna in Sicily, and Mount Canabolas in Orange New South Wales. As a general rule, for every 100m (328ft) of ascent, the mean temperature drops by 0.5-0.6°C (0.9-1.1°F). Higher altitudes are also associated with cooler nights and a greater diurnal temperature range, which enables grapes to ripen and concentrate flavour while preserving natural acidity.

In more marginal regions such as the Côte de Nuits and Mosel, vines are often planted on slopes. At higher latitudes, slopes can receive much more incident sunlight than plains, especially during the critical autumn ripening period. Slopes also benefit from thinner topsoil, better drainage, and increased air circulation from convection currents. In the northern hemisphere, many vineyards are planted on south-facing slopes to capture as much sunlight as possible, and vice versa in the southern hemisphere. In hot climates, vineyards may be planted on north-facing slopes to take advantage of the shadier and cooler conditions. In general, slopes that face south-southeast or southeast are most favoured as they receive the first sun and warm up and dry out more quickly. In many regions, they are also sheltered from the prevailing winds. Steep slopes can have some disadvantages: they are prone to erosion and the vines can be expensive and dangerous to access.

Water bodies such as oceans, rivers, and lakes also exert an important influence on climate. For example, the River Loire moderates temperatures, making viticulture possible at such high latitudes. Rivers also reflect sunlight, increase air circulation, and provide a source of water and a channel for transport. Sea mists that form off the Californian coast penetrate far inland into regions such as Mendocino Valley, exercising an important cooling influence; and mists from the River Ciron in Sauternes or Lake Neusiedl in Austria's Burgenland create ideal conditions for the development of noble rot (see later).

Even trees and other plants have a role to play. The *Forêt des Landes* shelters Bordeaux from strong, salt-bearing winds. On a much smaller scale, trees and hedges protect a vineyard from gales and storms and stabilize steeper slopes. Ground cover crops protect the soil from erosion and runoff, improve soil structure and fertility, provide a habitat for beneficial predators, and promote biological diversity. A monoculture of vines on a flat and featureless expanse of land treated with herbicides may be optimal for machine harvesting, but not for the quality of the grapes or the long-term health of the soil and environment. More and more, growers are learning to work with nature rather than against it.

Soils

Soils are complex, layered systems, with the visible topsoil of critical importance only to very young vines. As a vine ages and develops, its roots bury deep into the subsoil in search of water and nutrients. A vine must come under some stress to yield high quality fruit, and most vineyards are planted on thinner, poorer soils that not only stress the vine but also promote deep rooting into the mineral-rich subsoil. The best vineyard sites are seldom suited to other forms of exploitation, which in regions such as Burgundy, the Rhône, and the Duero has ensured their preservation through the ages.

Soils heavy in clay (particles up to 2µm in diameter) behave like a sponge, expanding and contracting in function of water content. They are compact and hard to penetrate, and in a dry spell can crack and damage the roots of the vine. A clay-based soil is only suitable for viticulture if it contains substantial proportions of larger particles such as silt (2µm-0.05mm) and sand (0.05mm–2mm), which lend it a lighter, loamier texture. Gravel (>2mm) is the lightest and best draining of all soil types with the added advantage of reflecting and retaining the sun's heat. Some varieties do best on gravelly soils, whereas others prefer clay-based soils. Thus, in Bordeaux, the gravelly Left Bank is heavily planted with Cabernet Sauvignon and the clayey Right Bank with Merlot. Sedimentary soils such as limestone and chalk that developed from fossilized seashells have been favoured for centuries: they are free-draining but, at the same time, retain moisture; they also facilitate deep rooting and preserve the acidity of the grapes. Such calcareous soils underlie the success of such diverse regions as Burgundy, Champagne, the Loire, Saint-Emilion, Châteauneuf-du-Pape, the Piedmont, and Jerez.

Other important soil types that crop up throughout this book are marl, a friable deposit composed of clay and lime (limestone can be considered as a purer, lithified form of marl); alluvium, a river deposit composed of clay, silt, sand, and gravel; granite, a hard and coarse-grained igneous rock composed of feldspars, quartz, and other minerals; tufa, a porous rock composed of silica and calcium carbonate and precipitated from a source of water such as a spring or lake; and schist, a coarse-grained metamorphic rock with a foliated, often flaky structure composed of mica and other minerals. Schist, slate and gneiss are foliated metamorphic rocks that originate from shale, which itself originates from the consolidation of clay. Whereas schist is a medium-grade metamorphic rock, slate is low-grade and gneiss high-grade.

Pests and diseases

The most devastating of all vineyard pests is the phylloxera louse (*Daktulosphaira vitifoliae*), native to North America. American vines are resistant to the louse, but not so *V. vinifera*. The louse disembarked in France in the early 1860s and proceeded to decimate the vineyards of Europe. The life cycle of the louse is complex: in a nutshell, the damage is inflicted by the crawling form of the insect, which disrupts the root system of the vine and exposes it to secondary infection. The discovery that resistance is conferred by grafting *vinifera* vines onto American rootstocks led to replanting on an unprecedented scale. Today, phylloxera continues to pose a near universal threat, and almost all *vinifera* vines are grafted onto American rootstocks. Geographical isolation and strict quarantine measures have so far preserved South Australia and much of Chile and Argentina from the pest, but it can only be a matter of time before it rears it ugly head.

Most other vineyard pests are insects such as beetles, flies, mites, caterpillars, moths, and locusts. Some of these pests can be controlled with sulphur or chemical pesticides, although 'integrated pest management' (IPM or *lutte raisonée*) is often a more effective, less damaging, and/or more acceptable alternative. IPM involves using chemicals in only small amounts and only as a last resort after having exhausted non-chemical interventions. Such interventions may include selecting disease-resistant varieties and rootstocks, and introducing or encouraging natural predators. Larger animals such as birds, boar, rabbits, kangaroos, monkeys, baboons, and snakes can destroy crops, damage vines, or pose a hazard to vineyard workers.

Prior to the phylloxera epidemic, the vineyards of Europe had been battling with powdery mildew or oidium (*Uncinula necator*), a fungal infection imported from America. Unlike most fungi, oidium prefers dry conditions. The first symptoms of infection are whitish powdery patches on the undersurfaces of basal leaves, but canes, flowers, and fruit can also be affected. Diseased berries fail to thrive and may split open. The original solution of spraying or dusting sulphur onto the vines is still practised, assisted by canopy management techniques that increase air and light penetration. Vines are also susceptible to a number of other fungal diseases such as downy mildew and grey rot, which, like noble rot (see later), is caused by *Botrytis cinerea*. Many of these diseases can be prevented by canopy management techniques and copper-containing sprays such as Bordeaux mixture, although harsher treatments may sometimes be required. Some fungal diseases, notably oak-root fungus, attack the roots of the vine and are difficult to detect let alone treat. Eutypa dieback is a fungal infection of the trunk and branches of the vine that may be introduced through grafts and transmitted on infected shears at the time of pruning. The damage is often confined to one arm of the vine, whence the byname 'dead arm'. Although there is no available treatment, other parts of the plant remain largely unaffected. 'Dead Arm Shiraz' is a premium wine made by d'Arenberg from old Eutypa-infected vines in McLaren Vale. Historically, rose bushes planted on the edge of vineyards alerted growers to fungal diseases such as powdery mildew and downy mildew, with the rose bushes developing signs of disease ahead of the vines.

Prevention is the most effective, and often the only, cure for bacterial and viral infections. This involves disinfecting the soil before planting, observing the strictest standards of hygiene in operations such as grafting and pruning, and, if possible, controlling vectors of disease. For example, Fanleaf virus is transmitted by nematodes that inhabit the vine's root system, and can be controlled by grafting vines onto nematode-resistant American rootstocks.

Life cycle of the vine

Vines are generally propagated through cuttings, which preserve the genetic makeup of a particular grape variety or clone. This can be achieved either by taking and planting cuttings or, less commonly, by burying a branch of an existing plant, so-called layering, which is still practised in some phylloxera-free vineyards. Layering preserves the identity and genetic diversity of a vineyard, but another and better method is 'massal selection', which involves taking cuttings from the most outstanding vines in the vineyard or nearby vineyards. In most places, *vinifera* cuttings must be taken to a nursery and grafted onto American rootstocks to protect them from phylloxera. Grafting onto American rootstocks can also protect against other pests and diseases and provide a root system that is better suited to the climate and soil type. Young vines are typically planted in rows so as to facilitate vineyard operations, but can also be planted pell-mell or *en foule*. Closely spaced vines compete with one another for nutrients and water, which can help to stress the vine into producing higher quality fruit. Old vines generally make better wine, if only because they are less vigorous and more restricted in yield. This, however, should not be overstated: the great frost of February 1956 required large scale replanting in Saint-Emilion and Pomerol in Bordeaux, but young vines did not prevent the 1961 vintage from achieving cult status. In fact, very young vines (within three to five years of the first harvest) are also associated with restricted vigour and yields, and thus produce very good grapes.

Training

After planting, vines need about three years to establish themselves and start bearing quality fruit. In these early years, they are especially vulnerable to harsh sunlight, droughts, frosts, insects, and so on. Being natural creepers, they require some form of support on which to develop and fruit. Trellises range from a single stake in the ground to elaborate overhead pergola systems. A simple structure, while cheap, may render vineyard operations more difficult and expensive. The choice of trellis is also contingent on other factors such as the chosen variety, the vigour of the vine, the aspect of the vineyard, and the potential for hazards such as storms and frosts. A vine is often trained along one or more horizontal wires so as to optimize the microclimate and facilitate vineyard operations. Some more common training systems are the Guyot system in which one or two canes are trained along a main wire, and the vertical shoot positioning system (VSP) which is similar to the Guyot system but with additional wires above the cordon (or fruiting wire) on which to support the foliage. The Guyot system dates back to the 19th century, when most vines were trained in a bush (gobelet) without supporting wires. This ancestral system is still favoured in some regions with dry climates, most notably Châteauneuf-du-Pape.

Pruning

Traditionally, pruning to remove old wood kicked off on 22 January, the Feast of Saint Vincent of Saragossa, patron saint of winemakers. Vines that are spur-trained are cane-pruned, and vines that are cane-trained are spur-pruned. With cane-pruned, spur-trained systems such as gobelet and Cordon de Royat, only the individual canes are pruned, leaving the main branch or cordon intact. With spur-pruned, cane-trained systems such as Guyot, there is no permanent cordon. The vine is pruned down to the spur, leaving just one or more short canes each with one or more fruiting buds. In short, with spur-pruning the fruiting buds are borne on spurs; with cane-pruning they are borne on canes. Vines that are spur-pruned usually have a thin, smooth main branch, whereas vines that are cane-pruned usually have a thick and gnarled cordon branch. Note that VSP can be either cane-pruned or spur-pruned.

On the road to harvest

The vine jumps to life in mid-spring: buds appear and tiny leaves and embryonic tendrils emerge from the buds. The vine is susceptible to spring frosts, and a single episode can destroy the year's entire harvest. Pruning late delays bud burst and can help to protect against spring frosts, as can sprinklers, smoke-belching smudge pots, wind machines, and helicopters, among others. The shoots grow rapidly over the coming months and need to be positioned according to the trellising system and pruned back to restrict vegetative growth. As the foliage develops it begins to affect the microclimate surrounding the flowers and grapes, and it may need to be thinned or adjusted to optimize the ripeness and quality of the grapes. Canopy management, a term coined in the 1980s by viticulturalist Richard Smart, can serve to expose the grapes to the sun or shield them from harsh sunlight, restrain vegetative growth, increase air circulation, and protect against vine diseases. Some growers, for example, of Marlborough Sauvignon Blanc, aim for a wine with both ripeness of fruit and a fresh grassy note, in which case they may prune the leaves such as to uncover only one half of the fruit. By early summer, bunches of proto-grapes—caps of fused petals—have developed. Flowering begins when these caps fall off and the tiny stamens are exposed for fertilization. This is another critical juncture in the vine's development: adverse conditions during the flowering period, which lasts maybe a week or a fortnight, can lead to *coulure* and *millerandage*, that is, unfertilized flowers and a correspondingly small crop. Cropping potential is determined not only by the weather conditions of the current vintage, but also by the weather conditions of the previous vintage during which the fruiting buds of the current vintage were forming.

Berries develop over the summer months, accumulating water, sugars, acids, and other flavour compounds. In late summer, the berries change from mid-green to black, red, or pale green. This colour change, called *véraison*, marks the beginning of the ripening process during which sugars accumulate more rapidly, the harsh acids soften, and the tannins, anthocyanins, and other phenolic flavour compounds develop and mature. Green harvesting around *véraison* to remove immature bunches of grapes can improve the rest of the crop, especially in regions with vigorous vines or high yields. In the autumn, the grapes reach optimum sugar and phenolic ripeness (ideally at the same time) and are ready for harvesting. The grapes are harvested by hand or by machine and whisked away to the winery where the fermentation process can begin. Meanwhile, the vine stores complex carbohydrates in its canes, trunk, and roots to sustain it over the winter. The leaves are shed, shoots lignify, and the plant falls into dormancy.

For sweet wines the grapes need to be left on the vine for a longer period, with one or several pickings required. Luscious botrytized wines are made from late harvest grapes infected by *Botrytis cinerea*. Unless the infection is carefully managed, it can lead to grey rot rather than noble rot. For noble rot to develop, the berries must have ripened to a potential alcohol of at least 7%, at which point the fungus can feed on the berry without damaging or splitting it. The fungus punctures the skin, gradually shriveling the berry and concentrating its sugars and phenolics. Mesoclimates suited to the development of noble rot such as Tokaji, Sauternes, and parts of the Loire feature autumn mists that dissipate in mid-morning to make place for dry and sunny afternoons. In some cases, grapes are left to dry on the vine and then harvested, or else harvested and then dried (*passerillage*). In others, they are left on the vine until partially frozen by a deep winter frost. They are then harvested in the dead of night and pressed to extrude the ice crystals and produce super-concentrated ice wine (Eiswein), which is a specialty of parts of Germany, Austria, and Canada.

Chapter 3

Principles of Winemaking

By and large, harvesting begins once the grapes have reached optimal phenolic and sugar ripeness. If it is not operationally possible to harvest all the grapes at optimal ripeness, then it is a matter of compromising. Grapes that are harvested too early can introduce unripe, 'green' notes into the wine, while grapes that are harvested too late can make for a flabby or jammy wine. Many wines are made from a blend of fruit from multiple vineyards, in which case the grapes may be harvested at the best time (or close to the best time) for each individual site. The grower must also take weather conditions into account: for example, if a storm is imminent, it may be judicious to bring in the grapes even if they are still slightly under-ripe.

In many cases, large harvesters are driven through the vineyards. These machines beat the vines with rubber sticks, shaking off the grapes onto a conveyor belt that transfers them into a holding bin. Harvesters enable the grapes to be harvested quickly, day and night, without the cost or labour associated with hand harvesting. Some modern harvesters can even be controlled remotely through computers and GPS tracking systems. On the other hand, harvesters are expensive, can only operate on flat or gently sloping land, and introduce restrictions on planting and trellising. They can also damage the grapes, colouring the juice and exposing it to oxygen.

Top producers invariably prefer hand harvesting, which is both gentler and more selective. Pickers can be trained to recognize and discard rotten or under-ripe bunches and even to select individual berries that have been affected by noble rot. They can also pick whole bunches, which can be either desirable, as in Champagne, or necessary, as in much of Beaujolais. After harvesting, the grapes must be transported to the winery as fast as possible to minimize oxidative damage, and some large estates operate a number of pressing stations in or near the vineyards. Otherwise, transiting grapes can be protected from oxidation with a dusting of antioxidant powder, typically potassium metabisulfite, or a blanket of carbon dioxide. Once the grapes have been pressed and transformed into juice, it becomes much easier to protect them from oxidation.

Crushing and pressing

Upon arrival at the winery, the grapes are spread onto a sorting table fitted with a conveyor belt and undesirable material is discarded, either by hand or through an automated process. This includes under-ripe and rotten grapes, leaves, twigs, and large insects.

At this stage, a decision must be made as to whether to de-stem the grapes. Stems, though adding to bulk and volume, create drainage channels that increase the efficiency of the pressing process. If the stems are ripe, they can also contribute good tannins and flavour, but, if not, they can introduce bitter tannins and vegetal notes. Stems can also absorb colour and alcohol. The process of de-stemming involves feeding bunches through a rotating drum perforated with grape-sized holes. The bare stems are sometimes collected and added back at a later stage, either to reduce cap compaction or contribute extra tannins and flavour.

Next, the juice must be extracted from the grapes by crushing and/or pressing. Less commonly, the grapes are left intact to ferment. In crushing, the grapes are passed through a pair of rollers and the grape skins are ripped open. The rollers mimic traditional crushing by the human foot, which is still practised in certain regions—most notably the Douro in Portugal. The crusher is carefully calibrated to avoid damaging pips or stems and releasing bitter tannins and vegetal notes into the free-run juice.

The lightest and most delicate white wines are made exclusively from the free-run juice obtained by crushing, which contains none of the colour and tannin of the grape skins, pips, and stems. However, many white wines benefit from at least a small degree of 'skin contact', with the free-run juice left on the skins for a short period of time. Rosés are made in a similar fashion (on the skins of black grapes), especially in the EU, which, with the notable exception of Champagne, forbids the blending of white and red wine. Depth of colour varies according to duration of skin contact, which for rosé is typically 1-3 days. As the juice of almost all grape varieties is clear, red wines depend for their colour (and most of their tannins) on contact with skins, pips, and sometimes also stems, which are said to be 'macerating' in the juice. Collectively, the juice and solid matter are referred to as the must.

For most white wines, the free-run juice is augmented by juice extracted by pressing the grapes. Indeed, some economy-conscious winemakers entirely forgo crushing in favour of pressing alone. Pressing releases juice from the cells on the inner surface of the grape skin, along with aroma, flavour, and polyphenols. A traditional wine press consists of a slatted basket with spaces between the slats and a lid that is screwed down to exert pressure on the grapes. Pressing inevitably involves the release of bitter polyphenols, and the winemaker must strike a balance between volume and quality. Today, most winemakers use more efficient presses such as the Willmes pneumatic press. With the Willmes, grapes are loaded into a horizontal, perforated cylinder with a rubber bladder running through the centre. The rubber bladder is then inflated with air so as to exert gentle pressure on the grapes. For red wines, the grapes are also pressed, but *after* fermentation. During fermentation, the skins macerate in the juice, releasing colour and tannin.

Crushing and pressing must be carried out efficiently, with minimal exposure to air. The addition of sulphur dioxide to the must can protect against oxidation but can also impede fermentation. This can be desirable if the must is to be clarified before fermentation, a process that can take several days. The high polyphenols in red wines offer some protection against oxidation; even so, some sulphur dioxide may be added to help with polyphenol extraction. The use of sulphur dioxide can be minimized by refrigerating the must prior to the onset of fermentation. True anaerobic pressing can be achieved with a tank press, which is essentially a Willmes enclosed in a tank flushed with inert nitrogen.

However, it is possible to take protection from oxidation too far, resulting in a 'reductive' wine that smells unpleasantly rubbery or sulphurous.

Prior to fermentation, the must may be adjusted to suit the winemaker's purposes. Especially in marginal climates, the must might be enriched with sugar ('chaptalized') to increase the potential alcohol of the wine. Cane or beet sugar is commonly used. The must might also be deacidifed by the addition of a carbonate or bicarbonate compound. Conversely, in hot regions, wines may be acidified by the addition of tartaric acid.

Fermentation

In essence, wine results from the fermentation by yeast cells of sugar into ethyl alcohol, or ethanol. The chemical formula for this reaction is:

$$C_6H_{12}O_6 \rightarrow 2C_2H_5OH + 2CO_2$$
Sugar (glucose:fructose = ~50:50) $\rightarrow$ ethanol + carbon dioxide

There are many different species of yeast, and, within each species, many different genetically distinct strains. The yeast most commonly used in winemaking is *Saccharomyces cerevisiae*, which is efficient at fermenting sugars into ethanol and able to tolerate high levels of its ethanol waste product.

The winemaker pumps the must into a fermentation vessel, which can range from an airtight stainless steel tank to an open-air concrete pool to an oak barrel. He can either inoculate the must with a commercially produced yeast culture, or rely on the yeast cells on the grape skins and winery equipment to start a 'natural fermentation'. With natural fermentation, the winemaker is unable to select the best-suited strain of yeast for the wine that he is seeking to create; however, many winemakers claim that natural fermentation, which typically involves several species of yeast, results in more complex flavours and aromas. Various yeast species can start the fermentation but it is inevitably *Saccharomyces cerevisiae* that finishes it, as it is (almost) the only yeast able to metabolise sugar in the presence of high levels of ethanol.

Throughout fermentation, carbon dioxide is being produced and protects the fermenting must from oxidation. This carbon dioxide needs to be let out of the fermentation vessel and, as it can lead to suffocation, the winery as well. Another by-product of fermentation is heat, and the temperature of the must may need to be controlled to keep it within the optimal range for the yeast to function. The temperature of the fermentation also has a bearing on flavour and aroma. For instance, the esters that make a wine (especially a white wine) seem 'fruity' are lost at higher temperatures.

In most cases, the fermentation naturally comes to an end when the yeasts run out of nutrients, typically after one to two weeks. The wine has then been fermented 'to dryness', meaning that there is very little sugar left. In some cases, the initial sugar levels are so high that the alcohol produced kills off the yeasts, resulting in a wine with substantial residual sugar. This is one way of making off-dry and sweet wines. Alternatively, the fermentation can be artificially terminated by filtering out the yeast or killing it off by, for example, pasteurization or the addition of sulphur dioxide or alcohol for fortification. Unless the wine is being fortified, artificial termination of fermentation typically results in a wine with low alcohol and high residual sugar.

While conversion of sugars to ethanol is the predominant reaction, it is only one of potentially thousands of biochemical reactions taking place during fermentation. As a result, wine contains trace amounts of a large number of organic acids, esters, sugars, alcohols, and other molecules. Wine is, in fact, one of the most complex of all beverages: the fruit of a soil, climate, and vintage, digested by a fungus through a process guided by the culture, vision, and skill of an individual man or woman.

White wines

There are almost as many approaches to fermentation as there are winemakers. This section covers the most common techniques for white wines, red wines, and rosés. The most common techniques for sparkling wines and fortified wines are covered in Chapters 11 and 21, respectively.

For white wines, the must is usually fermented in the absence of solid matter. Skin contact for the extraction of polyphenols, if any, occurs prior to the onset of fermentation. For a fresh, fruity, and vibrant style, fermentation is carried out in sealed, inert vats (usually made from stainless steel) with active temperature control to keep the must from becoming too warm. For a more complex wine rich in secondary aromas and flavours, a more traditional vinification is preferred. Large vats and small barrels made of oak have found particular favour, and can be used for both fermentation and maturation. The porous wood allows a small degree of air exchange, which facilitates the development of more complex aroma and flavour compounds. Other alternatives include vats of concrete or clay.

Red wines and rosés

Red wines depend on contact with the grape skins, pips, and sometimes also stems for colour and tannin. Rosés and light red wines may undergo no more than cold maceration before the juice is drained off for fermentation. However, most red wines are fermented together with solid matter for at least part if not all of the process. The carbon dioxide released from fermentation forces the solid matter to the top of the vat, where it is pressed into a hard cap. This cap needs to be broken up at frequent intervals to return the solid material to the fermenting juice. Punching down (*pigeage*) involves pressing the cap to the bottom of the fermentation vessel, traditionally with a flat disc attached to a pole. Punching down is a gentle process that minimizes the release of bitter tannins from the outermost cells of the grape skins. As the process is laborious, it has largely become automated. Pumping over (*remontage*) involves extracting the fermenting juice from the bottom of the vat and pumping it onto the cap, thereby re-submerging it. This can be achieved with anything from manually operated hoses to automated fermentation vats with nozzles that spray the fermenting juice onto the cap. Racking and returning (*délestage*) involves draining the juice in the fermentation vat into a second vessel and then returning it to the original vat by spraying it over the cap. Racking can also be used at other stages of the winemaking process to separate the juice or wine from solid matter that has accumulated or been deposited at the bottom of the vessel. At any point in the fermentation process, the wine may be pumped off the solid material to continue fermenting in a separate vessel. This is another method of making rosé wine. For red wines, it is a means of controlling colour extraction and the quantity and quality of tannins.

Carbonic maceration

In carbonic maceration, bunches of intact grapes are placed in a closed vat and smothered in carbon dioxide. The gas inhibits conventional fermentation; instead, fermentation takes place through an intracellular process driven by natural enzymes within the grape. This intracellular process releases further carbon dioxide that bursts the skins open. After 1-2 weeks, the semi-liquid must reaches an alcoholic strength of ~3%, after which it is usually pressed and transferred to another vat for a conventional yeast fermentation. Wines produced by carbonic maceration are invariably red, the archetypal example being Beaujolais Nouveau. These wines are noted for their vibrant, fruity, and estery aromas. They are approachable, easy drinking wines that can be ready for market within just a few weeks of harvest. Sometimes, only one component of a wine is made by carbonic maceration and blended in for a subtle estery effect. A variant of carbonic maceration is semi-carbonic maceration, in which bunches of intact grapes are placed into a vat. The berries at the bottom of the vat are crushed by the weight above them and undergo yeast fermentation. This releases carbon dioxide onto the berries higher up in the vat, which in turn undergo intracellular fermentation.

Secondary (malolactic) fermentation

After the alcoholic, or primary, fermentation, the wine may remain in the fermentation vessel to undergo a secondary fermentation. The most common type of secondary fermentation is malolactic fermentation (or, more properly, malolactic *conversion*), which involves the conversion of malic acid to lactic acid. Lactic acid bacteria such as *Oenococcus oeni* are naturally present in grape must and spontaneously begin the malolactic conversion once the alcoholic fermentation has been completed. Compared to malic acid (Lat. *malum*, apple), lactic acid is softer and richer on the palate. Lactic acid is found in high concentrations in soured milk products, and white wines that have undergone a malolactic conversion can have a yogurt or dairy note. Almost all red wines undergo malolactic conversion. For white wines, the winemaker may choose to retain the sharpness of the malic acid by suppressing the malolactic conversion, either by adding sulphur dioxide or by decreasing temperature. This is almost invariably the case with Sauvignon Blanc, but almost never the case with Chardonnay (or, at least, not in its Burgundian homeland).

Maturation

The simplest wines are bottled almost immediately after fermentation. Most wines, however, benefit from a period of post-fermentation maturation.

White wines might be kept in contact with the lees, which consist primarily of dead yeast cells, for some time after fermentation. This adds to the texture and complexity of the wine and also imparts it with a certain yeasty, toasty, or nutty quality. Champagne undergoes lees ageing after the second, bottle fermentation, and much quality Muscadet is left 'sur lie' for several months post fermentation. The lees may be stirred through the wine at regular intervals in a process called *bâtonnage*, which increases lees contact and encourages oxygen to percolate to the lees. In the relative absence of oxygen, the reactions involved in the enzymatic decomposition of the lees can lead to the accumulation of hydrogen sulphide, which has a very unpleasant odour.

Wine is commonly matured in oak barrels, which, though watertight, allow small amounts of air to filter into the wine. Too much oxygen can damage a wine, but a small amount—so-called natural micro-oxygenation—causes tannin compounds to polymerize and thereby 'softens' the wine. Similar reactions can also lead to greater colour stability and intensity. Oak, especially new oak, also imparts flavour to the wine. In the main, three species of oak are used: American oak (*Quercus alba*) and two species of French oak (*Quercus robur* and *Quercus sessiflora*). Oak trees too are influenced by terroir, and oak from particular forests may be favoured for their flavour profiles. American oak barrels are considerably cheaper than French oak barrels because American oak has a tighter structure that allows it to be sawn; in contrast, French oak has to be split along the grain of the wood if it is to remain watertight. American oak is low in tannins and high in aromatics, imparting notes of coconut and 'sweet vanilla' to the wine. French oak imparts more subtle notes of butter, vanilla, and toast. French oak is also high in tannins and can add appreciably to the structure of a wine. To make top quality barrels, staves of wood are seasoned outdoors for up to three years to leach out the bitterest compounds. The wood is then toasted over a brazier to bend the staves into shape. This charring process brings out certain flavour compounds, and the degree of toasting is an important determinant of a barrel's flavour profile.

The most common barrel sizes are the Bordeaux *barrique* of 225l and the Burgundy barrel of 228l. A barrel's surface area to volume ratio has an important bearing both on the micro-oxygenation effect and on the transfer of flavour compounds. With short maturation times, oak flavours can appear more obvious because they have not been given time to integrate into the wine through a series of slow chemical reactions. Maximum flavour is imparted from the barrel the first time that it is used, when it is referred to as new oak. Barrels that have been reused several times (old oak) are poor in flavour compounds but still retain their porous properties. Old oak barrels can be sanded and re-toasted, although this practice undermines the structural integrity of the barrel and is not to be recommended.

Some wines, for example, Bordeaux blends, Rioja, and Shiraz, are well suited to new oak; others, for example, Pinot Noir, Rhône reds, and many Italian reds, are better suited to old oak. Yet others, especially aromatic white wines such as Riesling or Sauvignon Blanc, are not generally suited to oak ageing, which masks or detracts from their qualities. There are of course important exceptions to these principles, such as Grand Cru Burgundy and Sauvignon Blanc from the Graves in Bordeaux, which are typically aged in new oak. A winemaker may mature a proportion of a wine in new oak and the remainder in old oak or a neutral vessel and then blend the two together.

A number of techniques have been developed that aim to replicate some of the properties of oak ageing at a small fraction of the cost. These include adding in 'oak flavour' powder or inserting oak staves or a giant teabag of oak chips into the wine. Unfortunately, the resulting oak influence usually comes across as clumsy and poorly integrated. To mimic the micro-oxygenation effect of oak ageing, some winemakers introduce small amounts of oxygen through a ceramic diffuser at the bottom of the vat, often with good results.

Bottling

After vinification and maturation, which may last anything from a few months to several years, the wine is prepared for bottling. In some cases, the wine may be blended from constituent components with the aim of improving quality, complexity, and consistency. These constituent components might include different grape varieties or fruit from different vineyards, vinification vats, or maturation vessels. The wine may also need to be clarified (to remove suspended colloidal particles) and stabilized. Racking the wine off the lees is the first step in the clarification process, although some winemakers employ a quicker but harsher centrifugation approach. A fining agent, traditionally egg white, is then introduced to remove soluble substances such as polymerized tannins, colouring phenols, and proteins that can make the wine appear hazy. Some wines, most notably Riesling, are susceptible to the gradual formation of tartrate crystals which some consumers consider unappealing. If the winemaker wishes to address this issue, he can chill the wine to under –4°C (25°F) to induce the tartrates to precipitate. Any microorganisms still present in the wine must be removed or killed to guard against spoilage. Sulphur dioxide may be added as a preservative or the wine may be filtered to remove the microorganisms, in which case the bottles and bottling equipment need to be kept sterile. Filters can also be used to remove particulate matter beyond a certain size. Alternatively, the wine may be bottled first and then pasteurized to kill off the microorganisms. With pasteurization, the wine is subjected to a high temperature for a short time, and the winemaker must take great care not to damage the wine. A wine crafted with patience and skill is naturally clarified and free of damaging microorganisms. Such a wine can be bottled without any of the above interventions—an approach favoured by winemakers bent on producing an artisanal, natural, or traditional wine.

Most wines are bottled in what has become a standard 750ml glass bottle. Other bottle sizes include piccollo (equivalent to 1/4 of a standard bottle), demi (equivalent to 1/2 a standard bottle), magnum (equivalent to 2 standard bottles), Jeroboam (4), Methuselah (8), Salmanazar (12), Balthazar (16), and Nabuchadnezzar (20). Sweet wines often come in a 500ml jennie, and Vin Jaune typically comes in a 620ml *clavelin*. As well as different sizes, bottles can have different shapes, which, in many cases, have become enshrined in EU law. Other vessels include plastic bottles, cardboard bricks, and metallic-plastic bags set in cardboard boxes, none of which outperform glass bottles for long-term storage.

Cork, the traditional closing method, is harvested from the cork oak tree (*Quercus suber*) and is elastic and watertight. It allows a tiny amount of air exchange, which is thought to prevent the development of reductive odours as the wine matures. Problems with cork hygiene from the 1960s when the wine industry was booming led to an increase in the frequency of 'cork taint'. This prompted the development of alternative closures such as stoppers made from reconstituted cork, synthetic 'corks', aluminium screw caps, and glass stoppers with a plastic washer seal. There continues to be a lot of debate and research into the 'best' closure. Some of the world's most prestigious producers are carrying out longitudinal studies with a single wine under multiple closures. As the finest wines can take decades to mature, a definitive answer may have to wait a bit longer. Meanwhile, the quality of cork is improving and instances of cork taint are less common than in the past. For many purists, the aesthetics of the customs, movements, and sounds associated with uncorking a bottle, and the quasi-Pavlovian association with care and quality, easily outweigh the small risk of cork taint. Today more than ever, the presence of a true cork is an indication of a quality wine intended to improve with age.

Bottle ageing

If stored correctly at a constant temperature of about 10–15°C (50–59°F) and out of direct sunlight, a fine wine continues to evolve through a diverse number of slow chemical reactions. These chemical reactions are poorly understood, but their net effect is to lend the wine 'tertiary' notes that complement the primary fruit profile and secondary notes of the winemaking process. Over time, often several years, the primary fruit recedes and tertiary notes such as earth, mushroom, and truffle come to the fore. The oak flavours become more integrated and, with red wines, the tannins polymerize and soften. The drinking window of a wine is perhaps best described as the period during which all its elements come into harmony. This is often a matter of taste: for example, the Bordelais prefer to drink their wines at about five to seven years old, whereas many British would look upon this as infanticide. Unfortunately, nothing lasts forever, and the process of maturation is also one of decay. Wait too long, and you'll be pouring yourself something that looks and tastes like death.

Wine faults

A lack of care in the winery or bottling plant can result in a faulty wine.

Cork taint

True cork taint is due to 2,4,6-trichloroanisole (TCA), formed when certain phenolic compounds react with chlorine-containing compounds used as disinfectants. This need not result from the cork, as TCA is also found in barrels and other winery equipment. If there is a high degree of cork taint, the wine smells musty ('like wet cardboard') and falls flat on the palate, without fruit or vibrancy. Some people are very sensitive to cork taint, others less so.

Brettanomyces

The benefits or otherwise of *Brettanomyces* in a wine is a source of controversy. The yeast is encouraged by a lack of hygiene in the winery. Some claim that it lends added complexity to a wine in the form of horsey or farmyard notes. Others that it is a taint, overlying the natural fruit character of the wine with 'unclean' notes of sticking plaster or rancid cheese. Some of the world's finest wines, most notably older vintages of Château de Beaucastel in Châteauneuf-du-Pape, carry an unmistakeable trace of Brett. Whether this is a benefit or a fault is ultimately a matter of personal preference: the least that can be said is that Brett should never dominate a wine.

Other microorganisms

If active yeasts and fermentable sugars remain in a wine, it will continue to ferment in bottle. This second fermentation and the carbon dioxide that it releases is exactly what is wanted in traditional method sparking wine (see Chapter 11) although not in other wines which will become inappropriately cloudy and fizzy. In severe cases, the bottle may even burst. Off-dry and semi-sweet wines are particularly susceptible to a second fermentation, and care must be taken to remove or kill all yeast cells prior to bottling.

Similarly, bacteria within the bottle can cause a wine to go off. Lactic acid bacteria make a wine smell like mouse droppings, while acetic acid bacteria convert ethanol to acetic acid, the acid ingredient in vinegar. Acetic acid reacts with ethanol to form ethyl acetate, an ester that smells like nail varnish. A small amount of this so-called volatile acidity can be tolerable, but, given time, the wine will go to vinegar.

Oxidation and reduction

Oxidation is probably the cause of most wine faults, although consumers often mistake the musty note of oxidation for cork taint. For both red and white wines, excess exposure to oxygen (beyond the small amount required for the development of tertiary notes) gradually leads to a brownish colour. The wine loses its fruit character, which is replaced by a musty, dusty, 'flat' note reminiscent of beef stock. Oxidation may result from careless winemaking, a poorly sealed bottle, or inadequate packaging. Corks degrade over time, especially if the bottle is stored upright such that the liquid is no longer in contact with the surface of the cork. For this reason, very old bottles need to be recorked. It should be noted that some wines, such as Madeira or Tawny Port, are made in a deliberately oxidative style that is part of their character and appeal.

Reduction is the opposite chemical reaction to oxidation and occurs when the wine is deprived of oxygen. Oxygen prevents the conversion of dissolved sulphur dioxide into hydrogen sulphide, a gas with an unpleasant smell of rotten eggs or drains. Reductive taint is most common in bottles closed by a screwcap, which forms an airtight seal and prevents the wine from breathing. Mild reductive taint ought to disappear as soon as the wine is swirled around in the glass and exposed to oxygen. Severe reductive taint can be treated with a copper coin, which precipitates the sulphide ions out of the wine.

Chapter 4

Blind Tasting Guide

Wine is a complex combination of acids, alcohols, sugars, phenolics, and other biochemicals suspended in an aqueous solution. These biochemicals may be experienced as colour, aromas and flavours, structure or mouthfeel, and by their effects—either pleasant or unpleasant, depending on the amount consumed—on the mind and body. Parameters such as grape variety, soil, climate, winemaking, and ageing express themselves through the ever-changing makeup of the liquid in the glass, and can be analysed and interpreted (or, depending on your style, divined) by the attentive or inspired taster.

Unfortunately, unconscious bias and suggestion are all too easily introduced into this process of identification and appreciation. Ideally, a wine ought to be evaluated objectively, with only an afterthought for such factors as price or prestige, the reputation of the region or producer, the shape of the bottle, the type of closure used, and the design on the label.

The only way to control for these factors is for the evaluator to be blinded to everything but the liquid itself, which is served naked in a standard wine glass. The wine may be tasted either on its own or in a flight, in which case it may also be compared with the other wines in the flight. The wines within a flight may or may not have certain things in common, for example, grape variety, country or region of origin, and/or vintage. If these commonalities are revealed prior to tasting, the wines are presented 'semi-blind'. The precise identity of a wine is only revealed once it has been thoroughly assessed and, for more advanced tasters, an attempt at identification has been made.

Aside from setting a standard of objectivity, there is much pleasure to be taken from this process, in

- Testing, stretching, and developing our senses
- Applying our judgement
- Relying upon and recalling old memories
- Comparing our analysis with that of our peers
- Getting it more or less right (or 'wrong for the right reasons')
- Discussing the wine and learning about it, and about wine in general
- Imbibing the wine with the respect and consideration that it deserves.

In refining their senses and aesthetic judgement, blind tasters become much more conscious of the richness not only of wine but also of other potentially complex beverages such as tea, coffee, and spirits, and, by extension, the flavours in food, the scents in the air, and the play of light in the world. For life is consciousness, and consciousness is life.

The less romantic, more rational among you may rest assured that blind tasting also has some more practical purposes: winemakers need to taste their wine as they are making it; wine buyers before adding it to their lists; journalists, critics, and sommeliers before recommending it to their readers or customers; and you, the drinker, before deciding to buy it. Especially as a student, you can enter into a growing number of national and international blind tasting competitions. You can also pursue more formal qualifications and give yourself the option of entering the wine trade, which is perhaps more life affirming than many other trades.

The components of wine

Wine is estimated to contain over one thousand different flavour compounds, half of which are made by yeasts during the process of fermentation. Some aromas leap out of the glass while others need to be coaxed out by stirring—a reflection of their relative volatility in solution. Over time, some compounds bind to one another, become insoluble, and precipitate out of solution, resulting in tannin sediment or tartrate crystals.

Apart from water, the most important component of any wine is ethyl alcohol, or ethanol, which is formed by the fermentation of sugars by yeast cells. Although ethanol does not taste of much, it does provide body or density to the wine and also alters the perception of other compounds. For example, a wine with a modest alcohol can come across as more savoury than a similar wine with a higher alcohol, while excessively high alcohol can obscure fruit flavours and aromas. Alcohol ought to be in balance with the other components of the wine, in which case it is perceived as unobtrusive or 'integrated'.

Next come organic acids. Wine grapes contain malic and tartaric acid and also a small amount of citric acid. Tartaric acid stabilizes the finished wine, but some of it may precipitate out in the form of tartrate crystals resembling shards of broken glass. Malic acid, named after the Latin for 'apple', gives green apples their characteristic bite. During the winemaking process, malic acid may be converted to lactic acid through a decarboxylation reaction variously referred to as secondary fermentation, malolactic fermentation, or malolactic conversion. This can occur naturally, but is often initiated by an inoculation of desirable lactic acid bacteria, usually *Oenococcus oeni*. Lactic acid is also present in soured milk products, whence the name, and is softer and richer than malic acid, leading to a rounder and fuller texture. With some fruity and floral white grape varieties, for example, Riesling and Gewurztraminer, the malolactic conversion may be inhibited to conserve a tarter and more acidic profile. Other acids in wine include succinic acid, which is a by-product of fermentation, acetic acid or vinegar, and butyric acid. Excessive amounts of acetic acid or butyric acid (which smells like spoiled milk or rancid butter) are bacteria-induced wine faults. Apart from preserving it, the acids in a wine contribute to freshness and depth or contrast; balance alcohol, sugars, and flavour components; and help to dissolve fats in accompanying food. A wine lacking in acidity can appear flat, dull, and uninteresting.

Grapes contain near equal amounts of glucose and fructose sugars, which are converted to ethanol during the fermentation process. Sometimes, the fermentation process is inhibited so that the wine is left with a certain amount of so-called residual sugar. During the fermentation process the yeast preferentially eats up glucose, such that most residual sugar is the sweeter tasting fructose. Dry wines have a residual sugar of 4g/l or less, which, in general, is undetectable or only indirectly detectable as offset acidity or a slightly fuller body. At the other end of the scale, some sweet wines can contain more than 100g/l of residual sugar. The sweetness of a wine can be masked by acidity and, to a lesser extent, tannins.

Polyphenols are a broad group of chemicals that are principally found in the grape skins. They account for much of the taste of a wine, and, over time, interact with other chemicals in the wine to form a vast array of secondary and tertiary flavour compounds.

Anthocyanins are a class of red, blue, and purple polyphenols that leach into red wine through skin contact during fermentation. They are unstable and, in the presence of oxygen, react with tannin molecules to form larger compounds that precipitate out of the wine, leading to some colour loss. At the same time, anthocyanins are antioxidants that preserve the wine and, according to some scientists, also the drinker.

Tannins are a group of polymerized polyphenols found in grape skins, pips, and stems. The tannin levels of a wine are related to, among other things, the degree and duration of contact with the skins and other solid matter. Although tannins are mostly associated with red wines, some white wines undergo a degree of skin contact to give them a slightly astringent texture. Oak barrels can represent an additional source of tannins for both red and white wines. Tannins are detectable as a textural or structural element together with a certain astringency and bitterness. They interact with saliva proteins to form large compounds that prevent the saliva from lubricating the mouth—experienced as a drying, puckering sensation. With increasing bottle age, they come across as softer and gentler, sometimes almost silky or velvety. The process by which this occurs is poorly understood.

The aroma and most of the flavour of a wine is perceived not on the tongue but in the nose, triggered by volatile compounds that escape the surface of the liquid and reach the olfactory bulb. These volatile compounds originate either in the grape itself or as a by-product of chemical reactions during fermentation or maturation. They include higher alcohols (or fusel oils), esters, aldehydes, lactones, and pyrazines. Short chain esters are responsible for fruity and floral notes, and long-chain esters for notes of perfume and soap. Aldehydes give rise to nutty, Sherry, or oxidized notes; lactones to vanilla and butter notes; and pyrazines to vegetal, leafy, grassy, and green pepper notes.

The perception of wine

Our sense of taste arises from specialized sensory cells in taste buds on the tongue, hard palate, soft palate, and in the throat. There are around 5,000 taste buds in the mouth, each with 50-100 sensory cells or chemoreceptors. These sensory cells are responsive to one of five groups of chemicals, with each chemical within a group interpreted as one of the five fundamental tastes: alkaloids as bitterness, sugars as sweetness, ionic salts as saltiness, acids as sourness, and amino acids as *umami* or savouriness. Although some parts of the tongue are more sensitive to certain tastes than others, the 'tongue map' that divides the tongue into discrete tasting areas very much overstates the case. Chemical sense of taste is supported by the physical and chemical sensation of the liquid in the mouth. The physical sense of touch, which is responsive to dissolved particles as small as three microns, transmits the temperature and texture (or 'mouthfeel') of the wine. The prickle of dissolved carbon dioxide is transmitted by chemesthesis, the same sense or sensibility by which chemical irritants such as chilli or mustard register their fieriness.

Sense of smell, or olfaction, is triggered by airborne chemicals acting on receptor cells in the olfactory bulb behind the nose. There are ~500 types of olfactory receptors which, through a form of combinatorial processing, are capable of discerning several thousand aromas. Sensitivity to aromas can differ significantly, both from one aroma to another and from one individual to the next. Indeed, some aromas are detectable in concentrations one hundred million times smaller than others! Receptor cells in the olfactory bulb may be triggered orthonasally, through the nostrils, or retronasally, from within the mouth. Much 'tasting' actually takes place retronasally, which explains why a runny or blocked nose can leave our food tasting bland.

The 'flavour' of a wine is an integrated interpretation by the brain of all the various sensory stimuli detailed above. Upon tasting the wine, the brain experiences something of a sensory overload, whence the frequent difficulty in pinpointing individual flavours and aromas. To make its job easier, the brain relies heavily on preconceptions, context, and memory to inform its interpretation of the sensory stimuli. For example, if a white wine with an aroma of lemons and apples is dyed red with food colourings, most people will describe red berry aromas; and if a table wine is served in a bottle labelled 'Grand Cru', most people will describe it as 'complex', 'balanced', and such-like. The olfactory bulb is part of the limbic system, an area of the brain closely associated with emotions and memories. Thus, smells and tastes can trigger strong emotions and vivid memories that colour the brain's interpretation of those smells and tastes and thereby 'bias' our perception of the wine. Similarly, our emotional state affects our appreciation of sensory stimuli, which explains, for example, why wine tastes better in good company. Fortunately blind tasting can help us overcome these biases, first, by removing a certain number of their sources, and, second, by encouraging us to hyper-focus on sensory stimuli, tease them apart, and assess and evaluate them.

In engaging intellectually with a wine, blind tasters activate not only their limbic system, but also parts of the brain responsible for cognition, which is a conscious, higher-order function. This process can be assisted and developed by writing tasting notes that seek to accurately describe the sensations produced by the wine. Given the limitations of language in accurately describing our sensations, this is no mean feat. Nonetheless, language is by far the best tool at our disposal for communicating our experiences to others and, indeed, to ourselves. The act of consciously describing the sensations produced by the wine alters the makeup of our brain, forging neural connections that, over time, affirm, develop, and refine our ability to taste and think about taste. As Wittgenstein famously remarked, 'the limits of my language are the limits of my world.'

Although some people do have a higher density of taste buds, this does not make them 'super tasters'. Tasting is not so much a function of the hardware (the nose and palate) as it is of the software (the mind or brain). Indeed, regardless of the sensitivity of their tasting apparatus, untutored tasters find it difficult to 'get their head round' more complex wines, and, as a result, derive greater enjoyment from simpler, more accessible wines. To them, it can seem as though the more experienced tasters are talking mumbo jumbo. But with enough experience and training, almost anyone can turn into a wine expert.

An approach to blind tasting

As a blind taster gathers increasing experience, he or she develops a memory bank of wine styles that makes identification faster and more instinctive. Even then, the blind taster needs a framework to fall back upon to confirm an initial impression or come to grips with an unfamiliar wine style. Even the most experienced blind taster can stumble upon *terra incognita*, and the sheer number and diversity of ever-changing (and evolving) wines is one of the many fascinations of blind tasting.

Preparing the tasting

Broadly speaking, a blind tasting can be horizontal, vertical, or a combination of horizontal and vertical. In a horizontal tasting, different wines (sometimes although not necessarily from the same vintage) are tasted, whereas in a vertical tasting different vintages of the same wine are tasted. Horizontal tastings in which grape varieties and regions and terroirs are compared are much more common than vertical tastings. A typical tasting consists of between six and twelve white and red wines, sometimes with a focus or theme such as 'Italy', 'the Rhône', or 'Oak'. The white wines are served first, to be followed by the red wines. This reduces the number of glasses required (and the washing up!), while still enabling white wines to be compared with white wines and red wines to be compared with red wines. Obviously, if the theme is 'Chardonnay', then only white wines can be served, so maybe choose a theme such as 'Chardonnay and Pinot Noir'.

The best glasses for tasting are long-stemmed and tulip-shaped. The long stem ensures that the wine does not warm up through contact with the hand. The tulip-shape concentrates volatile compounds inside the glass. As the bowl is wider than the rim, the wine can be swirled without fear of spillage, and the glass and its contents can be tilted to near horizontal for a proper inspection of colour. The ideal shape of the tulip varies according to the wine style, hence the Bordeaux glass, the red Burgundy glass, and so on. However, when blind tasting, it is best to use the same style of glass for all wines, thereby establishing a standard for making comparisons. The style of glass that is used in most blind tasting societies and blind tasting competitions is the International Standards Organisation (ISO) glass, which is cheap, sturdy, portable, and suitable for most purposes.

When conducting a blind tasting, the wines ought to be decanted into neutral, clear bottles or decanters. Bottle sleeves, which are available commercially, may be adequate for beginners' classes or if there is no variation in shape or type of closure among the selected bottles. Alternatively, wines may be poured into glasses by the organiser or a non-participating person. It is important to pour the right amount of wine into the glass: too little and it is difficult to smell or taste all the components; too much and the wine cannot breathe in the glass. A fingerbreadth in an ISO glass is ideal. At most, a bottle of wine can serve 18–20 portions.

The temperature of a wine influences the perception of its aromas and structure. At higher temperatures, there is more energy in the wine, such that more and larger molecules can escape the surface of the liquid. On the other hand, if the temperature is too high, much of the aromatic subtlety is lost and the wine becomes much less enjoyable. In practical terms, this means that most white, rosé, and sparkling wines ought to be served at around 8-10°C (46-50°F), sometimes referred to as 'fridge door temperature'. Highly aromatic sweet wines such as Sauternes are best served slightly cooler, while full-bodied, oaky white wines such as Meursault are best served slightly warmer. Red wines ought to be served at around 14-18°C (57-64°F). Pinot Noir and other light-bodied red wines with delicate bouquets are best served slightly cooler, while full-bodied red wines such as Australian Shiraz are (usually) best served at the warmer end of the quoted range. Eventually, the blind taster develops a feel for the temperature of a wine and the temperature range at which it ought to be served. If in doubt, err on the side of cool, as a wine that is too cool can easily be warmed up by cupping the glass in the hand. If the wine is still in the bottle, it can be cooled or kept cool with a thermic bag, frozen sleeve, or ice bucket. Depending on the weather, it might be possible to put the wine outside on a windowsill or even in a river or stream.

Other than glasses and bottles, you will need a foil cutter, a corkscrew, a pourer to minimize dripping (this is most commonly a metallic disc that is rolled into the neck of the bottle), a spittoon for spitting the wine (almost any receptacle will do), tasting sheets, writing materials, and someone to do the washing up! For further details on setting up a blind tasting, see Appendix A.

Assessing the wine: in the glass

Immediately after the wine has been poured, inspect it for any bubbles or 'spritz'. Spritz is carbon dioxide coming out of solution, and is indicative of reductive wine making. Obviously, sparkling wine releases a stream of carbon dioxide bubbles, the volume and rate of which can be suggestive of the method of winemaking (see Chapter 11).

On a white background (for example, a sheet of paper), examine the colour of the wine. Look at the wine from above to assess the depth of colour, which can be gauged from the visibility of the stem of the glass. Then gently tilt the glass and inspect the liquid to confirm its colour and clarity. Especially with red wines, the colour at the centre or 'core' may differ from that at the edge or 'rim'. Finally, note any deposits of tannin or tartrate crystals. Some people like to swirl the wine to generate legs or tears on the side of the glass. These tears are a marker of the density or viscosity of the wine, and, by extension, of its level of sugar, alcohol, and/or extract. However, these parameters are best assessed on the palate.

White wines range in colour from watery-white through to green, lemon, straw, golden, and even coppery-orange in the case of certain dessert wines. Wines at the 'greener' end of the spectrum are usually paler and vice versa. Red wines range in colour from orange-red through to brick-red, ruby, violet, and indigo—or even 'black' for the inkiest wines. However pale or opaque, red wines almost invariably start off as 'red' or 'purple'; with age, the colour softens, leading to more orange hues. Rosés are typically described as orange, salmon, or pink.

Assessing the wine: on the nose

The next step is to smell the aromas or bouquet of the wine by bringing the glass very close to the nose. Now swirl the wine to bring out the heavier volatile compounds and take another sniff. The terms 'aromas' and 'bouquet' are more or less synonymous, although, properly speaking, 'bouquet' refers more specifically to the tertiary aromas on a mature wine. The first thing to note is the intensity of the aromas: in other words, how easy is it to smell the wine? Certain wine styles such as New Zealand Sauvignon Blanc and Alsatian Gewurztraminer are intensely aromatic, others, such as Chablis or Muscadet, much less so. Consider also the complexity of the wine. If you cannot immediately come to grips with the wine, this may be a sign of complexity.

It can be difficult to find adequate descriptors with which to express and convey your subjective experience of a wine. The descriptors that you choose are but metaphors that aim to evoke your impressions of the wine. Although original descriptors, particularly if accurate, are to be welcomed, there is already an established lexicon of 'wine words' that are used repeatedly and that have come to be associated with, and therefore to connote, certain ideas. For example, 'apples' or 'lemons' suggests a cooler climate, 'vanilla' or 'butterscotch' suggests French oak, 'coconut' suggests American oak, 'cedar wood' suggests Cabernet Sauvignon, and 'undergrowth' and 'old books' suggest a mature wine. These 'wine words' are deeply rooted in European culture and experiences, which can make them especially challenging for people from other cultures.

Returning to the wine, begin by identifying the fruit aromas. Most fruit aromas originate in the grape itself; for beginners, such 'primary aromas' are generally easiest to identify. For white wines, there is an aroma spectrum that ranges from cool climate fruits such as apple, pears, lemons, and grapefruit, to tropical fruits such as passion fruit, pineapple, mango, and papaya. This reflects the ripeness of the grapes at harvest and, to a lesser extent, the grape variety. For red wines, the aromas can, broadly speaking, be grouped into red fruits (such as strawberries, raspberries, and redcurrants) and black fruits (such as blackberries, plums, and blackcurrants). The ripeness of the grapes is reflected in the quality of the fruit, for example, fresh, jammy, stewed, or dried.

Fruit aromas are one thing, but there are also many other, non-fruit aromas that originate in the grape itself. However, most other aromas are an expression of the winemaking processes ('secondary aromas') or bottle maturation ('tertiary aromas'). Non-fruit aromas can fall into one of several categories: floral (for example, lily, elderflower, rose, violet); vegetal (asparagus, grass, green pepper, tobacco leaf); mineral (slate, earth, petrichor); animal (meat, wool, leather, manure); spice (pepper, cinnamon, clove, vanilla); nutty (almond, hazelnut, walnut, coconut); autolytic (yeast, bread, brioche, toast); lactic (milk, yoghurt, cream); and 'other' (coffee, chocolate, honey, resin, rubber). Some particularly colourful non-fruit descriptors include 'wet dog' (suggesting aged Loire Chenin Blanc) and 'cat's pee on a gooseberry bush' (suggesting Loire Sauvignon Blanc).

Assessing the wine: on the palate

Take a sip of wine large enough to coat your mouth, but small enough that you can swish it around with your tongue. Don't drink the wine as you would water or milk. Instead, hold it in the mouth so that it can express itself. Assess the intensity of flavour together with its character. The flavours are not so much tasted by the tongue as sensed by the nose through retronasal olfaction, and ought to be very similar to the aromas that you identified by smelling the wine. Some aromas and flavours might be more forthcoming on the palate than on the nose, which can be helpful in confirming, developing, or rejecting some of your initial impressions.

Having ascertained the flavour of the wine, consider its structural elements, of which there are seven: acidity, alcohol, residual sugar, body, tannin, oak, and finish. Human beings are not calibrated scientific machines and cannot accurately assess structural elements such as acidity and alcohol content. A wine may be high in acidity or alcohol, but not seem so, for example, if acidity and alcohol are masked by high residual sugar, or if all structural elements are in near perfect harmony. Describing structural elements such as acidity or alcohol in such simple terms as 'high', 'medium', or 'low' may seem rather crude, but suffices for the purposes of blind tasting.

Acidity is primarily experienced as a tingling on the sides of the tongue. High acidity is also accompanied by a sharp taste. High residual sugar and/or a full body can mask acidity, such that luscious dessert wines are much more acidic than they appear. Acid stimulates the secretion of saliva from the parotid glands and other salivary glands. For a more objective assessment of acidity, try to gauge the saliva response. After spitting or swallowing the wine, tilt your head forward and note the flow of saliva into the front of the mouth.

Assess the level of alcohol by holding a small amount of wine in the mouth and gently breathing in through the lips. The degree of heat or 'burn' at the back of the throat is more or less proportional to the alcohol level. If alcohol level is markedly high, a similar burning sensation is produced in the nose upon sniffing the wine. Overly alcoholic wines tend to lack flavour intensity. Even when bone dry, they can produce a sensation of sweetness on the tongue. On the other hand, wines that are lacking in alcohol may come across as thin or insipid, unless, as with Mosel Riesling, the low alcohol is balanced by high residual sugar and intensity of flavour.

Wines with detectable residual sugar range from off-dry to medium-dry, medium-sweet, and sweet. Some wine styles, most notably Champagne, have prescribed terms for defined levels of residual sweetness (see Chapter 11). Assessing sugar levels can be quite challenging, especially with sweeter wines, which saturate sweetness receptors in the taste buds. Wines with high sugar levels call for high acidity to flush the sweetness receptors and balance the cloying sweetness with a sensation of freshness. However, this freshness can create the impression that the wine is less sweet than it actually is. In such cases, the wine's body provides a clue as to its actual sugar content. An accurate assessment of residual sugar in grams per litre is quite unnecessary; focus instead on whether the sugar is in balance with the other components of the wine and, in particular, with acidity. Assessing sugar and alcohol in tandem can hint at the ripeness of the grapes at the time of harvest and at the winemaking methods employed. Fortunately for us, most wines are dry!

Body refers to the overall feel of the liquid in the mouth. It is in large part a measure of density and viscosity, and related to levels of sugar, alcohol, and extract in the wine. A light-bodied wine may feel like water in the mouth, whereas a full-bodied wine feels more like milk. Full-bodied wines require higher levels of acidity to complement their weight. Conversely, light-bodied wines with excessive acidity come across as sharp. A certain creaminess to the body, especially if accompanied by a bread-like or floral aroma, suggests that the wine has spent time ageing on its lees (dead yeast cells). Lees ageing is much more noticeable on white wines than on red wines.

Oak enables the wine to 'breathe' through micro-oxygenation, facilitating a more harmonious integration of fruit flavours with the body of the wine. Much more than old oak, new oak leeches flavour compounds into the wine. Depending on such factors as the provenance of the oak, the age and toast level of the barrel, and the time spent in barrel and in bottle, oak ageing can contribute notes of vanilla, butter, toast, chocolate, coffee, roasted nuts, nutmeg, cedar, tobacco, and smoke. American oak is 'sweeter' than French oak, and less subtle, with dominant notes of coconut and white chocolate. Oak ageing promotes polymerization of tannins, which is experienced as a 'softening' of the wine. At the same time, heavily toasted barrels can introduce tannins that are harsher and more astringent than those already present. Finally, by promoting the malolactic conversion (see Chapter 3), contact with oak can alter the character of the acids in the wine. Oak staves, chips, or powder aim to replicate at least some of the influence of oak ageing.

Discussion of tannins is usually restricted to red wines. However, there are some white wines that are fermented or matured in oak, or that undergo significant skin contact, that contain discernible tannins. Tannins are usually experienced as astringency and/or a certain textural mouthfeel, together with a drying or puckering sensation on the gums and inner surfaces of the cheeks and lips. In assessing a red wine, you ought to consider both the quality and quantity of the tannins. Quality of tannins can be described in terms of size, texture (smooth, coarse, jagged), and flavour (ripe, bitter, green). Determining the quantity of tannins can be tricky, since coarse-grained tannins initially overwhelm the palate, leading to a false impression of high tannins; conversely, fine-grained tannins are only fully revealed in the delayed tannic 'grip' of the wine.

The finish of a wine describes the sensations that remain in the mouth after the wine has been spat or swallowed. Fine wines with a certain degree of flavour intensity will continue to resonate for seconds, sometimes minutes. Flavour compounds titillate the taste receptors in the throat and volatile compounds continue to rise to the olfactory bulb. Finish however is not just a question of duration, but also of character or quality and, perhaps most importantly, of harmony with what went before.

Interpreting your findings

You have dissected and analysed the various features of the wine as best as you could. The next step is to interpret your data and make an educated guess as to the grape variety or blend; the country, region, and appellation of origin; the vintage; and the quality and approximate price. In competitions and exams, most (and sometimes all) available marks are for interpretation rather than analysis, although you can still score very highly for 'getting it wrong for the right reasons'—particularly if the judges or examiners came to the same conclusions as you did.

Appearance

Spritz is indicative of anaerobic wine making in sealed stainless steel vessels. It is a common feature of white wines such as Sauvignon Blanc and Riesling, which are made reductively so as to emphasize freshness and fruitiness.

White wines that are fermented or matured in oak barrels are often deeper in colour than those fermented in inert vessels. In contrast, red wines fermented in oak tend to be paler or softer in colour, and red rather than purple. As they age, white wines become deeper in colour and red wines paler. Indeed, with increasing age, both white and red wines tend towards the same shade of orange-brown. A pronounced colour gradient from core to rim (typically red and darker in the core, and bronze and lighter at the rim) is a particular feature of red wines with significant bottle age. In forming conclusions about oak treatment or bottle age, do not rely solely on colour; seek to confirm your initial impressions on the nose and palate. Never fall into the trap of shoe-horning a wine into an initial impression: if something doesn't quite add up, you have probably got it wrong.

With young red wines and rosés, depth of colour is a function of duration of skin contact and thickness of the skins. Thin-skinned grape varieties such as Pinot Noir, Gamay, and Tempranillo impart relatively little colour compared to thick-skinned grape varieties such as Tannat, Malbec, and Corvina. Apart from providing a clue about grape variety, depth of colour also provides a clue about climate and, by extension, origin. High sunshine hours bring out deeper, purpler hues in a wine.

Thus, Pinot Noir from Central Otago is typically darker than that from Beaune; and whereas Malbec from Cahors is deep purple, Malbec from Mendoza is inky black.

Nose

Some grape varieties are more aromatic than others and tend to leap out of the glass. Red wines, which derive much of their aromatic content from prolonged skin contact, are invariably aromatic. By contrast, white wines, which receive little or no skin contact, vary more widely in their aromatic intensity. Some of the most aromatic white grape varieties include Sauvignon Blanc, Riesling, Gewurztraminer, Muscat, Albariño, Torrontes, and Viognier. More neutral white grape varieties include Chardonnay (in cool climate styles), Melon de Bourgogne, Pinot Blanc, Sémillon, and Trebbiano. With excessive heat, the vine starts to shut down, inhibiting the development of aromatic compounds. Thus, wines from excessively hot climates or vintages can fail to reach their full aromatic potential.

The primary aromas on the nose provide the biggest clues as to grape variety (or in the case of a blend, grape varieties). Some grape varieties, for example, Pinot Noir, Cabernet Sauvignon, Gewurztraminer, and Viognier are referred to in blind tasting circles as 'bankers' (wines with which you bank points) on account of their very distinctive aromatic profiles. A neutral wine may pose more of a conundrum, but at least you know what it is not! Blends too can complicate matters, although some classic blends, such as Sauvignon Blanc and Sémillon from Bordeaux, are relatively easy to recognize.

Primary aromas are also indicative of growing conditions. Cool climate white wines tend towards citrus and white fruit (such as apple and pear) aromas, whereas warm climate white wines tend towards stone fruit (such as peach and apricot) and tropical fruit aromas. Cool climate red wines tend towards fresh fruit aromas, whereas warm climate red wines tend towards baked or jammy notes and, at the hotter end of the scale, even raisins and dried fruit. Notes of raisins and dried fruit may also indicate a wine that has been made from dried grapes, for example, Amarone. Herbaceous notes, which can be pleasant in small degrees, are often a sign of unripeness. Botrytis or noble rot has a characteristic smell of honeysuckle and honey, sometimes accompanied by a faint antiseptic or musty note. The intensity of these aromas indicates the degree of botrytization. Note that botrytized wines are invariably white wines.

Primary aromas originating from the grape itself may be obscured by secondary aromas from the winemaking or tertiary aromas from bottle maturation. Autolytic notes such as yeast, rising bread dough, brioche, and biscuit (especially if accompanied by a certain creaminess on the palate) suggest that that the wine has been aged on its lees. The classic example of a still wine with prominent lees character is Muscadet Sur Lie. Skin contact usually masks autolytic notes, which is why they are much more prominent in white than red wines.

Evidence of oak on the nose (and, later, on the palate) speaks volumes about the wine, and more particularly about the winemaking, grape variety (as some grape varieties are never or rarely oaked), and origin. Oak is either old or new, French or American, which again can provide further clues. For example, Riesling is never oaked, Chianti is typically aged in old oak, and Rioja is typically aged in American oak. A wine with pronounced new French oak, which is very expensive, suggests a wine with pretensions. Oak can sometimes dominate a wine, but softens and 'integrates' with the passing years.

Tertiary aromas such as mushroom, truffle, wet leaves, leather, coffee, and butterscotch are indicative of bottle age. A mature fine wine dominated by tertiary aromas but still with a core of sweet and juicy fruit is a true wonder. But if left for too long, the wine starts to dry out, lose its fruit aromas, and develop oxidative notes reminiscent of Madeira or overcooked vegetables.

Palate

The nose normally anticipates the palate, which in turn confirms the nose. This is especially true for grape variety, winemaking techniques, complexity, and maturity. In addition, the palate enables an assessment of the structural components of the wine. Part of the pleasure of drinking wine is to take your time over it and let the nose 'whet the palate'. A disconnect between nose and palate could reflect on poor winemaking or over-maturation.

Acidity is an indicator of the climate in which the grapes were grown. Grapes grown in cooler climates tend to be higher in acidity. That said, early harvesting results in a more acidic profile, and some grape varieties are naturally high in acidity. In white wines, notes of green apples suggest high levels of malic acid and, by extension, suppression of malolactic fermentation. On the other hand, notes of dairy or yoghurt suggest higher levels of lactic acid, which is less sharp than malic acid. A sour 'tug' on the palate, experienced once the flavours have died back, is indicative of added tartaric acid. Citrus notes are unrelated to citric acid, which in wine is found in only minute concentrations.

Alcohol too is an indicator of ripeness at harvest and, therefore, of climate. Alcohol ought to be considered alongside residual sugar to provide an indication of total pre-fermentation sugar level in the grapes. A dry wine with high alcohol and a sweet wine with low alcohol can, at least in principle, have been made from the same crop of grapes. Wine identification ought to be guided by knowledge of regional terroirs and grape varieties. For instance, the banks of the River Mosel in Germany see some of the coolest average temperatures of any wine region; however, the long dry autumns combined with late harvesting enable the grapes to achieve high sugar levels. Conversely, the Hunter Valley in Australia, while very warm, is frequently clouded over: the heat promotes phenolic ripeness but the lack of sunshine restricts sugar accumulation, leading to wines with a relatively low alcohol. With regards to grape varieties, some, such as Merlot and Sémillon, accumulate sugars rapidly, while others, such as Cabernet Franc, Nebbiolo, and Riesling, are slower to ripen.

In red wines, tannin levels are related to the thickness of the grape skins and so to the grape variety. The blind taster is often tempted to correlate depth of colour with tannin levels. However, colour can be extracted from the skins, for instance, through cold maceration, without imparting much tannin to the wine. And some grape varieties, most notably Nebbiolo, are relatively light in colour but very heavy in tannins. The character or quality of the tannins reflects on grape variety, growing conditions, and winemaking. For example, harsh tannins suggest a crude, mechanized method of tannin extraction that damages pips and enables bitter compounds to leach into the wine.

Quality assessment

Wine professionals are usually more interested in assessing a wine's quality than in identifying it for sport, tallying price and quality in search of 'value for money'. Of course quality is in large part subjective, even if most wine amateurs do wind up developing a taste for more complex or refined wines. Owing to their growing knowledge and tasting skills, this need not mean ever more expensive labels. Top wines from unfashionable regions usually offer much more 'bang for your buck', and even fashionable regions are sure to hide some great bargains for those with a discerning palate. It is certainly possible to enjoy great wine at under £10/$15/€12 a bottle.

There are five criteria by which to assess the quality of a wine: balance, length, intensity, complexity, and typicity. If the wine is balanced or harmonious or integrated, the flavours complement one another like musical instruments in an orchestra, the palate is faithful to the promises of the nose, and none of the structural elements protrudes or dominates in the mouth. Length refers to the progression of flavours as the wine crosses the palate, triggering taste buds on the tongue, the roof of the mouth, and the throat. In the best of cases, the flavours and structure of the wine linger long after the wine has been spat or swallowed. Intensity refers to the apparent concentration of flavour and impact of the wine in the mouth—the fireworks, if you will. Intensity is related to length in that there cannot be length without intensity. Intensity and length are highly sought after in balanced wines, but in unbalanced wines serve only to prolong the torture. Again, it is just as with music—or speaking, or acting, or anything. Complexity refers to the number of players in the orchestra, and, by extension, the strands and textures in the music. As with other markers of quality, complexity begins with high quality, healthy grapes, preferably of a so-called noble grape variety. The role of the winemaker is then to conserve and craft what nature has given him, looking not only to complexity but also to balance, length, and intensity. Additional complexity can be imparted in the winery through blending, lees stirring, oaking, and ageing. Some styles are complex mostly for having been made from dried grapes or grapes affected by noble rot. A wine ought to reflect the style that it is associated with, most obviously by being faithful to its terroir: the soil, climate, and viticultural and winemaking traditions of its area and region of origin. This European concept of typicity is being adopted by an increasing number of New World producers bent on quality and authenticity. Unlike balance, length, intensity, and complexity, typicity is not an essential ingredient of greatness. There are many iconic wines, such as the original Super Tuscans, that defy the traditions of their region and, in time, even come to alter them. As Winston Churchill once said, 'Without tradition, art is a flock of sheep without a shepherd. Without innovation, it is a corpse.'

Examples

Wine 1: Recent vintage of Mosel Riesling

Tasting note:
- *Pale straw in colour.*
- *Highly aromatic with notes of fresh lime, green apple, sherbet, slate, and hints of pineapple and honeysuckle.*
- *Fresh fruit flavours on the palate: apple and lime dominate.*
- *No evidence of new oak.*
- *High in acidity with markedly low alcohol and medium residual sugar.*
- *Creamy in texture though still light in body.*
- *Moderate in length, with an elegant and tapered mineral finish.*
- *Well balanced, with the high acidity and low alcohol compensated for by the sugar, intensity of fruit, and creamy texture.*

Analysis:
The pale colour suggests that the wine is young and that is has seen little or no oak, initial impressions that are confirmed by the dominant fresh fruit aromas. The hints of pineapple and honeysuckle on the nose imply ripeness, as does the medium residual sugar. Taken together, the residual sugar and alcohol are indicative of high sugar levels at harvest and of arrested fermentation. At the same time, the high acidity is a marker of the overall cool climate. One is entitled to conclude that the wine most probably comes from a cool climate with a long and dry

autumn. The creamy texture indicates some ageing on the lees. The balance and elegant finish are markers of high quality.

From the aroma profile, acidity, residual sugar, and lack of oak, one can be fairly confident that the grape variety is Riesling. The pale colour, fruit-driven aroma profile, and lack of tertiary aromas such as butterscotch, toffee, smoke, and kerosene betray a very young wine, no older than one or two years. The aroma profile, in particular the sherbet, slate, and mineral, suggest that this is Riesling from the Mosel. This hypothesis is confirmed by the combination of high acidity, low alcohol, and medium residual sugar. It remains possible that the wine is in fact a New World imitation of Mosel Riesling, but the character and complexity of the nose and the creamy elegance of the palate are highly in favour of Germany. The wine could also be from the nearby Rheingau or Nahe, but these styles tend to be rounder and fuller with higher alcohol levels and rather less mineral character.

Wine 2: Californian Cabernet Sauvignon with eight years of bottle age

Tasting note:
- *In colour, medium-deep purple in the centre and brick-red at the rim.*
- *Moderately aromatic with jammy blackcurrant and mulberry fruit, meaty notes, and a hint of menthol, coconut, and sweet spice.*
- *Dry and full-bodied with high alcohol and low acidity.*
- *Intense jammy black fruit flavours with coconut and milk chocolate, suggesting American oak.*
- *Tannins moderate in quantity, with a soft and velvety quality.*
- *Moderate length with a finish dominated by fruit flavours and alcohol.*
- *Overall, a complex wine with clear development, but let down by low acidity relative to full body and high alcohol.*

Analysis:
The colour gradient and brick-red rim indicate a significant degree of bottle age, as later confirmed by the meaty notes. The moderate depth of colour eliminates overly thin- or thick-skinned grape varieties. The jammy fruit and other aspects of the aroma profile are suggestive

of a hot climate. Notes of coconut and sweet spice betray the use of American oak, which is corroborated on the palate. The wine, though complex, is let down by its lack of balance and in particular by its alcoholic flabbiness.

The menthol note is crucial to unmasking Cabernet Sauvignon as the grape variety. Cabernet Sauvignon is often marked out by blackcurrant and green pepper; however, the 'green' note can adopt a number of forms, including, especially in California, menthol. Taken together, the notes of menthol and jammy fruit, the high alcohol, and the use of American oak make California an obvious choice. Other possibilities include Australia or South Africa, which are similarly hot. Australian Cabernets capable of a similar degree of complexity typically arise from chalky soils, such as those of Coonawarra, that preserve acidity. Moreover, the 'green note' is usually expressed as eucalyptus rather than menthol.

Wine 3: 30-year-old Pinot Gris SGN (Sélection de Grains Nobles) from Alsace

Tasting note:
- *Deep gold and intense in colour.*
- *Dense, concentrated nose with a complex bouquet of mushroom, leather, honey, butterscotch, confected pear, peach, nutmeg, and white pepper.*
- *Intensely sweet on the palate with notes of peach, fig, date, and butterscotch.*
- *Full-bodied with moderate alcohol and moderate-to-low acidity.*
- *High residual sugar.*
- *Very long and tapered savoury finish that echoes the earlier aromas and flavours.*
- *A wonderfully complex sweet wine. The sweetness fades to a savoury, dry finish. The one slight damper is that the moderate-to-low acidity does not quite stand up to the high residual sugar.*

Analysis:
The deep golden colour and developed notes of mushroom, leather, and so on imply significant age. The complexity of the nose and palate

and the elegant, long, dry finish are some of the hallmarks of very high quality. The sweetness and honeyed notes suggest a dessert wine made from botrytized grapes.

This leaves only a few options: Auslese or Beerenauslese Riesling from Germany, sweet Chenin from the Loire, Sauternes from Bordeaux, Tokaji from Hungary, or a SGN from Alsace. The wine could not possibly come from the New World because New World producers were not making this style and quality of wine twenty or thirty years ago. With mature wines, the developed notes can obscure the original primary fruit aromas, leaving the blind taster to identify the wine more by elimination than anything else. The wine in question is too low in acidity to be Riesling, Chenin Blanc, Tokaji, or Sauternes. While SGN from Alsace could be made from Riesling or Gewurztraminer, it is more commonly made from Pinot Gris. Notes of pear and spice—rather than, say, vanilla custard (Sauternes) or apricot (Tokaji)—support the conclusion that the wine is indeed a Pinot Gris. It is usually difficult to pin an age on a very old wine, but any guess that makes it 'very old' ought to score full marks.

PART II

Chapter 5

Alsace

In the 1st century the Romans established the region of Alsace, then part of the province of Germania Superior, as a centre of viticulture. In more recent history, Alsace has at times been German and at other times French, but at all times, and above all, proudly Alsatian. Despite the centralizing tendency of the French Republic, the region still retains a strong and separate identity, with its own language, culture, cuisine, and wine tradition, which revolves around not French but Germanic grape varieties. Alsatian wines are, for the most part, single varietal white wines, with the most prized made from Riesling, Gewurztraminer, or Pinot Gris. As in Germany, it is common for the grape variety to be proudly and prominently displayed on the front label. If the grape variety does not feature on the front label, the wine is typically a blend of several grape varieties, sometimes labelled as *Gentil* or more modest *Edelzwicker*.

The lie of the land

The vineyards of Alsace are framed by the Vosges Mountains to the west and the River Rhine to the east, and centred on the picturesque towns of Colmar and Ribeauvillé, which is ~16km (10mi) north of Colmar and ~70km (43mi) south of the regional capital of Strasbourg. The best vineyards lie at the foot of the Vosges, forming a narrow strip that stretches from north to south over a distance of more than 100km (62mi). In general, the slopes face east, but hills and lateral valleys give rise to a number of south-facing and north-facing slopes. Indeed, many of the best vineyards have a southeast to southwest orientation. The slopes are usually worked by hand, with mechanical harvesting confined to the plains of the Rhine.

Climate

Alsace sits in the rain shadow of the Vosges Mountains, which provide shelter from the prevailing Atlantic winds. Colmar receives less than 500mm (20in) annual rainfall, which makes it the second driest place in France after Perpignan in the extreme south. In contrast, annual rainfall in Jurançon in the foothills of the Pyrenées is a surprising 1,200mm (47in). The winters are cold and long, as might be expected in such a northerly and continental location (although Alsace is actually south of Champagne), but the summers are hot and the autumns long and dry, which favours the finesse and elegant aromas associated with extended ripening. In some years, spring frosts and summer hailstorms can cause significant damage to the harvest.

Soils

As the vineyards of Alsace run along a collapsed fault line, the soils are very varied, sometimes even within a single vineyard. Whereas the soils on the plain are for the most part alluvial, those higher up can be almost anything. Rockier flint, granite, and schist soils tend to be associated with a mineral, petrol, and gunflint character and to be particularly suited to Riesling; heavy clay and marl soils tend to be associated with weight and broad fruit flavours and to be particularly suited to Gewurztraminer; and limestone soils tend to be associated with finesse and to be particularly suited to Muscat. Producers often choose their varieties according to the terroir available to them, but also seek to diversify their plantings so as to minimize the impact of a poor harvest for a particular variety.

Grape varieties

The seven major grape varieties of Alsace are Riesling, Gewurztraminer, Pinot Gris (formerly 'Tokay'), Pinot Blanc, Pinot Noir, Sylvaner, and Muscat. Over the years, there has been a trend to replace plantings of Sylvaner, once the most common grape variety, with Pinot Gris, Pinot Noir, and Riesling.

Almost all the wines are white except for those made from Pinot Noir, which are light red or rosé. A good quality sparkling wine, Crémant d'Alsace, is also made after the traditional method, and accounts for about a fifth of the region's total production. Grapes for Crémant d'Alsace are picked at the beginning of the harvest season, and permitted grape varieties include Pinot Blanc (aka Klevner), Pinot Gris, Pinot Noir, Riesling, and Chardonnay. Finally, there are late harvest wines, which may be classified as either *Vendange Tardive* ('Late Harvest', similar to *Auslese* in Germany) or *Sélection de Grains Nobles* ('Selection of Noble Berries', similar to *Beerenauslese* in Germany and made from botrytized grapes). Only the four so-called 'noble' grape varieties, namely, Riesling, Gewurztraminer, Pinot Gris, and Muscat are permitted for late harvest wines, whether *Vendange Tardive* or *Sélection de Grains Nobles*. Late harvest wines account for a very small fraction of total production, even in vintages that are favourable to late ripening and the development of noble rot. Straw wine (*vin de paille*, a wine made from dried grapes) and ice wine are also made, but in even smaller quantities.

Appellations

Almost the entire production of Alsace is *Appellation d'Origine Contrôlée* (AOC) as there is no *Vin de Pays* designation for the region (see Appendix C: The European Union and French Classification Systems). To make life simple there are only three AOCs: AOC Alsace (~74% of production) and AOC Crémant d'Alsace (~22% of production), which cover the entire region, and the more restrictive AOC Alsace Grand Cru (~4% of production), which covers 51 named vineyards, from Rangen in the south to Steinklotz almost 100km (62mi) further north. With a couple of minor exceptions, only the four noble grape varieties are permitted for Grand Cru wines. Some producers prefer to relinquish the Grand Cru designation in favour of historical names such as Clos Sainte Hune, part of Grand Cru Rosacker and probably the most vaunted name in Alsace wine. Terms such as *Réserve Personnelle* and *Cuvée Spéciale* have no legal status, but producers can include them to indicate a wine of higher quality, just as they can include the name of a particular locality (*lieu-dit*). Whereas bottles of crémant are the same shape as Champagne bottles, still wine is entered into tall and slender bottles called *flutes d'Alsace*. Unlike in Germany, this is actually a requirement of the appellation rules. The one exception is for Pinot Noir, which can also be entered into Burgundian bottles.

Wine styles

Compared to their German counterparts, the white wines of Alsace tend to be fuller in body and higher in alcohol, and also dryer— although perhaps not quite as dry as they once used to be. They are mostly unblended, unoaked, and un-softened by a second, malolactic fermentation, and therefore tend to be highly expressive of varietal character and terroir. Unfortunately, it can be difficult to gauge the sweetness of a particular wine (even a *Vendange Tardive*, which may be unexpectedly dry), since there is no labelling standard by which to indicate sweetness. Individual producers usually have a distinct house style: for example, Trimbach and Léon Beyer are reputed for their bone-dry wines and Rolly Gassmann for a rich and velvety sweetness. Other highly regarded Alsatian houses include Blanck, Marcel Deiss, Josmeyer, Ostertag, Schlumberger, Weinbach, and Zind-Humbrecht.

Riesling is the most aristocratic of the four noble grape varieties and also the most highly reflective of terroir. Alsatian Riesling tends to be drier, richer, and higher in alcohol than Riesling from across the Rhine. It can be steely and inexpressive in its youth, with aromas of mineral, apple, citrus fruits, stone fruits, jasmine, and honey. With age, it develops a complex bouquet dominated by pure fruit flavours and petrol or kerosene notes, typically with a long, dry finish that rides home on a backbone of high acidity.

Gewurztraminer is often easy to recognize, as it is opulent with high alcohol and smells like an oriental perfume shop! For just these reasons, it can seem sweeter than in actuality. In hot vintages, it can be flabby and lacking in acidity, and this too can contribute to an impression of sweetness. Blind tasters often look out for a pink tinge to the golden hue, but this is not invariably present or visible. Typical notes include spice, rose petals, lychee, grapefruit, peach kernel, and smoky bacon. Despite its relative lack of acidity, Gewurztraminer can be age-worthy. It is commonly used in *Vendange Tardive* and *Sélection de Grains Nobles*, even if most of the production is dry or off-dry.

Pinot Gris is noted for aromas of spice and pear or stone fruit with hints of honey and smoke and a certain earthy minerality. Alsatian Pinot Gris is much fuller and richer than Italian Pinot Gris (aka Pinot Grigio), which is often crisp and lean. Among Alsatian wines, it sits in the middle, combining the spiciness and alcohol of Gewurztraminer with some of the structure and acidity of Riesling. And like Riesling and Gewurztraminer, it can improve with age. Pinot Gris can achieve high levels of sugar and, like Gewurztraminer, it is commonly used in *Vendange Tardive* and *Sélection de Grains Nobles*.

Pinot Blanc is often blended with a similar grape variety called Auxerrois and sold as Pinot Blanc. It can be thought of as an understudy of Chardonnay, with which it shares several characteristics. At its best, it is round and medium-bodied with hints of ripe apples, pears, and spice and a clean and refreshing finish. Although distinctly Alsatian, it has less body than Gewurztraminer or Pinot Gris, less acidity and precision than Riesling, and less aromatic intensity than either of the three. It is not intended for ageing.

Pinot Noir from Alsace used to be distinctly pale and thin and unripe, but, with rising temperatures, the trend is for darker and fleshier offerings. Even so, world-class Alsatian Pinot Noir remains something of a rarity.

Sylvaner is a humble grape variety, although there do exist some very fine examples. Indeed, since 2005, it has been a permitted grape variety in Grand Cru Zotzenberg, prompting some to label it as the 'comeback kid' of Alsace. Typical examples are lean and fresh with hints of citrus and white flowers, sometimes marred by a slight bitterness or earthiness. Wines made from Sylvaner are not intended for ageing.

Muscat is usually a blend of Muscat Ottonel and Muscat Blanc à Petits Grains. It is delicate and floral, with a light body and low alcohol. Although it is dry, the signature grapey aroma can produce an impression of sweetness. Other notes include apple, orange, and mandarin. The intensity of the nose rarely follows through on the palate, particularly as acidity is often lacking. Wines made from Muscat are not intended for ageing.

Chapter 6

Burgundy

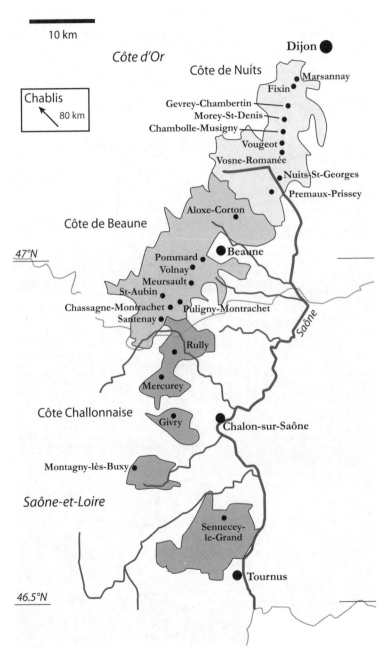

10 km

Côte d'Or

Chablis
80 km

Dijon ●

Côte de Nuits

Marsannay ●

Fixin ●

Gevrey-Chambertin ─── ●
Morey-St-Denis ─── ●
Chambolle-Musigny ─── ●

Vougeot ●

Vosne-Romanée ●

Nuits-St-Georges ●

Premaux-Prissey ●

Aloxe-Corton ●

Côte de Beaune

47°N

Beaune ●

Pommard ●
Volnay ●
Meursault ●
St-Aubin ●
Chassagne-Montrachet ● Puligny-Montrachet ●
Santenay ●

Saône

Rully ●

Mercurey ●

Côte Challonnaise

Givry ●

Chalon-sur-Saône ●

Montagny-lès-Buxy ●

Saône-et-Loire

Sennecey-
le-Grand ●

46.5°N

Tournus ●

Northern Burgundy

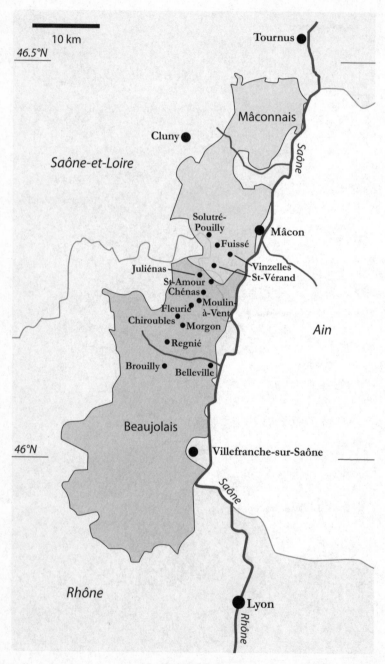

Southern Burgundy

The Celts were already making wine in Burgundy when the Romans conquered Gaul in 51BC. To supply their soldiers and colonists, the Romans propagated the vine all along the east-facing slopes of the Saône river valley. After the fall of the Western Roman Empire, the monasteries moved in and, through the gradual accretion of land, became the dominant force in wine making. Already in 591, Gregory, Bishop of Tours and author of the *History of Franks*, found it apt to compare Burgundy to the Roman Grand Cru Falernian.

The Benedictines, who founded the Abbey of Cluny in 910, and the Cistercians, who founded the Abbey of Cîteaux in 1098, became especially involved in wine making. These brothers in God soon became aware of the subtle influences of terroir and began to document vineyard and vintage observations with fastidious care. In 1336, the Cistercians created the first enclosed vineyard in Burgundy, Clos de Vougeot.

The proud monks invested so much time, effort, and skill into their wine that the Avignon popes soon began to take notice, purchasing vast quantities to ease the pangs of their Babylonian captivity. So as to uphold the quality and reputation of his wines, Philip II the Bold, Duke of Burgundy, banned the cultivation of the 'vile and disloyal' Gamay grape and the use of manure as fertilizer (which, by increasing yields, decreased concentrations). Thenceforth, red Burgundy could only be made from Pinot Noir. As for white Burgundy, it was then being made not from Chardonnay, but from Fromenteau, an ancestor of Pinot Gris.

In the 18th century, roads improved significantly, facilitating the export of wine out of landlocked Burgundy. The wines of Burgundy began to vie with those of Champagne, which were then predominantly still and red, for the lucrative Paris market. So fashionable did Burgundy become that, in 1760, the Prince de Conti acquired the Domaine de la Romanée and appended his name to the already famous estate.

After the absorption of Burgundy into the French crown in the late 15th century, the Church began to, figuratively and literally, lose ground. In the late 18th century, the French revolutionaries confiscated and auctioned off the Church's remaining lands. Over the course of several generations, these new, laical holdings became ever smaller owing to the *Code Napoléon*, which stipulates that any inheritance be equally divided among all children, including daughters. Today, there are no fewer than 80 growers in the Clos de

Vougeot, with some owning just a few rows of vines. This extreme parcellation has not occurred in Bordeaux, where many properties are owned by companies or structured as companies, and where the vineyards are not individually delineated and registered.

The parcellation of the vineyards of Burgundy encouraged the development of *négociant* houses, the first of which were established in the 1720s and 1730s. In 1847, King Louis-Philippe of France gave the village of Gevrey the right to append to its name that of its most famous Grand Cru, Chambertin. Not to be outdone, other villages soon followed suit, whence all the double-barrelled names in the area: Chambolle-Musigny, Morey-Saint-Denis, and so on. In 1855, the year of the Bordeaux Classification, one Dr Jules Lavalle published an influential book with the snappy title of *Histoire et Statistique de la Vigne et des Grands Vins de la Côte-d'Or*. Dr Lavalle's book included an unofficial classification of the vineyards of Burgundy, which informed the official classification adopted by the Beaune Committee of Agriculture in 1861. After the introduction of the French AOC system in 1936, most of the vineyards in the top tier of this classification acceded to the lofty Grand Cru status.

Like other wine growing regions, Burgundy then started to suffer, first from the phylloxera epidemic which arrived in Meursault in 1878, then from the Great Depression, and finally from the Second World War. Upon returning to their land, the growers began to enrich their devastated vineyards with chemical fertilizers. This worked well at first, but over time potassium accumulated in the soil, leading to a fall in acidity in the grapes and wines. The assiduous application of modern vineyard management techniques has largely reversed this trend.

The lie of the land

Burgundy has one hundred AOCs, that is, about 25% of the total number of AOCs in France and twice as many as Bordeaux. But if one excludes the Beaujolais, the actual area under vines is only a small fraction of that in Bordeaux, about 28,000ha versus 120,000ha (1ha = 2.47ac). To the north, just south of the regional capital of Dijon, lies the most illustrious section of the *vignoble bourgignon*, the Côte d'Or, which is the name both of the *département* and of the wine growing area. The Côte d'Or consists of the northerly Côtes de Nuits, which is especially reputed for its red wines and contains the great majority of the red Grand Cru sites, and the southerly Côtes de Beaune, which is especially reputed for its white wines. Still further south is the Côte Chalonnaise with some of the best bargains in Burgundy, then the Mâconnais, and, finally, the Beaujolais, which stretches almost as far south as Lyon. The picture is completed by Chablis, a satellite of Burgundy that is actually closer to Champagne than to the Côte d'Or.

Climate

The vineyards of the Côte d'Or, with the romantic town of Beaune more or less at their centre, run the length of an east-facing limestone escarpment, whence 'Côte d'Or' or 'Golden Slope'. According to some, the name is a diminutive of 'Côte d'Orient' or 'East-facing Slope', rather than a reference to the golden tinge of the slope. The climate here is northerly and continental, with cold winters, hesitant springs, and potentially hot summers. The shortish growing season is partly compensated for by east-facing slopes, long summer days, and, in good years, a dry and sun-drenched September. Aside from spring frosts, other weather hazards include heavy rain in May and June and hailstorms in the late summer. Unsurprisingly, there can be a lot of variation between vintages and even between different parts of Burgundy within a single vintage. While the marginal climate does pose certain risks, the overall cool temperatures preserve acidity and promote the development of complex aromatic compounds. Without its marginal climate, Burgundy would simply not be Burgundy.

Grape varieties

The grape varieties of Burgundy do not tax the memory. The principal varieties are Pinot Noir for the reds and Chardonnay for the whites; otherwise, Gamay goes into making Beaujolais and there is also some Aligoté. And that's pretty much it.

The name Pinot Noir is thought to allude to the grapes themselves, which are tightly clustered into bunches that resemble pinecones. As the variety is ancient, and as it is genetically unstable and prone to mutations, there are a large number of clones for growers to choose from. Even a single clone, if planted in different locations, can yield very different expressions. Indeed, Pinot Noir is extremely expressive of terroir, perhaps more so than any other variety. Unfortunately, it is not easy to work with: as the Californian winemaker André Tchelistcheff once put it, "God made Cabernet Sauvignon whereas the devil made Pinot Noir." The vine is intolerant of heat and drought and does best in cooler climates, especially when planted on well-drained limestone soils as in the Côte d'Or, its spiritual home and, arguably, its highest expression. As it flowers early, it is especially vulnerable to spring frosts and to *coulure* and *millerandage*, and as the grapes are tightly bunched and thin-skinned, they are prone to rot and disease and damage from hail. Compared to many other black grape varieties, Pinot Noir is lacking in pigment and tannin, which explains the characteristic pale colour and a reliance on high acidity for definition on the palate; if the grapes are overripe, the result is a soft and jammy offering that is flabby and lacking in interest. Planting densities, especially in Burgundy, are very high, up to 12,000 vines/ha, with the vines, which are single or double Guyot trained, less than 1m (3.3ft) apart. The yields are diminutive and, in some of the best vineyards, no more than 25hl/ha. The wines are light to medium in body, silky, and aromatic, distinguished by their savoury fleshiness and farmyard aromas—even if the current vogue is for a lighter, cleaner, and more fruit-driven style.

Unlike Pinot Noir, Chardonnay is relatively easy to work with, and, on a global scale, is more widespread than any other grape variety including Cabernet Sauvignon. It tends to do especially well on chalk, clay, and limestone, which are all highly prevalent in its Burgundian homeland. Chardonnay has a 'neutral' or 'malleable' profile, and is sometimes compared to a mirror that reflects the terroir that it is planted in, or, more commonly, the skill and ambition of the winemaker—in particular with regard to temperature of fermentation, extent of malolactic fermentation, amount of lees contact and stirring (*bâtonnage*), oak treatment, and bottle ageing. Generous yields of over 50hl/ha are easy enough to achieve and need to be restricted for premium wines. The choice of rootstock is important, both for limiting the vigour of the plant, and, on limestone soils, for reducing the risk of chlorosis. Like Pinot Noir, Chardonnay buds and flowers early, which makes it vulnerable to spring frosts—especially in Chablis, where the use of frost protection systems is common—and to *coulure* and *millerandage*. As it is thin-skinned, it is prone to rot and damage from hail; but as it also ripens early (just after Pinot Noir), it can often be harvested before autumn rains move in. Another reason not to delay the harvest is that acidity declines rapidly once the grape is fully ripe. Chardonnay produces a number of different styles, even within Burgundy itself, from lean, racy, and mineral Chablis to round, rich, and buttery Meursault. It is planted throughout Chablis, and is also found in the Côte d'Or (especially the Côte de Beaune), the Côte Chalonnaise, and the Mâconnais. The best-made Chardonnays of the Côte Chalonnaise—from the villages of Mercurey, Montagny-lès-Buxy, or Rully—can rival those of the Côte de Beaune, as can those from the Pouilly-Fuissé area in the Mâconnais.

Aligoté very much plays second fiddle to Chardonnay in the white wine stakes; as Chardonnay is so much more profitable, Aligoté has mostly been relegated to the poorer vineyard sites at the top and bottom of the slopes. Aligoté wines can be labelled as Bourgogne Aligoté AOC or, in the commune of Bouzeron in the Côte Chalonnaise, as Bouzeron Aligoté AOC. Yields for Bouzeron Aligoté AOC are capped at 45hl/ha, compared to 60hl/ha for Bourgogne Aligoté AOC. The wines are light and rather neutral with faint notes of apples and lemons, and a high acidity that can be either lively or angular. They do not benefit from oak treatment or ageing. Kir or *vin blanc cassis* is traditionally made by adding crème de cassis to Aligoté. Other, less widely planted white grape varieties in Burgundy are Pinot Blanc, Pinot Gris, Melon de Bourgogne, and Sauvignon Blanc, which has a variety-specific appellation in St Bris.

Appellations

About 61% of all the wine produced in Burgundy is white, about 31% is red (together with a very little rosé), and the rest is sparkling.

Broadly speaking, the wines of Burgundy can be divided into four levels: regional or generic, village or commune, Premier Cru, and Grand Cru. There are 23 regional AOCs, 44 commune AOCs (which encompass the Premier Crus), and 33 Grand Cru AOCs: the first account for 52% of the vineyard area, the second for 46.6%, and the third for just 1.4%. Within this, Premier Cru vineyards or *climats*, of which there are 635, account for some 11% of the total vineyard area. Each AOC is associated with a specific set of regulations.

Regional AOCs all begin with 'Bourgogne'. Some, namely, Bourgogne Rouge, Bourgogne Blanc, Bourgogne Aligoté, Bourgogne Grand Ordinaire (which can be red, white, or rosé and contain several grape varieties), and Bourgogne Passetoutgrains (which can be red or rosé and can contain up to two-thirds Gamay), cover the entire *vignoble bourguignon*; others, such as Bourgogne Hautes Côtes de Nuits, Bourgogne Hautes Côtes de Beaune, and Bourgogne Côte Chalonnaise are circumscribed to a defined area. There is no such thing as a regional *Vin de Pays* and there is no *Vin de Pays* for the *département* of the Côte d'Or; but there is a *Vin de Pays* for the Saône-et-Loire and for the Yonne.

Côte de Nuits-Villages and Côte de Beaune-Villages, despite covering diverse areas, are considered as village or commune appellations rather than regional appellations. Côte de Nuits-Villages is a red wine appellation that can be used by five communes, two in the extreme north of the Côte de Nuits (Fixin, Brochon) and three in the extreme south (Prissey, Corgoloin, Comblanchien). With the sole exception of Fixin, they cannot use their own name. Côte de Beaune-Villages is also a red wine appellation, available to a number of communes in the Côte de Beaune (all the communes except for Aloxe-Corton, Beaune, Volnay, and Pommard). Unlike with Côte de Nuits-Villages, these communes can choose between Côte de Beaune-Villages and their own name. Côte de Beaune-Villages AOC should not be confused with Côte de Beaune AOC, which applies to a delimited area in the vicinity of Beaune.

Next up come specific village or commune AOCs, which broadly apply to a specific commune. Examples are Pommard AOC, Chambolle-Musigny AOC, Chassagne-Montrachet AOC, and Pouilly-Fuissé AOC. For a commune AOC, the vineyard or *climat* can be included on the label, but it must be in smaller lettering—except if it is of Premier Cru status. A wine from a Premier Cru vineyard, say, les Perrières in Meursault, may be labelled as MEURSAULT LES PERRIERES or MEUR-SAULT PREMIER CRU. The designation MEURSAULT PREMIER CRU can also be used for a blend from several Premier Cru vineyards in Meursault. Note that there are no Premier Cru sites in the Mâconnais.

At the summit of the pyramid are the 33 Grand Crus, which, unlike the Premier Crus, are completely independent of the commune appellation. All but one of the red Grand Crus are in the Côte de Nuits, and all but one of the white Grand Crus (of which there are fewer) are in the Côte de Beaune. A couple of the red Grand Crus, namely, Chambolle-Musigny and Corton, also produce some white wine. The red Grand Crus occupy 356ha, the white Grand Crus 194ha. In 2010, about 2.5m bottles of Grand Cru were produced. Some of the largest individual Grand Crus are Corton (97.53ha), Corton-Charlemagne (52.08ha), and Clos de Vougeot (50.6ha); the smallest is La Romanée at a mere 0.85ha. Although every producer in, say, the Clos de Vougeot is entitled to label his wine as GRAND CRU CLOS DE VOUGEOT, the reputations and prices of the various wines vary widely.

Wine industry

The small size of many holdings makes co-operatives and *négociants* an important part of the landscape of Burgundy. Grapes, must, or wine are often sold on to *négociants*, who then make and/or blend the wines. Despite the rise of domaine bottling, especially in the more highly regarded communes, *négociants* remain an important force in Burgundy, with such big names as Bouchard Père et Fils, Louis Jadot, Joseph Drouhin, and Faiveley. These *négociant* houses also have significant vineyard holdings of their own, but as the law limits the extent of their holdings, they remain highly dependent on smaller growers and producers.

Wine styles

Chablis

Chablis is in the *département* of the Yonne, around 100km (62mi) to the northwest of Dijon. The vineyards are spread across some

20 communes centred on the small town of Chablis in the valley of the River Serein. The climate is cooler than in the Côte d'Or, with increased risk of frost damage and later harvests. The use of protection measures against frost such as aspersion systems and smudge pots is widespread. The soil consists of a limestone bed overlain by either Kimmeridgean or Portlandian clay, which both originated in the Jurassic period. Kimmeridgean clay is more highly sought-after than Portlandian clay, and consists of clay, limestone, and fossilized oyster shells. Only Chardonnay is, and can be, planted in Chablis, which, for many, has become synonymous with Chardonnay.

There are four appellations in Chablis: Petit Chablis AOC, Chablis AOC, Chablis Premier Cru AOC, and Chablis Grand Cru AOC. In recent decades, the area classified as Chablis AOC, and which accounts for the bulk of production, has controversially been expanded to include land on Portlandian clay. There are 40 Premier Cru vineyards, although the names of the smaller Premier Cru vineyards may or may not be subsumed under that of a nearby larger Premier Cru vineyard. There are 17 such 'umbrella' Premier Cru vineyards, including Montée de Tonnerre, Fourchaume, Vaillons, and Montmains. The seven Grand Cru vineyards—Blanchots, Bougros, Les Clos, Grenouilles, Preuses, Valmur, and Vaudésir—count as a single Grand Cru and occupy just over 100ha on the southwestern aspect of the slope along the right-bank of the River Serein. The Grand Cru wines most reliably capture the gunflint quality (*goût de pierre à fusil*) for which Chablis is reputed.

On the whole, Chablis winemakers privilege terroir over winemaking, and tend to avoid exposing their wines to significant oak treatment. Some Grand Cru wines do come into contact with some new oak, but even so the amount of char in the barrel is usually very light. About one-third of total output is overseen by the co-operative La Chablisienne, which makes wines at all levels including Grand Cru. In the glass, Chablis is classically pale lemon in colour with or without a greenish tinge. On the nose, there are green apples, citrus fruits, honeysuckle, cream, and a characteristic stony or smoky minerality. The palate is lean, dry, and austere with pronounced acidity, which is a key distinguishing feature. New oak is usually absent.

Mâconnais

The climate of the Mâconnais is considerably warmer than that of Chablis or even the Côte d'Or, with less risk of spring frosts and earlier harvests. The relief is not as marked as in the Côte d'Or, and vineyards are mixed in with other forms of farming. The most reputed wines of the Mâconnais are from south of Mâcon, where the land rises up to form the Mont de Pouilly and other limestone hills. Chardonnay predominates, but some Gamay and Pinot Noir are also planted, especially in areas that are relatively rich in sand and clay.

Aside from the regional appellations (Mâcon, Mâcon-Villages, and Mâcon + name of a commune), there are five commune-specific appellations, namely, Pouilly-Fuissé, Pouilly-Loché, Pouilly-Vinzelles, St Véran, and Viré-Clessé. Some of the *lieux-dits* in Pouilly-Fuissé are deserving of Premier Cru status, but, as it stands, there are no Premier Cru vineyards in Pouilly-Fuissé or indeed the Mâconnais. The Viré-Clessé appellation, which lies to the north of Mâcon, was created in 1999 from two highly regarded commune appellations, Mâcon-Viré and Mâcon-Clessé.

Compared to Beaune, Mâcon is simple and easy to drink and unlikely to improve with age. That having been said, certain villages and producers have built a good reputation for themselves and can offer great value for money. As with Chablis, much Mâcon is unoaked. However, Mâcon is much less acidic than Chablis. Compared to Beaune and especially to Chablis, it is deeper in colour, with riper aromas and a fuller and softer or richer body. The Pouilly wines, which are often oaked, tend to be richer and riper on the one hand, and finer and more complex on the other. Pouilly-Fuissé can be thought of as an enclave of St Véran, and the wines of St Véran, while less well regarded, share many similarities with those of Pouilly-Fuissé.

Côte Chalonnaise

The Côte Chalonnaise is named for the town of Chalon-sur-Sâone, an important Celtic and, later, Roman trading centre. The vineyards, which are interspersed with other forms of farming, are planted on a 25km (16m) stretch of gently undulating land that separates the

Mâconnais to the south from the Côte de Beaune to the north. The geology and climate are similar to those of the Côte d'Or, and four of the five village-level AOCs (from north to south, Rully, Mercurey, Givry, and Montagny) even boast a number of Premier Cru sites.

The wines of the Côte Chalonnaise are similar to those of the Côte d'Or, if not quite so grand, and the region is a reliable source of affordable Burgundy. Mercurey produces more wine than any other village-level AOC; so important is Mercurey that the Côte Chalonnaise used to be referred to as the 'Région de Mercurey'. As in Givry to the south, production is dominated by red wine, which is noted for its deeper colour, fuller body, and spicy cherry notes. Further south, the region of Montagny is devoted to white wine production, and boasts as many as 51 Premier Cru sites. To the north of Mercurey, Rully produces more white than red wine, and is also an important source of Crémant de Bourgogne. Bouzeron is a bit of a curio, in that it is the only village-level AOC for Aligoté.

Côte d'Or: Côte de Beaune

The escarpment that is the Côte d'Or divides the mountains of the Morvan to the west from the plain of the River Saône to the east. The soils at the top of the escarpment are too sparse, and those on the plain too fertile, for the production of truly great wine. Thus, the best vineyards are mostly located mid-slope, at altitudes of 250-300m (820-1,150ft), where the vines also benefit from better sun exposure and water drainage. The monotony of east-facing vineyards is broken by a number of streams and dry valleys (*combes*), which cut across the escarpment and alter the aspect of certain vineyard sites.

The soils in the Côte d'Or are essentially a mixture of Jurassic limestone and marl. In the Côte de Beaune, limestone tends to predominate, making it more suitable to the cultivation of Chardonnay than the Côte de Nuits. Although the Côte de Beaune contains all but one of the white wine Grand Crus, red wine production predominates. Red wines from the Côte de Beaune are lighter, suppler, more fruit-driven, and quicker to mature than those from the warmer Côte de Nuits. That said, red wines from Corton (which is the only red wine Grand Cru in the Côte de Beaune) and from the commune of Pommard tend to be more muscular and tannic, and more akin to those from the Côte de Nuits.

To the north of Beaune itself, the hill of Corton divides between the communes of Aloxe-Corton, Pernand-Vergelesses, and Ladoix. This hill is home to three partially overlapping Grand Cru AOCs, Corton for red and white wine, Corton-Charlemagne for white wine, and the little used Charlemagne for white wine. Corton-Charlemagne mostly occupies the higher parts of the hill, which are more suited to the cultivation of Chardonnay. Excluding Chablis Grand Cru, Corton-Charlemagne is the largest white wine Grand Cru in Burgundy.

Pommard, a red wine-only commune and appellation, lies just to the south of Beaune. The quality of Pommard is variable, but better examples can represent very good value for money, with the Premier Cru sites of Les Rugiens and Epenots being especially reputed. The muscular red wines of Pommard are often contrasted to the delicate and feminine wines of Volnay, which lies just a little further south, and is the most southerly red wine only appellation of the Côte d'Or. Compared to the soils of Pommard, which are rich in marl, those of Volnay are rich in limestone, such that the wines of Volnay are especially soft and fragrant, similar to (but lighter than) those of Chambolle-Musigny in the Côte de Nuits.

Further south, Puligny-Montrachet, Chassagne-Montrachet, and Meursault yield some of the finest white wines in the world. Puligny-Montrachet boasts four Grand Crus of which two, Montrachet and Bâtard-Montrachet, extend south into Chassagne-Montrachet, which has a Grand Cru of its own, Criots-Bâtard-Montrachet. Puligny-Montrachet is tight and structured. It can be difficult to distinguish from Chassagne-Montrachet, which does however tend to be nuttier. In contrast, Meursault is broad and buttery and rather extravagant—although some producers do favour leaner styles. Meursault does not count any Grand Crus, but it does boast some very high performing Premier Crus, especially Perrières, Genevrières, and Les Charmes. At the southern end of Chassagne-Montrachet, red wine production is once again dominant, as it is further south in Santenay. In a side-valley to the west lies Saint-Aubin, which, in contrast, is dominated by white wine production. Some of the white wines of Santenay and Saint-Aubin can be reminiscent of Chassagne-Montrachet.

Côte d'Or: Côte de Nuits

The Côte de Nuits, which extends from the city of Dijon to just south of the regional centre of Nuits-Saint-Georges, is world renowned for its red wines. Of its 14 communes, six produce Grand Cru wines, with the commune of Gevrey-Chambertin alone boasting no less than nine Grand Cru vineyards, all carrying 'Chambertin' in their name. The largest Grand Cru vineyard in Gevrey is Charmes-Chambertin, followed by Chambertin and Chambertin-Clos de Bèze (which under AOC regulations can be labelled as Chambertin). Gevrey also has 26 Premier Crus, and a Premier Cru from a reputed producer might fetch a higher price than a less pedigreed Grand Cru. All in all, the wines of Gevrey-Chambertin are noted for their deep colour, power, and structure: full, rich, but also silky and delicately perfumed.

Morey-Saint-Denis, directly to the south of Gevrey, counts four Grand Cru vineyards: Clos de la Roche, the largest and most reputed among them; Clos Saint Denis; and Clos de Tart and Clos des Lambrays, which, unusually, are both monopoles (in single ownership). Another Grand Cru vineyard, Bonnes-Mares, mostly lies in Chambolle-Musigny, but does extend a little into Morey-Saint-Denis. Lying as it does between the vaunted villages of Gevrey-Chambertin and Chambolle-Musigny, Morey-Saint-Denis is often overlooked, and, accordingly, can provide better value for money. The commune also counts 20 Premier Cru vineyards, a very small proportion of which is for white Morey-Saint-Denis.

Compared to those of Gevrey-Chambertin, the wines of Chambolle-Musigny can be described as 'feminine', that is, lighter, brighter, more delicate, more elegant, and more seductive, and not unlike those of Volnay in the Côte de Beaune which are however somewhat lighter. As in Volnay, the soils in Chambolle are relatively rich in limestone, and Le Musigny is the only Grand Cru vineyard in the Côte de Nuits for white wine as well as red (although most of the plantings are Pinot Noir). Bonnes-Mares, the other Grand Cru vineyard in Chambolle, is larger but less reputed than Le Musigny, which has been tagged as "queen of all Burgundy" and described as "an iron fist in a velvet glove". Some of the 25 Premier Cru vineyards in Chambolle, in particular Les Amoureuses (which borders on Le Musigny) and Les Charmes, are so highly regarded as to fetch Grand Cru prices.

The smallest village in the Côte de Nuits, Vougeot, contains its largest Grand Cru vineyard, the Clos de Vougeot, which, at 50.6ha, accounts for the bulk of the commune's production. The Clos, named for the River Vouge separating Vougeot from Chambolle, comprises a château that, since 1945, has served as the headquarters of the *Confrérie des Chevaliers du Tastevin*, an outfit devoted to upholding standards in Burgundy. Most highly regarded is the top, northwestern corner of the vineyard, which surrounds the château and borders on Le Musigny and Grands Echezeaux; least regarded is the bottom part of the vineyard, to the east and bordering on the N74. This, together with the large number of producers operating in the Clos de Vougeot, means that wines labelled 'Clos de Vougeot' can vary enormously in style, quality, and price.

The communes of Vosne-Romanée and Flagey-Echezeaux together count eight Grand Cru vineyards, among which Romanée-Conti, that most iconic of red wines. There is no separate appellation for Flagey-Echezeaux, and the village and Premier Cru vineyards in this commune come under the Vosne-Romanée AOC. The commune of Vosne-Romanée itself counts six Grand Cru vineyards: Romanée-Conti and La Tâche, which are both monopoles of Domaine de la Romanée-Conti; La Romanée, which is a monopole of Comte Liger-Belair; Romanée-Saint-Vivant; Richebourg; and La Grande Rue, a monopole of Domaine Lamarche and upgraded to Grand Cru status in 1992. The commune of Flagey-Echezeaux counts a further two Grand Crus, Grands Echezeaux and Echezeaux. The smallest of these eight Grand Cru vineyards is La Romanée at only 0.85ha, corresponding to about 300 cases a year, and the largest (by a very long way) is Echezeaux at 34.79ha. As with the Clos de Vougeot, a combination of large size and fragmented holdings means that wines labelled as 'Echezeaux' can vary considerably in style, quality, and price. Vosne-Romanée Premier Crus are highly regarded; those that are higher up the hill, such as Aux Raignots and Cros Parentoux, tend to be in a fresher style.

Nuits-Saint-Georges lies at the southern end of the Côtes de Nuits, directly to the south of Vosne-Romanée and stretching for five kilometres to Prémaux-Prissey. The Nuits-Saint-Georges appellation covers the communes of Nuits-Saint-Georges and Prémaux-Prissey, and can apply to both red and white wine (although white wine accounts for only 3% of production). For historical reasons, there are no Grand Cru vineyards but as many as 41 Premier Crus, including the sought-after Les Saint Georges, Les Vaucrains, and Les Cailles, which lie just south of Nuits-Saint-Georges. These wines are richer and more structured than those from the north of the appellation, which are more similar to Vosne-Romanée in style. In general, the wines of Nuits-Saint-George are quite masculine, full and firm, and dominated by black rather than red fruit.

In the north of the Côte de Nuits, in the shadow of Gevrey-Chambertin, are the communes of Fixin ("Fissin") and Marsannay. The Fixin AOC covers vineyards in both Fixin and Brochon, and can apply to both red and white wine (although white wine accounts for only 4% of production). Five of the vineyards are designated as Premier Cru and all the rest are at village level. The red wines of Fixin are similar to those of Gevrey-Chambertin, if somewhat less delicate and less intense. Created as recently as 1987, the Marsannay AOC covers vineyards in Marsannay-la-Côte, Couchey, and Chenôve, and can apply to red, rosé, and white wine (although red wine accounts for two-thirds of production and rosé, for which Marsannay is known, accounts for most of the rest). All the vineyards are at village level. Compared to other red wines in the Côte de Nuits, those of Marsannay tend to be softer and fruitier and generally more approachable.

In general, it is very difficult to tell communes apart (perhaps even more so than for the Haut-Médoc in Bordeaux), and the blind taster who can frequently differentiate Côte de Beaune from Mâconnais for whites and Côte de Nuits from Côte de Beaune for reds is already doing a very good job.

Beaujolais

Beaujolais—named after Beaujeu, the historical capital of the province—is important by volume if not by reputation. 99% of Beaujolais is red, and almost all of that is made from the thin-skinned Gamay grape, which, in the Middle Ages, was driven south onto the granite soils of Beaujolais by the edicts of Philip the Bold and, later, Philip the Good. Although Beaujolais is thought of in terms of Burgundy, most of the region is in Rhône-Alpes and the climate more nearly approximates that of the Rhône, with hot summers and cold winters. The northern part of Beaujolais, to the north of Villefranche, is made up of rolling hills of granite and schist; the southern part or Bas-Beaujolais is flatter and more fertile, with soils rich in sandstone and clay and patches of limestone. Owing to a combination of gradient and soil type, the grapes actually ripen earlier and more fully in the northern part, which tends to produce wines with greater structure and complexity, and contains all of the region's ten Crus and village level vineyards.

Beaujolais wines are typically pale in colour with a blue tinge, light in body, high in acidity, and low in tannins. Most Beaujolais is made by semi-carbonic maceration, which contributes estery notes of bananas and bubblegum to the red fruits of the Gamay grape. In contrast, Cru wines tend to be made by traditional vinification and can also be oaked, rendering them more tannic and difficult to recognize as Beaujolais.

Whereas most Beaujolais ought to be drunk within a year, the Cru wines benefit from some cellaring, with the best coming to approach Burgundy in style. Moulin-à-Vent, Morgon, Juliénas, and Chénas are the most long-lived Crus, and can develop for up to ten or fifteen years after harvest. The other six Beaujolais crus are St-Amour, Chiroubles, Fleurie, Regnié, Côte de Brouilly, and Brouilly, which contains the notorious *Pisse Vieille* (roughly translated as "piss, old woman!") vineyard. According to local lore, a devout Catholic woman once misheard the local priest's absolution to "*Allez! Et ne péchez plus*" ("Go! And sin no more") as "*Allez! Et ne pissez plus*" ("Go! And piss no more"). Upon learning of the priest's words, her husband is supposed to have exclaimed, "*Pisse Vielle!*" It should be noted that, unlike in the rest of Burgundy, the ten Beaujolais Crus refer not to individual vineyards but to entire areas of viticulture. Aside from the ten Crus, the other appellations of Beaujolais are Beaujolais-Villages AOC in a defined area in the north, Beaujolais Supérieur AOC (of which little is produced), and Beaujolais AOC.

Beaujolais Nouveau is not an appellation but a style: simple, approachable, and destined for early release and immediate drinking. After a short period of fermentation, Beaujolais Nouveau is bottled and put on sale, by decree, from midnight on the third Thursday of November. Beaujolais Primeur is another, less commercially important *vin de primeur* that can only be put on sale after 31 January. According to regulations, Beaujolais Nouveau and Beaujolais Primeur can be produced from any area of Beaujolais except the ten Crus; in practice, much of it comes from the Bas-Beaujolais. There is a sense in which Beaujolais has become the victim of the one-time success of Beaujolais Nouveau, which, in the end, caused lasting damage to the reputation of the region.

Chapter 7

The Rhône

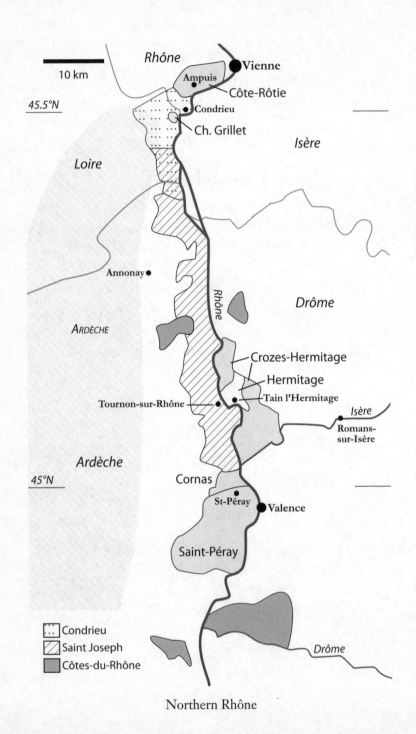

Northern Rhône

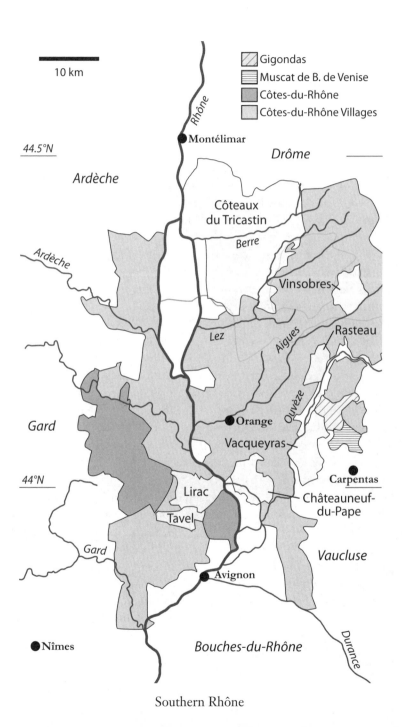

Southern Rhône

Syrah, the most important grape variety of the Northern Rhône, has given rise to much speculation about distant and exotic origins. However, extensive DNA typing has revealed it as an offspring of Dureza and Mondeuse Blanche, both varieties from southeastern France.

The history of wine in the Rhône is patchy. The 1st century naturalist Pliny the Elder noted that, in the region of Vienne, the tribe of the Allobroges produced and exported a highly prized wine. After the eclipse of Rome, viticulture in the Rhône fell into decline, only to be revived when, in 1308, Pope Clement V migrated the papal court from Rome to Avignon. His successor John XXII did much to improve viticultural practices; wines from the area came to be known as 'Vin du Pape' and, later, after John erected his famous castle, as 'Châteauneuf-du-Pape'. The Babylonian captivity of the Bishop of Rome also benefited Burgundy: when Petrarch wrote to Urban V pleading for his return to Rome, the Pope wryly noted that the best wines of Burgundy did not percolate south of the Alps.

In the 15th and 16th centuries, the city of Lyon and its hinterland began to prosper. However, from 1446, Burgundy banned Rhodanian wines on the grounds that they were *très petits et pauvres* ('very small and miserable'), effectively restricting access to northern markets. In the 17th and 18th centuries, Rhodanian wines began to develop a reputation in Paris and London, so much so that top Bordeaux producers such as Château Lafite took to enriching their wines with Hermitage. In time, some of these enriched wines came to fetch even higher prices than their unblended counterparts.

In the wake of the phylloxera epidemic, quality plummeted, and the practice of passing off inferior wine as Châteauneuf-du-Pape became depressingly common. In 1924, Baron Le Roy of Château Fortia founded the *syndicat des vignerons de Châteauneuf-du-Pape* and, in 1929, the *syndicat des Côtes-du-Rhône*. In 1933, he succeeded in defining and delimiting the appellation of Châteauneuf-du-Pape, thereby restoring the quality and reputation of the wines. In that same year, he co-founded the *Académie du vin de France*, and, in 1935, together with former minister of agriculture Joseph Capus, the *Institut national des appellations d'origine* (INAO), which did for France that which Le Roy had done for Châteauneuf-du-Pape.

The Northern Rhône too had suffered a marked decline, only to be revived in the late 20th century by such figures as Marcel Guigal and Robert Parker, who did a splendid job shouting about it and raising its international profile. Still today, compared to Burgundy and especially Bordeaux, the Rhône retains a rustic and agrarian feel.

The Northern Rhône

The entire Rhône region is defined and united by the River Rhône, which arises in the Swiss Alps, drives into and out of Lake Geneva, and veers south to carve out the *couloir rhodanien* (Rhône or Rhodanian corridor), a valley that separates the Massif Central from the Alps. The Northern Rhône, or *secteur septentrional*, stretches 80km (50mi) from Vienne in the north to Valence in the south. This area differs significantly in climate, topography, and geology from the Southern Rhône, or *secteur méridional*, which stretches 70km (43mi) from Montélimar in the north to Avignon in the south. These areas are not contiguous, and there is a gap of 30km (19mi) between the southern end of the Northern Rhône and the northern end of the Southern Rhône.

The landscape of the Northern Rhône, where the river valley is narrow and the inclines are steep, is much more dramatic than the Southern Rhône, with terraced vineyards that can only be worked by hand. The subsoil consists of granite and gneiss and the topsoil is sparse and prone to erosion by heavy rains. Most of the appellations of the Northern Rhône are on the western (east-facing) slope: all, in fact, but Hermitage and Crozes-Hermitage, which are on the eastern slope, just north of Valence and the confluence with the River Isère. In some areas, the plantings stretch into lateral valleys, which offer shelter from the full force of the Mistral, a cold, dry north-south gale that picks up speed as it is funnelled through the Rhodanian corridor. Winters are cold and summers hot, but tempered by the Mistral and cooler than in the Southern Rhône.

The Northern Rhône is home to some of the region's most celebrated wines, even though it accounts for only a tiny fraction of the total production of the Rhône, which, after Bordeaux, is the second largest quality wine region of France. Except in the small white wine appellations of Condrieu, Château-Grillet, and Saint-Péray, red wines are predominant, and are made of Syrah or a majority blend of Syrah together with one or two of the three white wine grapes: Viognier, Roussanne, and Marsanne. Of the red wines, Côte-Rôtie can be blended with up to 20% Viognier, Crozes-Hermitage and Hermitage with up to 15% Marsanne and Roussanne, and Saint-Joseph with up to 10% Marsanne and Roussanne. Cornas is the only red wine which calls for 100% Syrah. Of the white wines, Condrieu and Château-Grillet are made from Viognier; and Saint Péray and the white wines of Crozes-Hermitage, Hermitage, and Saint Joseph are made from Marsanne and Roussanne. There are no rosés in the Northern Rhône.

Let us begin with Hermitage, the grandest appellation of the Northern Rhône and the spiritual home of the Syrah grape. According to legend, the Chevalier de Stérimberg returned wounded from the Cathar Crusade, and was granted permission by Blanche of Castile, Queen consort of France, to build a small refuge and chapel in which to live out his days as a hermit. This hermitage gave its name to the appellation, which rises from Tain l'Hermitage and runs along the southern aspect of a steep granite hill that captures the best part of the sun's heat. The appellation, which stands at a mere 154ha (cf. Château Lafite, 107ha), is divided into a number of named *climats*; traditional Hermitage, such as that of JL Chave, is a blend of wines from several of these climats. Hermitage is dark, full-bodied, and tannic, with intense aromas of soft black fruits accompanied by red fruits, smoke, black pepper and spice, leather, cocoa, and coffee. The wine calls for age, and after a decade or so develops a certain sweetness of fruit and gamey complexity. The best examples from top vintages—such as the famous La Chapelle 1961—can keep for decades, and very old Hermitage can be almost impossible to distinguish from top claret of a similar age. At one time, the white wines of Hermitage were just as renowned as the red wines. With age, these noble blends of Marsanne and Roussanne develop notes of apricots and peaches together with a nutty finish. In some years, Chapoutier also makes a straw wine, which, owing to its scarcity, fetches very high prices.

Unlike Hermitage, Crozes-Hermitage and Saint-Joseph are larger appellations which, taken together, account for most of the production of the Northern Rhône. Crozes-Hermitage stretches across eleven villages centred on Tain-l'Hermitage. Over 90% of production consists of unblended red wines, which are generally softer and fruitier than Hermitage. The best examples are complex and full-bodied and similar to Hermitage, and can offer good value for money. However, wines from vineyards on flatter land, or those destined for early drinking which are made by semi carbonic maceration, tend to be less impressive. Among the best Crozes-Hermitage are Domaine de Thalabert, Les Chassis, and the offerings of Alain Graillot. The co-operative Cave de Tain is especially important here, as is Jaboulet.

The heart of Saint-Joseph lies around the communes of Tournon, on the right bank opposite Tain l'Hermitage, and Mauves, a little bit further south—indeed, Saint-Joseph used to be called *Vin de Mauves*. Today, the appellation is named for the vineyard of Saint-Joseph, itself named for the patron saint of manual labour and scorned husbands. After the creation of the appellation in 1956, the area under vines expanded six-fold, and, today, wines labelled with Saint-Joseph are just as variable as those labelled with Crozes-Hermitage. As the grapes ripen less fully than in Hermitage across the river, the wines are lighter, with notes of black fruit and pepper. They are mostly intended for early drinking.

The wines of Hermitage are sometimes described as masculine and compared and contrasted with the 'feminine' wines of Côte-Rôtie, which lies in the area of Ampuis, right up in the north of the Northern Rhône. Owing to a bend in the river, the vineyards face southeast on a slope that is even steeper than in Hermitage. The aspect and incline combine to maximize sun exposure, whence the name Côte-Rôtie ('Roasted Slope'). The site is also protected from the Mistral. Côte-Rôtie is sub-divided into two main areas, the Côte Brune on dark, iron-rich schist, and the Côte Blonde on pale granite and schist soils. According to legend, the areas were named for the brown- and blonde-haired daughters of a local lord; just like those girls, the wines have different characters, with Côte Brune being more tannic and full-bodied and Côte Blonde softer and more elegant. Traditionally, Côte-Rôtie was often a blend of Côte Brune and Côte Blonde. In recent years, there has been a trend towards single vineyard wines, and it is above all the single vineyard wines of Marcel Guigal that, in the early 1980s, led to the revival of the appellation. Côte-Rôtie is either 100% Syrah or a blend of Syrah and a very small amount (typically 5%) of Viognier, which is sometimes said to impart a floral fragrance to the wine. Côte-Rôtie marries power and finesse, with a complex nose of raspberry, blueberry, plum, bacon, green olives, violets, and leather.

At the other end of the Northern Rhône, south of Saint-Joseph, lies the highly regarded appellation of Cornas, which is smaller even than Hermitage. Here the land forms a sheltered amphitheatre which acts as a suntrap and protection from the Mistral—indeed, the name 'Cornas' is Celtic for 'burnt earth' (cf. Côte-Rôtie). Cornas is invariably 100% Syrah, as the appellation does not cover white wines and blending is not permitted. As one might expect, Cornas is fuller and richer than Crozes-Hermitage or Saint-Joseph, but more rustic than Hermitage. The fresher and more fruit-forward style of Cornas pioneered by Jean-Luc Colombo can be drunk earlier than traditional Cornas of the sort championed by Auguste Clape, the icon of appellation. Red Rhône can be confused with red Bordeaux, which tends to be higher in acidity with drier and grippier tannins and green or leafy Cabernet notes.

The white wines of the Northern Rhône, though relatively scarce, often make an appearance in blind tasting competitions. Condrieu is a small, white wine appellation that is entirely planted with Viognier. It extends south from Côte-Rôtie on steepish slopes with a south and southeastern aspect. The best areas are those in which the soil includes a fine layer of *arzelle*, which consists of decomposed chalk, flint, and mica. The essence of Condrieu is a full, almost oily body together with high alcohol, which are balanced by a pronounced perfume of peach blossom, apricots, white flowers, and violets. Modern Condrieu is usually dry in style, although the richness together with the high alcohol can produce an impression of sweetness. Acidity is not as high as for Chardonnay and can be distinctly low. Oak is usually absent, although there is more and more of it around. In general, Condrieu ought to be drunk at about three years of age, before it loses its freshness and perfume.

At the southern end of Condrieu lies the enclave of Château-Grillet, a mere 4ha of a soil that is lighter and more fragmented than in Condrieu. This too is a land of Viognier, planted in a natural granite amphitheatre that, as in Cornas, acts as a suntrap and a protection from the Mistral. Château-Grillet is a monopole and there is just the one wine, matured in oak for up to 24 months before being entered into signature brown bottles. The wine can be said to be more Burgundian than Condrieu: drier, lighter, more delicate and less perfumed, and able to improve for a decade or more.

The last appellation in the Northern Rhône is Saint-Péray, which is, again, a very small appellation. It lies at the southern end of the region, across the river from Valence. The bulk of production consists of a sparkling blend of Marsanne and Roussanne made by the traditional method. In stark contrast to Condrieu, still Saint-Péray is typically light and acidic and rather undistinguished, although the best examples can be gently floral. A number of well made still wines point to a brighter future for the appellation.

The Southern Rhône

In the Southern Rhône, the Rhodanian corridor opens up into a rugged landscape with sheltered valleys and a diversity of mesoclimates. The macroclimate is Mediterranean with mild winters and hot summers, and sparse rainfall during the summer months. Drought is a perennial problem. Rather than orchards as in the Northern Rhône, vineyards are interspersed with olive groves, lavender fields, and garrigue (Mediterranean scrubland). Some of the best are planted on alluvial deposits overlain by polished pebbles called *galets*, which absorb the heat of the sun by day and release it by night.

Unlike the Northern Rhône, which is dominated by its eight crus, the Southern Rhône puts out a great deal of modest Côtes-du-Rhône and Vin de Pays. The only appellation of the Southern Rhône that can compete with the likes of Hermitage and Côte-Rôtie is Châteauneuf-du-Pape, which is a blend of up to 13 grape varieties, eight black and five white. In contrast, the Northern Rhône counts a grand total of only four grape varieties. Other notable cru appellations of the Southern Rhône include Gigondas, Vacqueyras, and Tavel.

More wine is made in Châteauneuf-du-Pape than in the entire Northern Rhône. The 3,200ha of the appellation stretch across an undulating plateau on the left bank of the Rhône, between Orange and Avignon, and are crowned with the picturesque ruins of the summer palace of

John XXII. The soils are varied. In the north and northeast are the famous *galets*, deposited by Alpine glaciers and polished by the Rhône over several millennia. Although closely associated with the appellation, they are by no means essential to making great Châteauneuf. The most famous vineyard or *lieu-dit* in Châteauneuf-du-Pape is La Crau, which is principally held by Domaine du Vieux Télégraphe. Some 95% of the production of the appellation is red wine and the remaining 5% is white wine (there is no rosé). As many as 13 grape varieties are permitted, and Château de Beaucastel takes great pride in growing and blending each and every one of them. However, many producers use only three or four grape varieties, typically Grenache, Syrah, Mourvèdre, and Cinsault; some use only Grenache, most notably Château Rayas. Unlike in the Northern Rhône, the vines are typically trained as bushvines (gobelet). This traditional form of training offers greater resistance to wind and drought but is unsuited to fertile soils and humid conditions. Grenache accounts for over 70% of plantings, Syrah for over 10%, and Mourvèdre for about 7%. Syrah typically adds colour and spice to a blend, while Mourvèdre contributes structure and elegance. Grenache, which is prone to oxidation, is vinified in large cement tanks, while the other grape varieties are most commonly vinified in large old oak barrels. Red Châteauneuf-du-Pape is medium-to-deep ruby in colour, with notes of red and black fruit, game, tar, leather, and garrigue. On the palate, it is rich and spicy, with a higher alcohol and lower acidity than Bordeaux and Northern Rhône. It is rather tight in its youth but softens and opens up after about seven years, and can continue to evolve and improve for several more years, sometimes decades. Vinification by carbonic maceration or semi-carbonic maceration results in a lighter, earlier drinking style. White Châteauneuf-du-Pape, which can be made from Clairette, Grenache Blanc, Bourboulenc, Roussanne, Picpoul, and Picardan, ranges in style from lean and mineral to rich and oily, and is difficult to generalize about.

Gigondas ranks second in prestige in the Southern Rhône and can be very similar to Châteauneuf-du-Pape. The eponymous town was founded by the Romans for the recreation of the soldiers of the Second Legion, whence the name Gigondas (Lat. *jocunditas*, pleasure, enjoyment). It lies at the foot of the picturesque Dentelles de Montmirail, a small chain of mountains that divide the 1,200ha of the appellation into two distinct areas, one with a cooler mesoclimate and the other with a hotter. The bulk of production is red, although a small amount of rosé is also made. Red Gigondas is typically heavy in Grenache (up to 80% of the blend), but also contains a minimum of 15% Syrah and/or Mourvèdre and a maximum of 10% of other Rhône grape varieties excluding Carignan. Gigondas is typically rich and powerful, and more rustic and animally than Châteauneuf-du-Pape. The best examples can improve for a decade.

If Gigondas can be thought of as junior Châteauneuf-du-Pape, then Vacqueyras, which lies just to the south of Gigondas, can be thought of as junior Gigondas. The best vineyards of the 1,400ha appellation are situated on the Plateau de Garrigues. As in Gigondas, the bulk of production is red, although small amounts of rosé and white wine are also made. Vacqueyras typically consists of at least 50% Grenache (so often less Grenache than Gigondas) together with smaller proportions of Syrah, Mourvèdre, and Carignan.

Across the river from Châteauneuf-du-Pape lies the commune and appellation of Tavel, which, uniquely in the Rhône, produces only rosé. In the course of history, Tavel has found favour with, among others, the Avignon popes, Louis XIV, Balzac, and Hemingway, and many French people regard it as the *premier rosé de France*. The principal elements of the blend are Grenache and Cinsault, although eight other grape varieties are also permitted. The rosé is produced by the *saignée* (bleeding) method, which involves 'bleeding off' some of the juice from the must so as to concentrate colour and phenolics. Extended skin contact during fermentation imparts extra colour and tannin to the must. Tavel ought to be drunk chilled. At its best, it is full-bodied and structured on the one hand, and yet bone-dry and refreshing on the other. Alcohol is high, at around 13.5%. Tavel is often drunk young, but is unusual among rosés in that it can evolve and improve for several years.

The discussion so far has mostly centred on cru wines, which also include Lirac, Rasteau, Beaumes de Venise, and Vinsobres in the Southern Rhône. However, much of the wine produced in the Rhône falls under the more modest generic appellation of Côtes-du-Rhône, which is of tremendous commercial importance. In theory, this AOC can apply to red, rosé, and white wine from anywhere from Vienne to south of Avignon, so long as the alcohol is 11% or higher and the yield does not exceed 52hl/ha (cf. 35hl/ha for Châteauneuf-du-Pape). In practice, almost all Côtes-du-Rhône is red wine from the Southern Rhône. In the main production area south of Montélimar, the appellation rules stipulate a minimum of 40% Grenache and a minimum of 70% Grenache, Syrah, and Mourvèdre combined. There is also a more restricted higher appellation of Côtes-du-Rhône Villages with stricter regulations for alcohol levels, yields, and grape varieties. Within this higher appellation, a certain number of villages can also display their name on the label, for example, CAIRANNE, APPELLATION CÔTES-DU-RHÔNE VILLAGES CONTRÔLÉE. A significant amount of Côte-du-Rhône is made by carbonic maceration, and some of that is released *en primeur* to compete with Beaujolais Nouveau. The bottom line is this. Côte-du-Rhône wines are incredibly diverse, and the best, which are getting better all the time, can offer astounding value for money. Here more than anywhere else, it really pays to know your stuff.

Note: The Rhône also counts a number of satellite appellations, among which Côtes du Ventoux, Côtes du Lubéron, and Costières de Nîmes. Wine from within an appellation can be declassified to a Vin de Pays. Such wines are not dissimilar to Côtes-du-Rhône.

Chapter 8

Bordeaux

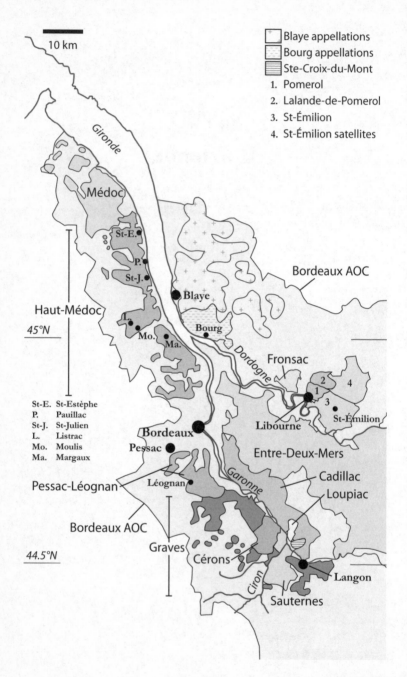

Bordeaux

The region of Bordeaux in Aquitaine lies around the confluence of the Rivers Garonne and Dordogne. This confluence gives rise to the Gironde estuary, the largest estuary in Europe, which flows northwest for some 65km (40m) before merging into the Bay of Biscay.

The Romans first carried the vine to Bordeaux, as attested by the 1st century naturalist Pliny the Elder and the 4th century rhetorician Ausonius, who is still remembered by Château Ausone in Saint-Emilion. In 1152, Henry II of England married the formidable Eleanor of Aquitaine: the region came under English rule and 'claret'—Bordeaux red wine—under great demand. By the end of the Hundred Years' War in 1453, France had regained control of the Bordelais; but, despite heavy export duties, the British Isles remained an important market for claret.

In the course of the 17th century, Dutch traders drained the marshland around the Médoc, which soon outclassed the Graves as the pre-eminent viticultural area of the Bordelais. Pierre de Rauzan, a grand bourgeois and manager of Château Latour until his death in 1692, accumulated the land that later became Châteaux Pichon Longueville Comtesse de Lalande, Pichon Longueville Baron, Rauzan-Ségla, and Rauzan-Gassies. Later, Nicolas Alexandre, marquis de Ségur acquired the epithet *Prince des Vignes* after coming into possession of the Médoc properties of Châteaux Lafite, Latour, Mouton, and Calon-Ségur. He turned some pebbles of Pauillac into buttons for his coat, which Louis XV once mistook for diamonds.

In 1855, Napoleon III ordered a classification of the top châteaux of Bordeaux for the *Exposition Universelle de Paris*. Bordeaux brokers ranked 61 châteaux into five *crus* or 'growths' based on a *savant mélange* of price and reputation. All of the 61 châteaux that made it into their classification are in the Haut Médoc, bar one—Haut Brion in the Graves.

Starting in the late 19th century, the Bordelais began to suffer from a succession of American imports, first oidium (powdery mildew) and then phylloxera. In the wake of phylloxera, the vineyards had to be replanted onto American rootstock, and the grape varieties that tolerated this best such as Cabernet Sauvignon, Cabernet Franc, and Merlot became dominant. But then came downy mildew and black rot, followed by war, economic depression, more war, the severe frost of

1956, and an oil crisis. In the late 20th century, many châteaux found themselves in a state of utter disrepair and in dire need of the restoration and regeneration that is still under way.

The lie of the land

The Bordeaux region, which boasts ~125,000ha of vineyards and 57 AOCs, can be divided into three main sub-regions. The Right Bank describes the area north of the Dordogne and Gironde, with Libourne at its centre. The Left Bank describes the area south of the Garonne and Gironde, with Bordeaux itself at its centre. Finally, the Entre-Deux-Mers is the rather large and undistinguished area between the Dordogne and the Garonne. The Left Bank is subdivided into the Médoc downstream of Bordeaux; the Graves upstream of Bordeaux; and, also upstream of Bordeaux, Sauternes, Barsac, and Cérons. By far the most notable areas on the Right Bank are Saint-Emilion and Pomerol, which are both very close to Libourne.

Climate

Bordeaux is on the 45th parallel, about halfway between the Equator and North Pole and at the same latitude as the Rhône valley, Piedmont, the Veneto, and Oregon. The climate is maritime, with high humidity from the Bay of Biscay and local river systems predisposing both to noble and ignoble rot: powdery mildew, downy mildew, grey rot, black rot, and eutypa dieback. Winters are short and mild, and summers increasingly warm. For all that, severe frost in the winter of 1956 killed off a large number of vines. During the growing season, spring frosts, unsettled weather around flowering time in June, midsummer heat spikes and storms, and September rains are the main threats to the size and quality of the harvest. However, a long, sunny autumn can burnish and even rescue an unpromising harvest. In April 1991, a night of severe frost destroyed half of that year's harvest: Château Pétrus beat the odds by flying a helicopter over its vineyards to displace the freezing air—not a measure that most other châteaux could easily afford!

Soils

The subsoil in the Bordelais is mostly limestone. On the Left Bank, the topsoil is likely to consist of quartz-rich gravel over clay and marl. The last ice age deposited five major gravel banks, four in the Haut-Médoc (in Saint-Estèphe, Pauillac, Saint-Julien, and Margaux) and one in Pessac-Léognan in the north of the Graves. These gravel soils have a number of qualities: rich in minerals and microorganisms, free draining, and heat retaining and reflecting. Further south on the Left Bank, the topsoil is mostly a mixture of clays and sands. On the Right Bank, the topsoil is likely to consist of clay and limestone, but here too there are some gravelly areas. Compared to gravel, clay is more damp and less heat retaining and reflecting. As a result, the vineyards are more susceptible to frosts and heavy rains and later to ripen. Gravel soils are best suited to Cabernet Sauvignon and Sauvignon Blanc, clay soils to Merlot and Sémillon.

Grape varieties

People often think of Bordeaux as a Cabernet Sauvignon dominated blend from the Médoc, but the most planted black grape variety is in fact and by far Merlot (62%). Compared to Cabernet Sauvignon (25%), Merlot is earlier to flower and ripen and thinner in skin and so more prone to rot. Because it is high yielding, it requires hard pruning if it is to produce wines of distinction. Cabernet Sauvignon is a smaller grape with a much higher skin to pulp ratio, whence the deeper colour and denser tannins. If Cabernet Sauvignon is Apollonian, then Merlot is Dionysian: the sugar and alcohol in Merlot are higher, which together with the lesser tannins translate into a certain softness, ripeness, and early approachability. The other four permitted black grape varieties are Cabernet Franc (12%), which is especially prominent in Saint-Emilion and Pomerol, Petit Verdot, Malbec, and Carmenère. Petit Verdot (which is on the up on the Left Bank) and Malbec account for only a very small proportion of plantings, and Carmenère for *trois fois rien* ('thrice nothing').

White wine production in the Bordelais has fallen to 11% of the total production of around 6m hectolitres, with the principal grape varieties involved being Sauvignon Blanc (54%), Sémillon (35.5%), and Muscadelle (6%). Compared to Sémillon, Sauvignon Blanc is higher yielding, thicker in skin, much lighter in body, much higher in acidity and aromatics, and very much on the make. But Sémillon is more prone to noble rot and better suited to oak, for which reasons it predominates in sweet white wines. Other permitted white grape varieties are Ugni Blanc, Colombard, Merlot Blanc, Mauzac, and Ondenc.

Viticulture

The number of growers in the Bordelais has fallen to ~10,000, with a significant proportion making their wines with at least some help from a co-operative. At the same time, the average holding size has increased to 13.5ha; some Bordeaux châteaux can be very large, with many estates, including the first growth Château Lafite, spreading over 100ha or more. The other three first growths in the Médoc are also quite large, with Château Mouton-Rothschild at 78ha, Château Margaux at 78ha, and Château Latour at 65ha. The fifth and final first growth, Château Haut Brion in the Graves, is a 'mere' 46ha. In the Sauternes, Château d'Yquem is 103ha, Château Suduiraut 90ha, Château Rieussec 75ha, and Château Climens 29ha. Châteaux in Saint-Emilion and Pomerol tend to be smaller, with, for example, Château Cheval Blanc at 36ha, Château Angélus at 23ha, Château Pétrus at 11ha, and the bijou Le Pin at only 2ha. In addition, the Right Bank is associated with a number of very small producers or 'garagistes' whose wines can (also) fetch exorbitant prices.

Vine densities are often very high, with up to 10,000 vines/ha in the Médoc. The training system is Guyot; single Guyot predominates on the Right Bank and double Guyot on the Left Bank. Common or important viticultural practices include spraying, de-leafing, and green harvesting. Hand harvesting is very much the norm at top châteaux. The harvest begins in September in all but the hottest years and may extend into October, with, in general, Merlot first, Cabernet Franc next, and Cabernet Sauvignon last. Sauvignon Blanc and Sémillon for dry wines are harvested earliest of all, and for sweet wines latest of all, with the selective harvesting of botrytized grapes sometimes stretching right into November.

Vinification and maturation

The process of vinification is led by the *maître de chai* (cellar master), often with help from a Bordeaux wine consultant such as the Boissenots, Denis Dubourdieu, or Michel Rolland.

Almost all Bordeaux wines are blended, with the individual components of a blend vinified separately. The process described here is that practised by the more ambitious châteaux.

After harvesting, bunches are sorted either in the vineyard or winery so as to remove any diseased or unripe fruit and extraneous material. Bunches are then de-stemmed and the grapes crushed. A small number of châteaux, notably Smith-Haut-Lafitte, do not crush the grapes at all.

Fermentation is carried out on the skins by ambient rather than cultured yeasts, most often in a stainless steel vat. The vat is held at a temperature of about 30°C (86°F), and fermentation completes over a period of about 14 days. Pumping over and sometimes also *pigeage* are used to promote extraction. Once fermentation is complete, the wine is left to macerate on the skins for several more days. The second, malolactic fermentation takes place either in the fermentation tank or in barrique (225l oak barrels). Micro-oxygenation may be used at the fermentation stage to defuse green and harsh tannins, although the very best châteaux try to ensure that there are no green and harsh tannins in the first place. Micro-oxygenation can also be used at the later stage of élevage, in this case to avoid racking and control oxygen exposure.

Once fermentation and maceration are complete, the free-run juice is racked off, either by pumping or by gravity, with any remaining matter entered into a basket (vertical) press or pneumatic press. Compared to free-run juice, press wine is coarser and more likely to go into a lesser wine. The wine is left to mature for up to 18-20 months in medium-toast oak barriques, with racking off the lees taking place every three months or so. A certain proportion of the barriques are new: at first growth châteaux such as Lafite or Latour, that proportion is a full 100%.

Blending occurs either before the wine is entered into barriques or in January or February after the harvest, in time for the *en primeur* tastings. The blending reflects not so much the harvest as the precise requirements of the vintage, with unused wine going into a lesser, second or third wine. For example, Merlot can be used to flesh out the mid-palate of a Cabernet Sauvignon dominated blend. Petit Verdot, which is regarded as a 'seasoning' variety, can be used to add not only structure and tannin, but also finesse and spiciness. Before bottling, the wine may be fined with egg whites or powdered albumen. And it might also be filtered.

Châteaux generally sell a large proportion of their wine as futures (*en primeur*) to *négociants*, who then slap on their markup and sell it on to importers in several batches or *tranches*. These *tranches* are usually sold at increasing prices, as determined by the judgments of various wine critics and journals but in particular of Mr Robert Parker. This only marks the end of the beginning: the wine still needs several more years to mature in bottle, and will not be released from bond for another 18 months or so.

With dry white wines, the imperative is often to preserve and enhance fruitiness, freshness, and varietal character. Depending on final style, likely differences include extended pre-fermentation skin contact (*macération pelliculaire*, a technique pioneered by Denis Dubourdieu for Sauvignon Blanc), a considerably cooler fermentation temperature, blocked malolactic fermentation, *bâtonnage* on the fine lees, and strategic use of sulphur dioxide. Sweet white wines are fermented very slowly so as to convert as much sugar as possible into alcohol before the fermentation comes to a standstill or is halted by cooling or sulphur dioxide. Cryoextraction, that is, freeze concentration, might be used in some vintages by some producers, including Château d'Yquem.

Appellations and classifications

There are in essence three levels within the AOC structure, regional (Bordeaux AOC or Bordeaux Supérieur AOC), district (for example, Haut-Médoc AOC, Saint-Emilion AOC, Sauternes AOC), and commune (for example, Pauillac AOC or Margaux AOC, which are both within the Haut-Médoc AOC). Compared to Bordeaux AOC, Bordeaux Supérieur AOC requires older vines, a longer élevage of 12 months, and a slightly higher minimum alcohol of 10.5%. Taken together, the regional appellations account for almost half the vineyard area and production of the Bordelais.

The Médoc appellations only apply to red wines, even if some excellent white wines are also produced within their delimited areas, for example, Château Margaux's Pavillon Blanc. Médoc AOC applies to the clayey northern Médoc; Haut-Médoc AOC to the larger, more gravely southern Médoc which also encompasses the six commune appellations of Saint-Estèphe, Pauillac, Saint-Julien, Margaux, Moulis, and Listrac. Of these commune appellations, Saint-Julien and Pauillac have the greatest proportion (over 60%) of Cabernet Sauvignon plantings, and Listrac the greatest proportion (almost 60%) of Merlot plantings.

Various classifications are superimposed upon the AOC structure, most notably the 1855 Classification, which has barely changed over time. In 1973 Château Mouton-Rothschild got bumped up to first growth level, whence its revised motto, from '*Premier ne puis, second ne daigne, Mouton suis*' ('First I cannot, second I deign not, Mouton am I') to '*Premier je suis, second je fus, Mouton ne change*' ('First I am, second I was, Mouton never changes'). Classed growths that regularly perform on a par with first growths are sometimes referred to as 'super-seconds'. A list of super-seconds might include the Pichons, Léoville-Las-Cases, Ducru-Beaucaillou, Cos d'Estournel, Montrose, and Palmer. The 1855 Classification includes a separate chapter on the sweet white wines of Sauternes and Barsac, which divides 26 châteaux into first and second growths with Château d'Yquem standing alone as a *Premier Cru Supérieur*. Médoc châteaux outside the 1855 Classification can apply each year for the *Cru Bourgeois* label, usually for their top cuvée.

The classification of the Graves and that of Saint-Emilion are relatively recent, dating back, respectively, to 1953 and 1955. In the Graves, there are seven châteaux (including Haut-Brion) that are classed for both their red and white wine, six for their red wine only, and two for their white wine only, making 15 châteaux and 22 *cru classés* in total. In Saint-Emilion, the classification is revised every ten years or so. The classification divides into *Premier Grand Cru Classé* (which further subdivides into A and B categories, with only Château Ausone, Château Cheval Blanc, Château Angélus, and Château Pavie in the A category) and *Grand Cru Classé*. *Grand Cru Classé* should not be confused with Saint-Emilion Grand Cru AOC, which is only slightly better than Saint-Emilion AOC. As for Pomerol, it continues to resist and defy classification.

Vineyards in Bordeaux are not individually delineated and registered. This means that, so long as the appended land is within the same appellation, a proprietor can easily expand the holdings held under the name of his château and still retain the same status in the classification.

Wine styles

The 1200ha of Pauillac are split into north and south by the Chenal du Gaer drainage channel. This Eldorado contains all of 18 classed growth properties, including the three first growths Château Lafite-Rothschild, Château Latour, and Château Mouton-Rothschild; the Pichons; Château Duhart-Milon; and 12 highly disparate fifth growths. Most reputable among these are Château Pontet-Canet, Château Grand-Puy-Lacoste, Château Lynch-Bages, Château d'Armailhac, and Château Clerc-Milon. At its best, Pauillac is the epitome of a Cabernet Sauvignon dominated blend. On the nose, it is complex and dominated by notes of cassis, appealing green/bell pepper, cedar, chocolate, cigar box, and vanilla from new French oak. On the palate, it is powerful yet elegant, with a medium body, fairly high acidity, medium alcohol, fine, structured tannins, and a long finish.

The Ruisseau de Juillac separates Pauillac from the 900ha of Saint-Julien to the south. The gravel is not quite so deep as in Pauillac, which might account for the absence of any first growths. There are however eleven classed growths of which five second growths, including Château Léoville-Las Cases which borders on Château Latour and is regarded as first among the super-seconds (and priced to match). Other highly performing properties are Château Léoville-Barton, Château Léoville-Poyferré, Château Ducru-Beaucaillou, and Château Gruaud-Larose. Overall, Saint-Julien is more consistent in quality than its northerly and southerly neighbours, and a seductive compromise between the power of Pauillac and the magic of Margaux, with a silkier texture and a drier finish.

Saint-Estèphe is the most northerly commune appellation of the Médoc, and its 1200ha are separated from neighbouring Pauillac by the La Jalle du Breuil drainage channel. The gravel here is not quite so abundant as in Pauillac, Saint-Julien, or Margaux, with more clay and therefore more Merlot and more moisture retention. Saint-Estèphe is nonetheless home to five classed growths including second growths Château Montrose and Cos d'Estournel and third growth Château Calon-Ségur. Compared to Pauillac, Saint-Julien, or Margaux, Saint-Estèphe tends to be deeper in colour, fuller or coarser in texture, with coarser, more rustic tannins, a touch more acidity, and a touch less perfume.

The 1500ha of Margaux are not contiguous with Saint-Julien, lying a fair distance further south. There are more classed growths in Margaux than in any other commune, of which Château Margaux, five second growths, ten third growths, three fourth growths, and two fifth growths. Soils and topography are more varied than further north, as a result of which quality is less consistent. Aside from Château Margaux, properties with a reputation for quality include Château Brane-Cantenac, Château Palmer, Château Rauzan-Ségla, and Château d'Issan. Archetypal Margaux is floral and feminine, exuding a refined perfume of acacia and violets.

Adjoining Margaux are the diminutive appellations of Moulis (550ha) and Listrac (650ha). Moulis and Listrac do not count any classed growths, and are much less favoured than the other four commune appellations of the Haut Médoc. However, the best properties are worth the detour and often represent excellent value for money. In Moulis, Château Chasse-Spleen (cf. Baudelaire, *Spleen et Idéal*) and Château Poujeaux are performing at classed growth level. In Listrac, some of the biggest names are Château Clarke, Château Fourcas-Dupré, and Château Fourcas-Hosten. Moulis is soft and fleshy, with more power but less finesse than Margaux, and maturing more quickly. Listrac is firmer and more tannic, similar to Saint-Estèphe but more rustic and with less ripe fruit, and also maturing more quickly. Although dominated by Cabernet Sauvignon, the wines of Moulis and Listrac often contain more Merlot than those of the other four communes.

On the Left Bank south of Bordeaux is the Graves, so named for its gravel soils. The northern enclave of Pessac-Léognan, an appellation that dates back only to 1987, encompasses all the top Graves properties. Château Haut-Brion in particular is the only property outside the Médoc to have been included in the 1855 Classification. Its principal wine contains considerably more Merlot and Cabernet Franc than the other four first growths. Other top properties include Château La Mission Haut-Brion, Château Pape-Clément, and Domaine de Chevalier. Compared to those of the Médoc, the wines of Graves tend to be lighter in colour, body, and tannins, with more fragrance, more Merlot character, and hints of smoke, minerals, and red bricks. Like the red wines, the white wines of the Graves can be among the finest in the world, combining the opulence of Sémillon with the verve of Sauvignon Blanc, and resulting in intense aromas of citrus fruit, peach, acacia, beeswax, and hazelnut. On the palate, they are medium in body, acidity, and alcohol, and often oaked. The relatively small amount of sweet wine that is produced in the Graves is labelled as Graves Supérieures AOC, a sweet wine appellation that is co-extensive with Graves AOC.

Within the southern Graves lie the appellations of Sauternes and Barsac, which, since the 18th century, have been internationally reputed for their sweet white wines. Barsac lies within the Sauternes, and Barsac wines—which are typically drier and lighter in body with higher acidity—are entitled to either appellation. The other communes within the Sauternes are Bommes, Fargues, and Preignac. The principal grape variety used for Sauternes is Sémillon, with some Sauvignon Blanc for freshness and aroma and, in some cases, a touch of Muscadelle for exotic perfume. The River Ciron, which arises from a cool spring, courses along the Sauternes-Barsac boundary under a shady canopy before losing itself to the warmer Garonne. In the autumn, the temperature differential between these two waters gives rise to evening mists that linger until mid-morning and promote the growth of noble rot. Some years see less mist, and so less noble rot, than others, which—together with diminutive yields (typically 12-20hl/ha), selective harvesting of individual berries with multiple pickings or *tries*, and oak ageing—adds significantly to production costs. But the result is intense sweetness balanced by crisp acidity, aromas of apricot, peach, passion fruit, orange marmalade, honey, honeysuckle, acacia, hazelnut, and vanilla, and a long, elegant finish. In time, the colour veers from gold to amber and copper, with notes such as old books, caramel, and crème brulée not uncommon. The very best examples can keep for over a century. The top name is of course Château d'Yquem, but other star performers include Château de Fargues, Château Suduiraut, Château Rieussec, and, in Barsac, Château Climens and Château Coutet.

Similar but less distinguished wines are produced in the neighbouring regions of Cérons on the Left Bank, and of Sainte-Croix-du-Mont, Loupiac, and Cadillac across the river. Premières Côtes de Bordeaux AOC, also across the Garonne, can apply to both sweet white wines (sometimes botrytized and mostly produced in the south of the appellation) and red wines (Merlot-dominated and mostly produced in the north of the appellation), but not to dry white wines, which can only be labelled as Bordeaux AOC. The appellation is dominated by red wine production, and can represent remarkable value for money.

The bulk of the extensive land between the Garonne and Dordogne falls under Entre-Deux-Mers AOC. Over recent decades, this area has seen a shift from dry white wine production to majority red wine production. As Entre-Deux-Mers AOC only applies to dry white wines, this red wine can only be labelled as Bordeaux AOC. Today, Entre-Deux-Mers AOC tends to be dominated by Sauvignon Blanc, which differs from Loire Sauvignon Blanc in being more expressive of tropical fruits and less so of grass and minerals.

The Right Bank produces some of the world's greatest Merlot wines. Pomerol is a small appellation of some 800ha. Demand for Pomerol outstrips supply, and some labels sell for considerably more than Left Bank first growths. The heart of the appellation is a plateau of gravel and clay, with sandier soils to the west yielding rather lighter wines. The subsoil contains seams of iron-rich clay known as *crasse de fer*, a major feature at Château Pétrus. Merlot is the dominant grape variety, representing about 80% of plantings (and 95% at Pétrus). Most of the rest is Cabernet Franc together with an even smaller amount of Cabernet Sauvignon. Pomerol is deep ruby in colour with notes of fresh black and red fruit (especially plums), spice, truffles, and vanilla from new French oak. On the palate, it is rich, often opulent, with less acidity and softer tannins than Left Bank Bordeaux. Alcohol ranges from medium to high in hotter years.

Top producers include Château Pétrus, Château Trotanoy, Le Pin, Vieux Château Certan, Château Lafleur, Château Gazin, Château l'Evangile, and Château La Conseillante. More affordable is Château La Croix de Gay. Across the Barbanne stream to the north of Pomerol is the somewhat larger Lalande de Pomerol AOC, which can sometimes match or at least evoke Pomerol or Saint-Emilion.

Adjoining Pomerol to the southeast is the much larger 5,500ha appellation of Saint-Emilion, with the town of Saint-Emilion at its centre. Of these 5,500ha, ~3,800ha is classified as Saint-Emilion Grand Cru AOC, with yields capped at 40hl/ha (vs. 45ha/ha) and a minimum alcohol of 11% (vs. 10.5%). Like Bordeaux Supérieur AOC, Saint-Emilion Grand Cru AOC is an almost meaningless designation. The soils can essentially be divided into four different types: the plateau of Saint-Emilion, rich in limestone; the surrounding slopes, a mixture of limestone and clay; the border with Pomerol with its five gravel mounds (two at Château Cheval Blanc and three at Château Figeac); and the plains to the west and south with lighter (and rather inferior) soils of sand and alluvium deposited by the nearby Dordogne. The average holding in Saint-Emilion is considerably larger than in Pomerol, but still small by Bordeaux standards. Merlot is rather less dominant than in Pomerol, with Cabernet Franc making up about 30% of plantings and Cabernet Sauvignon 10%. Château Cheval Blanc is, famously, Cabernet-Franc dominated, and Château Ausone, which is on the plateau, also contains a high proportion of Cabernet Franc. A third exception-that-proves-the-rule is Château Figeac, with less Merlot than either Cabernet Franc or Cabernet Sauvignon. Saint-Emilion has four satellites to the north and northeast, the biggest being Montagne Saint-Emilion and Lussac Saint-Emilion. The wines here are similar to Saint-Emilion in character, if more rustic, and can represent excellent value for money. Compared to Pomerol, Saint-Emilion is drier and more tannic and less obviously from the Right Bank.

To the west of Pomerol and Libourne are the appellations of Fronsac and Canon Fronsac. Fronsac is about the same size as Pomerol, and Canon-Fronsac much smaller. Both appellations, and Canon-Fronsac in particular, are reputed for powerful but refined Merlot-dominated wines.

Bergerac

Bergerac lies to the east of Bordeaux, across the Gironde departmental boundary and into the Dordogne. The wines of Bergerac are similar and often superior to those of Bordeaux, but find it difficult to shine in the shadow of their neighbour. As it stands, the bulk of production is destined for the domestic market. The principal grape varieties are the same as those in Bordeaux, with Merlot, Malbec, and Sémillon most commonly planted. The area comprises 13 appellations for reds, rosés, and dry and sweet whites. In terms of regional appellations, Bergerac AOC covers reds and rosés, Bergerac Sec AOC covers whites, and the superior Côtes de Bergerac AOC covers both reds and whites (*demi-sec*, *moelleux*, and *doux*). Côtes de Bergerac is to basic Bergerac what Bordeaux Supérieur is to basic Bordeaux, with slightly stricter requirements on yield and alcohol. Other appellations in Bergerac include Monbazillac, Saussignac, Rosette, Haut-Montravel, and Côtes de Montravel for sweet whites; Pécharmant for reds; and Montravel for dry whites and reds. The 2,000ha of Monbazillac are situated on the left bank of the River Dordogne in an area that is propitious to the development of noble rot. Monbazillac is broadly similar to Sauternes, except that it tends to have a higher proportion of Muscadelle in the blend. In its youth, it can be more giving than Sauternes. With age, it develops a creamy and nutty character. The wines of Saussignac, directly to the west, are similar to those of Monbazillac, if slightly less luscious.

Chapter 9

The Loire

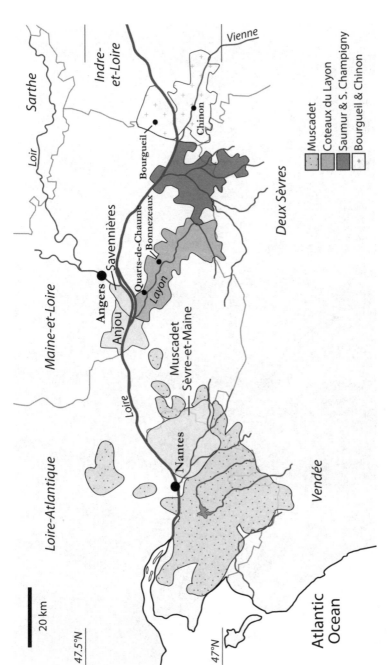

Western Loire

Legend:
- Muscadet
- Coteaux du Layon
- Saumur & S. Champigny
- Bourgueil & Chinon

Atlantic Ocean

20 km

47.5°N

47°N

Loire-Atlantique
Maine-et-Loire
Sarthe
Loir
Indre-et-Loire
Vienne
Deux Sèvres
Vendée

Nantes
Angers
Savennières
Anjou
Quarts-de-Chaume
Bonnezeaux
Layon
Muscadet Sèvre-et-Maine
Bourgueil
Chinon
Loire

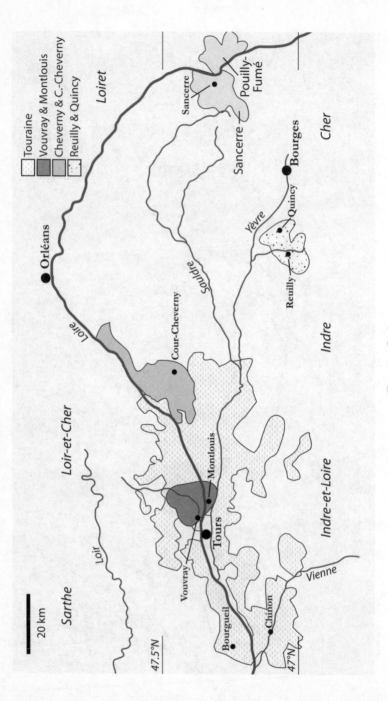

Eastern Loire

Touraine
Vouvray & Montlouis
Cheverny & C.-Cheverny
Reuilly & Quincy

Sarthe

Loir

Loir-et-Cher

Loiret

Loire

Orléans

Cour-Cheverny

Sauldre

Sancerre

Sancerre

Pouilly-Fumé

Cher

Bourges

Yevre

Quincy

Reuilly

Indre

Vouvray

Montlouis

Tours

Vienne

Indre-et-Loire

Bourgueil

Chinon

47.5°N

47°N

20 km

The diversity of wines made in this region reflects variations in soil, climate, and grape varieties along the lengthy course of the River Loire. The bulk of production consists of white wines made from Chenin Blanc, Sauvignon Blanc, and Melon de Bourgogne (Muscadet), but there are also red wines made from Cabernet Franc, together with rosé, sparkling, and dessert wines. In the 1st century, the Romans carried the vine to the Loire from the nearby regions of Bordeaux and Burgundy. The 4th century bishop Saint Martin of Tours is credited with spreading viticulture across the region. According to legend, his tethered donkey stripped some nearby vines of their leaves, thereby establishing the practice of pruning! Proximity of the Loire valley to Paris and the Atlantic coast greatly facilitated trade: in the High Middle Ages, Englishmen held the wines of the Loire in higher esteem than those of Bordeaux.

The lie of the land

The Loire comprises 70,000ha of vines spread across ~500km (310mi) and 14 administrative *départements*, from Muscadet near Nantes on the Atlantic coast to Sancerre and Pouilly Fumé to the southeast of Orléans in north central France. Sancerre is actually closer to Burgundy than to Muscadet, in terms not only of distance but also of climate and history. The Loire can be divided into four sections, from west to east along the river: The Nantais, Anjou-Saumur, Touraine, and Centre. The Nantais is mostly planted with Melon de Bourgogne, Anjou-Saumur and Touraine with both Chenin Blanc and Cabernet Franc, and Centre with Sauvignon Blanc.

Climate

The climate at this northerly latitude is distinctly marginal. Viticulture can only be sustained by the moderating influence of the Loire and its various tributaries, along which the vineyards are concentrated. The most highly prized sites are south facing riverbank slopes that make the most of the sunlight and riverine mesoclimate. The mild and humid

Atlantic climate of the Nantais stands in contrast to the continental climate of the Centre, which is marked by cold winters and hot but short summers. Anjou is protected from the prevailing winds by the forests of the Vendée and receives less rainfall than might otherwise be expected. Spring frosts and prolonged autumn rains are all too common in the Loire, and vintage variation can be very marked. Under-ripeness is a perennial problem.

Soils

Soils are extremely varied, as might be expected from a region that stretches over 500km (310mi). The soils of the Nantais are mostly sand with areas of clay, granite, schist, and gneiss; those of Anjou are mostly stony clay over schist; and those of Touraine are mostly flinty clay over limestone. The soils of Centre can resemble those of Chablis, with areas of limestone, chalk, and Kimmeridgian clay. In Saumur and Vouvray, the soils consist of *tuffeau*, a soft, free-draining and water-retaining calcareous rock. *Tuffeau jaune*, which is found in Chinon and Bourgueil, is sandier and softer than *tuffeau blanc* and especially suited to Cabernet Franc. The quarrying of *tuffeau* (mainly *tuffeau blanc*) to provide building material for the famous châteaux of the Loire gave rise to systems of caves that provided ideal conditions for wine storage and maturation.

Wine styles

The Loire can be thought of as a ribbon with crisp white wines at either end (Muscadet and Sancerre/Pouilly Fumé) and fuller bodied white and red wines in the middle. The white wines tend to be made from Muscadet in the west, Sauvignon Blanc in the east, and Chenin Blanc in the middle. For red wines, Cabernet Franc is dominant, but Pinot Noir and Gamay become increasingly important further up-river, nearer to Burgundy. There are however a number of trend-breakers such as Cour-Cheverny, an appellation in Touraine that is entirely planted with the obscure Romorantin grape. Chardonnay, Cabernet Sauvignon, and

Grolleau are also commonly planted. In general, the wines of the Loire are improving, but too many examples are made from overcropped, under-ripe grapes. Chaptalization is commonly practised and can help to compensate for under-ripeness. Malolactic fermentation and barrel ageing, especially in new oak, are both uncommon.

Sweet wines made from late harvest Chenin Blanc, which may or may not be botrytized, are capable of great complexity and longevity. The most notable appellations for sweet wines are Vouvray, home to top producers Huet and Foreau, and Coteaux du Layon together with its sub-appellations of Bonnezeaux, Chaume, and Quarts-de-Chaume. Whereas Sauternes is typically associated with peach and honey, the sweet wines of the Loire are more often associated with apple, apricot, and quince, together with a much higher natural acidity and rather less sugar and alcohol.

The Loire is an important producer of sparkling wines, third only to Champagne and Alsace. The most substantial among these is Crémant de Loire, which is made by the traditional method. Most Crémant de Loire is vinified in and around Saumur from blends of Chenin Blanc, Cabernet Franc, and Chardonnay, although a number of other traditional Loire grapes are also permitted. Appellation rules call for hand-harvested grapes and a minimum ageing period of one year (compared to nine months for, say, Saumur Mousseux). At its best, Crémant de Loire is long and complex with a floral, honeyed nose and a nutty finish.

The Nantais

Muscadet is made from Melon de Bourgogne, a frost-resistant and early ripening grape that came to dominate the area after the Great Frost of 1709. Of the three sub-regional appellations, Muscadet de Sèvre et Maine AOC is by far the most important, accounting for about three-quarters of all Muscadet production. Melon de Bourgogne is a neutral grape and *sur lie* ageing is often used to bring out greater flavour and texture, as is lees stirring and extended maceration. In addition, there has been some experimentation with extended lees ageing, barrel fermentation and ageing, and bottle ageing, leading to a diversity of styles. The *sur lie* process, which involves ageing on a natural sediment of dead yeast cells, should not be confused with malolactic fermentation, which is not used for Muscadet. To the blind-taster, Muscadet appears pale, sometimes almost watery. On the nose, the wine is distinctly unaromatic. On the palate, it is dry and light-bodied with high acidity and a touch of minerality or saltiness. Lees ageing contributes yeasty or nutty aromas and a rounder texture. At time of bottling, usually in the spring, some carbon dioxide may still remain in the wine, lending it a slight effervescence that can prickle on the tongue. Under AOC regulations, alcohol content is capped at 12%, the only instance of a maximum alcohol stipulation in France. Although the *sur lie* process does help to preserve freshness, most Muscadet is not intended for ageing. If you want to remember Muscadet, try it with oysters.

Anjou

Anjou is associated with a broad spectrum of wines. Particularly notable are the dry Chenin Blanc of Savennières and the sweet, often botrytized Chenin Blanc of Coteaux du Layon and more particularly of Bonnezeaux and Chaume and Quarts-de-Chaume.

Historically, Savennières AOC was sweet, but today the bulk of production is dry. Indeed, Savennières is the highest expression of dry Chenin Blanc, noted for its concentration of flavour, mineral intensity, and age worthiness. Though fuller in body than dry Vouvray, Savennières can be austere and unapproachable in its youth. Typical notes include apple, chamomile, warm straw, and beeswax. Acid and alcohol are both high. The crus of Savennières-Roche-aux-Moines AOC and Savennières Coulée-de-Serrant AOC are enclaves of Savennières AOC. Coulée de Serrant, first planted in 1130 by Cistercian monks, is considered by many to be the finest of the finest. It is currently a monopole of biodynamic producer Nicolas Joly.

The River Layon has carved out a valley that encourages the development of noble rot, although some grapes are simply very ripe or encouraged to dry on the vine (*passerillage*). Successive pickings at harvest time ensure that all the grapes are bursting with sugar, acidity, and flavour. Within Coteaux du Layon AOC, six villages—Beaulieu-sur-Layon, Faye-d'Anjou, Rablay-sur-Layon, Rochefort-sur-Loire, Saint-Aubin-de-Luigné, and Saint-Lambert-du-Lattay—can append their name to that of the appellation (as in, for example, 'Coteaux du Layon

Beaulieu') or, alternatively, use the name 'Coteaux du Layon-Villages'. A further two villages—Bonnezeaux and Chaume—have their own separate appellations, which are in effect sub-appellations of Coteaux du Layon. There is also a third sub-appellation, Quarts-de-Chaume AOC, for a particularly favoured enclave of Chaume that is shaped like an amphitheatre. Most of the land of Quarts-de-Chaume used to belong to the abbey of Ronceray d'Angers, which required tenant farmers to pay a tithe of one-quarter of annual production, whence 'Quarts-de-Chaume'. Compared to Vouvray, Coteaux du Layon tends to be fuller in body, sweeter, and lower in acidity. Coteaux de l'Aubance, along the River Aubance to the north of Coteaux du Layon, produces wines of a similar style to Coteaux du Layon. As with Coteaux du Layon, the wines can vary considerably in sweetness and in quality.

Rosé wines account for over 50% of Angevine production. First among them is Cabernet d'Anjou AOC, made from Cabernet Franc and Cabernet Sauvignon. Compared to Rosé d'Anjou AOC, which is made predominantly from Grolleau, Cabernet d'Anjou tends to be drier with higher alcohol and greater complexity and ageing potential.

With the exception of Anjou-Gamay AOC, red wines are all made from Cabernet Franc and Cabernet Sauvignon. Saumur-Champigny AOC is very similar to neighbouring Chinon AOC and Bourgueil AOC, both in Touraine.

Touraine

The most notable appellations in Touraine are Vouvray and Montlouis for white wines, and Chinon, Bourgueil, and Saint-Nicolas-de-Bourgueil for red wines.

Vouvray AOC, just to the east of the regional centre of Tours and on the right bank of the Loire, produces dry and sweet Chenin Blanc wines. A number of streams cut through the plateau of Vouvray to create sheltered south-facing slopes and promote the development of noble rot. In more favourable vintages, production shifts to sweet and botrytized wines; in cooler, unfavourable vintages, it shifts to dry and sparkling or semi-sparkling wines (which may however also be sweet). Sparkling Vouvray is also made according to the traditional method and can be either *pétillant* (semi-sparkling) or *mousseux* (fully sparkling). The harvest often lasts into November, with successive pickings required for the sweet wines. Compared to Coteaux du Layon, botrytis is less common and there is greater reliance on ripeness. Sweet wines may be *moelleux*, *doux*, or *liquoreux* (syrupy). Dry wines may be *sec* (dry), *sec-tendre* (gently dry), or *demi-sec* (off-dry). Vouvray is high in acidity, even though the acidity may be masked by sugar. Youthful Vouvray may be steely and unapproachable in its youth. In time, aromas of green apples, quince, and acacia blossom surrender to complex tertiary aromas dominated by honeysuckle, figs, and lanolin. Vouvray can have tremendous ageing potential, and this is especially true of the sweeter examples. Montlouis AOC, which sits on the opposite side of the river, used to be part of Vouvray, but in 1938 became a separate (and much smaller) appellation. The wines of Montlouis are similar to those of Vouvray in range and style, but tend towards less acidity and concentration.

Chinon AOC is encapsulated by some (untranslatable) verses by its most famous son, François Rabelais (1494-1553): '*Chinon, trois fois Chinon: Petite ville, grand renom, Assise sur pierre ancienne, Au haut le bois, au pied la Vienne.*' Chinon is about the same size as Bourgueil and Saint-Nicolas-de-Bourgueil taken together; although Chinon is more prestigious, the three appellations are very similar in style and more or less indistinguishable even to the seasoned blind-taster. Chinon has forever been associated with red wine, but also puts out a little rosé and a dash of white wine. The reds and rosés are made from Cabernet Franc, although up to 10% Cabernet Sauvignon may also be included. The soils are diverse and complex. In essence, gravelly, alluvial soils on the flats by the river yield a lighter and more fruit-driven style, while higher areas that are rich in limestone and *tuffeau jaune* yield a richer and more structured style. Chinon is classically described as having a nose of raspberries and pencil shavings. Unripe vintages may be marked, uncharitable souls might say marred, by a certain greenness or herbaceousness. On the palate, the wine is light- to medium-bodied with high acidity, medium alcohol, and fine and powdery tannins. Some Chinons can improve for 5-10 years, evolving earthy, spicy, and animally notes. The use of new oak is uncommon. Like so many wines of the Loire, Chinon can be very good value for money. Top producers include Olga Ruffault, Charles Joguet, and Bernard Baudry.

Bourgueil AOC and the smaller appellation of Saint-Nicolas-de-Bourgueil AOC lie across the river from Chinon. The slopes are south-facing and protected from cold, northerly winds by forests. Like Chinon, this is mostly red wine territory although some rosé can also be found. Bourgueil is made from Cabernet Franc together with up to 10% Cabernet Sauvignon. As in Chinon, gravelly, alluvial soils on the flats by the river yield a lighter and more fruit-driven style, while higher areas that are rich in limestone and *tuffeau jaune* yield a richer and more structured style. Compared to Bourgueil, Saint-Nicolas-de-Bourgueil has developed a lighter, more delicate and fruit-driven signature. Top producers in these appellations include Yannick Amirault, Max Cognard, and Delauney Druet.

Note: In practice it is very difficult to differentiate Saumur-Champigny, Chinon, Bourgueil, and Saint-Nicolas-de-Bourgueil.

Centre

The principal grape variety in the Centre is Sauvignon Blanc, with smaller plantings of Pinot Noir and Chasselas. The most notable appellations are Sancerre AOC and Pouilly-Fumé AOC, which almost face each other on opposite banks of the Loire. Sancerre used to be famed for its light-bodied red wines. However, since the mid 20th century, it has acquired a reputation for its white wines and has come to be considered as the spiritual home of Sauvignon Blanc. Today, most Sancerre is a white wine made from Sauvignon Blanc, although red and rosé wines made from Pinot Noir can also be found. In contrast, Pouilly-Fumé is invariably a white wine made from Sauvignon Blanc. Pouilly-Fumé is less than half the size of Sancerre. Its soils tend to be richer in silex, which translates into a smoky gunflint aroma (*pierre-à-fusil*). At the same time, calcium-rich limestone imparts a certain chalky quality. Both silex and limestone reflect light and retain heat, which helps the grapes of Sancerre and Pouilly-Fumé to ripen in the cool climate of the Loire. The wines are dry and high in acidity with a flavour profile that has been summarized as 'cat's pee on a gooseberry bush'. Notes of gooseberry and grapefruit are typically accompanied by hints of blackcurrant leaf, nettles, cut grass, and smoke. Notes of peach may be present, but notes (or even hints) of hotter climate tropical fruit are unusual. Malolactic fermentation and oak ageing are uncommon practices, and most Sancerre and Pouilly-Fumé is intended for early drinking. The quality of Sancerre in particular is very variable, and some Sancerre is not much different from generic Sauvignon de Touraine AOC from the Middle Loire. At the other end of the spectrum, the three villages of Bué, Chavignol, and Ménétréol-sous-Sancerre have achieved quasi cru status. Compared to, say, a Marlborough Sauvignon Blanc from New Zealand, Sancerre and Pouilly-Fumé are less fruit-driven with a cooler fruit profile and greater smokiness and minerality. In practice, it is very difficult to distinguish Sancerre from Pouilly-Fumé, although the latter tends to be subtly smokier. Wines labelled with just 'Pouilly' or 'Pouilly-sur-Loire' can be quite elegant, but are usually made from Chasselas rather than Sauvignon Blanc. Sancerre Rouge, which occasionally crops up in blind tastings, is a very pale, light, and delicate Pinot Noir with herbal notes and a just-ripe raspberry fruit profile.

Chapter 10

Other Notable French Regions and Appellations

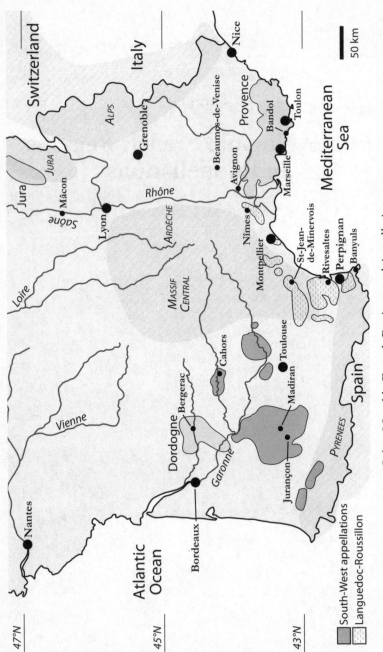

Other Notable French Regions and Appellations

South-West appellations
Languedoc-Roussillon

Atlantic Ocean

Nantes

Bordeaux

Dordogne

Bergerac

Garonne

Cahors

Jurançon

Madiran

Toulouse

PYRENEES

Spain

Loire

Vienne

MASSIF CENTRAL

ARDÈCHE

Nîmes

Montpellier

St-Jean-de-Minervois

Rivesaltes

Perpignan

Banyuls

Mediterranean Sea

Rhône

Lyon

Saône

Mâcon

JURA

Jura

Switzerland

ALPS

Grenoble

Beaumes-de-Venise

Avignon

Provence

Marseille

Bandol

Toulon

Nice

Italy

50 km

47°N

45°N

43°N

Jura

With less than 2000ha, the Jura is a small yet diverse wine region. The vineyards sit in the foothills of the Jura, ~80km (50mi) east of Burgundy and not far from Switzerland. The climate is cooler than in Burgundy, although the summers are fairly hot and sunny. The soils, which are rich in fossils, are clay and limestone with outcrops of marl. Five grape varieties are planted: Chardonnay and Savagnin for whites, and Poulsard, Trousseau (which thrives in the gravelly vineyards around Arbois), and Pinot Noir for reds—which, though vinified as reds, tend to be rather more salmon than actually red.

The relative isolation of the Jura has led to the preservation of a number of distinctive wine styles. Most notable is Vin Jaune made from very ripe Savagnin, which is left to mature under a flor-like strain of yeast for six or more years before being bottled in a 62cl clavelin. This process leads to oxidative nutty aromas similar to those of Sherry—although, unlike Sherry, Vin Jaune is not fortified. Other aromas include walnuts, honey, and "curry". Vin Jaune can be produced under the Arbois, Etoile, and Côtes du Jura appellations, but the richest examples are produced under the exclusive Château-Chalon appellation, which is home to top producers Jean Macle and Domaine Berthet-Bondet. Vin Jaune can potentially last for decades, if not centuries.

Also notable is a straw wine, Vin de Paille, which, like Vin Jaune, can be produced under the Arbois, Etoile, and Côtes du Jura appellations. This blend of Chardonnay, Poulsard, and Savagnin is pressed, normally in January, from dried grapes and aged in oak for at least three years. It is rich and complex with high alcohol and dominant notes of honey and dried or confected fruits.

Macvin du Jura AOC, which can be white (Chardonnay and Savagnin) or red (Poulsard, Trousseau, and Pinot Noir), is a *vin de liqueur* or mistelle made from the must of late harvest grapes. The must is oak-aged for 12 months without prior fermentation. Marc du Jura is then added in a ratio of 1:2, thereby halting fermentation and preserving the natural sugars. Further oak ageing finishes the process by harmonizing the flavours.

To round up on the six Jura appellations: any style of wine can be made under the Arbois and Côtes du Jura appellations, which are the most quantitatively important. In contrast, only white wines (including Vin Jaune and Vin de Paille) can be made under the Etoile appellation, and only Vin Jaune under the Château-Chalon appellation. Macvin du Jura is a regional appellation, as is Crémant du Jura AOC. This sparkling wine is made by the traditional method, most commonly from 100% Chardonnay.

Of the still 'regular' wines, the whites enjoy a greater reputation than the reds. These whites, which can be very terroir driven, are made from Chardonnay and/or Savagnin, either by the classic method (employed in other regions) or by the more oxidative regional and traditional method whereby the barrels are not topped up to compensate for evaporation. This oxidative style has long been the signature of this beautiful but isolated and often neglected wine region.

Provence

Although most people associate Provence, in the southeast corner of France, with its crisp and refreshing rosés, it is the smaller, more peripheral appellations that produce its most stunning wines, among which Bellet, Les Baux-de-Provence, Cassis, and, above all, Bandol.

The climate of Provence is Mediterranean with mild winters and hot, dry summers, and over 3,000 sunshine hours per year. The soils are very varied, with white grape varieties dominating outcrops of limestone as, for example, in Cassis. A large number of grape varieties are planted, including Rhône varieties such as Mourvèdre, Syrah, Grenache, Cinsault, and Roussanne; Atlantic varieties such as Cabernet Sauvignon and Merlot; and more local varieties such as Tibouren for rosés and Rolle (Vermentino) for white wines. The largest appellations in the Provence region are Côtes de Provence to the east and Côteaux d'Aix-en-Provence to the west.

To the south, between the cities of Marseille and Toulon, lies the sleepy fishing village and appellation of Bandol, which produces red wine and rosé together with a dash of white wine. The vineyards, which amount to some 1,700ha, are sheltered by the Montagne Sainte-Victoire and the Massif de la Sainte-Baume to the north and the Chaine de Saint-Cyr to the west. Moist sea breezes make up for any shortfall of rain. The soils principally consist of silicon and limestone. Yields are among the lowest in France, the equivalent of no more than one bottle per vine. The star grape variety is Mourvèdre, which ripens fully in this hot and dry climate. In contrast, Grenache runs the risk of over-ripening, and is usually planted on cooler, north-facing slopes.

Red Bandol consists of at least 50% Mourvèdre, usually completed by Grenache and Cinsault. Syrah and Carignan may also be included but are restricted to 15% of the blend and 10% individually. The wine is aged in old oak for at least 18 months prior to relase. Red Bandol is dark in colour with notes of black fruit, vanilla, spice, liquorice, leather, and red meat. On the palate, it is full-bodied, intense, and structured, with a high alcohol in the order of 14-15%. It improves with age and can be cellared for a decade or more. The rosé, which is made from a similar blend, is spicy and earthy in character, and not dissimilar to Tavel from the Southern Rhône. Bandol producers tend to be very reliable, with Domaine Tempier the most recognized.

Cahors

The South West wine region includes several disparate appellations situated south of, and inland from, Bordeaux. The most notable of these appellations are Cahors, Madiran, and Jurançon.

The 'black wines' of Cahors, the spiritual home of the Malbec grape (called Cot in Cahors), enjoyed a splendid reputation in the Middle Ages and right up into the 19th century. In the late 19th century, phylloxera reared its ugly head, and, in 1956, the Great Frost killed off all but 1% of the vines. Unsurprisingly, the area has taken a long time to recover.

Cahors is equidistant from the Atlantic and the Mediterranean. Compared to Bordeaux, the winters are colder, but the summers are hotter and drier. The vineyards are planted on gravelly slopes in the valley of the River Lot and up on the *causse* or limestone plateau. The plateau yields more tannic, longer-lived wines, while the slopes and alluvial valley floor yield softer, fruitier wines.

The appellation is for red wine only, with Malbec making up at least 70% of the blend and Merlot and Tannat accounting for any remainder. Cahors can be reminiscent of Bordeaux, but is darker in colour with more plum, chocolate, and minerals and heavier tannins that can make it austere and unapproachable in its youth. With age, it develops aromas of earth, forest floor, and animal. Acidity is high and body and alcohol only medium. The best examples are aged in oak. Compared to Cahors, Argentine Malbec is softer and riper with a heavier body, higher alcohol, and lower acidity.

Madiran

The appellation of Madiran, which is coextensive with the appellations of Pacherenc du Vic-Bilh and Pacherenc du Vic-Bilh Sec, lies to the southwest of Cahors, on the left bank of the River Adour. Madiran applies to red wines, Pacherenc du Vic-Bilh to white wines of varying degrees of sweetness, and Pacherenc du Vic-Bilh Sec to dry white wines. Summers are hotter than in Bordeaux and autumns often dry, facilitating late harvests. On the baked hills, the soils consist of flinty sedimentary rock, and in the valley of clay and sand. Madiran consists of Tannat and smaller proportions of Cabernet Franc, Cabernet Sauvignon, and Fer Servadou, although some of the finer examples are 100% Tannat. The wine is sensuous and yet structured, dark, full-bodied, alcoholic, and so tannic that Cabernet Sauvignon is looked upon as a softening grape. Techniques used to make the wine less astringent and more approachable in its youth include hand picking only the ripest grapes, de-stemming, and micro-oxygenation, first developed in Madiran by Patrick DuCournau. Top producers include Château Aydie, Domaine Berthoumieu, Château Boucassé, and Château Montus.

Jurançon

Henry IV of France and Navarre (nicknamed *le vert galant*) was baptized with a drop of Jurançon wine, and novelist Colette called Jurançon wine '*séduction du vert galant*'. "I was a girl when I met this prince; aroused, imperious, treacherous, as all great seducers are."

Jurançon lies to the south of Madiran, near Pau in the foothills of the Pyrenées. Warm and dry foehn winds extend the ripening season, with some harvests taking place as late as November and December. The soils are clay and sand, with some limestone at higher altitudes. Some vineyards contain *poudingues* (after the English 'pudding'), sedimentary rocks of calcareous clay studded with marble-sized pebbles or *galets*. The principal grape varieties are Petit Manseng and Gros Manseng, with smaller amounts of Courbu Blanc, Camaralet de Lasseube, and Lauzet. Gros Manseng is normally the principal grape variety for Jurançon Sec AOC, and Petit Manseng for the sweet and sometimes oak-aged Jurançon AOC, which is more sought-after and dominates production. As Petit Manseng has a thick skin, it is particularly suited to drying on the vine (*passerillage*).

The sweetness of Jurançon AOC can vary quite considerably depending on vintage conditions and time of harvest. On appearance, the wine is golden in colour, often with a greenish tinge. The nose delivers tropical fruits such as mango, pineapple, and guava together with flowers and sweet spice, and perhaps even beeswax, banana, and coconut. Acidity is high but sweetness can vary quite considerably depending on vintage conditions and time of harvest. Sweet Jurançon is more akin to Vouvray than to nearby Sauternes, both in terms of acid structure and aroma profile. Henri Ramonteu of Domaine Cauhapé is a highly regarded producer.

Note: Bergerac is covered in Chapter 8, on Bordeaux.

Chapter 11

Sparkling Wines

Champagne

Early sparkling wines were produced by the *méthode ancestrale*, with the carbon dioxide gas arising from fermentation in the bottle. The *méthode ancestrale* is still used in certain parts of France such as Gaillac and Limoux; but as the lees are not removed from the bottle, the end product can be cloudy.

Historically in the Champagne, cold weather halted fermentation, which then restarted in the spring. If the wine had been bottled, the carbon dioxide gas produced by this second fermentation of sorts often shattered the bottle. But if the bottle resisted, the result was a sparkling wine more or less similar to modern Champagne. For a long time, the Champenois considered such a wine to be faulty, even calling it *vin du diable* (devil's wine).

In contrast to the Champenois, the British acquired a taste for this accidentally sparkling wine and introduced it to the court of Versailles, then under the regency (1715-23) of Philippe II, duc d'Orléans. The Champenois rose to meet the increasing demand for the sparkling wine, but found it difficult to control the process and could not source bottles strong enough to reliably withstand the pressure.

The solutions to these problems came not from Champagne but from across the Channel. (1) In 1662 Christopher Merret presented a paper in which he correctly maintained that any wine could be made sparkling by the addition of sugar prior to bottling, and it is likely that the English were making the wine of Champagne sparkle long before the Champenois themselves. (2) English glassmakers of the 17th century used coal-rather than wood-fire ovens that yielded a stronger glass and stronger bottles. (3) The English rediscovered the use of cork stoppers (lost after the fall of the Roman Empire), which provided an airtight closure with which to seal in the sparkle.

Just six years after Merret presented his paper Dom Pérignon became cellar master at the Benedictine Abbey at Hautvillers. Dom Pérignon thought of sparkling wine as faulty and recommended using Pinot Noir to minimize the tendency to sparkle. Yet, he greatly improved practices of viticulture, harvesting, and vinification, perfecting the wines that would become sparkling Champagne. For instance, he advocated aggressive pruning and smaller yields, early-morning harvesting, the rejection of bruised or broken grapes, and rapid pressing to minimize skin contact.

Until the early 19th century, Champagne producers did not remove the lees from the bottle. While this preserved all the sparkle, it could make for quite a cloudy and unpleasant wine. The veuve Cliquot and her cellar master solved the problem by developing the process of riddling, which involves progressively moving the lees into the neck of the bottle and then ejecting it under the pressure of the wine. Today, this process has largely become mechanized.

The small amount of wine lost through riddling came to be replaced by a variable mixture of sugar and wine called the dosage, which then as today determined the final style of the wine. Throughout most of the 19th century, Champagne was very sweet. Champagne destined for the Russian market was sweetest of all, containing as much as 250-330g/l of sugar. At the other end of the spectrum, Champagne destined for the English market contained 'only' 22-66g/l of sugar. Today, the most popular style of Champagne, *brut*, only contains 6-15g/l of sugar; and the sweetest style, *doux*, can contain as little as 50g/l.

In the wake of the phylloxera epidemic and a seemingly endless succession of poor vintages, riots erupted in January 1911. Some producers had been making faux Champagne with grapes from other French regions, and the Champenois grape growers intercepted the trucks conveying this fruit and dumped it into the River Marne. To pacify them, the French government attempted to delimit the Champagne region, but the exclusion and then inclusion of the Aube provoked further riots that might have degenerated into civil war had it not been for the outbreak of World War I. The Great War brought destruction to buildings and vineyards, and many Champenois took refuge in the *crayères* (chalk cellars) normally used to store and mature Champagne.

The Champenois had barely begun recovering from the wounds of war when the lucrative Russian market was lost to the Bolshevik Revolution, and then the US market to Prohibition. The Great Depression also hit sales, as did the advent of the World War II. Since the end of World War II, Champagne has been in ever increasing demand. This has led to a quadrupling of production to over 330m bottles per year, but it has also led to a great number of imitators throughout France, Europe, and the New World; and, back home, to a controversial expansion of the Champagne delimited area.

Champagne: The lie of the land

The three grape varieties used in making Champagne are Chardonnay, Pinot Noir, and Pinot Meunier. All three varieties are planted across the Champagne AOC, which is the only major single-appellation region in France. This region is located ~85km (53mi) northeast of Paris at latitude 49-50°N, the northerly extreme of wine making. The climate is marginal with a mean annual temperature of 10°C (50°F) and all the problems that this entails, including severe winters, spring frosts, and hail. Mercifully, the chalk subsoil is good at storing the sun's heat. It is also good at retaining water, which is relatively scarce, and accommodates the cool and damp cellars in which the wines are made and matured. The vineyards themselves predominantly face south, east, and southeast on gently undulating to moderately steep terrain that combines high sun exposure with good drainage.

In Champagne, the badge of the quality of a terroir is not attached to an individual site as in Burgundy but, rather crudely, to an entire village. On the so-called Échelle des Crus, each village within the Champagne demarcated area is given a score ranging from 80 to 100%; villages with a score of 90 to 99% are classified as Premier Cru and villages with the top score of 100% as Grand Cru. There are currently 41 Premier Cru and 17 Grand Cru villages, altogether accounting for just over 30% of the entire demarcated area.

Most of these Premier and Grand Cru villages are located in just two of the five regional areas or districts, the Montagne de Reims to the north of Epernay and the Côte des Blancs to the south. The Montagne de Reims is a forested peak that is mostly planted with Pinot Noir, which contributes structure and depth of fruit to a blend. The Côte des Blancs is an east-facing slope that is mostly planted with Chardonnay, which contributes freshness and fine fruitiness to a blend. Compared to Pinot Noir, Chardonnay has the greater ageing potential. Some of the grandest Champagnes such as Taittinger's Comtes de Champagne and Ruinart's Dom Ruinart are 100% Chardonnay, so-called *blanc de blancs*. In contrast, almost no one deliberately sets out to make a *blanc de noirs*, that is, a 100% blend of black grapes (Pinot Noir and/or Pinot Meunier).

The Montagne de Reims and the Côte des Blancs are quasi contiguous with the Vallée de la Marne which runs west past Hautvillers and then for some 40 or 50km to a bit beyond Château-Thierry. The Vallée de la Marne is particularly suited to Pinot Meunier, with which it is mostly planted. Compared to Pinot Noir and Chardonnay, Pinot Meunier buds late, making it more resistant to the spring frosts to which the Vallée de la Marne is particularly prone. In a blend, Pinot Meunier contributes notes of flowers and bruised apples, and an early-maturing richness and fruitiness that make for immediate appeal. All the classified villages in the Vallée de la Marne are concentrated at its chalky, eastern end, not far from Epernay.

The other two districts, the Côte de Sézanne and Aube (also called the Côte des Bar) are effectively detached satellites to the south of the Côte des Blancs. Neither district contains any Grand or Premier Cru villages. Sézanne, which lies northwest of Troyes, is a small area mainly planted with Chardonnay. In contrast, Aube, which lies southeast of Troyes and which is actually closer to Chablis than to Reims, is mainly planted with Pinot Noir. Aube is also responsible for the Rosé de Riceys (which used to be a favourite of Louis XIV) and red Coteaux Champenois.

All in all, the Champagne delimited area stands at ~35,000ha spread across ~281,000 vineyard plots, 319 villages, and five *départements*. 67% of plantings are in the Marne, and the Marne, Aube and Aisne together account for some 99% of plantings. The remaining plantings are in the Haute-Marne and Seine-et-Marne. Of the three grape varieties, Pinot Noir is the most commonly planted, but Pinot Meunier and Chardonnay are a fairly close second and third.

In terms of viticulture, the plantings are dense with vines no more than 1.5m (5ft) apart. In all Grand Cru and Premier Cru vineyards, pruning must be by the *Taille Chablis* method, preferred for Chardonnay, or the *Cordon de Royat* method, preferred for Pinot Noir. Both methods retain a high degree of permanent wood that helps the vine to resist frost. The other pruning method used for Chardonnay and Pinot Noir is the Guyot method. Finally, Pinot Meunier is typically pruned by the *Vallée de la Marne* method. The maximum permitted yield used to be 13,000kg/ha, but from 2007 was increased to 15,500kg/ha.

Champagne: Method of production

Like many sparkling wines, Champagne is produced by the traditional or classic method, which is characterized by a second fermentation in the very bottle in which the wine will be sold.

The grapes that go into making Champagne require both high acidity and phenolic ripeness, a combination much easier to achieve in the cool Champagne region than in warmer climates. So as to preserve acidity, grapes are harvested early at a low must weight. This comes at the cost of sugar content, which is made up for by the subsequent addition of sugar in the form of *liqueur de tirage* and *liqueur de dosage*, and also, in some cases, by initial chaptalization. In black grapes it also comes at the expense of colour, which for Champagne is of course a benefit.

The vineyards are harvested by hand and whole bunches are taken. This prevents damage to the grapes and ensures that their juice can run off quickly along the stalks, which act as drainage channels in the press. The grapes are pressed without delay, traditionally in a basket or Coquard press although other types of press, notably the Vaslin horizontal press and the more delicate Wilmes horizontal press, are also used. Gentle pressure is applied so as to minimize the extraction of undesirable colour and tannin. Extraction is limited to a maximum of 102l of must per 160kg of grapes. The first 2l to emerge are discarded, the next 80l are the *cuvée*, and the remaining 20l are the *taille*, which may or may not be excluded. Anything beyond 102l is the *vin de rebèche*, which cannot be used for Champagne. After pressing, the must is clarified with some solids retained to facilitate the second fermentation. The must may also be chaptalized at this stage.

Next, the must is fermented to a still wine, normally in stainless steel vats although some producers such as Bollinger and Krug use (old) oak casks. The temperature of the fermentation typically ranges from around 18 to 22°C (64–72°F). Too cool a temperature encourages the formation of undesirable amylic aromas, which may mask some of the more subtle and complex notes of the finished Champagne. Many houses encourage malolactic fermentation, although some, most notably Lanson, prefer to avoid it.

Grapes from different plots and parcels are vinified separately. In the spring following the harvest these *vins clairs* (base wines) are blended along with varying proportions of reserve wine from older vintages. This process of blending or *assemblage* aims at balance and complexity, and also at creating a consistent house style. As so many parameters are vintage dependent, there can be no fixed recipe for the house style and every release is the product of the skill and judgement of a master blender.

The blended still wine, though full of promise, is not especially pleasant to drink. It is bottled together with the *liqueur de tirage*, a mixture of wine, sugar, and yeast. The purpose of the *liqueur de tirage* is to induce a second, slower fermentation or *prise de mousse* in the bottle. Around 24g/l of sugar are required to add around 1.2% of alcohol. This brings total alcohol to around 12% and also yields sufficient carbon dioxide for a bottle pressure of around 5–6atm—equivalent to 5–6 times atmospheric pressure at sea level or the pressure in a tire of a double-decker bus!

The bottles are sealed with a crown cap and laid horizontally *sur lattes* in a cool cellar. The *prise de mousse* takes place over a period of perhaps 4-8 weeks after which the wine is left to mature, in some cases for several years, on the lees. During this period of lees ageing, the gradual breakdown of yeast cells releases mannoproteins, polysaccharides, and anti-oxidative enzymes into the wine. This so-called yeast autolysis results in (1) a fuller body with a more unctuous mouthfeel, (2) reduced bitterness and astringency, (3) complex aromas of biscuit, bread dough, nuttiness, and acacia, and (4) enhanced ageing potential. By law, non-vintage wines must sit on the lees for at least 15 months and vintage wines for at least 36 months, although many producers largely exceed these minimum requirements.

Compared to blending and ageing on the lees, the remaining steps in the method of production of Champagne add relatively little to overall quality. The bottles are first agitated so as to loosen and consolidate the sediment, a process called *poignettage*. The yeast deposit is then gradually moved into the neck of the bottle. Traditionally, this is carried out over 8-10 weeks on a *pupitre*, a wooden frame with 60 holes bored at an angle of 45° on which bottles can be manually turned from horizontal to vertical. Nowadays, this process of riddling or *remuage* is far more likely to be carried out on a much larger scale and in a much shorter time by a mechanized gyropalette. With riddling complete, the bottle is left in its vertical, upside-down position (*sur pointes*) for a further period of maturation.

Next, the crown cap and lees are removed. This process of disgorgement used to be carried out by hand or *à la volée*. Today it is usually carried out in an automated process that involves freezing the material in the neck of the bottle and ejecting this ice plug under the pressure of the wine. The dosage or *liqueur d'expédition* is then added. The dosage is a mixture of the base wine and varying amounts of sugar that serves to balance acidity and determine the final style of the wine. By far the most common style is brut with added sugar of 6-15g/l. Other fairly common styles are extra brut with 0-6g/l and demi-sec with 35-50g/l.

A composite or agglomerated cork with whole cork attached to the base is inserted and held in place by a capsule and wire cage (*muselet*). However, the wine is not yet ready to drink, and a further rest period is required for the dosage to marry with the wine. During this period, a number of chemical reactions between sugar in the dosage and amino acids in the wine give rise to additional aromas of dried fruit, toast, and vanilla. Some authorities have argued that zero dosage wines (bone dry wines with no added sugar) are unable to benefit from this so-called Maillard reaction.

To produce the smallest and largest bottle sizes (half- and quarter-bottles and those beyond double magnum or jeroboam), the wine is disgorged into a pressure tank, the dosage is added to the tank, and the wine is rebottled—a process called *transversage*.

The method of production described above may be slightly adapted for different styles of Champagne. Vintage Champagne is not made every year but only in very good to exceptional years. The wines that go into the *assemblage* must all come from the same declared vintage and the minimum period for ageing on the lees is 36 months. Compared to non-vintage Champagne, vintage Champagne is richer and fuller and more apt to improve with bottle age. A producer may also indulge in a *cuvée de prestige*, normally a vintage Champagne made from premium grapes and aged for an even longer period. Pink Champagne, which accounts for ~7% of total production, results either from the addition of a small amount of still red wine prior to first fermentation or, less commonly, from the removal ('bleeding off') of some of the juice after limited contact with the skins (the *saignée* method). Champagne that is sold as 'recently disgorged' or similar is Champagne that has benefited from prolonged yeast ageing and that has been released for sale immediately after disgorgement. If consumed soon after release, this Champagne can taste especially fresh, fruity, and complex. Single vineyard and single village Champagnes are increasingly popular, but still very much occupy a niche market.

The Champagne industry

The Champagne industry is dominated by about one hundred big houses, so-called *Grandes Marques* or *négociants-manipulants* (identified as NM on bottle labels) such as Laurent-Perrier, Moët et Chandon, and Perrier-Jouët, which together account for almost 90% of all export sales. These big houses own only a small fraction (around 13%) of the vineyards, and many are heavily reliant on purchased grapes from some 15,000 growers or *récoltants*.

Some growers instead sell their grapes to a co-operative that may fulfil a number of functions such as pressing the fruit, completing the first fermentation, or, in the case of *co-opératives-manipulants* (CM), producing a finished Champagne that is ready for sale. Other growers, so-called *récoltants-manipulants* (RM), prefer not to sell their grapes but to produce something akin to a boutique Champagne. *Récoltants-manipulants* are gaining both in numbers and prestige, with wines that are often more terroir-driven than those of the *Grandes Marques*.

Other entities in the Champagne industry are *recoltants-co-opérateurs* (RC), growers who sell Champagne made in their co-operative under their own name and label; *sociétés de récoltants* (SR), growers who group together to produce a Champagne outside the co-operative system; and *négociants-distributeurs* (ND), *négociants* who buy a finished Champagne and market it under their own name and label. Similarly, *marque d'acheteur* (MA) is applied to a finished Champagne marketed under the label of a retailer such as a supermarket group.

The largest player in the Champagne industry is Louis Vuitton Moët Hennessy (LVMH), a luxury goods concern that is listed on the Paris stock market and that operates the brands Moët et Chandon, Krug, Veuve Clicquot, Ruinart, and Champagne Mercier. In 2011, LVMH sold 55.5m bottles of Champagne and accounted for as much as 50% of Champagne exports to the USA. Other important players in the Champagne industry include Lanson BCC, Vranken Pommery Monopole, and Laurent Perrier. Some of our favourite Champagne houses are Bollinger, Pol Roger, and Taittinger. All three remain family-run.

Other traditional method sparkling wines

Though the traditional method is often associated with Champagne, it is also used in a large number of other regions both in Europe and the New World. Indeed, some regions in France can claim to have been using the traditional method long before the Champenois came round to it.

The French term *crémant* traditionally referred to a sparkling wine with a lower pressure than that of Champagne. In 1994, the Champenois secured the exclusive use of the term *méthode champenoise*. In exchange, they abandoned the term crémant to a number of other French regions with a Crémant AOC status. Today, the term crémant is no longer tied to the pressure of a sparkling wine but to its provenance, and many modern crémants have a similar pressure to Champagne. If modern crémants differ from Champagne, this is principally in terms of grape varieties, yields, harvesting, pressing, time on lees, and, of course, regional differences in climate and terroir.

Alsace is the most important producer of crémant, with around 30m bottles per year in recent years (about 9% of the figure for Champagne). Permitted grape varieties for Crémant d'Alsace are Pinot Blanc, Pinot Gris, Pinot Noir, Riesling, Auxerrois, and Chardonnay. Whereas Chardonnay is not permitted in the still wines of Alsace, Gewurztraminer and Muscat are not permitted in the crémant on account of their pronounced aromatics. In practice, Crémant d'Alsace is often dominated by the relatively neutral Pinot Blanc. Maximum yields are high at 80hl/ha, although this figure can be adjusted according to the vintage. Hand harvesting is compulsory, no more than 100l of juice may be extracted from every 150kg of grapes (a slightly higher extraction ratio than for Champagne), and the wine must spend at least nine months on lees.

Burgundy produces about one-third less crémant than Alsace. Crémant de Bourgogne can be made in all areas of Burgundy except Beaujolais. Important regional centres are Auxerre and Châtillon-sur-Seine in the north, and Rully further south in the Côte Chalonnaise. Crémants from the north are typically tauter and leaner than the more generous offerings from the south. Permitted grape varieties are Chardonnay, Aligoté, Pinot Noir, Pinot Blanc, Pinot Gris, Gamay, Melon de Bourgogne, and Sacy. In practice, Crémant de Bourgogne is often dominated by Chardonnay and Aligoté. Just as in Alsace, hand harvesting is compulsory, no more than 100l of juice may be extracted from every 150kg of grapes, and the wine must spend at least nine months on lees. But unlike in Alsace, yields are capped at a lower 65hl/ha.

In the Loire, crémant production is centred upon the area of Anjou-Saumur although the appellation of Crémant de Loire also extends into Touraine. Producers around Saumur can choose to label their crémant as either Crémant de Loire AOC or Saumur Mousseux AOC. Crémant de Loire is considered to be the higher quality appellation. All the grape varieties permitted in the still wines of the Loire are also permitted in the crémants, with the single exception of Sauvignon Blanc which is considered too aromatic. The better quality wines consist mostly of Chardonnay with varying amounts of perhaps Cabernet Franc, Pinot Noir, and Chenin Blanc. Maximum yields are slightly higher than in Burgundy and vary according to the vintage. Other regulations are similar to those in Burgundy and Alsace, except that the wine must spend at least 12 months on lees. Typical production volumes approach around 8m bottles per year. Saumur Mousseux, though not called a crémant, is a fully sparkling wine made by the traditional method. It is mostly produced in poor vintages in which the grapes are not sufficiently ripe for more lucrative still wines. Chenin Blanc is invariably an important constituent of Saumur Mousseux, but Chardonnay, Pinot Noir, Cabernet Franc, and even Sauvignon Blanc can also be included in the blend. Maximum yields are actually lower than for Crémant de Loire, but the wine need spend only nine months on lees.

Much further south, the Languedoc is the home of Crémant de Limoux AOC and Blanquette de Limoux AOC. The climate is considerably warmer with a Mediterranean pattern of hot, dry summers. The best vineyards are on the hills, where cooler conditions conserve acidity. Blanquette de Limoux is at least 90% Mauzac, which has a distinct bruised apple character on the nose and palate. The remaining 10% or less is made up by Chardonnay and Chenin Blanc. Crémant de Limoux, by contrast, must contain between 50-70% Chardonnay and 20-40% Chenin Blanc, with perhaps a little space for a dash of Mauzac and/or Pinot Noir. For both Crémant de Limoux and Blanquette de Limoux, yields are capped at 50hl/ha. As in Burgundy and Alsace, hand harvesting is compulsory, no more than 100l of juice may be extracted from every 150kg of grapes, and the wine must spend at least nine months on lees.

Rest of Europe

By volume, Cava is the second most important sparkling wine in the world after Champagne. The *Denominación*, which dates back to Spain's 1986 entry into the European Union, covers five Spanish regions: Cataluña, Aragon, Navarra, País Vasco, and La Rioja—that is, all the regions bordering France plus La Rioja. There are fewer than 300 Cava producers, and the largest, Cordoníu and Freixenet, account for the bulk of production. Both operate from Sant Sadurni d'Anoia in Penedès, Cataluña. Today, about half of all Cava is dry or brut. The historically popular sweet semi-seco style still accounts for about a third of production, but is mostly destined for the domestic market. At either extreme, *brut nature* and *seco* each account for about a tenth of production.

The best vineyards for Cava tend, as in Limoux, to be at a relatively high altitude. Although the total area under vines is similar to that in Champagne (~32,000ha), production is only two-thirds that of Champagne partly because the vines are planted at a lower density and trained in bush. Maximum yields are 12,000kg/ha for white grapes and 8,000kg/ha for black, and only the first pressing or *cuvée* can go into making Cava—further reducing effective yields. Minimum lees ageing is nine months rising to 18 months for Reserva and 30 months for Gran Reserva wines. Pressure must be at least 4.0atm (although, as with Champagne, it is usually much higher) and alcohol must range from 10.8 to 12.8%.

The most obvious difference between Cava and Champagne is not in method of production but in grape varieties. For the most part, these are Macabeo (Viura), Xarel-lo, and Parellada. Macabeo lends a delicate aroma, Xarel-lo body and an earthy aroma (which is absent from Champagne), and Parellada acidity and subtle florality. Chardonnay is increasingly important, especially in top quality wines in which it might even constitute the majority component. For rosado wines, the traditional black grapes Monastrell (Mourvèdre) and Garnacha (Grenache) are preferred, as is the less traditional Pinot Noir. Unlike in Champagne, it is uncommon for black grapes to be used in the production of white wines.

Italy's most well-known sparkling wines, Prosecco and Asti, are not made by the traditional method, and Franciacorta is currently the only *Denominazione* that specifically calls for it. Franciacorta DOCG is produced just south of Lake Iseo, in Lombardy, north-central Italy. The climate is continental but the lake exercises a subtle moderating effect. Permitted grape varieties are Chardonnay (85% of plantings), Pinot Noir, and Pinot Blanc. The approach to winemaking is similar to that of Champagne. The vines are densely planted and 'big vine' training systems such as the pergola are forbidden. The rosé must include 15% Pinot Noir, and, as in Champagne, may be made by blending with a still red wine. Franciacorta Satèn is a *blanc de blancs* with a lower pressure of 4.5atm. Total annual production of Franciacorta is ~7m bottles.

Other notable traditional method sparkling wines in Europe are Vouvray Mousseux AOC, Crémant de Bordeaux AOC, Crémant de Jura AOC, and Crémant de Die AOC. Crémant de Die, made from the Clairette grape, is not to be confused with Clairette de Die Tradition AOC, mostly made from Muscat of Alexandria by the *méthode dioise*. The must is fermented to around 3% alcohol, cooled, and bottled, and then re-ferments in bottle to around 7-8% alcohol. After four months lees ageing, the wine is disgorged by the transfer method. It is in many ways similar to Asti (see later).

Traditional method sparkling wines can also be found in other parts of Europe (for example, some top quality Lambrusco or German Sekt) but these regions do not enshrine the traditional method in their regulations. Since some years, high quality English sparkling wines are being made using grape varieties and methods of production similar or identical to those in Champagne. English sparkling wines can be difficult to tell apart from Champagne, but do tend to be drier and more acidic.

New World

Many top-quality bottle-fermented sparkling wines from the New World are made by a variant of the traditional method called the transfer method. The transfer method is identical to the traditional method up to the riddling stage. Instead of being riddled, the wine is disgorged into a pressurized tank, the lees are filtered out, and a dosage is added. The wine is then rebottled under pressure, circumventing the trouble and expense of the riddling process.

Many New World traditional method or bottle-fermented sparkling wines are Champagne clones made from Chardonnay and Pinot Noir (and, to a much lesser extent, Pinot Meunier). But there are also some styles, such as sparkling Shiraz or Zinfandel, that are unique to a particular country or region and very distinct from Champagne. Many Champagne clones struggle to achieve the same balance of high acidity and phenolic ripeness as in Champagne.

The two largest producers of New World sparkling wine are the USA and Australia. Over 90% of US sparkling wine hails from California, which in the past 40 years has received considerable investment from a number of larger Champagne and Cava houses. Notable regions include the Anderson Valley in Mendocino County; Carneros at the southern end of Sonoma and Napa; Sonoma itself, especially sites in the Green and Russian River Valleys; and certain sites in the Central Coast that are close to the ocean. Despite the cooling influence of the ocean, conditions are not as propitious as in Champagne, with the winemaker caught between an early harvest that preserves acidity but risks under-ripe, 'green' aromas and a later harvest of riper fruit that risks a flabby and overly alcoholic wine. The principal grape varieties are Chardonnay and Pinot Noir; other grape varieties include Pinot Meunier, Pinot Blanc, and Pinot Gris. Sparkling Zinfandel is an off-dry rosé with a distinct note of 'strawberries and cream'. It is most commonly made by the tank method (see later).

Like California, Australia has received significant investment from Champagne houses. The principal grape varieties are Chardonnay and Pinot Noir, and the most notable regions are the Yarra Valley and Tasmania. The nearby ocean and high altitudes (up to 470m or 1,542ft) exert a moderating influence on the climate of the Yarra Valley. Tasmanian production is tiny, but there has been a lot of interest in this coolest of Australian regions and, in particular, the sub-regions of Tamar Valley and Piper's River. Australia's equivalent of California's Central Valley is the Big Rivers zone, which is the source of vast quantities of basic bubbly. The weather in Australia and California is far more reliable than in Champagne. As a result, the blending focus is a lot more horizontal (across vineyards and sub-regions, and even across regions) than vertical (across vintages). Sparkling Shiraz is a unique piece of Australiana with roots in 19th century Victoria. The best examples of this deep red, semi-sweet wine are made by the traditional method, mostly from Shiraz but also from Merlot or Cabernet Sauvignon. Sparkling Shiraz is typically high in alcohol (14%) and tannins, and some examples may have spent time in oak. It is said to be ideal for a barbecued Sunday brunch.

In New Zealand, most traditional method sparkling wine production is concentrated in Marlborough and carried out on a very small scale. The important exception is Montana, which produces most of New Zealand's sparkling wine. Montana's top *cuvée*, Lindauer Grandeur, is traditional method, as is the celebrated Deutz Marlborough Cuvée.

In South Africa, production of traditional method sparkling wine ('Méthode Cap Classique') is on a very small scale with fewer than two-dozen producers, mostly working with Chardonnay and Pinot Noir. Sparkling Chenin Blanc and Sauvignon Blanc tend to be produced by the tank method.

Latin America has received investment from some bigger Champagne and Cava houses. Most of the production, which remains very small, is consumed domestically or in other Latin American countries. Sites with great potential such as the Limarí Valley in Chile and the Rio Grande del Sul in Brazil are yet to be fully explored. Argentina is currently the biggest producer of sparkling wine in Latin America, with Mendoza accounting for about 70% of Argentine output.

Other sparkling wines

The autolytic character and long ageing associated with the traditional method is well suited to Chardonnay and Pinot Noir, but not, for instance, to the Prosecco grape Glera.

The other major method of making sparkling wine is the tank method (*cuve close*, Charmat). The tank method is cheap and consistent and preserves freshness and varietal character; on the other hand, it requires a large upfront investment and a skilled operator to prevent any loss of pressure, and lacks the charm and cachet of the traditional method. Sugar and yeast are added to the base wine in a large pressurized tank, which may be fitted with rousing paddles to increase yeast contact. Once the second fermentation has taken place, the wine is cooled, clarified by centrifugation and filtration, and enriched with a dosage. Prosecco, most Lambrusco, and most Sekt (among others) are made by the tank method.

Prosecco is made in the area of Treviso in northeast Italy, where the cool continental climate is ideally suited to the late-ripening Glera grape. The DOCG delimited area covers 4,100ha extending into the pre-Alps and Dolomites to the north. Most Prosecco is made in the Conegliano and Valdobbiadene area. Prosecco from the 107ha of the hill of Cartizze is said to be especially rich and creamy. The bulk of Prosecco production is *spumante* (fully sparkling) and most of the rest is *frizzante* (lightly sparkling). Prosecco should be drunk young. It is light, fresh, and intensely aromatic with primary fruit flavours, alcohol of ~11%, and a trademark slightly bitter finish. The traditional style is off-dry with 16-17g/l of sugar, but most Prosecco on the export market is dry.

Lambrusco is mainly a red *frizzante* made from the eponymous Lambrusco grape, a black grape that encompasses several genetically unrelated grape varieties and that has been in cultivation since Roman and even Etruscan times. In the 1970s and 80s, when pink and white Lambrusco were more common, it was the most important import wine in the United States. Lambrusco is made in four areas of Emilia-Romagna and one area of Lombardy. The climate is Mediterranean, the soils are fertile, and yields can be high. Most Lambrusco is made in co-operatives by the tank method and is of rather ordinary quality. Of the five Lambrusco DOCs, Lambrusco di Sorbara is the most highly regarded; the best examples are made by the traditional method. Lambrusco is characterized by sour cherries, high acidity, and a dry or off-dry sweetness.

90% of Sekt is made from inexpensive base wine sourced from

outside Germany—mainly Italy, France, and Spain. The remainder is Deutscher Sekt, that is, Sekt made from German grapes. The bulk of Sekt and Deutscher Sekt is made by the tank method and sold under the label of a large and inexpensive brand. The small amount of traditional method Deutscher Sekt is likely to consist of Riesling, Chardonnay, or the Pinot varieties, with the most prestigious examples carrying the vineyard name and vintage on the label. Sekt is big business in Germany: three of the world's five largest producers of sparkling wine are German.

Asti (formerly Asti spumante, which suffered from a poor reputation) is made from Muscat Blanc à Petits Grains in southeast Piedmont, Italy. The method of vinification is the Asti method or single tank fermentation method. The must is transferred into large tanks and chilled to almost 0°C (32°F) to inhibit fermentation. The tanks are sealed and pressurized and the temperature is raised to 16-18°C (61-64°F) for a single fermentation to 7-7.5% alcohol and a pressure of around 5 atm. The wine is then cooled to 0°C to halt fermentation and membrane filtered to remove the yeast and yeast nutrients. Finally, it is bottled under pressure by cool sterile bottling. Asti can also be made by double fermentation, with a second fermentation from 6% to 7.5% taking place in a sealed tank to build up pressure. The wine is fresh and intensely fruity and floral with dominant aromas of peach and musk and enough acidity to balance out the 3-5% residual sugar. Asti should not be confused with Moscato d'Asti, which is made from the same grape in the same region, but which is *frizzante*, sweeter, and even lower in alcohol.

Chapter 12

Germany

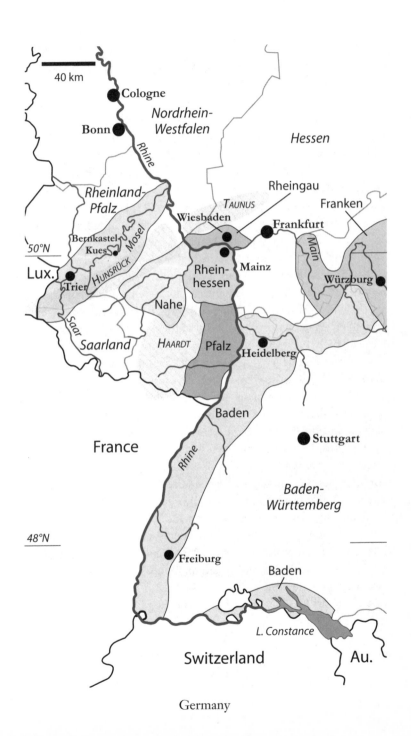

Wine is mostly produced in the southwest of the country, along the River Rhine and its tributaries. The Romans founded Trier (Augusta Treverorum), modern Germany's most ancient city, on the Mosel. In 370, Ausonius lauded the beauty of the region's steep vineyards in his poem *Mosella*. Little is known about the style or quality of these and other early 'German' wines, although, in about 570, the poet Venantius Fortunatus did make mention of a red wine from the region.

During the Middle Ages, Christianity spread east, bringing with it churches and monasteries and the cultivation of the vine. Riesling is first documented in or near the Rheingau from 1435, and Pinot Noir from 1470. However, the most common grape varieties in the 15th century were Elbing and Silvaner, probably planted pêle-mêle along with other varieties such as Muskat and Traminer. Viticulture reached a high point around 1500, with the area under vines four times larger than today. The vines receded for a number of reasons including competition from beer, the Thirty Year's War (which ended in 1648 with Alsace becoming a French province), the expropriation of the monasteries, and the Little Ice Age, which made viticulture difficult in more marginal climates.

Paradoxically, quality improved as unsuitable land was abandoned and lesser grape varieties were replaced with Riesling. The first Riesling monoculture was planted in 1720 at Schloss Johannisberg, then a Benedictine abbey in the Rheingau. In 1775, the courier delivering the permission to begin the harvest arrived at Schloss Johannisberg so late that most of the fruit had been affected by Botrytis. This vintage of 'rotten' grapes became legendary, inaugurating a number of late harvest styles. In the early 1800s, Napoleonic France seized the Church's vineyards and parcelled them out. Owing to strict inheritance laws, vineyards became ever smaller, creating an important demand for co-operatives.

At the height of their renown in the 19th century, the wines of the Rhine could fetch higher prices than first growth Bordeaux. But then came vine diseases, wars, and economic upheaval. Whatever remained of the lustre of the golden age was completely tarnished in the 1970s when Germany began blending and exporting cheap semi-sweet wines such as Liebfraumilch that, in foreign eyes, came to epitomize the country's entire wine offering. However, among enthusiasts, Germany's reputation is still founded on aromatic, elegant, complex, and long-lived Rieslings that range across the entire spectrum of sweetness. The best examples are among the finest wines in the world and enough to make anyone believe in a Roman Catholic God.

The lie of the land

At ~100,000ha, Germany's vineyard area is much smaller than that of France, Italy, or Spain. Production is concentrated in the federal state of Rhineland-Pfalz, which boasts six of the country's thirteen regions for quality wine. The pre-eminent regions of the Mosel and Rheingau, which lie on the 50th parallel, are among some of the most marginal wine regions in the world. Without the Gulf Stream, viticulture would simply be impossible. Weather events such as spring frosts, summer hails, and autumn rains can lead to very significant vintage variation. On the other hand, autumns tend to be long and dry, which enables grapes to concentrate flavours while preserving acidity, and to be harvested selectively at different levels of maturity. In this cool continental climate, it is crucial to seek out every possible natural advantage, with even the slightest difference in temperature or sunlight being reflected in the wines. Several wine regions lie in the shelter of hills or mountains. Vineyards tend to be concentrated in river valleys with more temperate mesoclimates and reflected sunlight. The best vineyards are sited on steep, south- or southwest-facing slopes with slate soils that absorb solar heat and release it overnight.

Grape varieties

The most commonly planted grape variety is Riesling, followed by Müller-Thurgau and Pinot Noir (Spätburgunder). Müller-Thurgau and Silvaner have been in steady decline. Conversely, there has been a marked increase in Pinot Noir and other black varieties such as Dornfelder and Portugieser; since 1990, black varieties have risen from 16 to 35% of plantings. Less commonly planted varieties include Pinot Gris (Grauburgunder, Ruländer), Pinot Blanc (Weissburgunder), and Kerner. But for us, Germany is mostly about Riesling, arguably the most noble of all white varieties. Unlike, say, Chardonnay, which is very much a 'made wine', Riesling is very much a 'grown wine' and highly reflective of terroir. Fermentation and maturation take place in stainless steel tanks (although some top producers retain large old oak casks) and malolatic conversion is averted. A fine German Riesling can be extremely long-lived.

Quality levels and classifications

There are four quality levels. Basic wines, that is, *Deutscher Tafelwein* and *Deutscher Landwein*, only account for a negligible proportion of total production. The next level up is *Qualitätswein bestimmter Anbaugebiete* (QbA), wine from one of the 13 regions for quality wine (*Anbaugebiete*). That too is fairly basic, although there are exceptions. Liebfraumilch is a QbA from Rheinhessen, Pfalz, the Rheingau, or the Nahe. It consists of at least 70% Riesling, Müller-Thurgau, Silvaner, and Kerner (although in practice there is very little Riesling) and has a residual sugar of at least 18g/l. The highest level is *Prädikatswein* (formerly *Qualitätswein mit Prädikat*, QmP), which must be produced in one of the 39 sub-regions (*Bereich*) of the 13 *Anbaugebiete*. There are six ripeness levels, more accurately regarded as styles, that call for progressively higher levels of sugar: Kabinett, Spätlese, Auslese, Beerenauslese, Trockenbeerenauslese, and Eiswein. Sugar content (and therefore potential alcohol) is measured by must weight, and the minimum must weight for each quality level varies according to grape variety and region. For example, in the Mosel, the minimum must weight is 70°Oe (i.e. 1070g/l) for Kabinett, 83°Oe for Auslese, and 150°Oe for Trockenbeerenauslese. Any delineated and registered vineyard (*Einzellage*) in an *Anbaugebiet* can produce both QbA and *Prädikatswein*. Compared to QbA, the minimum must weight for *Prädikatswein* is higher, blending can only be carried out from within the *Bereich*, and chaptalization is forbidden. On the other hand, the addition of *Süßreserve* is permitted up to the level of Auslese. *Süßreserve* is unfermented grape juice; as it is added after fermentation, the sugar that it contains is not converted to alcohol. Even so, quality-conscious producers tend to avoid using it. Note that it is not uncommon for *Prädikatswein* to be declassified to QbA.

Kabinett is usually dry or off-dry, delicate and with crisp acidity. Spätlese ('late harvest') is intended to be fuller and fruitier although the style does overlap with Kabinett. Spätlese is usually off-dry. Auslese ('select harvest') is made from very ripe hand-selected bunches that may or may not be affected by noble rot. It can be made in diverse styles, but is most often medium-sweet. Beerenauslese ('select berry harvest') is made from overripe individually selected grapes that are often affected by noble rot. It is typically rich and sweet. Eiswein (ice wine) is made from grapes that have been naturally frozen on the vine. As the ice/water is left behind in the press, Eiswein is highly concentrated in sugar and flavour. Trockenbeerenauslese ('select dry berry harvest') is made from individually selected overripe and shrivelled grapes usually affected by noble rot. It is extremely concentrated. The amount of Beerenauslese, Eiswein, and Trockenbeerenauslese that can be produced in any one vintage is very variable. Trockenbeerenauslese is especially rare and expensive.

The label of any QbA or *Prädikatswein* displays the producer's name and address, the vintage, the village and *Einzellage* (for example, Graacher Himmelreich, from the Himmelreich vineyard in Graach), the grape variety and ripeness (for example, Riesling Spätlese), the *Anbaugebiet*, the alcohol content, bottling information, the quality classification, and the quality control number. In some cases, the collective name for a group of vineyards, or *Großlage*, of which there are ~170, may be used instead of that of an *Einzellage*. Unfortunately, it is impossible to distinguish a *Großlage* from an *Einzellage* from the label alone. Piesporter Goldtröpfchen and Piesporter Michelsberg may sound similar, but the former is an *Einzellage* and the latter a *Großlage*. Needless to say, Piesporter Goldtröpfchen is of much higher quality. There are also a handful of historical *Einzellagen* such as Schloss Johannisberg and Schloss Vollrads that are dispensed from displaying the village. In addition to all this, the label might indicate the residual sugar content of the wine (which is a different concept to the ripeness of the grapes), with *trocken* (dry, up to 9g/l residual sugar) and *halb-trocken* (half-dry, up to 18g/l residual sugar) being the most common descriptors used. *Goldkapsel* (gold capsule) is an unregulated designation that indicates that the producer regards the wine as especially fine. Stars, for example ***, indicate that the grapes have been harvested at a higher ripeness level than the minimum required.

The German classification system dates back to 1971. It is founded on the notion that, in such a marginal climate, only vineyards in the very best sites can produce fully ripe grapes. Ripeness is measured by sugar content, and the 'quality level' of a wine is determined by the sugar content of the grapes at the time of harvest. Unfortunately, ripeness is but one indicator of quality (vineyard soils, for example, being an important other), and the sugar content of the grapes at the time of harvest need not reflect the sugar content of the wine itself, which is also a function of winemaking. As it is based on ripeness and sugar content, the classification system inherently undervalues drier wines, which are of ever more commercial importance. Apart from being confusing and potentially misleading, the classification system has had unintended consequences, with some growers replacing Riesling with less distinguished grape varieties that reliably achieve high sugar levels. To quote Stephan Reinhardt in his book, *The Finest Wines of Germany*, "The [classification system] guarantees equality of opportunity—for Riesling hand-picked on the steep slope of a historically validated vineyard, as well as for Huxelrebe machine-harvested in a potato field; but it excludes consumers. It may be politically correct, but it is a disaster for wine lovers."

To address these problems, the *Verband Deutscher Qualitäts- und Prädikatsweingüter* (VDP), an association of some 200 top German producers, has inaugurated an alternative terroir-driven classification for top white and red dry wines. This stringent VDP classification divides into four tiers: *Grosse Lage* (Grand Cru), *Erste Lage* (Premier Cru), *Ortswein* (village wine), and *Gutswein* (estate wine). The dry wine of a *Grosse Lage* is designated *Grosses Gewächs* and labelled *Qualitätswein trocken*, while a sweeter wine is labelled with one of the traditional *Prädikats* such as Kabinett or Auslese. Members of the VDP often feature the VDP logotype, a stylized eagle with a cluster of grapes, on their labels; needless to say, it is a very reliable indicator of quality.

Another, and independent, measure to address the problems of the classification system has been the introduction of the 'Classic' and 'Selection' designations for drier wines of a certain quality. A Classic wine label indicates region, producer, and grape variety, whereas a Selection wine label indicates region, producer, grape variety, and vineyard site. The principal aim of this scheme is to simplify matters for consumers, who need only remember that Classic wines are representative of the best quality of a specific region, while Selection wines, also dry, are premium wines from a specific vineyard site.

Principal regions

Only the six most important and internationally recognized wine regions are discussed here. These are the Mosel, the Rheingau, the Nahe, Rheinhessen, Pfalz, and Baden. The Mosel, the Nahe, Rheinhessen, and Pfalz are in the federal state of Rheinland-Palatinate (Rheinland-Pflaz), the Rheingau is (only just) in Hessen, and Baden is in Baden-Württemberg. Rheinland-Palatinate accounts for over 60% of Germany's vineyard area, and has been nicknamed 'Weinland-Pflaz'.

The Mosel

The Mosel, formerly Mosel-Saar-Ruwer, covers the valleys of the meandering Mosel and its tributaries the Saar and Ruwer. The Middle Mosel is the most important area, with a litany of famous vineyards starting with the 3.26ha Doktor vineyard in Bernkastel (Bernkasteler Doktor), which lays claim to the title of most expensive agricultural land in Germany. Upstream from Bernkastel are Brauneberger Juffer-Sonnenuhr ('Virgin-Sundial') and Piesporter Goldtröpfchen ('Little Drop of Gold') in its natural south-facing amphitheatre. Downstream are Graacher Himmelreich ('Kingdom of Heaven'), Graacher Domprobst, Wehlener Sonnenuhr, Urziger Würzgarten ('Spice Garden'), Erdener Treppchen ('Little Stairs'), and Erdener Prälat. The Middle Mosel is noted for its steep slopes of porous slate, with Bremmer Calmont on an incline of 65°—reputedly the steepest vineyard in the world. Many of the best vineyards have no topsoil at all, just broken slate that needs to be carried back to the top of the vineyard in buckets. Ungrafted vines (phylloxera never hit the Middle Mosel) are individually staked to the ground so that vineyard workers can move horizontally rather than vertically, which is less tiring and less perilous. Cost and safety are major issues, and some of the more vertiginous slopes are being abandoned. Top producers of Riesling in the Middle Mosel include Dr

Loosen, Joh Jos Prüm, Fritz Haag, Markus Molitor, and Reichsgraf von Kesselstatt, among others. The star producer in the Saar, which is cooler and wetter than the Middle Mosel, is Egon Müller at Scharzhof. Riesling cannot fully ripen on the flatter lands of the Mosel, which tend to be planted with grape varieties such as Müller-Thurgau. The region is also responsible for an unremarkable wine called Moseltaler, which is similar in style to sickly-sweet Liebfraumilch.

The Rheingau

Although it accounts for only 3% of Germany's vineyards, the Rheingau ('Rhine district') boasts the highest proportion of Riesling (around 80%, with Pinot Noir making up most of the rest) of the 13 regions, and is home to some of the country's most vaunted estates such as Schloss Johannisberg and Kloster Eberbach, not to forget the oenological research and teaching institutes at Geisenheim. The entire region counts only one *Bereich*, so-called Bereich Johannisberg, with which it is co-extensive, from Hochheim on the River Main to Lorch on the River Rhine. The greater part of the Rheingau is situated on the right bank of the River Rhine as it swings west at Wiesbaden for some 30km (19mi) resuming its northward flow at Rüdesheim. With the Taunus Mountains to the north, most of the vineyards are on sheltered south-facing slopes that run to the river. The climate is relatively dry and sunny, which enables Riesling to ripen fully. Soils are varied and include slate, quartzite, sandstone, gravel, and loess. Assmanhausen, to the west of the region, stands out for its steeper slopes planted with Pinot Noir and produces arguably Germany's finest red wine. Notable Rheingau producers include Domdechant Werner, Franz Künstler, Georg Breuer, Josef Leitz, Prinz von Hessen, Robert Weil, and Schloss Johannisberg.

The Nahe

In terms of vineyard area, the Nahe is not much larger than the Rheingau, accounting for only ~4% of Germany's vineyard area. First defined in 1971, the region is bordered by Rheinhessen to the east and the Rheingau and Mittelrhein to the north. It is defined by the River Nahe, which flows parallel to the Mosel and meets the Rhine at

Bingen. In the lee of the Hunsrück Mountains, which lie to the north of the region, the climate is comparatively warm and dry, and warmer downriver in Bad Kreuznach and the Lower Nahe than in the Upper Nahe. Owing to the diversity of soils and grape varieties the region is rather lacking in identity, but Riesling is the most planted grape variety with the best vineyards on steep slopes around Niederhausen and Schlossböckelheim in the Upper Nahe. Riesling from the Nahe can offer excellent value for money. The region's top houses include Weingut Hermann Dönnhoff and Schlossgut Diel.

Rheinhessen

This region lies opposite the Rheingau, on the other side of the Rhine. Unlike the Rheingau, and despite its name, it is in Rhineland-Pflaz rather than Hesse. This 'land of a thousand hills' is enclosed to the north and east by the Rhine, to the west by the River Nahe, and to the south by the Haardt Mountains. Unlike in the Mosel or Rheingau, vineyards are mixed in with orchards and other forms of agriculture. Rheinhessen is Germany's most important wine region by volume, producing white wines from Müller-Thurgau, Riesling, and Silvaner, and some red wines, mostly from Dornfelder. It is a region of contrasts, the home of Liebfraumilch (named for the Church of Our Lady or *Liebfrauenkirche* in Worms) and yet also some very fine and underrated Rieslings. The best terroir in the region is the *Roter Hang* (Red Slope, from the iron-rich sandstone) above Nierstein and Nackenheim in the steeper and more highly reputed Rhein Terrace area. The other area of note is Wonnegau to the south, home to Klaus-Peter Keller and Philipp Wittmann, the region's most iconic producers. Both are founding members of 'Message in a Bottle', a group of young, ambitious, and dynamic winemakers with hopes of returning Rheinhessen to its former glory. Along with Pflaz, Rheinhessen is one of the most vibrant and exciting wine regions in Germany.

Pfalz

To the south of Rheinhessen is Pflaz (Palatinate, formerly Rheinpfalz or Rhein Palatinate), the second largest German wine region. Pfalz lies in the lee of the Haardt Mountains, an extension of the Alsatian Vosges. Pfalz has much in common with Alsace, not least a warm and dry climate and a great diversity of soils. Almost the entire production is dry. Riesling, the most common grape variety, accounts for just over a fifth of plantings. The Riesling heartland is the Mittelhaardt to the north, which is richer in limestone; the villages of Forst, Wachenheim, and Deidesheim are especially reputed. Black grape varieties account for 40% of plantings, with Dornfelder, Portugieser, and Pinot Noir in the lead.

Baden

In terms of vineyard area, Baden is the third largest German wine region after Rheinhessen and Pfalz, and similar in size to Alsace across the Rhine. It is the most southerly wine region and also the longest, stretching ~400km (250mi) along the right bank of the Rhine from the shores of Lake Constance in the south to Franken in the north. Baden is divided into nine *Bereiche*, more than any other German wine region. The central part lies in the Rhine rift, sheltered by the Vosges to the west and the hills of the Black Forest to the east. This is Germany's warmest wine region and the only one in EU wine growing zone B rather than A. Riesling plays a smaller role than in other wine regions and over half the vineyard area is given over to the Pinot varieties: Pinot Blanc, Pinot Gris, and especially Pinot Noir. The region's finest vineyards are in the sundrenched Kaiserstuhl ('Emperor's seat'), an extinct volcano to the north of Freiburg. Kaiserstuhl Pinot Noir is finely etched and mineral on the one hand, and ripe, rich, full-bodied, and tannic on the other. Tuniberg to the south produces similar wines in a lighter style. In the north, the wines are similar to those of Franken and sold in the round *Bocksbeutel*. Gutedel (Chasselas) is a specialty of the Markgäflerland, close to the Swiss border. Baden is dominated by co-operatives, which handle ~85% of production.

Wine styles

Rieslings from the Middle Mosel are pale in colour, sometimes with a touch of effervescence. On the nose, they are intensely fragrant, more floral than fruity with notes of stony rainwater and sherbet. On the palate, they are filigree and delicate, with a mineral or salty finish. Alcohol is very low and acidity very high, but balanced by sugar and extract. Sweeter examples may be botrytized. Rieslings from the Saar and Ruwer valleys are steelier. Compared to Riesling from the Middle Mosel, Riesling from the Rheingau is more masculine: deeper in colour with a firmer structure and texture, riper fruit, and higher alcohol. Riesling from the Nahe is often a halfway house between that from the Middle Mosel and that from the Rheingau. Riesling from Rheinhessen is similar to that from the Rheingau but tends to be softer. Riesling from Pflaz is typically fuller-bodied and higher in alcohol than that from the Rheingau although not quite as dry and austere as that from Alsace. It is impossible to generalize about German Pinot Noir, some of which is on a par with fine Burgundy.

Note: For German Sekt, see Chapter 11.

Chapter 13

Austria

Czech Republic

20 km

Kamp

Kamptal

Kremstal

Wachau

Danube

Weinviertel

Slovakia

Wagram

Vienna

Wien

Carnuntum

Traisen

48°N

Niederösterreich

Thermen-
region

Neusiedlersee-
Hügelland

L. Neusiedl

NIEDERE TAUERN

Mittel-
burgen-
land

Hungary

Steiermark

Süd-
burgen-
land

47°N

Graz

Südoststeiermark

West-
steiermark

Sud-
steier-
mark

Slovenia

Traisental

Neusiedlersee

Austria

In 1985, it emerged that a small number of Austrian wine brokers had been adulterating their light and acidic wines with diethylene glycol to increase body and sweetness. This 'antifreeze scandal' hit the international headlines, almost completely destroying the reputation of Austrian wines. Like the phoenix rising out of its ashes, Austria moved away from medium sweet, mass-market wines and reinvented itself as a producer of quality wines.

The lie of the land

The four wine regions of Niederösterreich (Lower Austria), Burgenland, Wien (Vienna), and Steiermark (Styria) are all in the east of the country, bordering on the Czech Republic, Slovakia, Hungary, and Slovenia. Niederösterreich, Burgenland, and Steiermark are divided into districts, of which there are, including Wien, a total of 16. Burgenland sits on the edge of the vast Pannonian Plain and is a much flatter region than the other three. The most important or prevalent soils are a varying thickness of loess over granite in Niederösterreich, sand over limestone in Burgenland, and clay over limestone in Styria.

Climate

Austria is a landlocked country with a frankly continental climate marked by cold winters and hot summers. Autumns are long, enabling grapes to ripen and sweet wines to be made. High diurnal temperature variation throughout the growing season promotes concentration of sugar and phenolics while preserving natural acidity. In Niederösterreich, the River Danube and its tributaries exercise an important moderating influence on temperatures, as does, in Burgenland, the Lake Neusiedl (Neusiedlersee), which also creates ideal conditions for the development of noble rot. Burgenland in particular also benefits from warm easterlies from the Pannonian Plain. Most vines in Austria (although not those devoted to the finest wines) are trained high on the Lenz Moser system, which offers some degree of frost protection and reduces labour costs.

Grape varieties

Austrian wines are mostly dry white wines, although sweeter white wines are also made. Twenty-two grape varieties are permitted for quality Austrian white wine, but the best are made from Grüner Veltliner or Riesling, with Grüner Veltliner by far the most planted grape variety. Other important white grape varieties are Welschriesling (which is unrelated to Riesling), Müller-Thurgau, Pinot Blanc (Weißburgunder), Chardonnay, and Sauvignon Blanc. Red wines account for some 30% of production, and are most often made from Blaufränkisch and local grape varieties such as Zweigelt (Blaufränkisch x Saint Laurent). Although plantings are relatively small, Pinot Noir (Blauburgunder) punches above its weight on the export market. All in all, 13 grape varieties are permitted for quality Austrian red wine.

Classifications

There are three separate classifications operating in Austria. The traditional classification system is modelled on that of Germany (see Chapter 12), with four principal levels based on must weights: Tafelwein, Landwein, Qualitätswein, and Prädikatswein. The bulk of production is either Qualitätswein or Prädikatswein; given the choice, many producers prefer to label their wine as Qualitätswein to circumvent a German style of labelling. In addition to Kabinett (which in Austria is included under Qualitätswein rather than Prädikatswein), Spätlese, Auslese, Beerenauslese, Trockenbeerenauslese, and Eiswein, there are two additional styles, Ausbruch and Strohwein (straw wine). Ausbruch is made from botrytized grapes to which grape must or late harvest wine may be added to assist with the pressing operation. Minimum must weight for Ausbruch is higher than for Beerenauslese. For each classification level, minimum must weights in Austria are higher than in Germany. As in Germany, chaptalization is permitted for Qualitätswein, although not for the higher level of Kabinett. Unlike in Germany, the addition of *Süßreserve* is not permitted for Prädikatswein.

In addition, eight of Austria's sixteen wine regions adhere to a geographical appellation system, *Districtus Austriae Controllatus* (DAC), first introduced in 2003. As with other geographical appellation systems, each DAC has specific requirements intended to bring out the particular characteristics of a recognized regional style. The DACs are Weinviertel (for Grüner Veltliner), Mittelburgenland (for Blaufränkisch), Traisental (for both Riesling and Grüner Veltliner), Kremstal (for both Riesling and Grüner Veltliner), Kamptal (for both Riesling and Grüner Veltliner), Leithaberg (for Grüner Veltliner, Pinot Blanc, Chardonnay, Neuburger, and Blaufränkisch), Eisenberg (for Blaufränkisch), and Neusiedlersee (for Zweigelt: 100% Zweigelt for Klassik and at least 60% Zweigelt for Reserve Cuvée Blend).

The Wachau operates a separate classification, the *Vinea Wachau Nobilis Districtus*. This has three ascending categories, all for dry wines: Steinfeder, Federspiel, and Smaragd, the last named after an emerald lizard of the vineyards.

Regions

Niedösterreich

Niederösterreich is the country's largest and most important wine region, accounting for eight of the sixteen districts and over half of total production. The extreme west of the region harbours the small and premium district of Wachau, with vineyards on steep terraces that stretch along the Danube from Melk to Krems. Wachau is famous for its rich and concentrated Grüner Veltliners and Rieslings. The district is home to a large but highly rated co-operative, the Freie Weingärtner Wachau. Immediately to the east of Wachau is Kremstal, in which the Danube valley opens up into gently rolling hills. Like Wachau, Kremstal is especially noted for its Grüner Veltliners and Rieslings, which qualify for the Kremstal DAC. To the northeast of Kremstal is Kamptal, which stretches out around Langenlois with the best vineyards on steep south-facing terraces overlooking the River Kamp. These vineyards are particularly suited to Riesling, with both Rieslings and Grüner Veltliners qualifying for the Kamptal DAC. Closer to the Danube, the side valley opens up and black grape varieties become more common. Wagram stretches from Kamptal to Vienna along the Danube. The deep loess soils are particularly suited to Grüner Veltliner although other grape varieties are also planted. Founded in 1114, Klosterneuburg Abbey in the east of the district is one of the oldest and largest wine estates in Austria. To the west of Wagram and south of Wachau, Kremstal, and Kamptal lies the small district of Traisental. Grüner Veltliner, Riesling, and other grape varieties are planted on steep terraces overlooking the River Traisen, with Grüner Veltliners and Rieslings qualifying for the Traisental DAC. The Weinviertel ('Wine Quarter') is the largest district in Niederösterreich and indeed Austria, accounting for about half of plantings in Niederösterreich and one third of plantings in Austria. The land is mostly flat and fertile and planted with Grüner Veltliner, which is made in a fresh and fruity style. Many other grape varieties are also planted, but in much smaller quantities. Sekt is made from Riesling and Grüner Veltliner in the far northeast around Poysdorf. South of the Weinviertel and south of the Danube lies the hilly district of Carnuntum. With its deep soils and warmer climate, Carnuntum is particularly suited to black grape varieties, with Blaufränkisch and Zweigelt dominating plantings. To the southwest of Carnuntum is Thermenregion, named after Roman thermal baths. Thermenregion is noted for a white wine blend of indigenous grape varieties Zierfandler (Spätrot) and Rotgipler. Black grape varieties are also planted, Portugieser first among them.

Vienna

Vienna is fiercely proud of its vineyards, all 600ha of them. Land on the left (northern) bank of the Danube is mainly planted to Grüner Veltliner, Chardonnay, Riesling, and Pinot Blanc, and land on the right bank to black grape varieties. Vienna is noted for Gemischter Satz, a blend of several grape varieties cultivated *en foule* in the same vineyard. Punters can drink the latest vintage of Gemischter Satz by the jug in one of the city's many wine taverns or *Heurigen*, which are signposted with sprigs of pine over the door.

Burgenland

Burgenland is home to four DACs: Neusiedlersee, Leithaberg, Mittelburgenland, and Eisenberg. The Neusiedlersee district in the north of the region is reputed for its botrytized wines made from Welschriesling or a number of other grape varieties other than Riesling (sometimes in a blend). However, the Neusiedlersee DAC is exclusively for red wines dominated by Zweigelt. To the west, on the opposite shore of the lake, which is never deeper than 1.8m (6ft), lies Neusiedlersee-Hügelland ('Hill Country'). This district of diverse terrains produces sweet white wines (including the famous Ruster Ausbruch, Austria's answer to Tokaji), dry white wines, and dry red wines. The Leithaberg DAC is for white wines made from Grüner Veltliner, Pinot Blanc, Chardonnay, and Neuburger, and red wines made mostly from Blaufränkisch. Mittelburgenland, nick-named 'Blaufränkischland', on the Pannonian Plain is the spiritual home of Blaufränkisch, which accounts for more than half of the district's plant-ings. The other DAC for Blaufränkisch is Eisenberg ('Iron Mountain'), to the south in the small district of Südburgenland.

Note that 'Weinland Österreich' refers to Niederösterreich and Burgenland, which together account for more than 90% of Austria's vineyard area. The main *raison d'être* for this legal entity is to enable Landwein to be blended across a very large area.

Steiermark

Steiermark stands out for its small size, rugged terrain, and warmer and wetter climate with marked diurnal temperature variation. The bulk of the region's production is consumed locally. The soils of Südoststeiermark are largely volcanic in origin, lending themselves to the cultivation of grape varieties from the Traminer family. Other grape varieties are also planted. The wines are crisp, aromatic, and full-bod-ied with notes of spice and mineral. Sudsteiermark is very mountain-ous, with vineyards planted on steep, south-facing slopes. The district is reputed for its Sauvignon Blanc and noted for its 'Junker' (young, fruity wines). Westersteiermark counts only 500ha of vines. It is known for Schilcher, a cult rosé-style wine of searing acidity made from the indigenous Blauer Wildbacher grape.

Wine styles

Like Alsatian Riesling, which it resembles most closely, Austrian Riesling is dry with high acidity, medium-to-high alcohol, and pronounced minerality. However, it is typically less austere and dominated by riper stone fruit. 'Hints of lime' is another common tasting note. Riesling from Kremstal and Kamptal is often fuller than that from Wachau.

Grüner Veltliner is very much an Austrian specialty. It is produced in a range of styles and qualities, and is often reminiscent of Burgundy or Alsace. Grüner Veltliner from Wachau is often pale gold with hints of green. It is typically dry with notes of celery, white pepper, spice, and minerals. Depending on ripeness, fruit can range across the spectrum from apple and grapefruit to distinctly tropical fruit. Body is medium to full, acidity is high, alcohol is medium-high or high, and oak is absent. The best examples can develop honeyed and toasty aromas with age. Grüner Veltiner from Kremstal and Kamptal is often fuller than that from Wachau.

Blaufränkish is usually dark purple in colour with notes of red currants or cherries, blackberry, pepper and spice, and liquorice. On the palate, body is medium, acidity high, alcohol medium, and tannins firm and grippy. New oak may be evident in some examples. Blaufränkish is sometimes blended with other grape varieties such as Zweigelt, in which case it typically contributes acidity and structure to the blend. Owing to the red, iron-rich soils, Blaufränkisch from Eisenberg is typically spicier than Blaufränkisch from Mittelburgenland.

Zweigelt is fresh and fruit-driven. It is often deep ruby in colour, with notes of red cherries and soft spice such as cinnamon and nutmeg. On the palate, it is light-to-medium bodied with a supple acidity reminiscent of Barbera, medium alcohol, and soft and subtle tannins. Oak is usually absent.

Chapter 14

Hungary

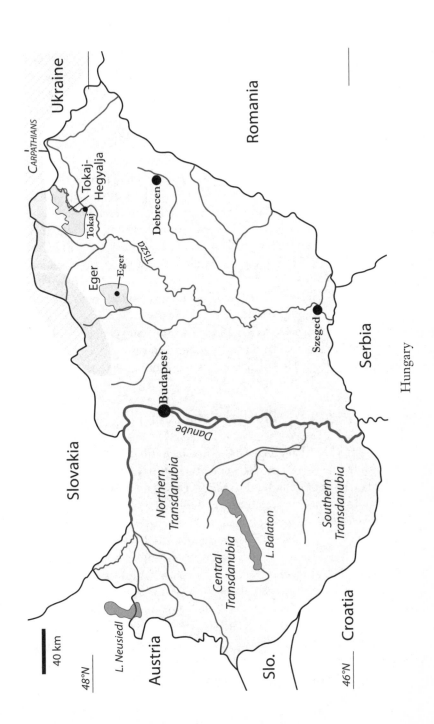

The history of wine in Hungary dates back to the Pannonia of Roman times (Sanskrit *pani*, 'water'). Today, the country counts 22 separate and diverse wine regions. The bulk of Hungarian wine production is destined for domestic consumption. Furmint aside, exports often consist of international grape varieties such as Pinot Grigio, Chardonnay, and Gewurztraminer. With regard to black grape varieties, the most significant are Blaufränkisch (Kékfrankos), Zweigelt, and the Bordeaux varieties. Beyond these, there are also a number of indigenous varieties.

The big names, especially on the export markets, are Tokaji and, to a much lesser extent, Bull's Blood of Eger (*Egri Bikavér*). Louis XV of France held Tokaji in such high esteem as to christen it *Vinum Regum, Rex Vinorum* (Wine of Kings, King of Wines). Franz Josef, Emperor of Austria and Apostolic King of Hungary, had a tradition of sending Queen Victoria Tokaji for her birthday. He gifted her one bottle for every month that she had lived, sending her a grand total of 972 bottles on her final, eighty-first, birthday.

Under communism, overcropping, oxidation, and pasteurisation led to a general fall in quality. Since 1989, heavy investment, especially in the region of Tokaj-Hegyalja, has begun to root out the rot.

The lie of the land

Hungary (and the Pannonian Basin in which it lies) is bisected north-to-south by the River Danube, which flows through the capital city of Budapest. To the east and south is the Great Plain, which, owing to its sandy soils, has been spared from phylloxera. To the east and north are the volcanic hills of Upper Hungary, with the best vineyards planted on steep, south-facing slopes. The entire area to the west of the Danube is referred to as Transdanubia. Transdanubia can be divided into three principal wine producing regions: Northern Transdanubia, Central Transdanubia around Lake Balaton, and Southern Transdanubia. The climate in Hungary is continental, with hot summers and cold winters. Autumns are long and relatively dry. To the east, the arc of the Carpathian Mountains encloses the Pannonian Basin and protects it from cold continental winds. To the west, Lakes Balaton and Neusiedl give rise to distinct and favourable mesoclimates.

Tokaji

The delimitation of Tokaj-Hegyalja (Foothills) and the classification of its vineyards predate those of the Douro in the mid 18th century (see Chapter 20). The 1920 Treaty of Trianon left a small part of this delimited area outside Hungary in Czechoslovakia (modern-day Slovakia). Tokaj-Hegyalja lies on a small plateau in a nook of the Carpathian Mountains, at the confluence of the Rivers Tisza and Bodrog and the meeting point of hot and cold air streams. During the long Indian summer, morning mists dissipate into sunny and breezy afternoons. These conditions could not be more ideal for the development of noble rot and the shrivelling of berries on the vine. The soils are clay or loess on volcanic subsoil, with the best vineyards planted on sun-exposed south-facing slopes. The average vineyard size is very small, and the dominant state winery contracts grapes from almost 3,000 growers. Six grape varieties are permitted: Furmint (60% of the area under vines), Hárslevelü (30%), Muscat Blanc à Petits Grains (5%), Zéta (Furmint x Bouvier), Kabar (Hárslevelü x Bouvier), and Kövérszóló.

Several styles of wine are produced, ranging from dry white wines to Eszencia, the sweetest wine in the world. However, it is Aszú for which the region is especially reputed. Aszú (shrivelled and botrytized) berries are individually picked and trampled into the consistency of a paste. This so-called aszú dough is mixed with must or wine and stirred from time to time. After about 24-48 hours, the wine is racked into Hungarian oak casks and left to mature for at least three years in cool cellars carved into the subsoil. These cellars are coated in a thick black growth of *Racodium cellare*, a fungus that feeds on the alcohol vapours and maintains humidity in the range of 85-90%. Once matured, the wine is entered into 500cl bottles labelled with a puttony number ranging from 3 to 6. This number traditionally referred to the number of puttonyos (wooden tubs) of aszú dough added to a Gönc cask (136l barrel) of must or wine. Today, it simply reflects the residual sugar content, with 3 puttonyos equivalent to 60g/l and each additional puttony adding 30g/l. Eszencia, which is made from the free run juice (or syrup) of aszú berries, typically has a sugar content of 500-700g/l! Eszencia is added to Aszú wine to adjust sweetness, but can also be fermented and bottled pure. The fermentation process takes at least four years to complete (yes, four years), at which point the alcohol level ranges from 2 to 4%.

The extreme longevity of Aszú wines can be attributed to Furmint, and in particular to its high levels of acidity and sugar. Furmint also imparts spicy notes, which can help to distinguish Aszú wines from Sauternes. Other markers of Aszú wines are a darker, copper colour; higher acidity; and notes of apricot, orange zest, barley sugar, and tea. Dry Furmint is an entirely different animal, lemony in colour, with notes of smoke, pear, and lime, together with hints of mandarin, apricot, honey, and spice. On the palate, it is light and crisp, with high acidity, medium-high to high alcohol, and a mineral backbone. The finish can be quite long.

Other styles of Tokaji are Szamorodni, made from bunches of grapes with a high proportion of botrytized grapes; Fordítás, made by pouring must on spent aszú dough; Máslás, made by pouring must on aszú lees; and late harvest wines ready for release from just one year after harvest. Depending on the proportion of botrytized grapes, Szamorodni comes both in a dry (*száras*) style, made under flor like a fino Sherry, and a sweet (*édes*) style.

Chapter 15

Italy: North East

Northeastern Italy

Italy has a long history of wine production that stretches back to the Etruscans and early Greek settlers. Today, the country ranks first in terms of wine exports, second in terms of wine production (after France), and third in terms of area under vines (after France and Spain). Italy boasts a range of favourable climates and terrains, over 2,000 indigenous grape varieties, and countless wines. Of its 20 wine regions, three are in the northeast (Veneto, Trentino-Alto Adige, Friuli-Venezia Giulia), five are in the northwest (Piedmont, Lombardy, Emilia Romagna, Liguria, Valle d'Aosta), six are in the centre (Tuscany, Umbria, Lazio, Marche, Abruzzo, Molise), four are in the south (Campania, Basilicata, Puglia, Calabria), and the remaining two are the islands of Sicily and Sardinia. The most important regions by volume are Sicily, Puglia, and Veneto; and by quality Piedmont, Tuscany, and Veneto. This chapter and the next three cover all the Italian regions except Aosta, Emilia-Romagna, Liguria, Molise, Calabria, and Sardinia.

Classification

Since its inception in 1963, the Italian wine classification has undergone a number of modifications and additions. Wines with a geographical indication can be classified as either DOP (*Denominazione di Origine Protteta*) or the broader and less restrictive IGP (*Indicazione Geografica Protteta*). There are a total of 403 DOPs, of which 330 DOCs (*Denominazione di Origine Controllata*) and 73 DOCGs (*Denominazione di Origine Controllata e Garantita*). Italy's DOCGs are mostly concentrated in just three regions: Piedmont, Veneto, and Tuscany. DOCGs are subjected to the strictest regulations and to quality analysis and tasting prior to bottling; and the bottles carry numbered seals across the neck to improve traceability and deter fraudsters. Introduced in 1992, the IGP classification caters for those wines that sit outside a DOP or do not conform to DOP regulations relating to grape varieties or styles. While most IGP wines (labelled with the trigram IGT, *Indicazione Geografica Tipica*) are fairly simple, some, most notably the premium 'Super Tuscans', can be of the highest quality. To be promoted to DOC a wine must have been an IGP for at least five years; to be promoted to DOCG it must have been a DOC for at least ten years. In 2006, a dozen flagship producers launched the unofficial *Comitato Grandi Cru d'Italia*, and they have since been joined by scores of other top producers. Some common terms that may feature on an Italian wine label are 'Classico', 'Superiore', and 'Riserva'. Broadly speaking, 'Classico' denotes a wine produced in the historical or original part of a denomination; 'Superiore' denotes a higher alcohol and more restricted yield; and 'Riserva' denotes a longer period of ageing. Note that, in the case of Chianti, 'Classico' is integral to the name of the appellation, 'Chianti Classico DOCG'.

Veneto

The three northeast regions of Veneto, Trentino-Alto Adige, and Friuli-Venezia Giulia are collectively referred to as the *Venezie*, after the old Venetian Republic and, prior to that, the Roman region of Venetia et Histria. Veneto is the most important of the three regions and the most important DOP producer in Italy, with over 20% of production qualifying for DOC or DOCG status. Its natural boundaries are the Alps to the north, the Adriatic Sea to the east, and Lake Garda to the west. Aside from the regional capital of Venice, other important centres include Padua, Verona, and Vicenza. The most notable appellations are Soave and Prosecco (see Chapter 11) for white wines and Vapolicella and Bardolino for red wines; overall, the region produces slightly more white than red wines.

Soave

Just east of Verona is the Soave delimited area, part of which is DOC and another part, Soave Superiore, DOCG. The delimitations and their associated regulations are controversial, and some producers have protested against them by declassifying their wines to IGP/IGT status. The soils in the hilly Classico district are much less fertile than those in the alluvial plains of the River Adige, which are responsible for the undistinguished bulk of production. Within the Classico district, the soils to the west near the commune of Soave are richer in limestone, which retains heat and promotes a riper, fuller style. Soave DOCG from the hillsides outside the Classico district is labelled as Soave Colli Scaligeri Superiore DOCG. To meet DOCG regulations, Garganega must contribute at least 70% to the blend, with any remainder made up by Verdicchio (Trebbiano di Soave) and Chardonnay. Garganega is a late-ripening grape variety with a thick skin that protects it against the autumn mists that rise in from the Po valley. The bulk of Soave production is dry and still, but there is also a spumante and a late harvest *recioto*, that is, a straw wine (*passito*) made from raisined grapes. The Cantina di Soave co-operative, which numbers over 2,000 members, is responsible for almost half of Soave DOC production. Top producers include Anselmi, Ca' Rugate, Gini, Inama, Pieropan, Pra, Tessari, and the Cantina di Monteforte co-operative. Quality Soave is typically straw in colour, with notes of citrus fruits and almonds and hints of flowers and spice, a body ranging from light to fairly full, crisp acidity, medium alcohol, and a mineral or creamy finish with a slightly bitter edge. The best examples can be quite long and complex.

Valpolicella

After Chianti, Valpolicella is the biggest producer of DOC wine in Italy. The demarcated area lies to the north of Verona, linking Soave in the east to Bardolino in the west. Valpolicella is principally made from three grape varieties: Corvina Veronese, Rondinella, and Molinara. Of the three, Corvina is certainly the most distinguished. Much Valpolicella is light and simple, made in a *novello*, early-release style similar to Beaujolais Nouveau. Beyond this, Valpolicella Classico is made from grapes from the traditional Classico district in the Monte Lessini foothills. Valpolicella Valpantena is similar, and made from grapes from the highly regarded Valpantena district. Valpolicella Superiore is Valpolicella with an alcohol of at least 12% that has spent at least one year in oak. At the top of the pyramid, there are late harvest Recioto and Amarone, and a Ripasso made from Valpolicella re-fermented ('re-passed') on the grape skins left over from the fermentation of Recioto or Amarone. The Recioto and Amarone come under a separate DOCG, and the Ripasso comes under a separate DOC. In contrast to Recioto, Amarone is fermented dry such that there is less residual sugar and more alcohol. Amarone is then matured for at least two years, usually in large barrels of old Slovenian or French oak. Grapes used for Recioto and Amarone often come from the best vineyard sites. Co-operatives account for about half of the total production of Valpolicella. Some of the best producers include Allegrini, Corte Sant-Alda, Giuseppe Quintarelli, and Novaia.

At the bottom of the pyramid, Valpolicella *normale* is a simple, fruity, and refreshing quaffing wine that is sometimes served slightly chilled. It is light in colour and body with vibrant cherry or berry fruits, high acidity, and low tannins. Valpolicella Classico Superiore is fuller in body and considerably more structured and complex, with more tannins and a discernible old (sometimes new) oak influence. Ripasso is a further step up, darker, richer, more complex, and more tannic, with soft, rounded tannins and a sweet finish. Amarone is deep ruby in colour. The wine is rich, full-bodied, and concentrated with high alcohol, crisp acidity, velvety tannins, and a long, bitter finish. Its complex flavour profile is often compared to that of port, with notes of raisins, stewed cherries, dark chocolate, and liquorice. If matured in oak, there are accents of vanilla and spice. A more modern style of Amarone is also made, lighter and purer in fruit. Amarone can improve for a decade or more.

Bardolino

Like Valpolicella, Bardolino DOC is mostly made from a blend of Corvina, Rondinella, and Molinara. However, Bardolino generally contains less Corvina and more Rondinella, making it lighter in colour and body. Cool air from the Alpine foothills to the north and reflected sunlight from Lake Garda help to account for Bardolino's fresh and fruity signature. Almost half of production comes from the Bardolino Classico delimited area although differences in terroir are not so marked as in Valpolicella or Soave. Other styles include a Superiore with DOCG status, a rosé (*chiaretto*), a frizzante, and a novello similar to Beaujolais Nouveau. Bardolino ought to be drunk young and slightly chilled.

Pinot Grigio

The DNA profiles of Pinot Gris and Pinot Noir are almost identical, and the vines are so similar as to be distinguishable only by the colour of the fruit. Pinot Grigio is the Italian clone of Pinot Gris. In its Burgundian homeland, Pinot Gris (Fromenteau) used to be planted *en foule* with Pinot Noir and served to soften the must. However, poor yields and unreliable crops led to its gradual decline and quasi disappearance. This fall from grace has been offset by the recent success of its Italian clone. From 1990 to 2010, plantings of Pinot Grigio in Italy have risen from 3,500ha to 12,000ha. Most of these plantings are in the northeast and more specially in Veneto. Compared to Pinot Grigio from Friuli or Alto Adige, Pinot Grigio from Veneto can be rather neutral owing to high yields and, in some cases, blending with cheaper grape varieties such as Trebbiano. Pinot Grigio owes its enduring appeal to a combination of simplicity and savvy marketing. Compared to Riesling and Sauvignon Blanc, which are high in acidity and aroma, and Chardonnay, which can be dense and alcoholic, Pinot Grigio is versatile and uncomplicated: fresh, light, and easy to drink and pair with food. Compared to Alsatian Pinot Gris, it is less ripe, with a lighter colour, leaner body, tighter structure, and higher acidity. It is invariably dry and unoaked, with notes of pear, citrus fruits, white fruits, and flowers. At the time of writing (2014), Pinot Grigio accounted for 40% of all Italian wine sold in the UK.

Trentino-Alto Adige

Trentino-Alto Adige is located in the far north of Italy, in the foothills of the Alpine Dolomites. The region is bisected by the valley of the River Adige and consists of two provinces, Trentino in the south and Alto Adige (Südtirol) in the north. Alto Adige belonged to Austria until 1918 and still feels very Germanic, with a high proportion of German bilingual speakers. The province is so mountainous that only the valley of the River Adige can be cultivated, with vines planted on terraces on the valley sides. Trentino-Alto Adige is relatively small in terms of production, but boasts a higher proportion of DOC wine than any other Italian region. Much of the production is exported, not least because many Austrians still retain a fondness for the region's red wines made from Schiava (Trollinger) and Lagrein. Despite Trentino-Alto Adige's northerly latitude (on par with central Burgundy), high altitude, and rugged terrain, the wines are often ripe and rich owing to warm alpine air currents and a relatively dry and sunny climate. High diurnal temperature variation makes the region particularly suited to white wine production, even if red wine production still dominates. Trentino and Alto Adige each contain one large catchall DOC and manifold smaller ones. A large number of grape varieties are planted. The principal black grape varieties are Lagrein, which is often blended with Schiava to add colour and extract; the indigenous Schiava, Teroldego, and Marzemino; and Cabernet Sauvignon, Cabernet Franc, Merlot, and Pinot Noir. The principal white grape varieties are Pinot Blanc, Chardonnay, Pinot Grigio, Riesling, Muscat, Gewurztraminer (the village of Tramin is actually in Alto Adige rather than Alsace), Sauvignon Blanc, Müller-Thurgau, Sylvaner, Grüner Veltliner, and Kerner. Trentino-Alto Adige is dominated by cooperatives, many of which are excellent.

Friuli-Venezia Giulia

Friuli-Venezia Giulia, or Friuli, is especially reputed for unoaked white wines that emphasize varietal character, freshness, and fruitiness. Nestled in the far northeast corner of Italy, the region comes under Italian, Germanic, and Slavic influences, which accounts for the large number of grape varieties and wine styles. A large proportion of production is DOC, and, of this, more than half is Friuli Grave DOC. Other notable DOCs are Collio DOC and Colli Orientali DOC, each of which encompasses a large number of varietal wines. All in all, there are eleven DOCs and three DOCGs. Most of the region's vineyards are in the south, protected from cold northerly winds by the Julian Alps in the north. The climate is influenced by the Adriatic Sea and cool Alpine air, with warm days and cool nights. In the hills of Collio and Colli Orientali near the Slovenian border, the soils consist of calcareous marl with alternating layers of sandstone (called 'ponka', 'flysch', or 'flysch of Cormons'). In contrast, the undulating plain of Friuli Grave sits on gravelly soils, whence 'Friuli Grave'. Friuli wines are relatively expensive because arable land is scarce, and because the region is dominated by quality-conscious, technologically advanced small-scale producers.

The region's most reputed wines come from Collio and Colli Orientali, which are both predominantly white wine areas. In general, the wines of Collio have more delicacy and bouquet than those of Colli Orientali, which however have greater body and depth. The most important grape varieties in Collio are Friulano (formerly Tocai Friulano), Ribolla Gialla, Malvasia Istriana, Chardonnay, Pinot Bianco, Pinot Grigio, and Sauvignon Blanc. Friulano wines are crisp and floral, developing notes of nuts and fennel as they age. Collio Rosso is usually a blend of Merlot, Cabernet Franc, and Cabernet Sauvignon. Compared to Collio, Colli Orientali produces more red wine and more sweet wine. Friulano is the most important grape variety, accounting for almost one third of plantings. Other white grape varieties include Sauvignon Blanc, Pinot Grigio, Verduzzo, Pinot Bianco, and Ribolla Gialla. Black grape varieties include Merlot, Cabernet Sauvignon, Pinot Noir, Pignolo, Refosco dal Peduncolo Rosso, and Schioppettino. There are two DOCGs for sweet wines made from Picolit in the passito style. Picolit is prone to diseases and mutations, which limits its supply. The other DOCG is for Ramandolo, a sweet wine made from Verduzzo, also in the passito style.

Chapter 16

Italy: North West

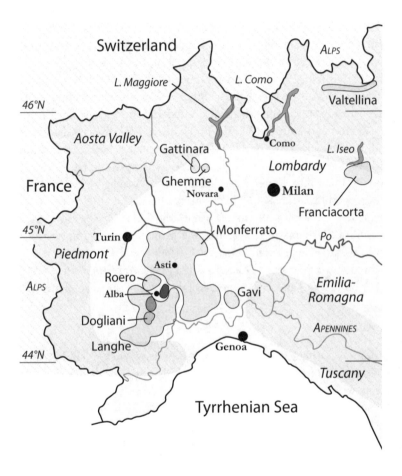

40 km

Switzerland

ALPS

L. Maggiore

L. Como

Valtellina

46°N

Aosta Valley

Gattinara

Como

L. Iseo

France

Ghemme

Novara

Lombardy

Milan

Franciacorta

45°N

Turin

Monferrato

Po

Piedmont

Asti

Emilia-
Romagna

ALPS

Roero

Gavi

Alba

Dogliani

APENNINES

44°N

Langhe

Genoa

Tuscany

Tyrrhenian Sea

Northwestern Italy

Piedmont

Piedmont means 'at the foot of the mountain'. The region is enclosed to the north and west by the Alps and to the south by the Apennines, which seal it off from Liguria and the Mediterranean coast. Much of the terrain is unsuited to viticulture, consisting either of mountains or the flat valley of the River Po, which opens out onto Lombardy in the east. The principal wine areas are situated in the Alpine foothills to the east and southeast of the regional capital of Turin, around the centres of Alba and Asti. Piedmont boasts more DOCGs and DOCs, and produces more quality wine, than any other Italian region including Veneto and Tuscany. Although especially noted for Barolo and Barbaresco, production is dominated by Asti and Moscato d'Asti (see Chapter 11) and, to a lesser extent, Barbera d'Asti. Unusually, there is no regional IGP/IGT; instead, the region is covered by the generic DOC appellations of Piemonte, Langhe, and Monferrato. As may be inferred from the geography, winters in Piedmont are harsh, but the ripening season is long and relatively dry. The principal black grape varieties are Nebbiolo, Barbera, and Dolcetto; the principal white grape varieties are Moscato, Cortese, and Arneis. Nebbiolo and Barbera tend to be planted on warmer sites, Dolcetto and Moscato on cooler sites. Several other indigenous and international grape varieties are also planted.

Barolo

Although Barbera is the most planted grape variety, Nebbiolo is the most noble, not only in Piedmont but also in Italy. It is very late to ripen, with harvests typically taking place in mid-to-late October, after the autumn fogs (*nebbie*) have risen. Nebbiolo underlies several DOCs and DOCGs, including Barolo, Barbaresco, Roero, and Gattinara.

Back in 1980, Barolo obtained one of the first three Italian DOCGs together with Brunello di Montalcino and Vino Nobile di Montepulciano (see Chapter 17). The Barolo delimited area lies in the Langhe hills south of Alba and the River Tanaro. The bulk of it sits on five communes: Barolo, La Morra, Castiglione Falletto, Monforte d'Alba, and Serralunga d'Alba. Though smallish, the area harbours a plethora of subtly different mesoclimates, soil types, altitudes, and aspects. Broadly speaking, it consists of two valleys: the Central Valley encompassing the communes of Barolo and La Morra, and, to the east, the Serralunga Valley encompassing the communes of Castiglione Falleto, Monteforte d'Alba, and Serralunga d'Alba. The soils are primarily calcareous clay, but those of the Central Valley are richer in calcareous marl and yield more delicate and perfumed wines, while those of the Serralunga Valley are richer in sandstone and yield more full-bodied and tannic wines. Average holding size is very small and emphasis on quality very strong, leading to comparisons with Burgundy. Although there is no official cru system as in Burgundy, some vineyards are considered superior and their wines priced accordingly. DOCG regulations for Barolo call for 38 months ageing (62 months for the Riserva), of which at least 18 in oak—traditionally large casks (*botti*) to avoid contributing even more tannins to the wine.

Although full-bodied, Barolo is light in colour, typically with a brick or rust red tinge that can make it seem older, sometimes much older, than it really is. The nose is potentially very complex and often short-handed as 'tar and roses'. Other notes include damsons, mulberries, dried fruit, violets, herbs, dark chocolate, liquorice, and, with increasing age, leather, camphor, tobacco, forest floor, mushrooms, and truffles. The palate is marked by high acidity and alcohol, and, above all, very high tannins, which, in the best of cases, are experienced as a silky or velvety texture. There is also a more modern, earlier drinking style of Barolo that is fruitier and less austere, often with obvious new French oak influence. Some traditional producers argue that the more modern style is unfaithful to the spirit of Barolo, and seem to be gaining the upper hand in the 'Barolo Wars' against the modernists. However, even the staunchest traditionalists employ some modern techniques in their wineries, and, at least in that much, their Barolo is a compromise between the traditional and the modern.

Barbaresco

Barbaresco lies to the east of Alba, fewer than 10 miles from Barolo with which it is often compared. The delimited area is considerably smaller than that of Barolo and can be broadly divided into three areas: Barbaresco, Treiso, and Neive. The soils of calcareous marl are similar to those of Barolo but lighter and more uniform. The climate is warmer and drier, enabling the grapes to ripen a full fortnight earlier. In terms of style, there is some overlap with Barolo, but Barbaresco tends to be more feminine, that is, more aromatic, elegant, and refined, with softer fruit and suppler, riper tannins. Although tight and tannic in its youth, it requires less cellaring time and is less long-lived. According to DOCG regulations, it must be aged for one year fewer than Barolo. The region's star producer is Gaja. Note that wines from Barolo and Barbaresco can, if required, be declassified to Langhe Nebbiolo DOC.

Other notable Piedmont Nebbiolos

Roero is a small, recently promoted, DOCG that lies across the river from Barbaresco. The soils are sandier than in the Langhe, resulting in a wine that is lighter, more delicate, and earlier maturing. DOCG regulations stipulate that Roero must contain 95-98% Nebbiolo and 2-5% Arneis, and be aged for 20 months (32 months for the Riserva) of which six in cask.

Further north, north of Novara, are the small, neighbouring areas of Gattinara and Ghemme. The climate here is cooler than in the Langhe, and, despite the steep south-facing slopes, the wines are even more tannic, acidic, and long-lived than Barolo. Gattinara DOCG consists of 90% Nebbiolo (Spanna) along with Bonarda (Uva Rara) and Vespolina to 'soften' the wine. Ghemme DOCG consists of the same blend, but with 75% Nebbiolo. Both Gattinara and Ghemme must be aged for at least three years prior to release.

The best Nebbiolo wine from outside Piedmont is Valtellina Superiore DOCG from Lombardy.

Barbera

Barbera accounts for half of Piedmontese plantings. Although it plays second fiddle to Nebbiolo, it can produce wines of great distinction, especially within the delimited areas of Barbera d'Asti DOCG, Barbera del Monferrato Superiore DOCG, and Barbera d'Alba DOC (which overlaps with Barolo and Barbaresco). Compared to Nebbiolo, it is higher yielding and earlier ripening, and much more adaptable. In the mid-1980s a number of Piedmontese producers added methanol to their Barberas, killing over thirty people and blinding many more. Barbera's reputation is still recovering from this scandal. Barbera ranges in style from light and delicate to heavy and powerful. It is typically deep ruby in colour with an intense and mouth-filling fruitiness (often dominated by black cherries), very high acidity, low tannins, and a dry finish. Some modern examples are aged in oak, which imparts tannins and notes of vanilla and spice.

Dolcetto and other black grape varieties

Being adaptable and early to ripen, Dolcetto is often planted on cooler, less distinguished sites. It is generally made as a simple and undemanding 'early to market' wine, generating income for the producer while his Nebbiolos and Barberas are still maturing. Dolcetto skins are rich in anthocyanins, yielding a dark colour that ranges from deep ruby to purple. A short and gentle fermentation that aims to limit tannin extraction produces a wine that is soft, fruity, and uncomplicated—often thought of as Italy's best answer to Beaujolais. Notes of black cherry, soft spice, and liquorice are accompanied by moderate acidity, high alcohol, and a characteristic dry, bitter almond finish. Piedmont has a number of DOCGs and DOCs for Dolcetto, most notably Dogliani DOCG and Dolcetto d'Alba DOC.

Other black grape varieties in Piedmont include Grignolino, Freisa, and Brachetto, the latter being made into a medium sweet, semi-sparkling wine.

Cortese

The spiritual home of Cortese is in the steep chalk-clay hills around Gavi in the far southeast corner of Piedmont. Its most famous incarnation is Cortese di Gavi DOCG, the first Italian white wine to achieve international acclaim. Cortese di Gavi from Gavi itself is labelled 'Gavi di Gavi'. Cortese wines are characterized by their zesty acidity, which can be searing in cooler vintages. Cortese di Gavi is light and dry, fruity and floral, with notes of lime, peach, and white flowers, hints of grass or herbs, and a citrusy finish. The wine can improve with some age.

Arneis

The historical function of Arneis (Piemontese, 'little rascal') was to soften and perfume Nebbiolo. Despite being difficult to grow, naturally lacking in acidity, and prone to oxidation, Arneis can yield delicate and character-ful wines. It is most at home in the Roero Hills, and, in the main, bottled as either Roero Arneis DOCG or Langhe DOC. It is rather full-bodied, oaked or unoaked, with dominant notes of ripe pears, apricots, white flow-ers, and hops, and a dry finish with an aftertaste of almonds.

The principal white grape variety in Piedmont is neither Cortese nor Arneis but Moscato, which underpins sparkling Asti and semi-sparkling Moscato d'Asti. These Moscato wines are discussed in Chapter 11.

Lombardy

Of Lombardy's thirteen wine producing areas, three are of special sig-nificance: Franciacorta, Valtellina, and Oltrepò Pavese, which alone accounts for over half of regional quality wine production. Franciacorta, which produces mostly sparkling wine, is covered in Chapter 11.

Valtellina is in the Alpine north of Lombardy, close to the border with Switzerland. The high altitude vineyards are planted on steep south-facing slopes along the valley of the River Adda. Nearby peaks offer protection from cold winds and vineyard stones soak up the sun's heat, enabling Nebbiolo (Chiavennasca) to ripen. The best wines are labelled as Valtellina Superiore DOCG, and are noticeably less acidic and tannic than their Piedmontese counterparts. The area is also responsible for Sforzato DOCG, an amarone-style wine.

Oltrepò Pavese ('in Pavia across the Po'), in the foothills of the Apennines close to the River Po and Milan, benefits from favourable soils and a relatively dry climate. It is responsible for a range of tradi-tional and modern style wines: Pinot Noir-dominated sparkling wines which are increasingly being made by the traditional method; white wines from Chardonnay, Sauvignon Blanc, Welschriesling (Riesling Italico), Riesling, Malvasia, Moscato, Cortese, or Pinot Grigio; and red wines from Pinot Noir, Cabernet Sauvignon, Barbera, Croatina, or Uva Rara. The latter three grape varieties are sometimes blended as Oltrepò Rosso.

Chapter 17

Italy: Central

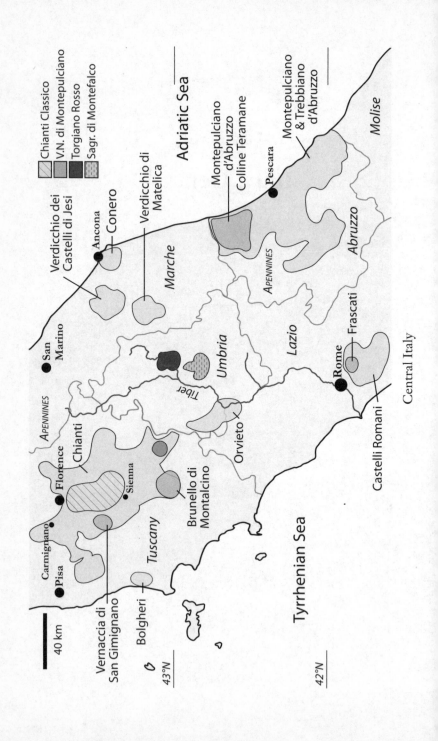

Central Italy

Legend:
- Chianti Classico
- V.N. di Montepulciano
- Torgiano Rosso
- Sagr. di Montefalco

Adriatic Sea

Tyrrhenian Sea

40 km

43°N

42°N

Pisa
Carmignano
Florence
Chianti
APENNINES
San Marino
Sienna
Vernaccia di San Gimignano
Bolgheri
Tuscany
Brunello di Montalcino
Tiber
Umbria
Orvieto
Lazio
Rome
Frascati
Castelli Romani
Verdicchio dei Castelli di Jesi
Ancona
Conero
Verdicchio di Matelica
Marche
APENNINES
Montepulciano d'Abruzzo Colline Teramane
Pescara
Abruzzo
Montepulciano & Trebbiano d'Abruzzo
Molise

Tuscany

Viticulture in Tuscany can be traced back to the Etruscans in the 8th century BC. Today, the region boasts some of the biggest names in wine, including Brunello di Montalcino, Vino Nobile di Montepulciano, and, of course, Chianti, Italy's most recognized red wine. Over 50% of production is DOC or DOCG, making Tuscany the third largest producer of quality wine after Piedmont and Veneto.

Tuscany enjoys a diversity of mesoclimates, with the Tyrrhenian Sea and inland hills exercising moderating effects. Most vineyards are planted on hilly or undulating terrain at altitudes of 150-500m (492-1,640ft). On these elevated slopes, the grapes benefit from greater direct sunlight, cooler summer temperatures, and a higher diurnal temperature range.

Red wine accounts for over 80% of Tuscany's production and the principal grape variety is Sangiovese (Lat. *Sanguis Jovis*, Blood of Jove). Other names for Sangiovese include Brunello, Montepulciano, Morellino, Pignolo, Sangioveto, and Prugnolo Gentile. With the rise of the Super Tuscans from the 1970s (see later), international grape varieties such as Cabernet Sauvignon and Merlot have become more prominent. Other commonly planted black grape varieties include Canaiolo, Colorino, Malvasia Nera, and Mammolo. The principal white grape varieties are Trebbiano, Malvasia Bianca, Vermentino, and Vernaccia, the basis of the region's finest white wine, Vernaccia di San Gimignano DOCG.

Vin Santo ('Holy Wine') is a type of passito wine that is also made in other regions of Italy but that is particularly associated with Tuscany. The most prominent style of Vin Santo is the blend of Trebbiano and Malvasia produced in the Chianti Classico area, but there are many other styles of Vin Santo including Sangiovese-based reds and rosés.

Chianti

The first delimitation of the Chianti area took place in 1716 under Cosimo III de'Medici, Grand Duke of Tuscany. The modern incarnation of Chianti as a Sangiovese-dominated blend dates back to the mid 19th century and the Baron Bettino Ricasoli (later Prime Minister of the

Kingdom of Italy). In 1932, the Chianti area was expanded and divided into seven sub-areas: Classico, which encompasses the original delimited area, Colli Aretini, Colli Fiorentini, Colline Pisane, Colli Senesi, Montalbano, and Rufina. Today, the Chianti area stretches right across the central Tuscan hills and is responsible for more wine than any other Italian appellation. In 1996, an eighth sub-area, Montespertoli, was carved out from Colli Fiorentini. At ~7,000ha, Chianti Classico is larger than all the other sub-areas combined. Of these other sub-areas, Colli Senesi (at ~3,500ha) is the largest and Rufina the most reputed. Wine from outside the sub-areas (or made from a blend from more than one sub-area) is labelled 'Chianti DOCG'—although, technically, the Chianti DOCG area overlaps with the DOCG areas of Brunello di Montalcino, Vino Nobile di Montepulciano DOCG, Carmignano, and Vernaccia di San Gimignano. Chianti Classico accounts for about one-quarter of total Chianti production and enjoys a separate DOCG. Members of the Chianti Classico Consortium can display a black rooster seal (*gallo nero*) on their bottlenecks. Chianti Classico Riserva must be aged for at least 27 months prior to release, although, unlike with Brunello, there is no minimum stipulation for cask versus bottle ageing. Outside the Classico sub-area, Chianti that meets a more stringent set of criteria can be sold as Chianti Superiore.

The topography and soils of Chianti Classico are quite varied. Vineyards are planted at altitudes of 250 to 610m (820 to 2,000ft), typically on soils of weathered sandstone (albarese) or bluish-grey chalky marlstone (galestro). Albarese is more prevalent in the south of the area and galestro in the north. The traditional grape varieties for Chianti are Sangiovese, Cannaiolo Nero, Malvasia Bianca, and Trebbiano. In recent years, it has become possible to make Chianti from 100% Sangiovese and the use of white grape varieties in Chianti Classico has been prohibited. Today, Chianti Classico consists of 80-100% Sangiovese and 0-20% other black grape varieties including Cannaiolo, Cabernet Sauvignon, Merlot, and Syrah. The wine is far more likely to be sold in a Bordeaux bottle than in the traditional *fiasco*, a squat bottle partially covered with a close-fitting basket of *sala*, a swamp weed sundried and blanched with sulphur. Glassblowers had an easier time making rounded bottles, and the sala baskets provided these bottles with a flat base.

Typically, Chianti is medium ruby in colour with notes of cherries, strawberries, raspberries, plums, soft spice, and herbs—and, with increasing age, tea leaves, tobacco, and leather. Top examples may display additional notes of French oak. On the palate, body is medium, acidity high, alcohol medium to high, and tannins firm. The finish is agreeably dry and accompanied by a note of bitter almonds. Compared to Chianto Classico, Chianti Rufina is typically fuller in body and higher in acidity.

Brunello di Montalcino

The success of Brunello is built on prestige and scarcity. The first records of a red wine from Montalcino date back to the early 14th century. In 1831, the marchese Cosimo Ridolfi, a future prime minister of Tuscany, praised the wines of Montalcino above all others in the region. In the mid 19th century, Clemente Santi, a local farmer, isolated a Sangiovese clone that yielded a wine that could be extensively aged. In 1888, his grandson Ferrucio Biondi-Santi made the first modern Brunello, which, at the time of release, had spent more than ten years in barrel. Over the next six decades, the Biondi-Santi firm declared only four vintages of its Brunello (1888, 1891, 1925, and 1945) and the rich elixir acquired a reputation for almost mythical scarcity. In 1980, the Italian authorities conferred the first ever DOCG to Brunello di Montalcino; and, in 1999, a panel of experts selected a 1955 Biondi Santi Brunello as 'best of the century', the only Italian wine to make the cut.

The high and consistent quality of Brunello is the product of several factors, most notably: the unique Sangiovese clone that is perfectly adapted to the terroir, the terroir itself, the process of vinification and maturation, and the option of declassifying substandard produce into Rosso di Montalcino DOC. The vineyards are planted on slopes with a diversity of aspects, altitudes, and soil types including limestone, clay, schist, marl, and volcanic soil—features that contribute significantly to quality and complexity. The climate is warmer and drier than in Chianti, enabling Sangiovese to ripen more fully and consistently; at the same time, a maritime breeze promotes air circulation and cooler nights.

Vinification involves extended maceration and oak ageing. DOCG regulations stipulate that Brunello must be released at least four years after harvest (five for Riserva), including at least two in barrel. Created in 1984, Rosso di Montalcino DOC is co-extensive with Brunello DOCG and enables producers to declassify substandard produce or release their wine earlier. In 2008, the Italian authorities impounded the 2003 vintage of four Brunello producers on charges of bulking up their wine with varieties such as Cabernet Sauvignon and Merlot. Laboratory tests demonstrated that the confiscated wines had not been blended or adulterated, except for a small proportion that tested inconclusively. Today, the so-called Brunellogate scandal has mostly been forgotten. Producers have reaffirmed their commitment to the strict production code, with only 4% voting to change it. Compared to Chianti, Brunello is darker and richer, more full-bodied, tannic, and alcoholic, and also more complex.

Vino Nobile di Montepulciano

The name 'Vino Nobile' dates back to the 1930s and Adamo Fanetti, although the wine itself has a much longer history. It is mentioned in Voltaire's *Candide*: 'Thereupon he accosted them, and with great politeness invited them to his inn to eat some macaroni, with Lombard partridges and caviar, and to drink a bottle of Montepulciano.' In contrast to Montepulciano d'Abruzzo, which is made from the Montepulciano grape, Vino Nobile di Montepulciano is made from Sangiovese (minimum 70%), with any balance made up by Canaiolo Nero and/or other varieties such as Merlot, Syrah, and Mammolo. The climate is warmer than in Chianti Classico and the vineyards face east to southeast on slopes that range in altitude from 250 to 600m (820 to 1,968ft). The soils are sandier than in either Chianti Classico or Montalcino and contain less limestone. DOCG regulations stipulate that the wine must be aged for at least two years (three years for the Riserva) prior to release, including at least 12 months in barrel—typically large Italian *botti*. Other wines from Montepulciano include Rosso di Montepulciano DOC, which is earlier to mature, and Vin Santo di Montepulciano. Compared to Chianti, Vino Nobile di Montepulciano is weightier and more alcoholic, with firm tannins and high acidity and a drying 'tea-leaf' finish. In a sense, it sits between Chianti and Brunello in body and style, although it does not quite match the best of either in finesse or complexity.

Carmignano

In 1716 Cosimo III de' Medici legislated to protect the fine wine of Carmignano. In the 18th century Carmignano winemakers developed a tradition of blending Sangiovese with Cabernet Sauvignon, a practice that became commoner in the 20th century. The appellation comprises a mere 100ha around the village of Carmignano on the eastern slopes of Monte Albano ~10 miles northwest of Florence. The vineyards are planted on lime-rich, free-draining soils, and their relatively low altitude of 50 to 200m (164 to 656ft) enables Sangiovese to ripen fully. Carmignano used to be sold as Chianti Montalbano until it acquired separate DOC status in 1975 (the DOCG came in 1990). Current regulations call for at least 50% Sangiovese, 10-20% Cabernet Sauvignon or Cabernet Franc, 0-20% Canaiaolo, 0-10% Trebbiano, and 0-10% other grape varieties such as Merlot and Syrah. In practice, Canaiolo and Trebbiano are seldom used. Riserva status calls for three years ageing including 12 months in cask. Substandard produce can be declassified into Barco Reale DOC, which is made in a fresher, more modern style. Vin Santo is also made, including a rosé Vin Santo, Occhio de Pernice ('eye of the partridge', similar to the French *oeil de perdrix*). Carmignano is rather soft and elegant, with lower acidity and more pronounced tannins than Chianti Classico. It tends to benefit from blending with Bordeaux varieties. Despite its early recognition and protection, it can be thought of as the original Super Tuscan. The most recognized producer in Carmignano is Capezzana.

Vernaccia di San Gimignano

Vernaccia di San Gimignano has long been considered one of Italy's finest white wines, and is even spoken of in Dante's *Divine Comedy*: '[Pope Martin IV] Has held the holy Church within his arms... and purges by his fasting Bolsena's eels and the Vernaccia wine.' In 1966, Vernaccia di San Gimignano was the first Italian wine to be granted DOC status, upgraded to DOCG status in 1993. Vernaccia is made from Vernaccia di San Gimignano (which is distinct from other Vernaccia grape varieties) in and around the picturesque hilltown of San Gimignano. The DOCG regulations stipulate that the wine must consist of at least 90% Vernaccia, with any balance made up by a number of approved white grape varieties. For Riserva status, the wine must be aged for at least twelve months, either in stainless steel or oak, and a further four months in bottle. Vernaccia di San Gimignano is gold in colour, with notes of lime, camomile tea, and flowers. On the palate, it is rich and full-bodied but also dry, with crisp acidity and a mineral and slightly bitter finish.

Super Tuscans

The first true Super Tuscan is Tenuta San Guido's Sassicaia, first released in 1971. In the 1960s and 1970s, many producers in Chianti regarded the DOC regulations as too restrictive. In particular, the regulations insisted upon blending white grape varieties into red wine, while leaving no place for Bordeaux grape varieties such as Cabernet Sauvignon and Merlot. A number of producers set out to make wines outside the DOC regulations (and, in many cases, outside the DOC delimited area), leaving them with no option but to label their wines as modest *vino da tavola*. The movement soon attracted international attention and some of the new style wines achieved iconic status.

Today, Super Tuscans can be varietal wines based on Cabernet Sauvignon or Merlot; Bordeaux blends; non-traditional blends, for example, Cabernet Sauvignon and Syrah; blends of Sangiovese and Bordeaux grape varieties; or varietal wines based on Sangiovese. Sassicaia is 85% Cabernet Sauvignon and 15% Cabernet Franc, and Tignanello—another prototype Super Tuscan—is 80% Sangiovese and 20% Cabernet Sauvignon. Since the 1960s and 70s, the legal situation has changed considerably: the DOC regulations have become more flexible and accommodating, and the legal entities of IGT Toscana and DOC Bolgheri have been created. Some Super Tuscans have re-entered the fold of DOCG Chianti. Others are labelled as IGT, which, although not DOC, still represents a big step up from *vino da tavola*. And yet others have fallen into the Bolgheri DOC delimited area in Alta Maremma, along the Tyrrhenian coast. This is the case of Sassicaia, which, uniquely, enjoys a separate DOC within Bolgheri: DOC Bolgheri Sassicaia.

Umbria

The climate of hilly, landlocked Umbria is similar to that of Tuscany but without the moderating Mediterranean influence. Though relatively small in terms of overall production, the region is particularly noted for Orvieto Classico DOC and Sagrantino di Montefalco DOCG.

The Orvieto delimited area, which accounts for the bulk of Umbrian quality wine production, is centred on the eponymous commune and extends south into the neighbouring region of Lazio. The soils in the Classico zone consist of *tufo* similar to the *tuffeau* in parts of the Loire Valley. Orvieto is made from a blend of Grechetto, Trebbiano Procanico, and other white grape varieties. Historically it was often made from grapes affected by noble rot (*muffa nobile*); but today sweet and semi-sweet styles account for only a small fraction of total production. At its best, Orvieto is fresh and clean, with notes of apples, pears, flowers, and peaches, and an aftertaste of citrus fruits or bitter almonds. Body, acidity, and alcohol are all medium. Caveat emptor: Orvieto with a high proportion of Trebbiano does tend to blandness.

In recent years, Sagrantino di Montefalco has overtaken the Sangiovese-dominated Torgiano Rosso Riserva DOCG as Umbria's premier red wine. Sagrantino di Montefalco is made from Sagrantino from a delimited area in the Province of Perugia. The dominant dry style is aged for 30 months of which at least 12 in oak barrels. A historical passito style is also made, but in much smaller quantities. Everything about Sagrantino di Montefalco is superlative. On approach, it is inky purple in colour, with an intense and complex bouquet of red and black fruit, ripe plums, soft spice, and earth. In the mouth, it is full-bodied, with high acidity, alcohol, extract, and tannins, and a long, sweet-seeming finish.

Lazio (Latium)

Production in Latium is dominated by white wines, first among them Frascati Superiore DOCG. The principal viticultural area is Castelli Romani in the Alban Hills to the southeast of Rome. Castelli Romani, so-called because Roman aristocrats used to summer there, is a collection of 14 communes including Frascati. The area's volcanic soils are rich and fertile, promoting high yields and a tendency to favour quantity over quality. Frascati is typically a blend, or primarily a blend, of Malvasia (Malvasia di Candia and Malvasia del Lazio) and Trebbiano (Trebbiano Toscano and Trebbiano Giallo). It is typically light, dry, crisp, and rather neutral, and perfectly suited to the local climate.

Marche

The principal grape varieties in Marche are Verdicchio, Sangiovese, Montepulciano, and Trebbiano. Verdicchio goes into making still, sparkling, and straw wines, and finds its finest expression in Verdicchio di Matelica Riserva DOCG from the province of Macerata and Verdicchio dei Castelli di Jesi Riserva DOCG from the nearby province of Ancona. The latter appellation is considerably smaller than the former, with more restricted yields and a fuller, more concentrated, and less variable character. In the glass, Verdicchio is characterized by a pale colour with hints of green (whence 'Verdicchio'), a crisp, citrusy acidity, subtle herbaceous undertones, and a bitter almond finish. The most distinguished red wine from Marche is Conero Riserva from Monte Conero just south of Ancona. Conero Riserva DOCG is typically 100% Montepulciano, and darker, weightier, and more intense than Rosso Conero DOC and nearby Rosso Piceno DOC, which are blends of Montepulciano and Sangiovese.

Abruzzo

Abruzzo is a rugged, mountainous region harbouring a diversity of mesoclimates. Fertile soils and tendone vine-training systems contribute to often very high yields. The bulk of production is concentrated in the Chieti province, but some of the finer wines are crafted in the northern Teramo and Pescara provinces. Quality wine production is dominated by Montepulciano d'Abruzzo DOC (which is not related to Vino Nobile di Montepulciano) and Trebbiano d'Abruzzo DOC. The finest expression of Montepulciano d'Abruzzo is Montepulciano d'Abruzzo

Colline Teramane DOCG in the north of the region. This inky-black wine is rich and powerful, yet subtle and complex, with notes of black cherries and plums, earth, spice, and smoke, soft tannins, and medium or low acidity. In the middle of the 20th century, Emidio Pepe and Edoardo Valentini (the 'Lord of the Vines') introduced innovative methods of winemaking to the region, and Valentini's Trebbiano d'Abruzzo is one of Italy's most distinctive and distinguished dry white wines.

Chapter 18

Italy: South and Sicily

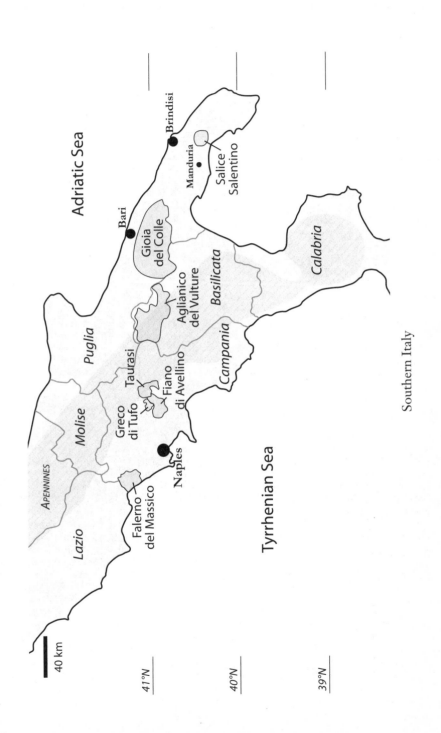

Adriatic Sea

Brindisi

Bari

Gioia
del Colle

Manduria

Salice
Salentino

Puglia

Aglianico
del Vulture

Basilicata

Calabria

Taurasi

Campania

Greco
di Tufo

Fiano
di Avellino

Molise

APENNINES

Naples

Lazio

Falerno
del Massico

Tyrrhenian Sea

40 km

41°N

40°N

39°N

Southern Italy

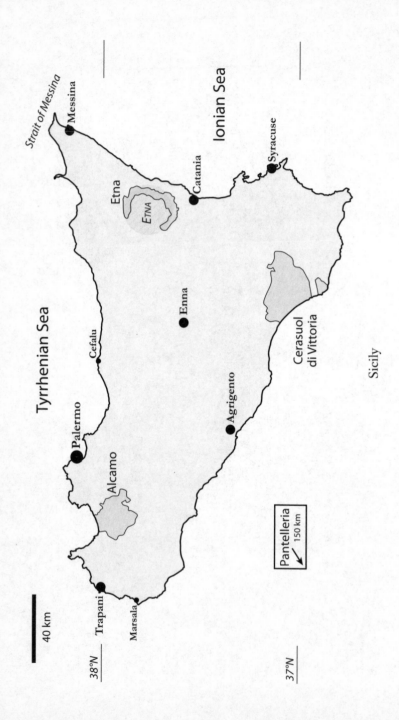

Tyrrhenian Sea

Strait of Messina

Messina

Ionian Sea

Etna

Etna

Catania

Syracuse

Palermo

Cefalu

Enna

Cerasuol
di Vittoria

Alcamo

Agrigento

40 km

38°N

Trapani

Marsala

Pantelleria
150 km

37°N

Sicily

Campania and Basilicata

Many of the best vineyards in Campania lie inland from Naples in the hills around Avellino. The key grape varieties are Fiano and Greco (Greco Bianco) for the white wines and Aglianico for the red wines.

The ancient Roman wine Apianum was made from *vitis apiana* (Lat. *apiana*, 'of the bees'), thought by some to be the same grape variety as Fiano. Today, Fiano finds its finest expression in Fiano di Avellino DOCG, which is also permitted to carry the name 'Apianum'. Fiano di Avellino is at least 85% Fiano, with Greco, Coda di Volpe ('Fox's Tail'), and/or Trebbiano making up any remainder. The wine is straw coloured, dry, crisp, and mineral, with medium body and alcohol and notes of pears, quince, honey, orange blossom, and—with age—spice and hazelnuts.

Greco finds its finest expression in Greco di Tufo DOCG. 'Tufo' is the name of one of eight communes within the delimited area, and also the name of the volcanic soil that underlies this commune. Greco di Tufo is at least 85% Greco, with Coda di Volpe making up any remainder. The wine is deep in colour, with notes of lemons, pears, peaches, foliage or herbs, and toasted almonds. On the palate, it is bone dry and austere, with crisp acidity and a sustained mineral finish. It matures more quickly than Fiano di Avellino.

Aglianico is the grape variety behind Taurasi DOCG, 'The Barolo of the South'. Despite the ancient origins of Aglianico, Taurasi is a relatively recent phenomenon, brought into the international spotlight by its original champion Mastroberardino. Taurasi is either 100% Aglianico or a blend of at least 85% Aglianico together with Piedirosso, Barbera, and/or Sangiovese. It must be aged for three years of which 12 months in cask, or, for the Riserva, four years of which 18 months in cask. Deep ruby in colour, the wine is big and brooding with intense aromas of black cherries and plums, cigar smoke, chocolate, ground coffee, leather, earth, and game. It is high in acidity and tannins and needs time to soften and develop.

Aglianico is a late ripener that performs best on steep slopes and volcanic soils. The other notable Aglianico varietal wine is Aglianico del Vulture Superiore DOCG. The delimited area is situated on the extinct Vulture volcano, 65km (40mi) south of

Taurasi in the rugged and depopulated region of Basilicata (Lucania). Aglianico del Vulture is similar to Taurasi, offering very good value for money.

Back in Campania, Falerno del Massico DOC is produced in the same region as the famous ancient wine Falernian (Falernum). The delimited area lies to the north of Naples, on a coastal hillside of volcanic origin. The red wines are made from Aglianico and Piedirosso, sometimes with the addition of Primitivo and/or Barbera. Alternatively, they are made from Primitivo, with up to 15% Aglianico, Piedirosso, and/or Barbera. The white wines are made from Falanghina.

Puglia

The hot and dry climate of Puglia (Apulia) is moderated by sea breezes, especially on the Salento peninsula to the south—the 'heel' of Italy. The region is an important producer of bulk wine, even if certain pockets have been upping their game. The north of the region is hillier with several of the same grape varieties as in central Italy. By contrast, the Salento peninsula is mostly flat, with a host of indigenous grape varieties that trace their lineage back to Greco-Roman times. Red wines account for more than four fifths of total production. The most notable grape varieties are, for red wines, Primitivo ('early ripener'), Negroamaro ('black bitter'), and Nero di Troia (Uva di Troia), and, for white wines, Verdeca and Bombino. Primitivo is genetically identical to Calfornia's Zinfandel. The principal appellations for Primitivo are Primitivo di Manduria DOC, called *mirr test* ('hard wine') in the local dialect; Primitivo di Manduria Dolce Naturale DOCG, which is made from grapes that are dried on the vine; and Gioia del Colle DOC. Negroamaro is more widespread than Primitivo, with varietal Negroamaro produced in several DOCs including Salice Salentino and Brindisi. Red wines from Castel del Monte DOC, which sits on a limestone plateau in central Puglia, are typically blends of Nero di Troia and other grape varieties. There are also three recent Castel del Monte DOCGs: Nero di Troia Riserva (minimum 90% Nero di Troia), Rosso Riserva (minimum 65% Nero di Troia), and Bombino Nero (minimum 90% Bombino Nero).

Sicily

It is Dionysus who brought the vine to Sicily, the largest island in the Mediterranean Sea and the largest region in Italy. Of all the Italian regions, Sicily has the largest area under vines and the largest volume of production. As in the rest of southern Italy, only a small fraction of total production is DOC level, although many fine wines fall under the banner of IGT Sicilia, which, confusingly, has recently been replaced with both DOC Sicilia and IGT Terre Siciliane.

Sicily offers close to ideal conditions for viticulture, with infertile soils, a rugged terrain, and hot, dry, sun-drenched summers. In the 20th century, this led to some very high yields, currently in the process of being tamed by quality-conscious producers. The east of the island is dominated by Mount Etna, with Etna DOC benefiting from high altitudes and mineral-rich volcanic soils. Other notable eastern DOCs are located further south in the area of Syracuse, on the slopes of the Iblei Mountains. Although less dramatic, the west of the island accounts for the bulk of production with a large number of DOCs including the fortified Marsala.

The most notable grape varieties in Sicily are the indigenous Nero d'Avola, Frappato, and Nerello Mascalese. Nero d'Avola is often compared to New World Shiraz, dark and full-bodied with fine tannins and notes of wild plums, mulberry, chocolate, and pepper. Leading examples are balanced, complex, and long-lived, and much in the same league as Taurasi and Aglianico del Vulture. In the southeast of the island, Nero d'Avola is blended with Frappato to produce Cerasuolo di Vittoria, Sicily's only DOCG. 'Cerasuolo' means 'cherry-like', and the wine can be reminiscent of Beaujolais. Etna DOC is made from Nerello Mascalese, sometimes in a blend with the more rustic Nerello Cappuccio. Wines made from Nerello Mascalese are fresh, delicate, and mineral, and have been compared to fine Burgundy. The principal white grape variety is Catarratto. Cataratto is a Marsala grape (although top producers of Marsala prefer to use the traditional Grillo and Inzolia grapes) and also the principal component of Bianco d'Alcamo DOC. Moscato and Malvasia are made into passito wines all over Sicily and also in the islands of Lipari and Pantelleria. The sublime Moscato di Pantelleria is made from Muscat of Alexandria (Zibbibo) rather than Muscato Bianco. As in other Italian regions, there is a secondary focus on international grape varieties such as Chardonnay, Cabernet Sauvignon, Merlot, and especially Syrah, which is well suited to the climate of the island. Sicily produces many varietal wines, but blending—including between indigenous and international grape varieties—is both traditional and common. Some top producers in Sicily include Corvo, COS, De Bartoli, Donnafugata, Planeta, Tasca d'Almerita, and Tenuta di Fessina.

Chapter 19

Spain

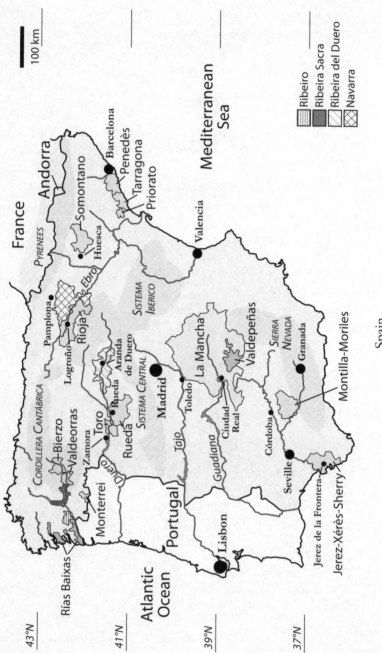

The Phoenicians, the Carthaginians, and the Romans all cultivated the vine in Spain. Under the Romans, trade in Hispanic wines surpassed trade in Italian wines, with Hispanic amphorae unearthed by archaeologists as far as Britain and the Germanic frontier. The Moors conquered much of Spain from the Visigoths in the 8th century. Despite their Islamic faith, they tolerated the blood of Christ and sometimes even drank it themselves. They also maintained vineyards for trade, grapes, raisins, and medicinal purposes. With the Spanish *Reconquista*, vineyards expanded and trade reopened. In 1364, the court of Edward III regulated the prices of wines sold in England, placing Spanish wines on a par with those from Gascony. As the relationship with England deteriorated, Spain became increasingly dependent on exports to its colonies, and, under Philip III, even ordered colonists to uproot their vines. In the late 19th century, French winemakers escaping from phylloxera crossed the Pyrenees into Rioja, Navarra, and Catalonia, bringing with them their grape varieties, methods, and technologies. By the time phylloxera caught up with them (it arrived in La Rioja in 1901), the remedy of grafting European vines onto American rootstocks had already been discovered. In the course of the 20th century, the Spanish wine industry suffered from marked civil and political upheaval. The Franco dictatorship came to an end in 1975 and Spain entered the EU in 1986. Today, Spain counts 1.2m hectares of vines, more than any other country, and is the third largest wine producing country after France and Italy. Its reputation as a producer of premium wines is relatively recent, and the industry remains in a state of flux.

The lie of the land

A parched plateau, the Meseta Central, occupies much of central Spain. To the east and south, the long Mediterranean coast is tempered by its proximity to the sea. To the northwest and north, the climate is influenced by the Atlantic Ocean and the Pyrenees, and is much cooler and wetter. Spain's many mountains and rivers very much complicate this overall picture: for example, the Cordillera Cantábrica, which can be looked upon as an extension of the Pyrenees, shelters regions such as Rioja and Ribera del Duero from the influence of the Atlantic. The country's principal rivers are the Miño, Duero, Tajo (Tagus), Guadalquivir, and Ebro: the first four flow to the Atlantic and the last oppositely to the Mediterranean. Many vineyards are planted at higher altitudes where cooler nights enable grapes to concentrate flavour while preserving natural acidity.

Grape varieties

Vines are planted across all of Spain's 17 administrative regions, including the Canary and Balearic Islands. Over 600 grape varieties are cultivated, of which only a score are commercially important. The most widely planted grape variety is the hardy and drought-resistant Airén, on the decline but still of importance in the manufacture of brandy. The second most widely planted grape variety is Spain's most noble, Tempranillo, which is also called, among others, Cencibel, Tinto Fino, and Ull de Llebre. Other important black grape varieties are Grenache (Garnacha), Mourvèdre (Monastrell), Carignan (Cariñena), Mencia, and Bobal. Other important white grape varieties are Albariño and Verdejo. Cava (see Chapter 11) is mostly made from Macabeo, Parellada, and Xarel-lo, and Sherry (see Chapter 21) from Palomino. Plantings of international grape varieties such as Cabernet Sauvignon, Chardonnay, Sauvignon Blanc, Merlot, and Syrah are becoming increasingly important.

Much of Spain is arid and infertile, with low-density plantings of old bush-trained vines. Yields are often very low, sometimes as low as ~20hl/ha (compared to, say, >100hl/ha in many parts of Germany). The widespread use of irrigation, legalized in 1996, has increased yields but potentially decreased quality. Owing to the heat, flabby and alcoholic wines are all too common, but modern winemaking methods, in particular, temperature-controlled fermentation in stainless steel tanks, are yielding fresher and fruitier styles. At the same time, the tradition of long barrel ageing, typically in American oak, is thriving. The Spanish wine industry is still dominated by small growers belonging to a cooperative, although there are also some very large concerns.

Classifications

The first *Denominación de Origen* (DO) was created in the early 1930s for Rioja. As with the AOC system in France or the DOC system in Italy, a DO indicates a clearly defined and tightly regulated geographical origin and style. There is a higher rung called *Denominación de Origen Calificada* (DOCa), similar to Italy's *Denominazione di Origine Controllata e Garantita* (DOCG), but this has only been granted to Rioja and Priorat. In contrast, the *Vinos de la Tierra* (VT) category, which is similar to France's *Vin de Pays*, captures not a particular terroir, style, and quality, but a broad geographic region such as Andalucia or Castile. On the bottom rung is *Vino de Mesa* (VdM), similar to France's *Vin de Table*, made from the produce of unclassified or intentionally declassified vineyards. There are two other categories: *Vino de Calidad Con Indicación Geográfica* (VC) and *Vino de pago* (VP). VC is similar to France's defunct *Vin Délimité de Qualité Supérieure* (VDQS), and is effectively a stepping-stone towards DO status. VP is granted to high-end single estates that deserve recognition but are outside a DO or do not qualify for a DO.

In addition, many Spanish wines are labelled according to time spent in oak.

- Vino Joven ('young wine') has undergone little, if any, oak ageing.
- Crianza has been aged for at least two years of which at least six months in oak. White and rosé Crianza has been aged for at least one year of which at least six months in oak.
- Reserva has been aged for at least three years of which at least one year in oak. White and rosé Reserva has been aged for at least two years of which at least six months in oak.
- Gran Reserva has been aged for at least five years of which at least 18 months in oak and 36 months in bottle. White and rosé Gran Reserva has been aged for at least four years of which at least six months in oak.

For Rioja, Ribera del Duero, and Navarra reds, Crianza has to spend at least 12 months (instead of six months) in oak, and Gran Reserva has to spend at least 24 months (instead of 18 months) in oak. Finally, there are three other terms that are used to indicate the age of a wine: *Noble* for a wine that has been aged for at least one year, *Anejo* for a wine that has been aged for at least two years, and *Viejo* for a wine that has been aged for at least three years in a distinctively oxidative style. Unlike Crianza and so on, the use of these terms does not call for or imply oak ageing. Not all wines are improved by lengthy barrel ageing; some may even be harmed.

Principal regions and wine styles

Galicia

Galicia in the far northwest is much cooler and wetter than the rest of Spain, with greater vintage variation. The granitic hills of Galicia are green and lush, with a coastline of steep cliffs alternating with inlets called *rías*. Four of the region's five DOs, Rías Baixas, Ribeiro, Ribeira Sacra ('Sacred Shore'), and Valdeorras, are in the valleys of the River Miño; Monterrei, the outlier, is in the Douro basin, and in the rain shadow of the Sierra de Larouca. Although adjacent to Valdeorras and in the valley of the Miño, Bierzo is actually in Castilla y León and so covered in the next section.

Galicia is renowned for its white wines, typically varietal Albariño but also blends and other varietal wines such as Godello (Verdelho, the specialty of Valdeorras), Loureiro, Torrontes, and Treixadura. Red wines are also made, often from Mencia, the specialty of Ribeira Sacra. Rías Baixas is the most notable of the five DOs, with five subzones all dominated by Albariño. Albariño from Rías Baixas is among Spain's finest white wines, and can bear a striking similarity to Vinho Verde from Monção in Portugal (see Chapter 20). There is a theory, albeit fanciful, that the grape variety descends from Riesling carried by German pilgrims on the path to Santiago de Compostela.

Albariño from Rías Baixas is pale in colour with hints of gold and green. On the nose, it is aromatic, with notes of white peach, apricot, almonds, honeysuckle, and jasmine. On the palate, it is medium in body with high citrusy acidity, medium alcohol, and a dry or pithy mineral finish. Most Albariño is fermented in stainless steel, so oak is usually absent. Albariño is often confused with Riesling, Pinot Gris, Viognier, or Grüner Veltliner. Compared to Riesling, it is fuller in body and lacks the tartness and petrol or fusel oil notes; compared to Pinot Gris, it is drier and higher in acidity; compared to Viognier, it is lighter in body and much higher in acidity; and compared to Grüner Veltliner, it is less acidic and austere and lacks the white pepper note.

Castilla y León

Stretching from just north of Madrid to just south of Bilbao, Castilla y León is more a country than a region, occupying about one fifth of Spain's total area. It sits on a plateau bounded to the north by the Cordillera Cantábrica, to the south by the Sistema Central, and to the east by the Sistema Iberico. The Cordillera Cantábrica blocks off any Atlantic influence, such that the climate is frankly continental, with hot summer days tempered by much cooler nights. The most notable DOs in Castilla y León are Ribera del Duero, Toro, and Rueda along the River Duero, and Bierzo along the Miño. This is red wine country and Tempranillo is king in all but Bierzo, which specializes in Mencia. White wines are also made, most often from Verdejo and Viura.

Ribera del Duero stretches ~110km (68mi) along the Duero around Aranda de Duero and upstream from Valladolid. The gently undulating terrain ranges from 700 to 900m (2,297 to 2,953ft) in altitude: frosts present a serious threat and diurnal temperature variation can be extreme. Soils consist of silt and clay on alternating layers of limestone, marl, and chalk; some vineyards have such a high chalk content as to appear almost white. In recent decades, production has shifted from Garnacha rosés to Tempranillo reds. These reds consist of at least 75% Tempranillo, with any balance made up by Cabernet Sauvignon, Merlot, and Malbec. Up to 5% of the white grape variety Albillo is sometimes added to lighten and soften the blend. Crianzas, Reservas, and Gran Reservas are aged in French and American oak casks. The best examples are complex, intense, and very long-lived, and count among Spain's finest red wines. Producers such as Vega Sicilia, Tinto Pesquera, and Emilio de Moro have made big names for themselves and for the region. The Tempranillo of Ribera del Duero (called Tinto Fino by locals) has thicker, darker skins than that of Rioja, and is also higher in acidity. Compared to most Rioja, the wines are dark and brooding: more full-bodied, concentrated, alcoholic, and tannic, and dominated by black fruits and plums rather than red fruits.

The historic winemaking region of Toro ('Bull') lies in the province of Zamora, downstream from Ribera del Duero and immediately to the west of Rueda. In the late 19th century, Toro exported large quantities of wine to a France ravaged by phylloxera. The sandy and pebbly limestone soils protected vineyards from the louse such that many Spanish regions ended up being replanted with Toro vines. Toro is at a similar altitude to Ribera del Duero and the climate is even more continental. The region is especially reputed for its red wines, which consist of at least 75% Tempranillo (Tinta de Toro) with any balance made up by Garnacha. Also on offer are rosés made from 50% Tempranillo and 50% Garnacha, and white wines made from Verdejo or Malvasia. In recent years, Toro has become very fashionable, attracting investment from companies in Rioja and Ribera del Duero, and even from the Lurtons in Bordeaux. Top producers include Pintia and Bodegas Fariña. Toro is similar in style to Ribera del Duero, but more exuberant and (often) more rustic, with a signature spicy note.

After falling to phylloxera, the historic winemaking region of Rueda turned to the production of bulk wine. In the 1970s, major investment by the Rioja winery Marqués de Riscal brought a change in direction, and Rueda acquired a reputation for fine white wines based on the Verdejo grape. Rueda is immediately east of Toro and the climate is very similar, with summers that are hot although not quite as hot as in south central Spain. Modern practices such as temperature-controlled fermentation in stainless steel tanks, mechanical harvesting at night, and inert gas blankets to protect the grapes from oxidation contribute greatly to preserving freshness. The stony soils of Rueda, rich in lime and iron, are mostly planted to Verdejo. Other authorized white grape varieties are Sauvignon Blanc, Palomino, and Macabeo (Viura). Some red wine is also made from Tempranillo, Cabernet Sauvignon, Merlot, and Garnacha. Rueda Verdejo is aromatic, fresh, and elegant, and, along with Albariño from Rías Baixas, ranks among Spain's finest white wines. Notes of gooseberry, peach, melon, and herbs are accompanied by a citrusy acidity. The texture is soft and full, but the finish is distinctly dry. The addition of Sauvignon Blanc or Macabeo to the blend can bring added complexity.

Phylloxera devastated the historic mining and winemaking region of Bierzo, which has been turned around most notably by Alvaro Palacios of Priorat fame. Bierzo combines some of the best features of Galicia and Castilla y León, enjoying a climate that is cooler and wetter than those of Ribera del Duero, Toro, or Rueda. The mountainous terraced vineyards and mineral-rich soils of slate and granite of Bierzo Alto contrast with the broad and fertile plain of Bierzo Bajo. The specialty of Bierzo is Mencía. Garnacha is also planted but is mainly used in blends. A small amount of white wine is made from Dona Blanca, Godello, and Palomino, and there is also a rosé based on Mencía. The red wines of Bierzo tend to be somewhat lighter and more refreshing than those from other parts of Castilla y León. They can be either fruity with soft, supple tannins, or more concentrated and powerful with notes of dark cherry fruit, spice, and earth, and pronounced minerality.

Rioja

Rioja is named for the Rio Oja, a tributary of the Ebro, and extends some 100km (62mi) along the Ebro as it flows southeast to the Mediterranean Sea. The region is enclosed by mountains, to the north and west by the Cordillera Cantábrica and to the south by the Sierra de la Demanda. The climate is more continental than Atlantic, and there is also an influence from the Mediterranean Sea—especially in Rioja Baja, which is warmer and drier than Rioja Alta and Rioja Alavesa.

About 90% of Rioja is red, and traditionally a blend of Tempranillo (typically ~60%), Garnacha (typically ~20%), Graciano, and Carignan (Mazuelo). Garnacha contributes body and alcohol; Graciano aroma; and Carignan colour, tannin, and acidity. Cabernet Sauvignon is also authorized but only for some producers. White Rioja is mostly if not entirely Macabeo (Viura), with any balance made up by Malvasia and Grenache Blanc (Garnacha Blanca). Rosés are mostly Garnacha. The reds are commonly aged in 225l American oak casks that impart characteristic and often pronounced aromas of vanilla and coconut. Many producers exceed the ageing requirements: Marqués de Murrieta only released its 1942 Gran Reserva in 1983! Generally speaking, ageing periods are shortening and the use of French oak (or a blend of French and American oak) is becoming more common. Oak ageing for white Rioja is currently very unfashionable and the traditional nutty and oxidative style has become hard to source.

Although there is a trend for single varietal and even single vineyard wines, many red Riojas remain merchant blends of fruit from Rioja Alta, Rioja Alavesa, and Rioja Baja. Rioja Alta stretches from the regional centre of Logroño in the east to Haro in the west. Most vineyards are to the south of the Ebro, on soils of clay rich in iron oxide. Owing in part to the higher altitudes, the growing season is shorter than in Rioja Baja, with wines that are finer, lighter, more acidic, and less alcoholic. Rioja Alavesa, by far the smallest of the three sub-regions, lies to the north of Logroño and the Ebro, extending beyond the autonomous community of La Rioja into Alava province in the Basque Country. The conditions are similar to those in Rioja Alta if slightly cooler and wetter. The clay soils are rich in chalk and limestone, without the iron oxide deposits that characterize large parts of Rioja Alta and Rioja Baja. The wines of Rioja Alavesa are similar to those of Rioja Alta but somewhat fuller and higher in acidity. Rioja Baja to the east is the largest of the three sub-regions and extends north across the Ebro and into Navarra. As in Rioja Alta, most vineyards are to the south of the Ebro. The climate in Rioja Baja is much warmer and drier, translating into wines that are deeper in colour, higher in alcohol, and often lacking in acidity. More modest Riojas are commonly made from Rioja Baja harvests. Top producers in Rioja include Marqués de Riscal, Martínez Bujanda, Muga, La Rioja Alta, Allende, Benjamin Romeo, Roda, and Artadi.

Traditional Rioja with a certain amount of age is pale in colour, brick red or garnet with a bronzing rim. It is distinctly dusty, with notes of cooked strawberries and raspberries, tobacco leaf, game, nuts, leather, soft spice, and vanilla and coconut from the American oak. On the palate, body is medium, acidity is medium to low, alcohol is medium, and tannins are ripe and silky. Compared to traditional Rioja, 'international style' Rioja generally spends less time in oak and is denser in colour and fruit, with more plum and blackberry. Compared to Ribera del Duero, Rioja is lighter in colour and body, with lower acidity, alcohol, and tannins, and dominated by red rather than black fruits.

Navarra and Somontano

Immediately north of Rioja, Navarra DO extends south from the regional centre of Pamplona across the southern half of the autonomous community and ancient kingdom of Navarre. Already in the 12th century, guidebooks recommended the wine of Navarra to pilgrims making the journey to Santiago de Compostela in Galicia. The terroir evolves from the rolling foothills of the Pyrenees to the flat Ebro valley, with the DO divided into five diverse sub-zones: Valdizarbe, Tierra Estella, Ribera Alta, Baja Montaña, and Ribera Baja. There are interregional differences in climate and soil, but, broadly speaking, the climate is continental and the soils are loam over gravel underlain by limestone. Compared to Rioja Alta, temperatures are cooler and rainfall is higher. At higher altitudes there is significant risk of damage by frost and storms. Most vines are trained on trellises, in part so as to maximize sun exposure. Under the tutelage of local oenological research institute EVENA, the region has turned from rosé to quality red wine. Black grape varieties account for 95% of plantings and include Tempranillo, Garnacha, Cabernet Sauvignon, Merlot, Graciano, and Carignan (Mazuelo). White grape varieties include Macabeo (Viura), Chardonnay, Garnacha Blanca, and Muscat (Moscatel). In recent years, emphasis has shifted from Joven wines to Crianzas, Reservas, and even Gran Reservas. Although co-operatives account for the bulk of production, the region boasts several dynamic and innovative independent producers. Hard though it be to generalize, the wines are similar to Rioja, if perhaps more New World in style, with a deeper colour, darker blackberry fruit from the use of international grape varieties such as Cabernet Sauvignon and Merlot, and, in many cases, French rather than American oak.

Navarra DO can be compared to Somontano DO further east along the Ebro, in the foothills of the Aragonese Pyrenees. Somontano ('under the mountain') is lusciously green with a high diurnal temperature range and soils that are ideally suited to viticulture. Local producers are brimming with energy and enthusiasm and are building a fashionable reputation for, among others, their avant-garde blends of traditional and international grape varieties. The DO only dates back to 1984, and the style is modern, fresh, and balanced. Both Navarra and Somontano can offer very good value for money. Top producers

in Navarra include Chivite, Guelbenzu, and Ochoa; and in Somontano
Viñas del Vero and Enate.

Priorat

Spain's other DOCa is a remote and mountainous region in central
southern Tarragona, an unlikely contender for the super-premium
niche appellation that it has become. In mediaeval times, the prior of
the Carthusian monastery of Scala Dei (Lat. Ladder of God) ruled as
feudal lord over much of the area, whence 'Priorato' or 'Priorat' in
the local Catalan. The state expropriated the monks in 1835 and distributed their vineyards to smallholders. Priorat rose to fame in the
1990s under the aegis of René Barbier (Clos Mogador), Álvaro Palacios
(l'Ermita), and others, attaining DOCa status in 2000. The appellation
encompasses the valleys of the Rivers Siurana and Montsant, with vineyards planted on terraced slopes at altitudes ranging from 100 to 700m
(328 to 2,297ft). Although close to the Mediterranean coast, the climate
is extreme continental, with diverse mesoclimates created by the Serra
de Montsant. Priorat is especially noted for its unique *llicorella* soils
of red and black slates and mica (quartzite) that conserve and reflect
the sun's heat. This schist is part of the same stratum that runs right
across northern Iberia through the finest vineyards of the Douro, Toro,
and Ribera del Duero. The porous topsoil is ~50cm deep, encouraging
roots to dig down into the subsoil. Above the ground, the vines are
trained in bush although some younger vines are trained on trellises.
Garnacha is the dominant grape variety; other black grape varieties
include Carignan (Cariñena), Cabernet Sauvignon, Merlot, and Syrah.
White grape varieties account for only 4% of plantings. Priorat wines
are Garnacha blends, often released as a *vino de guarda* after 18 months
in 300l oak casks (typically French oak) and a further few months in
bottle. The combination of old vines and diminutive yields makes for
concentrated, powerful, and long-lived wines that demand several years
of bottle ageing.

Priorat is very dark in colour with an intense aroma of ripe but
savoury black and red fruits, minerals, earth, spice, liquorice, chocolate, and, in some cases, vanilla from new French oak. On the palate,
it is full-bodied with high alcohol, crisp acidity, big and chewy tan-

nins, and a long, dry, and structured finish. The Priorat demarcated area is almost entirely surrounded by Montsant DO, which produces wines in a similar style. Priorat can easily be confused with Ribera del Duero, with l'Ermita and Vega Sicilia seemingly vying for the title of 'most expensive Spanish wine'. Compared to Ribera del Duero (which is Tempranillo rather than Garnacha dominated), Priorat often comes across as more tannic, more acidic, and more mineral.

Penedès

Penedès, north of Priorat and just south of Barcelona, is a diverse region better known for Cava than for still wines. The producer Miguel Torres (father and son) revolutionized the region, overseeing its transformation from mass production to quality and innovation—a movement taken up in other parts of Spain. The DO is split into three limestone-rich areas: Baix-Penedès on the coast, Mitja-Penedès on the rolling hills further inland, and Alt-Penedès even higher up on the fringes of the Meseta Central. Mitja-Penedès is responsible for the bulk of the region's production. The climate is Mediterranean with hot and dry summers and mild winters. With altitudes ranging from sea level to ~800m (2,625ft), there are a number of distinct mesoclimates. Baix-Penedès is the warmest area and dominated by black grape varieties. Frost and especially hail can present problems, as can fungal diseases and parasitic infestations. There are over 121 native grape varieties in Penedès. The principal white grape varieties are the Cava grapes Parellada, Macabeo, and Xarel-lo along with Malvasia and Chardonnay. The principal black grape varieties are Garnacha, Cariñena, Tempranillo, Monastrell, Merlot, and Cabernet Sauvignon. The region is responsible for a broad spectrum of styles and qualities. White and red wines are often made from a blend of local and international grape varieties, and, on the whole, the white wines enjoy the better reputation. Wines made from grapes grown at higher altitudes tend to have less alcohol, more acidity, and more finesse.

Castilla-La Mancha

Castilla-La Mancha (Arabic, *al mansha*, 'parched earth') lies in south central Spain. The region is famed for Don Quixote, Manchego cheese, and acre upon acre of sprawling vines. It produces more than half of Spanish grapes and is defying its reputation for bland and characterless bulk wines suitable for little more than distillation into brandy. The most important appellations in Castilla-La Mancha are La Mancha and Valdepeñas.

With ~200,000ha under vines, La Mancha DO is Europe's largest delimited wine area. It sits on a 600m (1,969ft) high plateau with an extreme continental climate. Summer daytime temperatures can rise to 45°C (113°F) and annual rainfall averages only 350mm (14in). The best vineyards are on soils that are rich in moisture-retaining limestone and chalk. Vines are widely spaced and trained in bush; unless the vineyards are irrigated, yields are diminutive. The principal grape varieties are Airén and Tempranillo, although a number of other varieties are also planted. The region has attracted investment from such luminaries as Alejandro Fernández (El Vinculo) and Martinez Bujanda (Finca Antigua), and some of the wines being produced are distinctly fresh and modern.

Valdepeñas DO ('Valley of Rocks') lies at the southern end of La Mancha, by which it is almost entirely surrounded. The Tempranillo wines of Valdepeñas are sometimes referred to as 'the poor man's Rioja' on account of their excellent value for money. The appellation is also known for a distinct style of light red or rosé wine called *aloque* or *clarete*, which is made from a blend of red and white grapes. As in La Mancha, the most commonly planted white grape variety is Airén, which still accounts for over half of plantings.

Chapter 20

Portugal

Portugal

Portugal is, of course, famous for its fortified wines, in particular Port and Madeira (see Chapter 21), but is also building a reputation for table wines. These wines often boast unique and distinctive characters, and are not to be conflated with those from neighbouring Spain. For much of the 20th century, Portugal stood in relative isolation from the rest of Europe: although the Salazar dictatorship hampered the country's wine industry, it also led to the preservation of a large number of indigenous grape varieties which today sit alongside pan-Iberian varieties such as Tempranillo (Tinta Roriz) and international varieties such as Cabernet Sauvignon and Chardonnay.

Although relatively small, Portugal is far from uniform and offers a host of climates and terrains. The moderating influence of the Atlantic Ocean quickly tails off, with inland regions marked by progressively drier and more continental climates. The south is dominated by rolling plains and divided from the mountainous north by the River Tagus (Tejo). The north is especially noted for terroir-driven red and white wines, and the south and centre for rich, ripe, and accessible red wines.

Portugal joined the European Economic Community (EEC) in 1986, leading to a rise in single estates (*quintas*) and the introduction of modern practices such as destemming and temperature-controlled fermentation in stainless steel tanks. As in other European countries, the wine classification divides into quality and table wines: *Denominaçã de Origem Controllada* (DOC) and *Indicação de Proviniência Regulamentada* (IPR) for quality wines, and *Vinho Regional* and *Vinho de Mesa* for table wines. The Vinho Regional designations, of which there are 14, are of especial importance to innovative winemakers using international grape varieties. The Portuguese term *Garrafeira* refers to certain red or white wines from exceptional vintages with higher alcohol and a longer maturation period.

Principal regions and wine styles

Vinho Verde

Vinho Verde DOC is produced in the large Minho region, which is bounded to the north by the River Minho and the border with Spain. The River Douro crosses the south of the Minho region, but Vinho Verde could not be more different from the Douro Valley's Port wine.

The prevailing winds from the Atlantic Ocean bring in plenty of rain, which promotes high yields and rot. The vines are planted on granitic soils and trained high, traditionally on pergolas, to reduce rot and make space for mixed farming. The region is dominated by small producers, with over 30,000 producers for 35,000ha—some 15% of Portugal's total vineyard area. The 'Verde' in 'Vinho Verde' means 'green' in the sense of 'fresh and youthful'. Despite its name, Vinho Verde can be white, red, and, increasingly, rosé. The most notable grape varieties for white Vinho Verde are Loureiro, Treixadura (Trajadura), and Arinto; and for red Vinho Verde Vinhão (Sousao), Azal Tinto (Amaral), and Espadeiro. White Vinho Verde is straw coloured, slightly effervescent, with a light body and very crisp acidity. Red Vinho Verde is dark purple, light in body, tannic, and astringent. Flavour profiles vary according to the constituent grape variety or varieties. The Vinho Verde DOC is divided into nine sub-regions, the most notable of which is Monção in the north. Vinho Verde from Monção is made from Albariño (Alvarinho) and can reach 13% alcohol compared to the maximum 11.5% permitted in the rest of the region. Though still fresh and light, this style is fuller and richer with dominant notes of green apple and tropical fruits.

Douro

The first notable Douro table wine, Barca Velha, dates back to 1952; but it is only in recent years that the Douro DOC has begun to make a mark. The Douro Valley is largely sheltered from the influence of the Atlantic Ocean by the Marão and Montemuro Mountains, such that its upper reaches are much drier than its more coastal areas, with hotter summers and colder winters. Although the Douro is especially noted for Port, table wine accounts for about half of regional production. Vineyards dedicated to Port tend to be planted on schistous soils, those dedicated to table wine on granitic soils. Douro table wines are typically made from the same grape varieties as Port, most notably Touriga Nacional, Touriga Franca, Tinta Barroca, and Tempranillo (Tinta Roriz). Wines made from international grape varieties, most commonly Cabernet Sauvignon, fall under the banner of Vinho Regional Terras Durienses. A small amount of white wine is also made, principally from the same grape varieties as White Port such as Gouveio, with the best examples usually hailing from higher altitude vineyards. Blending is an important practice in the Douro, both across grape varieties and vineyard sites. Douro reds are often reminiscent of Port, with notes of ripe fruit, herbs, and peppery spice, a full body, firm tannins, and crisp acidity. For more on the Douro Valley, see Chapter 21.

Dão

The Dão lies to the south of the Douro in north central Portugal. Most of the vineyards are planted along the River Dão, a tributary of the River Mondego. The region is enclosed on three sides by the granite mountain ranges of Serra da Estrela, Serra do Caramulo, and Serra da Nave. As a result, the climate is mild, with long dry summers and wet winters. The best vineyard sites are at higher altitudes of 150 to 450m (492 to 1,476ft), with stonier soils, better sun exposure, better ventilation, and a greater diurnal temperature range. Several grape varieties are planted, the most important being Touriga Nacional. Red wines account for the bulk of production, and are made from Touriga Nacional, Tempranillo (Tinta Roriz), Mencia (Jaen), Alfrocheiro Preto, and others. For white wines, Encruzado is the most important grape variety. Dão reds can be overly dry and tannic, but shorter periods of fermentation and cask ageing are resulting in fresher, fruitier wines.

Bairrada

Bairrada lies to the west of the Dão, in the coastal half of the same, Beiras region. Bairrada is named for its limestone-rich clay soils, 'bairro' being the Portuguese for 'clay'. In the mid 18th century, Bairrada wine was being passed off as Port or blended with Port, and so the Marquês de Pombal, First Minister of Portugal, dramatically ordered the uprooting of all the vines in Bairrada. Today, the region is still recovering from this near-fatal insult. The principal grape variety in Bairrada is the late-ripening Baga. The early advent of autumn rains in this maritime region can pose a threat to the Baga harvest, which often needs to be brought in early to avoid rot. Baga wines are deeply coloured, highly acidic, and very tannic, with dominant notes of peppery blackcurrant fruit. They are sometimes made less astringent through blending with

Touriga Nacional and other grape varieties, including international varieties such as Merlot and Pinot Noir. The best can develop considerable complexity with age. Other black grape varieties in Bairrada include Castelão (Periquita) and Rufete. White wine, often sparkling, is also made, principally from Fernão Pires (Maria Gomes) and Bical (Borrado das Moscaos, 'Fly Droppings').

Ribatejo

The Ribatejo ('banks of the Tagus') lies to the northeast of Lisbon. The DOC is divided into six sub-regions, each of which can append its name to the appellation. The climate is warm and dry, but tempered by the river. Most vineyards lie on the flat, fertile valley floor; high yields often dilute quality, and the best wines originate from stonier soils outside the floodplain. The most notable black grape variety is Castelão (Periquita), which, at its best, can yield structured, long-lived wines with crisp acidity and notes of red berries, spice, and game. International grape varieties are also planted but fall outside the DOC. The most notable white grape varieties are Fernão Pires, Arinto, and Trincadeira-das-Pratas.

Alentejo

Alentejo ('Beyond the Tagus') is a large DOC in southeastern Portugal. The region is especially noted for its cork production. The climate is hot and dry, with a mere ~600mm (24in) annual rainfall. The undulating plains present a range of soils, including granite, schist, and clay. Alentejo is making a name for its rich and yet soft red wines: 'New World wines from the Old World'. The most notable black grape varieties are Tinta Amarela (Trincadeira), Tempranillo (Aragonez), and Castelão (Periquita). Tinta Amarela wines are dark and jammy, with good acidity and high alcohol and notes of raspberries, plums, herbs, chocolate, and coffee. The use of French, American, and Portuguese oak is on the increase. The most notable white grape varieties are Roupeiro, Antão Vaz, and Arinto, the latter often blended to add acidity. International grape varieties such as Cabernet Sauvignon and Syrah are also planted. Alentejo is divided into eight sub-regions, each of which can append its name to the appellation.

Chapter 21

Fortified Wines

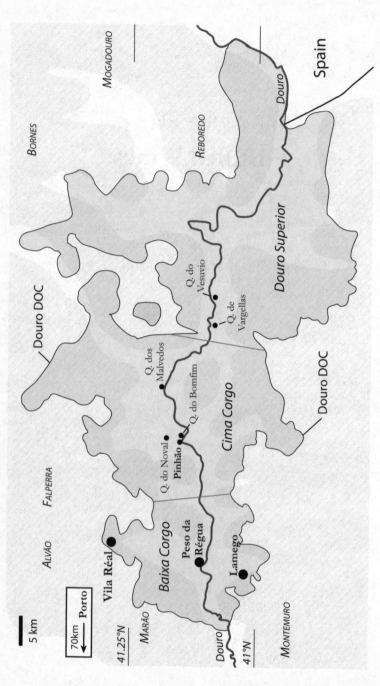

The Douro Valley

Port

Port is a fortified, typically red and sweet, wine that is made in a number of styles. It is produced in a demarcated region in the Douro Valley in northern Portugal, inland from the eponymous city of Porto (Oporto).

Non-fortified wine has been made in the Douro Valley since Roman times, and became an important export in the aftermath of the creation of the Kingdom of Portugal in 1143. The 1386 Treaty of Windsor established close trading and diplomatic links between England and Portugal, with many English merchants settling in Portugal and exporting wines back to England from Viana do Castelo on the broad estuary of the River Lima. These light and astringent wines came from the nearby Minho region, and compared poorly to the more expensive wines of Bordeaux.

In 1667, Colbert, first minister to Louis XIV, restricted the import of English goods into France, provoking Charles II to prohibit the import of French wines. The English merchants at Viana do Castelo stepped in to fill the gap in supply. To satisfy English tastes, they began sourcing more robust, full-bodied wines from the then remote upper Douro Valley. As they could not transport these wines overland to Viana do Castelo, they relocated a few miles south to Porto near the mouth of the River Douro.

The trade in the wines of Porto or 'Port wines' received a further fillip from the Methuen Treaty of 1703, which, among other things, lowered the duty on Portuguese wines exported to England. Port wines soon became a victim of their own success, with some producers and shippers enriching their often thin, overstretched offerings with sugar or elderberry. In 1756 (just one year after the cataclysmic Lisbon earthquake) these problems together with a resulting fall in demand impelled the then prime minister of Portugal the Marquês de Pombal to regulate production. This led to the demarcation of the Douro vineyard area by 335 stone pillars (*marcos pombalinos*), and, in the following year, to a classification of the vineyards according to quality.

Shippers sometimes added a small amount of brandy or grape spirit to stabilize Port wine on its voyage to England. Over time, it became common practice to add the brandy before the wine had finished fermenting as this resulted in a fresher, sweeter, and more appealing wine. The fortified wines benefited from a vastly superior ageing potential, and, as bottles became progressively more elongated, it became possible to store them on their side and cellar the wines. 1820 produced such an exceptional vintage that subsequent vintages had to be fortified simply to hold comparison, and by 1850 the practice of fortification had become near universal.

During the occupation of Porto by Napoleon's army from 1809 to 1811, the Port trade came to a virtual standstill. Trading also suffered from political turmoil in the 1820s and early 1830s, which culminated in the Portuguese Civil War and the 1832 Siege of Porto. Having withstood these setbacks, the Port trade flourished in the latter part of the 19th century, and it is in this period that it became customary to 'declare' the finest vintages. These Halcyon years came to an abrupt end in 1868 with the arrival of phylloxera, which ruined several long established producers. The Port trade did not fully recover until the 1890s, by which time most vines (with the notable exception of vines in the Nacional area of Quinta do Noval) had been grafted onto phylloxera-resistant American rootstocks. The delapidated small terraces (*mortórios*) were abandoned in favour of wider and steeper terraces that allowed for a higher planting density.

Until well into the 20th century, Port was carried downriver to the cellars of Vila Nova de Gaia (just across the river from Porto) on flat-bottomed vessels called *barcos rabelos*. To navigate the treacherous rapids, the *barcos rabelos* were equipped with a long steering oar operated from the top of a raised platform. A broad sail enabled them to make the return journey upriver, although in places they required assistance from oxen straining on a towpath. Historically, a waterfall in a narrow gorge had obstructed passage into the remote Douro Superior. The opening of this gorge to river traffic in the 1780s led to the establishment of some of the finest Douro estates. Today, the Douro has been dammed and is comparatively easy to navigate, but Port is sent to sea by road rather than river. The last commercial voyage of a *barco rabelo* took place in about 1961.

The lie of the land

The Douro (Duero in Spanish) is one of the most important rivers of the Iberian Peninsula, flowing almost 900km (560mi) through northern

Spain and Portugal to its mouth at Porto. The Douro delimited area or *vinhateiro* in northeastern Portugal is blocked off from any moderating Atlantic influence by the Marão and Montemuro Mountains to the northwest. The climate is continental with cold winters and hot and arid summers, with annual rainfall in the Douro Superior only a small fraction of that in Porto. Whatever rainfall there is tends to be concentrated in the spring and autumn, and the timing of the autumn rains (and even hail) can make or break a vintage.

Over time, the Douro has carved out the local schist and granite into a river valley with hills culminating at over 600m (1,969ft). The Douro *vinhateiro* can be divided into three sub-regions, the Baixo Corgo nearest Porto and the sea, the Cima Corgo or middle section, and the Douro Superior far inland and closest to the Spanish border. Some authors refer collectively to the Baixo Corgo and Cima Corgo as the Alto Douro, which is not to be confused with the Douro Superior. The Baixo Corgo enjoys the mildest climate and most rainfall, but its vineyards are not as reputed as those of the Cima Corgo and Douro Superior. The Cima Corgo, centred on the village of Pinhão, has the largest vineyard area and boasts many of the most celebrated vineyards such as Quinta do Noval, Quinta do Bomfim, and Quinta dos Malvedos. The Douro Superior is the hottest and driest of the three sub-regions, and also the least and last planted, but does boast some especially fine vineyards such as Quinta de Vargellas and Quinta do Vesúvio.

Of the 45,000ha under vines in the Douro, only ~26,000 are authorized for the production of Port, and the DOC produces just as much non-fortified as fortified wine (see Chapter 20). All in all, there are almost 40,000 growers, each with an average holding of 1ha across maybe three or four vineyard sites. The classification system for vineyard sites is run by the *Instituto dos Vinhos do Douro e Porto* (IVDP) and is similar to that operating in Champagne. Each vineyard site is graded from A to F on a complex system called the *cadastro* and then given an annual production quota called the *benefício*. The cadastro grading is based on a number of factors, among which altitude, aspect, yield, location, and soil type. The benefício is based not only on the cadastro grading but also on the quality of the vintage and the prevailing market conditions. Note that the IVDP classification system does not apply to non-fortified wines.

Generally speaking, the best vineyards of the Douro *vinhateiro* are to be found on sloping, schistous terrain converted into a series of horizontal terraces. In the 1970s, the traditional walled terraces or *socalcos* began to give way to so-called *patamares*, which are terraces cut by bulldozers and supported by earth banks. Each terraced level bears one or two rows of vines organized to permit some degree of mechanization. Higher density vertical planting permits the highest degree of mechanization, but is circumscribed to gentler slopes. Vines are trained low, with cordon training tending to replace the more common and traditional Guyot system. Average yield is ~30hl/ha and maximum permitted yield 55hl/ha.

Grape varieties

The grape varieties permitted for Port are often associated with small, dense fruit with intense and concentrated aromas. About 30 grape varieties are permitted, of which five are widely planted: Touriga Nacional, Touriga Franca (formerly Touriga Francesa), Tempranillo (Tinta Roriz), Tinta Barroca, and Tinta Cão. In selecting a grape variety, a grower seeks to match it to terroir and to balance quality with diversity. Single varietal Ports are rare, and older vineyards are still planted with a jumble of grape varieties. Touriga Nacional is the most highly regarded grape variety, but the yields obtained from its small, thick-skinned berries are restrictive and it is not as widely planted as Touriga Franca. Touriga Franca is heat and drought tolerant and so often planted on south-facing slopes. Both Touriga Nacional and Touriga Franca produce dark, concentrated wines with big tannins, but wines produced from Touriga Franca are softer and more aromatic. Tinta Roriz is the second most widely planted grape variety after Touriga Franca. It is associated with relatively high yields but is rather heat intolerant and best suited to cooler sites. It can take on great elegance and complexity with age. Less tannic than Tinta Roriz (and, of course, Touriga Franca and Touriga Nacional) is Tinta Barroca, which, like Tinta Roriz, is often planted on north-facing slopes, at altitude, or in cooler or shadier parts of the vineyard. It ripens early and produces soft, luscious, and fragrant wines. It is sometimes thought of as the Merlot of the Douro. Tinta Cão is particularly suited to the Douro's poor soils and hot and arid summers. It produces wines with great elegance and ageing potential, but yields are diminutive (1kg/vine versus 1.2kg for Touriga Nacional) and it is the least planted of the top five grape varieties.

Vinification

The grapes are hand-harvested at around 12-14 on the Baumé scale for the density of liquids (distilled water = 0). Only a small amount of Port is still produced by the traditional method of treading the grapes in square, three-foot high granite or cement tanks called *lagares*. Two hours of organized treading are followed by two hours of dancing in the lagar in what is in fact a very arduous and labour intensive process. The 'robotic lagar' with mechanical treading pistons first appeared in the late 1990s and, despite its alienating charmlessness, produces good results. After the four-hour crushing period, the wine ferments for 36-48 hours *in situ* in the lagar. The grape skins rise to the top of the lagar and are punched down with paddles so as to extract as much colour and tannin as possible. After about half the natural sugar has been converted into alcohol (leaving about 80-110g/l), the must is drawn off into large wooden or stainless steel vats and the fermentation is interrupted with 77% natural grape spirit (*aguardente*). Arguardente is added in a ratio of about 1:4, bringing the alcohol from ~6% to ~20%.

Since the early 1960s, most Port has been made by autovinification. The grapes are crushed mechanically and fermented in large stainless steel tanks, with the carbon dioxide produced forcing the juice from the bottom of the tank into a raised chamber from which it is sprayed over the cap. As with the traditional method, the must is drawn off into large wooden or stainless steel vats and the fermentation is interrupted by the addition of aguardente. An alternative or complement to autovinification is pumping over (*remontagem*), which only became possible with the arrival of a reliable electricity supply to the Douro. In the spring, the Port is transported downriver to the lodges of Vila Nova de Gaia to mature in the more temperate climes of the Atlantic coast and, in due course, to be evaluated and graded.

Styles

Port can be matured either oxidatively in wood or reductively in bottles. The four principal styles of reductive Port are Ruby, Late Bottled Vintage

(LBV), Crusted, and Vintage. Ruby is the most ubiquitous style of Port. It is a blend of the most recent harvests matured for no more than one to three years. Before bottling, it is fined and cold filtered and so does not require decanting. It is deep red in colour (whence its name), fresh and fruit-driven with a medium body and lesser tannins than Vintage Port. It is ready to drink upon release and does not tend to improve with age. Port labelled with 'Reserve' is essentially premium Ruby, sourced from better vineyards and matured for a longer period of four to six years. Compared to simple Ruby, it is richer, denser, and more complex.

LBV is a single vintage Port that is sourced from better vineyards and that spends four to six years in wood (considerably longer than Vintage Port, whence LBV). It used to be made only in non-vintage years from grapes that would otherwise have gone into the Vintage Port; today the main idea is to accelerate the maturation of a quality Port by exposing it to oxygen for several years longer than a Vintage Port. LBV is commonly fined and filtered prior to bottling, in which case it does not require decanting. Unfortunately, the process of filtering does strip the wine of some of its substance, and unfiltered LBVs derive greater benefit from bottle ageing. These unfiltered Traditional LBVs tend to be made in better years and must spend a further three years in bottle prior to release. Rather than a stoppered cork, they are capped with a conventional cork which is more conducive to bottle ageing.

Though the standard-bearer for the Douro, Vintage Port accounts for no more than 2% of total Port production. Needless to say, it must be made entirely from grapes of a declared vintage year. The decision to declare a full vintage is made by each individual Port house in the spring of the second year following the harvest. Historically, the most reputed Port houses have declared a full vintage about three times a decade. If a Port house does not declare a full vintage, it may still declare a top-quality single quinta. In non-vintage years, a Single Quinta Vintage Port is often declared so as to prevent the grapes from the best vineyards from going into a lesser Port. This is the case, for example, with Graham's Quinta dos Malvedos and Taylor's Quinta de Vargellas. Vintage Port is matured in wood for up to 30 months and often requires another 10-30 years in bottle before being ready to drink. Old Vintage Port is extremely rich, balanced, and complex, with aromas of cocoa, coffee, cedar, spice, fennel, and liquorice.

Crusted Port is a blend of several recent vintages, with the date on the label pertaining to the year of bottling rather than the year of the vintage. Crusted Port spends at least three years in bottle and is ready to drink right from release, making it an affordable and undemanding alternative to Vintage Port. At the same time, it is also capable of improving with bottle age. As Crusted Port has not been filtered, it deposits copious sediment ('crust') and requires careful decanting. It is, in effect, a super-premium unfiltered Ruby Port that resembles Vintage Port in both style and substance.

The three styles of oxidative Port are Tawny, Colheita, and Garra-feira. Tawny refers to the oxidized, golden-brown hue that quality Port acquires from long maturation in small casks with frequent racking. So as to accelerate the ageing process, some Tawnies are aged in the baking hot Douro rather than the more temperate climes of Vila Nova de Gaia. Inexpensive Tawny Port is a blend of lighter Ruby Port and White Port, and tends to be pink rather than truly tawny in colour. In contrast, premium Tawny Port is made from high quality grapes not included in Vintage and Single Quinta Vintage Ports. It may be sold either with an indicated age (10, 20, 30, or 'more than 40' years) or simply as 'Old Tawny', typically about eight years old. Older Tawnies in particular can be incredibly complex and balanced, dominated by aromas of burnt toast, nuts, dried fruit, coffee, and the products of esterification. Colheita is essentially Tawny from a single vintage. Garrafeira, which is an uncommon style, is Port from a single vintage that has been matured oxidatively in wood for about three to six years and then reductively in large glass demijohns for at least a further eight years.

Port is not invariably red. White Port is made from white grape varieties, and ranges in style from dry to very sweet. White Port darkens with age, such that a very old white Port can be virtually impossible to distinguish from a very old red Port.

Industry

As in Champagne, the landscape is dominated by a large number of growers who sell on their grapes, must, or wine to a commercial winery. There are some 90 commercial wineries, most of which are heavily export-oriented. The dominant players on the export market are the Symington

Family (Dow, Graham, and Warre), the Fladgate Partnership (Taylor, Fonseca, Croft, and Delaforce), and Sogrape (Sandeman, Ferreira, and Ofley). In recent decades, France, Belgium, and the Netherlands have overtaken the UK in terms of volume, but the UK still remains the most important market for premium Port. In 2011 the UK accounted for ~1m of ~9m cases produced, including over half a million cases of premium Ports. In recent years, Port consumption in the UK has been in gentle decline. Port continues to be associated with fusty elitism or thought of solely in terms of a Christmas or after-dinner drink. In truth, Port can be very versatile and generally represents excellent value for money.

Madeira

The volcanic archipelago of Madeira lies about 600km (370mi) off the coast of Morocco. Discovered in 1419 by sailors in the service of Henry the Navigator, it became a regular port of call for ships bound for Africa, the Indies, and the Americas. Agriculture prospered, principally sugarcane, but also wheat and, of course, the vine. In 1478 the Duke of Clarence was convicted of high treason, and, according to tradition, was drowned in a butt of Malmsey wine from Madeira. The earliest Madeira wines were unfortified and had a bad habit of spoiling at sea. Sailors took to adding a small amount of distilled alcohol to stabilize the wines, a practice that had become routine by the mid 18th century (much earlier than for Port). One day, a ship that had sailed out across the Equator returned to Madeira with some leftover wine. Producers tasted this wine and found that the intense heat and constant movement of the sea voyage had had a beneficial effect on its taste. So-called *vinho da roda* ('round-trip wine') soon became very popular. To save on the phenomenal costs of shipping wine half way around the world and back, producers began heating and ageing the wines on Madeira itself, either on trestles or in special rooms called *estufas*. In 1852 the vineyards of Madeira were devastated by powdery mildew, and in 1872 by phylloxera. The industry had barely recovered when the Russian Revolution and American Prohibition cut off its most important markets. The American vines that had been imported in response to phylloxera began to take over the vineyards and quality plummeted. Madeira wine never recovered the prestige that it enjoyed in the late 18th century, when it had been used to toast the 1776 United States Declaration of Independence. Much as Marsala, it came to be regarded as little more than 'cooking wine'. Founded in 1979 in a bid to drive up quality, the *Instituto do Vinho da Madeira* (IVM) decreed that thenceforth Madeira could only be made from *Vitis vinifera* grapes. In 2006, the IVM merged to become the *Instituto do Vinho, do Bordado e do Artesanato da Madeira* (IVBAM) and continues to promote and incentivize the replanting of the traditional grape varieties. Some of its other remits are to fix harvest dates, control quality, and promote Madeira.

The lie of the land

The archipelago of Madeira consists of the inhabited islands of Madeira and Porto Santo and the uninhabited islands of Ilhas Desertas and Ilhas Selvagens. At 55 by 22km (34 by 14mi), Madeira is by far the largest island, with rugged, mountainous terrain and a peak altitude of 1,861m (6,106ft). The climate is subtropical with a mean temperature of 19°C (66°F), mild winters, hot summers, and high rainfall and humidity. Vineyards are mostly planted on man-made terraces of red and basaltic bedrock called *poios* and irrigated from historical irrigation channels called *levadas*. Given the high temperatures and humidity, rot is a constant threat, and vine canopies are frequently raised off the ground on trellises called *latadas*. There are ~4,500 growers cultivating ~600ha of vineyards, with rows of vines often interspersed with market vegetables.

Grape varieties

Madeira grape varieties are classified as either 'permitted' or 'recommended', with almost all Madeira being made from the latter. Recommended grape varieties include Sercial, Verdelho, Bual, and Malvasia (Malmsey). Sercial and Verdelho do best at higher altitudes, and Bual and Malvasia at lower altitudes. Terrantez and Bastardo (which, in contrast to the other five, is a black grape variety) are both extremely rare. All six are varieties of *Vitis vinifera*. From 1993, a bottle labelled with any one grape variety must contain at least 85% of that variety. Broadly speaking, Sercial is dry, Verdelho off-dry or medium dry, Bual medium rich, and Malmsey rich. Madeira that does not bear a grape variety on the label or that predates 1993 is likely to have been made mostly or entirely from Tinta Negra Mole (TNM), a black grape variety that is often described as the workhorse of Madeira. After phylloxera hit in the late 19th century, producers turned to TNM for its disease resistance and prolific yields; today, it still accounts for well over half of total production. TNM is a chameleon that, at best, can imitate if not quite match the quality of the other, noble grape varieties.

Vinification

The harvest is mostly manual, with Malvasia picked first and Verdelho and Sercial last. The grapes are crushed, pressed, and fermented in stainless steel tanks or oak casks. Malvasia and Bual are traditionally fermented on their skins to extract more phenols and balance the high residual sugar. As with Port, fermentation is interrupted with 95% grape spirit. The precise timing of interruption depends on the amount of residual sugar desired, so, for example, very early for Malmsey and very late for Sercial.

Next comes the idiosyncratic *estufagem* process that seeks to reproduce the effects of a long, tropical sea voyage. The fortified wine is entered into a lined concrete vat or stainless steel container. It is then gently heated to 45-55°C (113-131°F) and maintained at this temperature for at least three months. After a rest period of three more months, it is entered into oak casks and aged and oxidized for 3-15 years. Finally, the individual wines are blended, often across several vintages, to produce a consistent and harmonious house style. Unlike with Port, the indicated age pertains to the youngest wine in the blend.

A more expensive alternative to *estufagem* is *canteiro*. The fortified wine is entered into 480l pipes or casks that are then placed on a beam (or *canteiro*) in the roof of a south-facing room for 20-100+ years. Five years of *canteiro* is equivalent to only three months of *estufa*, and so *canteiro* is used only for the very finest wines. Compared to *estufa*, *canteiro* is a gentler process that results in less caramelization and more freshness and fruitiness. The world is just incredible, isn't it? You just couldn't make this stuff up.

Styles

Madeira must be made from *Vitis vinifera* grape varieties, which account for just over half of vineyard plantings on Madeira. Of these, TNM is the most commonly planted, and is often an important component of a brand name such as Blandy's Duke of Clarence. Plantings of the four noble grape varieties remain small, and Madeira labelled with one of the noble grape varieties is relatively expensive. Sercial is pale in colour with aromas of almond and citrus fruit, razor sharp acidity and a drying finish. In comparison, Verdelho is less dry and more rounded with a smoky complexity and aromas of dried fruits, honey, and maybe a touch of caramel. Bual is still darker in colour and fuller in body, with aromas of dried fruits, orange peel, caramel, molasses, and coffee. Malmsey is a little lighter in colour than Bual, luscious, and distinguishable from PX Sherry by the high and balancing acidity that is the mark of quality Madeira. Malmsey is extremely long-lived, and can keep for a century or more.

The age of a Madeira is indicated on the label: either three years (Finest), five years (Reserve), 10 years (Old Reserve), 15 years (Extra Reserve), or more than 20 years (Vintage). Very old vintages may make mention of a solera system (see later), in which case the stated year is that of the establishment of the solera. Despite its name, Finest is usually destined for cooking. Madeira with one of the noble grape varieties on the label must be aged for a minimum of five years (to Reserve), often without any artificial heating. Vintage is made from the harvest of an exceptional year, and must age for at least 20 years followed by a further two years in bottle. A more recent style is Colheita or Harvest, which is vintage-dated Madeira that has been aged for at least five years (or, in the case of Sercial, seven years) versus 20 years for Vintage. With increasing age the appearance of Madeira tends towards mahogany with a yellow-green rim, which, together with high acidity, can help to distinguish it from other fortified wines.

Industry

The largest producer of Madeira is the Madeira Wine Company (MWC), which includes Blandy and many other brands. In 1989, the

Symington family acquired a controlling stake in the MWC. In 2011, it sold most of this stake back to the Blandy Group, which thereby regained overall control. Other than the MWC, there are only a small handful of Madeira producers. The principal market for Madeira is the EU, which in 2011 accounted for 81% of the 3.01m litres of Madeira produced. The largest national markets are France, Portugal, the UK, and Germany, even though much of the Madeira exported to France is of the cooking variety. In 2011, the UK imported 306,000 litres of Madeira. Sales over recent years have been stagnant at best.

Vins Doux Naturels

Vins doux naturels (VDNs) designate French fortified wines that are made by *mutage*, that is, by arresting fermentation with 95% grape spirit. This fortifies the wine to at least 15%, usually about 15-18%, and retains any unfermented sugars. It is, of course, the same process by which Port and Madeira are made. VDNs fall under the umbrella EU term of *vin de liqueur*, which designates all fortified wines including those, called mistelles, which have not undergone any fermentation prior to the addition of grape spirit. Mistelles are lacking in secondary fermentation characteristics and taste primarily of spirit and grape juice. There are a number of VDNs with an AOC in southern France, with most being made—albeit in different styles—from Grenache or Muscat. Their spiritual home is the Catalan region of Roussillon, where the 13th century physician and alchemist Arnaldus de Villa Nova perfected the process of mutage.

Rivesaltes

Rivesaltes AOC and Muscat de Rivesaltes AOC cover the same, very large, delimited area centred upon Rivesaltes in the Roussillon. Muscat de Rivesaltes AOC must be made from either Muscat Blanc à Petits Grains or Muscat of Alexandria. Once fortified, Muscat de Rivesaltes is protected from oxidation so as to preserve its fresh, citrusy, grapey, Muscat aromas. Rivesaltes AOC can be either red or white. Red Rivesaltes is made from Grenache, which may be blended with Grenache Gris, Grenache Blanc, Macabeo (Macabeu), and Tourbat. White Rivesaltes is made from these latter four, and may also include up to 20% of Muscat Blanc à Petits Grains and Muscat of Alexandria. A large number of different styles of Rivesaltes are produced: Grenat, Ambré, Tuilé, Hors d'Age, and Rancio. Aside from the blend of grape varieties, the most important differentiating parameters are oak ageing and oxidative handling. The Rancio style, which calls upon extended oxidative ageing in oak, is especially prized for its rich, complex, and delicate aromas of nuts, raisins, dried figs, dried dates, and coffee.

Banyuls

Banyuls AOC is a small area in Roussillon tucked between the Spanish border and the Mediterranean Sea and centred upon the small and beautiful fishing port of Banyuls, birthplace of the Catalan sculptor and painter Aristide Maillol. Banyuls AOC must contain at least 50% Grenache, rising to 75% for Banyuls Grand Cru AOC. This may be blended with Grenache Gris, Grenache Blanc, Macabeo (Macabeu), Tourbat, and/or Muscat along with a maximum of 10% Syrah, Cinsault, and/or Carignan. Harvest typically takes place in October, with the grapes having partially shrivelled on the vine. The must is fortified while still on the skins, after which it is left to macerate for several weeks. Banyuls must spend at least 12 months in oak and Banyuls Grand Cru 30 months, with these minima very often exceeded. The wines may also be aged in 20l glass flagons (*bonbonnes*) exposed to the sun. As with Rivesaltes, a number of styles are produced, including Rancio and Solera. The aromas of baked fruits, prunes, and coffee associated with Banyuls can sometimes be difficult to distinguish from those of Port; however, Banyuls tends to be lower in alcohol, typically 16% versus 20%. Note that the dry, unfortified wines produced in this same region fall under Collioure AOC.

Maury

Like Banyuls AOC, Maury AOC is an enclave within Rivesaltes AOC. It is centred upon the town of Maury in the Agly Valley inland from

Perpignan. In contrast to most of the Roussillon, the soils here are rich in schist. The red wines consist of at least 75% Grenache, with Grenache Gris, Grenache Blanc, Macabeo (Macabeu), Carignan, and/ or Syrah making up any remainder. The white wines consist of the very same grape varieties that go into making white Rivesaltes. Both the red and white wines must be aged in oak for at least 12 months. The red wines are similar to those of Banyuls but deeper in colour and more tannic, and do not quite achieve the same degree of finesse. Production is greater than that of Banyuls and dominated by the co-operative Les Vignerons de Maury. The leading independent producer is Mas Amiel.

Saint-Jean-de-Minervois

The Languedoc is home to four appellations of fortified Muscat: Saint-Jean-de-Minervois, Lunel, Frontignan, and Mireval. Saint-Jean-de-Minervois stands out by its elevated position at the southern end of the Massif Central, with grapes ripening a full three weeks later than in the other three, more coastal appellations. This, combined with poorer, better draining soils, results in a finer wine with more complex and delicate aromas. Saint-Jean-de-Minervois is entirely made from Muscat Blanc à Petits Grains. It is gold in colour with honeyed aromas of citrus fruits, orange blossom, apricot, and lychee, an alcohol of 15%, and around 125g/l of residual sugar.

Beaumes de Venise

This Southern Rhône appellation produces a VDN entirely from Muscat Blanc à Petits Grains that is similar to, and even finer than, Saint-Jean-de-Minervois. In his *Natural History*, the 1st century naturalist Pliny the Elder wrote that 'the Muscat grape has been grown for a long time in Beaumes and its wine is remarkable'. The vineyards are located in the Vaucluse around the foot of the Dentelles de Montmirail, a vertical comb of rock that reflects the sun's rays back onto the appellation's better vineyards. There is a touch less residual sugar than in Saint-Jean-de-Minervois, which makes for a more refreshing, elegant wine.

Sherry

'Sherry' is an English corruption of Jerez, an Andalusian city on the Atlantic seaboard near the crossing of the seas. The major centres of the Sherry trade are Jerez de la Frontera, El Puerto de Santa María, and Sanlúcar de Barrameda. Although Sherry comes in a number of distinct styles, it is—with the single exception of Pedro Ximénez—invariably made from the Palomino grape. Unlike, say, Port or Madeira, Sherry is not fortified by mutage but only once fermentation has been completed. It is then matured in a solera system involving a continuous process of fractional blending across several vintages (see later).

According to the 1st century Greek geographer Strabo, the Phoenicians and founders of nearby Cádiz planted the vine in the region of Xera as far back as 1100BC. By the time the Romans took over from the Carthaginians in 206BC, the region that they renamed Ceret had already acquired a reputation for its winemaking. Under the Arabic name of Šeriš ('Sherish'), it continued to produce wine throughout the Moorish occupation of 711-1264, with vineyards being maintained for trade, raisins, medicinal purposes, and other pretexts.

During the reign of Henry VIII, Anglo-Spanish relations deteriorated (think Catherine of Aragon), and exports of Sherry (or 'sack') to England declined. In 1587, Sir Francis Drake captured the harbour of Cádiz together with 2,900 pipes of Sherry destined for South America. Drake had the pipes delivered to Queen Elizabeth, and Sherry returned to favour in England. In *Henry IV*, Shakespeare has Falstaff say, 'If I had a thousand sons, the first humane principle I would teach them should be, to forswear thin potations and to addict themselves to sack'. However, at that time sack was still unfortified and in other ways quite unlike modern Sherry.

The War of the Spanish Succession (1701-1714) and later Napoleonic Wars (1799-1815) together with the increasing popularity of Port left many Sherry merchants with a large excess of stock. This Sherry sat and aged in oak barrels, which the merchants regularly topped up with younger wines. In this proto solera system, the Sherry began to acquire characteristics of ageing and oxidation under a layer of flor yeast, the growth of which had been stimulated by the repeated addition of the younger wines. Taking a leaf from their rivals in the Douro, the merchants began experimenting with fortification, which sometimes had the effect of killing off the flor and promoting further oxidation—resulting in yet another style of Sherry.

Throughout the 19th century, Sherry struggled to compete with poor imitations from France, Germany, and across the seas. Then, at the close of the century, phylloxera took its toll and the vineyards required replanting. Despite the creation of the appellation in 1935 and subsequent efforts to protect and promote it, sales have struggled to take off, with Sherry seemingly unable to kick off its 'cheap and fusty' image.

The lie of the land

The climate in Jerez is Mediterranean with 300 days of sunshine a year and only 600mm (24in) of rainfall. The mean annual temperature is a balmy 18°C (64°F). Summer highs often exceed 30°C (86°F), and the southeasterly *levante*, which picks up in North Africa, periodically delivers temperatures of around 40°C (104°F). At the same time, Atlantic breezes can exert a cooling effect of as much as 10°C on more coastal areas. Climatic differences within the Jerez are such that flor in coastal Sanlúcar de Barrameda thrives all year round, whereas that in inland Jerez de la Frontera, with its hotter summers and colder winters, mostly thrives in the spring and autumn, leaving the wine partially exposed to oxygen in the summer and winter. During the parched summer months, the vines are kept alive by the region's white, reflective albariza soils. Albariza is a unique compact of chalk, clay, and sand that is able to store up moisture and release it throughout the hot, arid summer. An additional source of summer moisture is the *blanduras*, very fine dews that form in certain areas of the Jerez.

In the wake of phylloxera, the number of grape varieties planted declined from over one hundred to just three: Palomino, Pedro Ximénez, and Muscat (Moscatel), with most outcrops of albariza replanted with Palomino. These outcrops of albariza are designated as Jerez Superior, and cluster around Jerez de la Frontera with smaller patches around Sanlúcar de Barrameda, Puerto de Santa Maria, and a number of other centres. Of the ~9,000ha under vine, ~90% are designated as Jerez Superior. The other soil types are barros, which is dark brown with a high ferruginous clay content, and arenas, which is yellowish with a high sand content. Pedro Ximénez, which is harder to cultivate and less productive than Palomino, tends to be planted on lesser albariza and barros. Moscatel tends to be planted on barros and arenas, especially around Chipiona.

Jerez counts 2,900 growers working in individual vineyards (*pagos*) that vary enormously in size, with the larger ones best regarded not as vineyards but as entire areas or sub-regions. Palomino accounts for over 90% of plantings in the Jerez delimited area. It is a high-yielding variety, although DO regulations do stipulate a maximum yield of 80hl/ha. Vines are planted at a density of around 4,000 vines/ha, typically on gently sloping ground, and are either free standing (*en vaso* or *en cabeza* with the head of the vine trained downwards) or, increasingly, wire trained. In either case, the vines are pruned according to the *vara y pulgar* or 'stick and thumb' method. This is similar to the Guyot system, with a single cane of some seven buds and a short replacement cane of a couple of buds.

Method of production

The aroma profile of Palomino is fairly neutral and the grape variety can be thought of as a blank canvas for expressing the method and skill of the winemaker. The grapes are hand-harvested during September and usually destemmed prior to pressing. The first press (*primera yema*) accounts for 65% of the maximum extraction of 72.5l/100kg, and tends to go into making finos. Any subsequent presses go into making olorosos, light wines, or even brandy or vinegar. The more delicate the must, the more likely it is to go into making finos, with the most delicate musts coming from albariza soils in cooler coastal areas. The musts are low in acidity, for which reason tartaric acid is often added at this stage together with the selected yeast culture.

Fermentation takes place in temperature-controlled stainless steel vats, with must destined for finos fermented at a cooler temperature. Fermentation may also take place in traditional American oak butts (600-650l barrels), not so much to impart oak flavours as to season the butts for later use as maturation vessels. In either case, the end result is a fairly non-descript pale, dry wine with an alcohol of 11-12%. This *añada* (young or single vintage) wine is fortified and placed, unblended, into clean butts which are filled to about 5/6 so as to facilitate either oxidative ageing or biological ageing under flor. After 6-12 months, the cellar master or *capataz* reassesses the wines for style and quality. The presence of a thick, healthy layer of flor—most notably *S. beticus*—confirms that a wine is able to continue its life as a fino. Otherwise, it continues as an oloroso.

Flor only forms if the alcohol ranges from 14.5 to 16%, for which reason wines destined to become finos are fortified to 15 to 15.5%. Under these conditions, flor yeasts metabolize aerobically, not only breaking down alcohol but also yielding acetaldehyde and other compounds that account for the characteristic aromas of dry finos. Flor yeasts also metabolize glycerol, which helps to explain the light body and intense dryness of finos. If the alcohol drops below 14.5%, the flor yeasts begin to produce acetic acid, turning the wine into vinegar. This can be prevented by entering the wine into a traditional oak butt and then into a solera: the butt allows just enough evaporation to maintain the right level of alcohol, with the solera periodically providing the flor with a supply of fresher, more alcoholic and nutrient-rich wines. Temperature is also important, which is why flor thrives all year round in coastal Sanlúcar de Barrameda but seasonally recedes in Jerez de la Frontera. To maintain temperatures within the ideal range of 15-20°C (59-68°F), traditional bodegas are built with high roofs and aligned so as to funnel the prevailing sea breeze.

In contrast to finos, olorosos are aged in a deliberately oxidative style and may be left in solera for a decade or more. In some cases, they may even be left outside under the hot sun. In time, they turn brown in colour and develop characteristic nutty aromas. Gentle evaporation during the ageing process results in a high alcohol of up to 24% for older olorosos. This dry oloroso is commonly sweetened with wine made from sun-dried Pedro Ximénez or Moscatel. The sweetest style, 'cream', was created by Harvey's of Bristol for the British market; though not highly regarded by the cognoscenti, Harvey's Bristol Cream still remains the best selling Sherry label. 'Pale cream' refers either to cream that has been discolored by charcoal treatment or to a fino that has been sweetened with concentrated grape must (*arrope*).

A solera is a fractional blending system that consists of stacked rows of oak butts in which older wines 'teach' younger wines to take on their refined character. After having been assessed for style and quality, the *añada* wine is poured into the top row or *criadera* of barrels, which are filled to about 5/6 of total capacity so as to facilitate either oxidative ageing or biological ageing under flor. Wine for bottling is withdrawn from the bottom *criadera*, which is (confusingly) also called the *solera*. This draws down the wine from upper rows such that it is blended both vertically across vintages and horizontally across barrels, with the end result being a consistent yet highly complex wine. Although pumps and pipes have been introduced, the process remains highly labour intensive. A maximum of one third of the wine in a butt on the solera level may be withdrawn at any one time, and only three times in any given year. This ensures than any Sherry inevitably contains a small amount of stuff dating back to the foundation of the solera—in some cases, more than 200 years ago. While it is impossible to put a date on a Sherry, the finest specimens can spend several decades ageing in solera. The designations *Vinum Optimum Signatum* (Very Old Sherry, VOS) and *Vinum Optimum Rare Signatum* (Very Rare Old Sherry, VORS) designate blends that are, respectively, at least 20 and 30 years old. Finos require a high flow of nutrients to aliment the flor, such that large amounts of wine (often the maximum) need to be withdrawn from the solera level. Thus, soleras for finos often have up to 14 *criaderas* compared to just three or four for olorosos—which, for the finest, may only move by some 5% a year.

Prior to bottling, Sherry undergoes cold stabilization to remove tartrate crystals. Fino wines are also filtered or fined with egg white to remove yeast cells.

Styles

Prior to bottling, a true fino spends its entire life under flor. It is pale, elegant, and dry, with a final alcohol of about 15.5%. A fino that spends some time under flor followed by a period of oxidative ageing is called an amontillado. This style results if the flor dies down, either naturally after a number of years or by deliberate fortification. Such 'true' amontillados may be aged in dedicated soleras, and should be distinguished from mere blends of fino and oloroso. True amontillados are yellow-brown in colour, with rich nutty notes yet a finer, lighter body than olorosos. An amontillado that has undergone only a short period of oxidative ageing is called a fino amontillado.

After having been assessed for style and quality, an *añada* wine with flor development may be fortified to about 17% and 'redirected' to age oxidatively. The end result is a palo cortado, an uncommon style with the body of an oloroso but the aromas and finesse of an amontillado.

Most fino hails from inland Jerez de la Frontera, where it undergoes a small degree of oxidation as the flor recedes in the summer and winter. This is less the case in Sanlúcar de Barrameda and Puerto de Santa María. A fino from Sanlúcar is called a manzanilla, and can also fall under the DO of Manzanilla de Sanlúcar de Barrameda. Manzanilla pasada, manzanilla amontillada, and manzanilla olorosa are the Sanlúcar equivalents of fino amontillado, amontillado, and oloroso, each with increasing degrees of oxidative ageing. A fino from Puerto de Santa María is called a Puerto fino, with a character between that of Jerez fino and manzanilla.

The greatest incarnations of the above styles are all dry, but many commercial styles are sweetened with wine made from sun-dried Pedro Ximénez or, less commonly, Moscatel—or else with concentrated grape must. The original example is Harvey's Bristol Cream.

Finally, there is a wine made from 100% Pedro Ximénez and called Pedro Ximénez or simply PX. Very little Pedro Ximénez is grown in Jerez DO, with most of it being legally imported from the nearby DO of Montilla-Moriles. The grapes are picked late and then left on straw mats for 1-2 weeks to raisin further. Once fermented, the wine is fortified and entered into a solera for oxidative ageing. The end result is one of the world's finest fortified dessert wines: a dark, syrupy, intensely sweet wine redolent of raisins and molasses, and just perfect with (or on) a scoop of vanilla ice cream.

Chapter 22

New Zealand

New Zealand: North Island

100 km

North Island

40°S

Cook Strait

Nelson
Blenheim

Marlborough

Tasman Sea

Waipara

*SOUTHERN
ALPS*

Canterbury
Christchurch

Timaru

Queenstown

Waitaki Valley
Oamaru

Central Otago

Dunedin

Pacific Ocean

45°S

Stewart Island

New Zealand: South Island

The vine arrived in New Zealand in the early 19th century, borne across the seas by English missionaries. Since then, the story of New Zealand wine has been one of chronic stagnation capped by a sudden and spectacular ascent. In the wake of phylloxera, growers neglected to graft their European vines onto American rootstocks, preferring instead to plant inferior American vines. A decline in quality together with a number of cultural, economic, and legislative obstacles impeded the growth of the wine industry, and, for a long time, most of the wine produced was being either fortified or distilled. Following the UK's entry into the EEC in 1973, New Zealand could no longer rely on exports of lamb, beef, and dairy products to the former colonial power. As the economy diversified, viticulture grew in importance. At about the same time, some deregulation of pubs and restaurants and a surge in international travel led to a transformation in domestic attitudes to wine. In 1973, on advice from University of California, Davis, Montana planted Sauvignon Blanc in Marlborough, and, within a generation, the region boasted one of the world's most celebrated wine styles. Dr Richard Smart, the government viticulturalist in the 1980s, inaugurated a more scientific approach to viticulture with effective canopy management becoming standard practice. Technological expertise honed in the dairy industry led to improvements in winemaking, in particular, cool fermentation in stainless steel tanks. These changes led to the clean, fresh, and punchy style of Sauvignon Blanc for which New Zealand has become famous. By the mid-1990s, both Sauvignon Blanc and Chardonnay had overtaken the unexciting Müller-Thurgau, which had been widely planted under the misguided notion that growing conditions in New Zealand resembled those in Germany. Today, Sauvignon Blanc accounts for just over half the country's ~33,000ha under vines, an area that is still growing very fast. Other grape varieties, notably Chardonnay and Pinot Noir, and, more recently, Riesling and Pinot Gris, have also been established. Consolidation of existing wine regions and development of new ones is still ongoing with winemakers busy matching grape varieties, clones, and rootstocks to the country's diverse soils and climates. Their journey so far has been nothing short of astonishing.

The lie of the land

Although only about half the area of France, New Zealand spans 12 degrees of latitude from 34° to 46°S. The vine is planted along most of the length of the country, a distance more or less equivalent to that separating Lugano from south of Tunis. The climate is considerably cooler than the latitude range might suggest owing to the moderating influence of the Pacific Ocean and chilly southerlies that travel unimpeded from Antarctica. Central Otago, nestled in the Southern Alps and blocked off from the prevailing winds, is the country's only truly continental viticultural region.

Climate

Overall, the South Island is considerably cooler and more temperate than the North Island, the northern part of which is subtropical. The prevailing winds are westerly such that the east coast is drier than the west coast. Marlborough, which lies in a rain shadow, is the country's sunniest wine region and can be affected by drought. Irrigation is unregulated, but ambitious producers use it only sparingly. Owing to the hole in the ozone layer, sunlight can be harsh, and canopy management aims in part to reduce ultraviolet burning of the fruit. Frosts too have become a problem over the last decade, with cold spells exacerbated by deforestation in areas such as Marlborough that have undergone a rapid expansion in vineyard area.

Soils

In stark contrast to Australia, which lies over 1,400km (870mi) across the Tasman Sea, New Zealand is one of Earth's youngest landmasses. Its position on a tectonic boundary gives rise to its mountainous spine and to frequent seismic and volcanic activity. Vineyard soils predominantly consist of free-draining deposits of greywacke gravel brought down from the mountains by braided rivers. The country's most renowned gravel vineyards include Gimblett Gravels in Hawke's Bay and the

Wairau and Awatere Valleys in Marlborough. The Waitaki Valley in northeast Otago and Waipara in North Canterbury are the only wine regions with significant limestone deposits. In many areas, the combination of fertile soils and humid conditions promotes the growth of foliage, with the principal function of canopy management being to ensure that sunlight can percolate to the grapes.

Regions

North Island: Auckland

Auckland is New Zealand's largest city, and the wine region can be taken to include the Northland district extending to the northernmost tip of the island. The subtropical climate is associated with disease pressure throughout the year and potential dilution of grape sugars at harvest time. However, ample cloud cover protects the grapes from the scorching sun and drier sites are well suited to Cabernet Sauvignon and Syrah, which can struggle to ripen in other parts of the country. Some of the best terroirs are to the west of the city around the town of Kumeu and on the island of Waiheke. Kumeu is home to descendants of Croatian Dalmatian settlers such as the Brajkovich family of Kumeu River, which is particularly noted for its Chardonnays. Waiheke Island to the east of Auckland is drier than the mainland, enabling the late-ripening Cabernet Sauvignon to thrive. The soils are more clay than gravel, and, accordingly, Merlot is also planted. Waiheke produces arguably the country's finest Bordeaux blends, and the Stonyridge and Man o' War wineries are especially reputed. Syrah too is making inroads. Of particular note is that the average Auckland estate is a mere 2ha, around one hundred times smaller than in Marlborough.

North Island: Gisborne and Hawke's Bay

Gisborne occupies the eastern extremity of the North Island and can boast the world's most easterly vineyards. With fertile loam soils and plenty of sunshine, yields are high and harvests early. The region is dominated by white wine production, especially Chardonnay, which is made in a distinctive tropical Gisborne style. Gisborne is also noted for its fragrant Gewurztraminers and Viogniers. Further south around the twin towns of Napier and Hastings is the Hawke's Bay region, which is the second most important by vineyard area. The region is sheltered from the prevailing winds by mountains and also benefits from abundant sunshine and cooling sea breezes. The soils are a complex mosaic ranging from fertile loam to poorer alluvial gravels. The most noted area in the region is Gimblett Gravels, a former riverbed of deep, free-draining greywacke gravel. The favourable climate and diverse soil types give rise to a variety of wine styles, first among which are Bordeaux blends. Although Cabernet Sauvignon is planted on warmer gravel deposits, it does not always achieve full ripeness, and the Bordeaux blends tend to be dominated by Merlot. Syrah is a relative latecomer, with a recognized expression that is distinct from its counterparts in Australia and the Rhône. Among the white wines, Chardonnay and Sauvignon Blanc predominate. Pinot Blanc, Cabernet Franc, and other grape varieties are also planted.

North Island: Wairarapa and Martinborough

Wairarapa is much smaller than Marlborough across the Cook Strait, and dominated by small producers intent on quality. Martinborough, the principal town, lends its name to the area that produces the country's most celebrated Pinot Noirs. The climate is similar to that of Marlborough, if slightly warmer. The Rimutaka Range protects the region from the wet winds that batter the capital of Wellington, some 65km (40mi) to the west. Sunny summers with cool nights preserve freshness and acidity, while long and dry autumns promote phenolic ripeness. Summer drought can present a challenge, and limited irrigation is common. The soils are varied, with some of the finest vineyards on free-draining gravels overlain by silt loam. The conditions are ideal for Pinot Noir, which has come to account for more than half of plantings. Pioneers such as Ata Rangi, Te Kairanga, Dry River, and Martinborough Vineyard began planting Pinot Noir in the 1980s, and today their wines compete with those of Burgundy. Although eclipsed by Pinot Noir, Sauvignon Blanc accounts for a large minority of plantings, and Riesling, Pinot Gris, Gewurztraminer, and Chardonnay are also to be reckoned with.

South Island: Marlborough

First planted in 1973, Marlborough has come to account for over 60% of the country's vineyard area. The region lies in a rain shadow near the northern extremity of the South Island. The regional centre is Blenheim, and the main areas are the Wairau and Awatere river valleys. Long and sunny days, cool nights, and (often) dry autumns combine with alluvial topsoils and gravelly subsoils to provide next to ideal growing conditions. Spring frosts and summer droughts can present problems, and the use of drip irrigation is common. Compared to that in Wairau, the climate in Awatere is drier and cooler with a greater diurnal temperature range. Marlborough is, of course, especially reputed for its Sauvignon Blanc, which alone accounts for 75% of the region's vineyard area. Much of the output is rather generic, but quality producers such as Greywacke, Dog Point, Saint Clair, and Vavasour have a focus on single vineyard wines and even produce oaked Bordeaux-style cuvées. Marlborough is also New Zealand's largest producer of sparkling wine, mostly Champagne blends of Pinot Noir and Chardonnay. Cloudy Bay's Pelorus is a regional benchmark for traditional method Champagne blends, although some less ambitious producers prefer to use the cheaper tank method. Pinot Noir reds are distinguished for their lightness and freshness, which set them apart from those of Martinborough or Cental Otago. Aromatic grape varieties are also planted; especially noteworthy are sweet botrytized Riesling and dry, lean Pinot Gris.

South Island: Nelson

Nelson, to the northwest of Marlborough, is similar in size to Wairarapa but has yet to forge a distinct identity for itself. The climate is similar to that of Marlborough, if a touch cooler and wetter, with abundant sunshine in the lee of the Southern Alps and Tasman Mountains. The vineyards are planted on hilly slopes or flatlands on a variety of soils including both clay and alluvial loam. As in Marlborough, Sauvignon Blanc is the most planted grape variety, although the region also has a fine reputation for Pinot Noir and Chardonnay. The long autumns are ideal for late harvest sweet wines, which are made from Riesling and other grape varieties. The small, family-owned Neudorf winery is the region's star performer.

South Island: Canterbury and Waipara

Vineyards are planted on the vast Canterbury Plains around Christchurch and in the volcanic hills of Banks Peninsula, but the region's most exciting wine area is the Waipara valley, 70km (43mi) north of Christchurch. Waipara sits on a rare outcrop of limestone and is sometimes thought of as the Burgundy of the southern hemisphere. The Teviotdale Hills shelter Waipara from the cool easterly winds without however obstructing the warm and dry 'Nor'wester'. The climate is milder than that of Burgundy and indeed the Canterbury Plains, with warm summers and long autumns. Waipara is recognized for its Pinot Noir and Chardonnay, and is also making a name for its Riesling, with styles ranging from dry, lean, and mineral to ripe and sweet and low in alcohol (similar to Mosel Riesling). Pegasus Bay is a highly regarded producer, and relative newcomer Black Estate is developing an impressive focus on terroir. Away from the main valley floor, Bell Hill and Pyramid Valley both make some rather fine Pinot Noir.

South Island: Central Otago

Enclosed by the Southern Alps, Central Otago is the only truly continental climate region in New Zealand, with extreme seasonal and diurnal temperature variations. Although summers are short, they are hot and sunny and cede to a dry autumn. The best sites are on north-facing slopes with maximal sun exposure, and many vineyards are planted near the banks of the region's several lakes and rivers. The soils are mostly light loess, which, owing to steep inclines and poor water retention, often require irrigation. There are also some gravel deposits over a subsoil of schist. The region is especially reputed for its Pinot Noir, which accounts for the greater part of plantings. Felton Road, Mount Difficulty, and Rippon perhaps best exemplify the signature rich and velvety style. Harvests take place in mid-to-late April compared to late February or early March in the country's more northerly regions. To the northeast of Central Otago, near the town of Oamaru on the Pacific coast, is the limestone-rich Waitaki Valley, which is currently attracting a lot of prospective interest.

Wine styles

New Zealand's cool and yet overall sunny climate is hospitable to grape varieties such as Sauvignon Blanc, Pinot Noir, Chardonnay, and Riesling that are at home in northern France. Varieties such as Merlot, Cabernet Sauvignon, and Syrah have colonized a few warmer regions. In general, the New Zealand style is typified by bright, pure fruit flavours and zingy acidity.

Marlborough Sauvignon Blanc has become a benchmark for Sauvignon Blanc. It has a clean, pungent aroma that combines ripe fruit and fresh vegetal notes. A typical tasting note might include gooseberry, passion fruit, asparagus, fresh grass, and blackcurrant leaf. Acidity is high but somewhat disguised by a smooth texture and, often, a touch of residual sugar that contributes roundness rather than sweetness. The finest examples can boast a more 'serious' austerity, and, as in Bordeaux, may be fermented and matured in oak. Sauvignon Blanc from the North Island is often lighter in style and more driven by tropical fruit. Compared to Sauvignon Blanc from the Loire, Sauvignon Blanc from New Zealand is typically riper, higher in alcohol, and less chalky or mineral.

Ripe (although not tropical) fruit and high acidity are often the hallmarks of New Zealand Chardonnay. Typical notes are ripe apple and stone fruit, sometimes accompanied by a distinct yoghurt note. The finest examples exhibit Burgundian winemaking techniques, especially oak ageing, with American oak less common than it used to be. Chardonnay from the North Island is often riper, but it is hard to generalize.

When it comes to Riesling, New Zealand looks more to Europe than to Australia, with generally lighter and more delicate styles. The wines are typically crisp and clean with a fresh lime character, as opposed to the pungent lime cordial note of many Australian Rieslings. There are, however, a range of styles, including delicate, Mosel-like styles and late harvest dessert styles. The climate preserves Riesling's natural searing acidity. With some age, the best examples can develop appealing petrochemical notes.

New Zealand Pinot Gris is much closer to Alsatian Pinot Gris than to Italian Pinot Grigio. The wines are usually dry or off-dry with notes of fresh pear, apple, honeysuckle, and white pepper. The palate bears the oiliness of an Alsatian Pinot Gris, although often with more marked acidity. There may also be suggestions of lees stirring or barrel ageing. Pinot Gris is an emerging grape variety in New Zealand and, so far, most of it is of a high standard.

Ultra-clean fruit and high acidity are the hallmarks of New Zealand Pinot Noir. Most of the production is intended for youthful drinking, but more ambitious examples can develop notes of earth and game. Pinot Noir from Central Otago is deep violet in colour with notes of black fruit and cherry and, often, a hint of greenness. On the palate, the wine is full-bodied for Pinot Noir, often with a high alcohol and firm, round tannins. Marlborough Pinot Noir is lighter, both in weight and colour, and dominated by red fruit such as cranberry and raspberry with finely etched, peppery tannins. Martinborough Pinot Noir is often from older vines and most similar to Burgundy. It is weightier than Marlborough Pinot Noir and more complete and complex than Central Otago Pinot Noir. Notes of cherry and plum mingle with game, spice, and chocolate. The Waipara style is still emerging, but seems to be lighter than Central Otago with red fruit, beetroot, game, and pepper notes.

A New Zealand style of Syrah (New Zealanders call it Syrah rather than Shiraz) is emerging that is quite distinct from that of Australia or the Rhône. Even in the best sites, the fruit can struggle to ripen, leading to light, earthy wines with just-ripe black fruit flavours, an appealing greenness, and crisp acidity. The pepper notes are unmistakably Syrah, as are the tannins, which are big but elegant.

Most New-Zealand Bordeaux blends are Merlot-dominated, with those from Waiheke Island (if you can find them) the likely exception. Merlot alone can be in an easy-drinking style, chocolately with ripe (although not jammy or baked) plum notes. More ambitious wines are likely to include components of Cabernet Sauvignon, Cabernet Franc, and/or Malbec. Compared to the real McCoy, New Zealand Bordeaux blends have more vibrant fruit and a savoury, mineral aspect.

Chapter 23

Australia

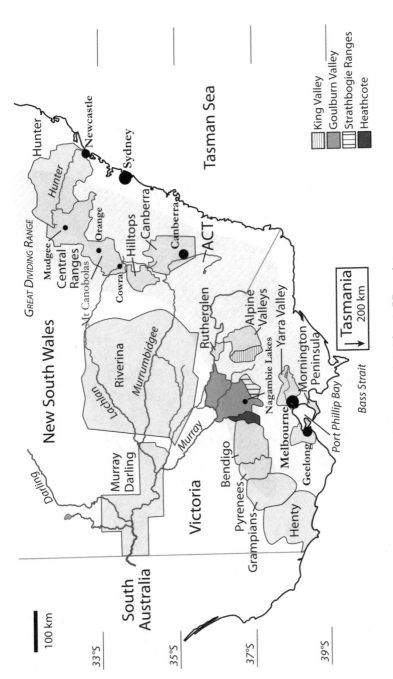

New South Wales & Victoria

King Valley
Goulburn Valley
Strathbogie Ranges
Heathcote

Tasman Sea

Tasmania
200 km

South Australia

New South Wales

Victoria

100 km

Great Dividing Range

Hunter
Hunter
Newcastle
Sydney
Mudgee
Central Ranges
Orange
Mt Canobolas
Cowra
Hilltops
Canberra
Canberra
ACT

Darling

Lachlan

Riverina
Murrumbidgee

Murray Darling

Murray

Rutherglen

Alpine Valleys

Nagambie Lakes

Yarra Valley

Bendigo
Pyrenees
Grampians
Henty
Geelong
Melbourne
Mornington Peninsula
Port Phillip Bay

Bass Strait

33°S

35°S

37°S

39°S

South Australia

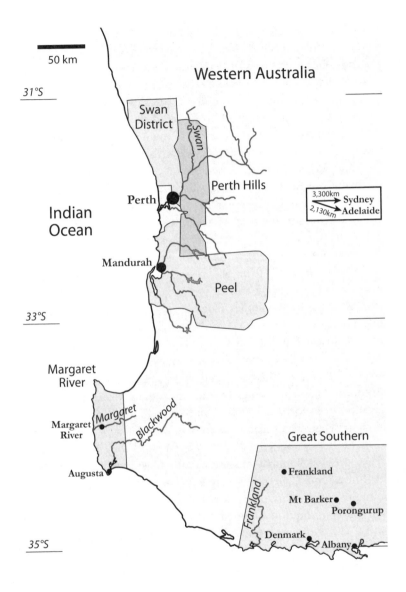

50 km

Western Australia

31°S

Swan
District

Swan

Perth Hills

Perth

Indian
Ocean

| 3,300km | Sydney |
| 2,130km | Adelaide |

Mandurah

Peel

33°S

Margaret
River

Margaret

Blackwood

Margaret
River

Great Southern

Augusta

● Frankland

Frankland

Mt Barker ●
● Porongurup

35°S

Denmark ● Albany

Southern Ocean

Western Australia

In 1788, the First Fleet of 11 ships landed in Botany Bay, now part of Sydney, with 1,500 British settlers on board. Over the next 80 years, thousands upon thousands of people immigrated to Australia, among them convicted criminals, soldiers, explorers, farmers, and fortune-seekers. The vine came with the first settlers, who had collected cuttings from Cape Town en route to Botany Bay. In 1832, James Busby, the 'Father of Australian Viticulture', brought hundreds of vines from France and Spain and established vineyards in the Hunter Valley in New South Wales. Around a decade later, Silesian settlers began making wine in the Adelaide Hills and Barossa Valley in South Australia. Phylloxera arrived in Australia in the late 19th century, seemingly through Geelong in Victoria. Victoria, then the most productive state in Australia, took the best part of a century to fully recover from the devastating effects of the pest. The Hunter Valley and South Australia have so far been spared from phylloxera, and can lay claim to some of the oldest vineyards in the world.

In 1901, the state colonies federalized. Australia exported significant amounts of mostly fortified, Port-style red wine to Britain and other countries. The Second World War and the demise of Imperial Preference damaged Australia's wine industry, and it was not until the 1970s that the country began once again to be recognized as a producer of quality wine. In the intervening decades, tastes had moved on from fortified wines to full-bodied red wines and the fresh and fruity white wines made possible by the advent of cold fermentation. The release of Tyrrell's Vat 47 Hunter Valley Chardonnay in 1971 spurred a national obsession with Chardonnay, which, along with Shiraz and Cabernet Sauvignon, has become one of the most commonly planted grape varieties in Australia. Wine exports and domestic consumption boomed throughout the 1980s, feeding the growth of large corporations and of 'cask wine', that is, bulk blends sold in bag-in-box casks. Unfortunately, cask wine and its bottled successors—competent, keenly priced, but very simple—have damaged Australia's image as the quality producer that it has increasingly become. Today, Australia counts ~150,000ha of vines and ~2,500 wineries. With an annual production of over 1.1bn litres, it has become the seventh largest wine producing and fourth largest wine exporting country in the world.

The lie of the land

Australia is almost the same size as the contiguous United States, at once the world's largest island and smallest continent. Yet, it counts fewer than 23m inhabitants, most of which live within just 50km (31mi) of the coastline. The Australian mainland ranges in latitude from 10.4°S in Queensland to 39.1°S in Victoria, with the island of Tasmania lying even further south. The Australian mainland is framed by the Indian Ocean to the west, the Southern Ocean to the south, and, to the east, the Tasman Sea. The stereotype of Australia as hot and dry, while not exactly inaccurate, belies the complexity and diversity of the continent's climate. Most of the country's interior is arid desert, but there are also tropical rainforests, temperate forests, fertile pasturelands, and even large ski fields in the Great Dividing Range. Viticulture is concentrated in coastal areas in the southern half of Australia and around the inland Murray-Darling River system. The climate in many wine regions is maritime and either warm or hot—not dissimilar to that of the southern Mediterranean. The Hunter Valley is subject to a subtropical climate, with warm temperatures and high humidity and cloud cover. Inland wine regions, especially in Victoria and South Australia, are subject to a continental climate, albeit with hotter summers and milder winters than in central Europe. The south coast, especially southwestern Western Australia and southern South Australia, experiences hot summers moderated by cool southern winds and waters. Some of the country's coolest and wettest climates are to be found in coastal Victoria and Tasmania. Exposure to harsh or extreme conditions has led to a number of technological innovations, most notably by Dr Richard Smart, who pioneered canopy management and developed the Smart-Dyson trellising system. Australian winemakers are very scientifically minded, so much so, in fact, that some of their wines have been criticized as 'too clinical'. Within the space of just a few decades, they have transformed Australia into one of the world's leading wine producing countries.

Classification

Australian wine regions are divided into Geographical Indications (GIs), in large part to conform to the European Union's export regulations.

A GI can be a zone, region, or sub-region. Zones are large tracts of land within a state or, sometimes, co-extensive with a state. Regions are parcels of land with a discrete and homogenous terroir, and sub-regions are designated areas within a region. GI wines featuring a region, grape variety, or vintage on the label must match that region, grape variety, or vintage by at least 85%. Blended wines often include the names of the predominant grape varieties, which must be listed in decreasing order of importance. The largest GI is the super-zone of South Eastern Australia, which encompasses 95% of Australia's vineyard area! It is typically used for cheap, bulk wine from the Murray-Darling corridor. The three large areas that make up this corridor are Riverina, Murray-Darling and Swan Hill, and Riverland. Together, they account for some three-quarters of Australian wine production. The only fine wine style made in these regions is a botrytized Semillon from Riverina. In particular, De Bortoli makes a very good Sauternes imitation called 'Noble One'.

New South Wales

New South Wales accounts for around one-third of Australia's wine production, although most of this is bulk wine from Riverina and Murray-Darling. The Hunter Valley to the north of Sydney is the country's oldest and most visited wine region. Newer, cool climate regions such as Orange and the Canberra District are stirring up excitement as they realize their potential.

Hunter Valley

The Hunter Valley region is formed around the Hunter River, with most production concentrated in the Lower Hunter Valley closer to the mouth of the river. The climate in the Hunter Valley is essentially subtropical, with the 750mm (30in) annual rainfall concentrated in the critical growing and harvesting season of January to April. Badly timed rainstorms can destroy entire crops, as with the 2012 Shiraz harvest. One upside of the humidity is the significant cloud cover, which restricts sugar accumulation in the grapes. Vineyards are planted on relatively infertile soils of volcanic basalt and red clay. So far, they have been spared from phylloxera, enabling the Hunter Valley to lay claim to some of the oldest vines in Australia. Today, the region is internationally reputed for its dry Semillon, 'Australia's gift to the wine world', with complex notes of toast, nuts, beeswax, and tarragon, high acidity, and low alcohol. A benchmark for the style is McWilliam's Mount Pleasant. The Hunter Valley is also noted for its Shiraz, which, compared to many other Australian styles of Shiraz, is more meaty, peppery, and medicinal, with more muscular tannins and a touch less alcohol. A benchmark for the style is Brokenwood's Graveyard Vineyard. Chardonnay is a relative latecomer, with Tyrrell's 1971 Vat 47 Hunter Valley Chardonnay serving both as prototype and archetype for Australian oaked Chardonnay. Cabernet Sauvignon is the other main black grape variety but, owing to the autumn rains, harvests can be unreliable. The Hunter Valley's 2,660ha of vineyards account for less then 2% of the national total; with thirsty Sydney on the doorstep, little wine leaves New South Wales let alone Australia.

Mudgee, Orange, and Cowra

The Central Ranges zone consists of three regions, inland of the Hunter along the line of the Great Dividing Range. From north to south they are: Mudgee, Orange, and Cowra.

Mudgee ('Nest of Hills') is encircled by a ring of hills. Summers are as hot as in the Hunter Valley, but with less cloud cover and much less rainfall. Black grape varieties dominate, with plantings of Shiraz, Cabernet Sauvignon, and Merlot outnumbering those of Chardonnay and Semillon by three to one. Soils of sandy loam and clay range in altitude from 450 to 1,000m (1,476 to 3,281ft), making them among the highest in the country. Altitude mitigates the summer heat to such an extent that the harvest takes place at least one month later than in the Hunter. Lack of irrigation water restricts yields, leading to grapes with concentrated flavours and high acidity. Cabernet Sauvignon and Chardonnay are the region's star performers. Semillon also does very well.

While Mudgee is the oldest region in the Central Ranges, Orange is the newest and also the coolest. The landscape is dominated by Mount Canobolas, an extinct volcano that culminates at 1,395m (4,577ft). Vineyards must lie above 600m (1,969ft) to qualify for the Orange appellation. Vines are planted on ancient basalt clays interspersed with patches of gravel and shale. The soils are fairly fertile and growers seek to restrict vine vigour with appropriate training systems. Before being overtaken by vineyards in the 1980s, Orange was reputed for its stone fruit. The warm, sunny summers and long, dry autumns are ideal for ripening peaches and plums, and, of course, late harvesting grape varieties. Shiraz and Chardonnay may dominate plantings, but Riesling and Pinot Noir are stirring the most excitement. The region also produces a lightly floral style of Sauvignon Blanc that is quite distinct from grassy Sancerre and tropical Marlborough. Philip Shaw is perhaps the most recognized producer, while Hedberg Hill and Cumulus Wines exemplify the region's range. Printhie Wines makes exceptional red wines, especially Merlot.

The climate in the flat plains of Cowra is hot and dry. Chardonnay, which is usually harvested early, is the region's best performer. Red wines are typically soft, juicy, and high in alcohol. Cowra is still in the process of establishing a clear identity.

Canberra District and Hilltops

The Canberra District region, part of the southern New South Wales zone, encompasses the Australian Capital Territory and surrounding hills in New South Wales where most of the vineyards are located. The hills to the east of the district block off the influence of the sea, leading to a continental climate with cold winters (by Australian standards) and hot and dry summers. Vineyards are planted at altitudes of 500 to 850m (1,640 to 2,789ft) where temperatures are cooler than in the plain. The clay and shale subsoils are poor at retaining water and drought is common. Despite this, cool climate grape varieties such as Pinot Noir and Riesling flourish. Dry autumns suit Cabernet Sauvignon, which is planted on warmer sites, and a cool-climate style of Shiraz is taking off. The region's wine industry dates back to the 1970s and most wineries are small, boutique operations. Clonakilla is one of the oldest and makes exemplary wines.

The vineyards in the nearby region of Hilltops, which experiences a similar climate, lie at a lower altitude of around 450m (1,476ft). Cabernet Sauvignon is emerging as the region's premier grape variety.

Victoria

Before phylloxera arrived in the 1890s, Victoria accounted for more than half of Australia's wine production. Today, Victoria is staging a comeback. It is the third largest wine producing state, yet counts more wineries than South Australia. Its climate is very diverse: coastal regions around Melbourne are cool and wet, while inland Victoria experiences very hot and dry summers. Accordingly, wines come in a broad range of styles, from cool climate Pinot Noir and Chardonnay to the celebrated liqueur Muscats from Rutherglen.

Mornington Peninsula

The Port Phillip zone encompasses those regions clustered around Port Phillip Bay, including Mornington Peninsula, Geelong, and the Yarra Valley. These regions are dominated by small, boutique operators with a focus on quality. Melbourne, the state capital and second largest city in Australia, sits at the top of Port Phillip Bay.

The Mornington Peninsula, at ~38°S, lies south of Melbourne on the eastern side of the bay. With water on three sides, the climate in Mornington Peninsula is ultra maritime. Rainfall averages 740mm (29in) per year, with the long growing season only slightly less wet than the winter. Vines are planted on gently sloping hills up to 250m (820ft) in altitude. The soils consist of a mix of clay, sandy loam, and volcanic elements. Site aspect and orientation are critical for ripening grapes and reducing disease pressure. The most important grape varieties are Pinot Noir and Chardonnay, and Mornington Peninsula is one of Victoria's rising stars for traditional method sparkling wine. On the whole, the climate is better suited to Chardonnay, with a fresh, Burgundy-influenced style emerging. Pinot Noir is yet to achieve the same finesse as across the Bass Strait in Tasmania. Pinot Gris offers a lot of promise. Stonier is one of the region's star producers, making standout Chardonnay and Pinot Noir.

Geelong

Geelong, on the western side of Port Phillip Bay, experiences a climate similar to that of the Mornington Peninsula. Soils are mostly red clay loam. Chardonnay and Pinot Noir dominate plantings, and are made into both traditional method sparkling wines and still, varietal wines. Further inland, the growing season is warmer, and Shiraz and Cabernet Sauvignon are more commonly planted; but even here, they can struggle to ripen in cooler, wetter years.

Yarra Valley

The Yarra Valley is the most important region in the Port Phillip zone, boasting some of Australia's most highly regarded cool climate wine styles. The region is defined by the Yarra River, which traces its path over 242km (150mi) from the Yarra Ranges to Melbourne and Port Phillip Bay. Vines are planted on steep slopes and along flat alluvial riverbeds. Pinot Noir and Chardonnay dominate plantings. Traditional method sparkling wine is a mainstay, with the Yarra Valley home to Moët et Chandon's Australian venture. The hilly topography, free-draining soils, and drier conditions than in Mornington are a boon to Pinot Noir, and Yarra Valley Pinot Noir has surfaced as a classic Australian style. Cabernet Sauvignon, Merlot, and Shiraz ripen reliably at lower altitudes. The Giant Steps wines by Innocent Bystander epitomize the Yarra style of Chardonnay and Pinot Noir. Mount Mary Vineyard makes an iconic Bordeaux-style blend, albeit in miniscule quantities. Phylloxera first arrived in Australia through Geelong, but, until as recently as 2006, had kept out of the Yarra Valley.

Goulburn Valley

The Central Victoria zone encompasses five regions to the north of Melbourne, reaching inland to the border with New South Wales. The most northerly and heavily planted of these is the Goulburn Valley. Vineyards are located on the relatively flat valley floor of the Goulburn River, which provides water for irrigation. The climate, although hot and dry, is mitigated somewhat by rivers and lakes. The climate and fertile soils of sand and gravel make for rich, generous wines. The principal black grape varieties are Shiraz and Cabernet Sauvignon, which are made into powerful, concentrated, full-bodied styles, typically with high sugar and low acidity. Most are very fruit-forward, but the best evolve notes of chocolate and leather. The principal white grape variety is Chardonnay, which is made into a rich, full-bodied style with notes of peach and tropical fruits. Fruit from the neighbouring, cooler region of Strathbogie Ranges is often included for added acidity and citrus notes. The Goulburn Valley is especially noted for its plantings of Marsanne, which are the oldest and largest in the world. Tahbilk, in the Nagambie Lakes sub-region, makes an iconic wine from Marsanne vines planted in 1927.

Heathcote

The region of Heathcote lies to the west of the Goulburn Valley. Cool southerly winds channelled by the Mount Carmel Range temper the hot summer heat and extend the growing season. Rainfall is fairly evenly distributed throughout the year. Premium vineyards are planted on the red calcareous clay soils of the mountain slopes. Shiraz utterly dominates plantings, and with good reason: Heathcote Shiraz is a unique style, dark and brooding with notes of blackberry, plum, cherry, black pepper, leather, coffee, and aniseed, vibrant acidity, firm, mouth-coating tannins, and a long finish. Jasper Hill, which uses fruit from dry-farmed vineyards, is one of the region's top producers.

Bendigo

Bendigo, to the west of Heathcote, is a relatively large but sparsely planted region. Summers are hotter and drier than in Heathcote although altitude (vines are planted up to 390m or 1,280ft) can take the sting out of the summer heat. Stony clay soils restrict yields and concentrate flavours. Pockets of quartz translate into a mineral steeliness, especially in Chardonnay. The dominant grape variety is Shiraz. Bendigo Shiraz is typically big and brooding, often with a note of mint or eucalyptus. Other important grape varieties include Cabernet Sauvignon and Sauvignon Blanc.

Pyrenees

The Western Victoria zone stretches west from the Bendigo region to the border with South Australia. Pyrenees, immediately to the west of

Bendigo, is the oldest and smallest of the zone's three regions. Unlike in the European Pyrenees, the terrain is hilly rather than mountainous. Viticulture is only made viable by altitude and irrigation, and the region is noted for its full-bodied, concentrated wines. Soils are predominantly sandy loam, which suits the most planted grape varieties, Shiraz and Chardonnay. Compared to Heathcote Shiraz, Pyrenees Shiraz is fruitier, with less spice and smoother tannins.

Grampians

Viticulture in the Grampians region to the west also dates back to the Victorian Gold Rush. Grampians has never fallen to phylloxera, and the Nursery Block at Best's Wines, planted in 1867, is a catalogue of the region's early grape varieties. Vineyards are planted on sandstone soils on elevated sites in the Grampians Range, at the western extremity of the Great Dividing Range. Owing to the higher altitude, the climate is cooler than in Pyrenees, with the average temperature during January being just 20.2°C (68.4°F). This translates into a style of Shiraz with more pepper, liquorice, and game than in Pyrenees. Compared to other Victorian (and South Australian) Shiraz expressions, acidity is higher and tannins are more structured. Producer Mount Langi Ghiran exemplifies the Grampians style of Shiraz. The dry conditions suit late-ripening black grape varieties, and Cabernet Sauvignon is also widely planted. Perhaps surprisingly, the region has a long association with sparkling wines, including sparkling Shiraz for which it is responsible. Traditional method sparkling wines are made from Pinot Noir and Chardonnay sourced from the region's coolest areas and from neighbouring Henty. Leading producers of sparkling wine in Grampians include Best's and Seppelt Great Western.

Henty

Henty, to the southwest of Grampians, stretches south to the coast and west to the border with South Australia. The region is large and diverse, with Shiraz the most planted grape variety overall. Coastal sites are cool enough to grow Chardonnay, Pinot Noir, and (unusually in Australia) Pinot Meunier for the production of sparkling wines. For still wines, Riesling offers the most promise in a style that is less 'limey' than the classic south Australian styles.

Rutherglen

The North East Victoria zone, to the east of the Goulburn Valley, encompasses five regions with extremely varied topography. Rutherglen is internationally reputed for the richness, depth, and complexity of its fortified wines. Tucked against the border with New South Wales, the climate in Rutherglen is very hot. Vineyards are planted on rich loamy soils or on the lighter sandy soils along the Murray River. The principal grape varieties for the fortified wines are Muscat à Petits Grains Rouge (Rutherglen Brown Muscat) and Muscadelle (Tokay). In the long and dry autumn, the grapes are left on the vine until they are semi-dry. After fortification, Rutherglen Muscat is barrel aged for a period of five to 105 years, often in a modified solera system. Rutherglen Muscats are classified based on richness and complexity into one of four categories: Rutherglen Muscat (average age 3-5 years), Classic Rutherglen Muscat (average age 6-10 years), Grand Rutherglen Muscat (average age 11-19 years), and Rare Rutherglen Muscat (average age 20+ years). Rutherglen Tokay (Topaque) can be just as impressive as Rutherglen Muscat, if lighter and finer and dominated by candied fruits, honey, toffee, and black tea rather than molasses, raisins, and chocolate. The nearby Glenrowan region shares Rutherglen's reputation for fortified Muscats and Tokays. Both regions are also noted for their full-bodied light wines, most commonly from Shiraz.

King Valley and Alpine Valleys

The neighbouring King Valley region and Alpine Valleys region extend south along the King and Ovens Rivers into the Great Dividing Range, reaching almost as far as Victoria's highest peak, Mount Bogong. The diverse terrain is planted with a large catalogue of grape varieties including Sangiovese, Marzemino, Durif, and Tempranillo alongside the more conventional Chardonnay, Cabernet Sauvignon, and Shiraz. Varying altitudes and slopes, cooling mountain breezes, and high diurnal temperature variation are some of the factors that underpin the quality of the wines from these regions.

Tasmania

Across the Bass Strait from Victoria lies the Australian island state of Tasmania, which is about the same size as the Republic of Ireland. The capital Hobart is on the same latitude line as the Waipara region in New Zealand. Overall, the climate is cool, wet, and windy, with harvests taking place as late as April. The many mountains that speckle the island offer some protection from the storminess of the seas. Viticulture is concentrated in the drier areas around Launceston in the north and Hobart in the southeast. In the north, vineyards are concentrated around the Tamar Valley and other river valleys. Chardonnay, Pinot Noir, Sauvignon Blanc, Pinot Gris, and Riesling are among the most planted grape varieties. The climate on the south-east coast is more marginal. Pinot Noir thrives here, and a distinct, cool-climate style of Cabernet Sauvignon is emerging from warmer, sheltered sites. Other grape varieties are also planted, in particular Chardonnay. Tasmania is seen as up-and-coming for cool climate styles but production is still miniscule. To date, the island's greatest claim to fame is perhaps its traditional method sparkling wine made from Chardonnay and Pinot Noir.

South Australia

South Australia, which has never been plagued by phylloxera, has come to account for about half of Australia's wine production. Much of this is made from fruit grown across state borders in the irrigated regions along the Murray-Darling corridor. But the state is also home to several of Australia's premium wine regions and iconic wines. The Australian Wine Research Institute in the state capital Adelaide ranks alongside the *Institut des Sciences de la Vigne et du Vin* in Bordeaux and UC Davis in California as one of the foremost centres of viticultural and oenological expertise. Much of South Australia is hot and dry and unsuitable for viticulture. In the southeast near Adelaide, the climate is moderated by cool waters from the Southern Ocean, which travel far inland up Gulf St Vincent and Spencer Gulf. Viticulture is concentrated in the southeast of the state, in particular, the Fleurieu Peninsula south of Adelaide;

the hills, valleys, and highlands to the east and north of Adelaide; coastal regions in the far south near the border with Victoria; and the productive Riverland region along the Murray-Darling River, which forms an estuary in Lake Alexandrina southeast of Adelaide. There are also limited plantings on Kangaroo Island across from the Fleurieu Peninsula and in the Southern Flinders Ranges 240km (150mi) north of Adelaide.

Barossa Valley and Eden Valley

Silesian settlers established the vine in the Barossa in 1842. This Germanic heritage is still evidenced in the architecture and cuisine of the region, the important place of Riesling, and the names of winemaking families.

The Barossa zone encompasses the Barossa Valley and Eden Valley regions. The broad Barossa Valley lies to the northeast of Adelaide, sheltered from the sea by the Mount Lofty Ranges of which the Barossa Ranges form a part. The climate is continental and marked by hot and dry summers. Vineyards are established on the valley floor and, increasingly, on cooler sites in the Barossa Ranges. Irrigation is often a necessity although some older vines are dry farmed, with their roots digging through the infertile soils of clay and sand to drink at the water table. Owing to the hot, dry, and infertile conditions, the grapes are remarkably concentrated. Black grape varieties make up about two-thirds of plantings. Shiraz reigns supreme, and some Shiraz vines predate the European phylloxera epidemic. Barossa Shiraz is an Australian classic: intensely dark and full-bodied with a jammy or stewed black fruit profile, notes of milk chocolate, sweet spice, black pepper, and eucalyptus, and soft and velvety tannins. Shiraz can also be integrated with old vine Grenache and Mourvèdre (Mataro) in a Southern Rhône-style blend, or else with Cabernet Sauvignon, which thrives in cooler sites. The most planted white grape variety is Semillon; other important white grape varieties are Chardonnay and Riesling.

The Eden Valley lies in the Barossa Ranges immediately southeast of the Barossa Valley. Owing to altitude, growing conditions are significantly cooler than in the Barossa Valley, and the hills are exposed to strong winds that have stripped their rocky faces of any high nutrient soils. The grapes develop intense concentration, much as they do in the Barossa Valley but with less sugar and greater acidity. Black grape varieties account for just over half of plantings, but the Eden Valley is chiefly reputed for its dry, austere, and textural Riesling. The best examples, such as Yalumba's Pewsey Vale 'The Contours', are made in a very Germanic style. The Eden Valley is also noted for an expression of Shiraz that is lighter in body, higher in acidity, and more savoury than that of the Barossa Valley. The region is home to one of the icons of Australian Shiraz, Henschke's Hill of Grace. While Hill of Grace is sourced from a single vineyard in the Eden Valley, Penfold's Grange, a Shiraz-dominated blend that is often thought of as Australia's 'first growth', is sourced from vineyards all around South Australia.

The history of the Barossa is so long and rich that there is a host of eminent producers to choose from. Family-owned Yalumba makes a range of typical Barossa Valley and Eden Valley wine styles, including single vineyard wines that highlight terroir variations within the Barossa. Yalumba also boasts the largest plantings of Viognier in the world, and the wine produced from these holdings is itself an Australian benchmark. Peter Lehmann epitomizes Barossan red and white wines, while Charles Melton's Nine Popes is a beautiful homage to Châteauneuf-du-Pape. The now corporate giant Jacob's Creek still makes excellent fine wines on a small-scale. Seppeltsfield, the original homestead of the Seppelt wine family, embodies the region's fortified wine heritage with their Para Tawny, which is released after one hundred years in barrel!

Adelaide Hills

The Mount Lofty Ranges, with their peak at 936m (3038ft), span a 300km (186mi) arc from the Fleurieu Peninsula to just north of the Clare Valley. The Adelaide Hills region corresponds to the section of the Mount Lofty Ranges that lies to the east of Adelaide and that borders on the Barossa in the north and McLaren Vale in the south. In most cases, vineyards must be planted above 400m (1,312ft) to qualify for the GI. The climate is significantly different from that of either the Barossa or Adelaide. Spring and even summer nights can be chilly, and spring frosts and hail can threaten harvests. The soils are mostly sandy loam. Chardonnay, established in the 1970s by one of the region's pioneers Brian Croser, is the most planted grape variety. Sauvignon Blanc, which has met with little success in other parts of Australia, occupies a very honorable second place. The cool nights make for acidity and delicacy, while ample sunshine and high daytime summer temperatures ensure full phenolic ripeness. Pinot Noir is the most commonly planted black grape variety. Much of the Pinot Noir harvest is blended with Chardonnay to make traditional method sparkling wine, of which Petaluma, established by Croser, is one of the top exponents. Shaw + Smith and The Lane Vineyards make exceptional Burgundy-inspired Chardonnay, while Tapanappa, Croser's more recent venture, is a new cult favourite.

McLaren Vale

McLaren Vale lies in the north of the Fleurieu peninsula, to the south of Adelaide and southwest of Adelaide Hills. This famed region boasts some very old vineyards, including one that dates back to 1838—Australia's oldest. The climate in MacLaren Vale is Mediterranean, tempered by sea breezes from Gulf St Vincent. Cool nighttime air that descends from the hills increases the diurnal temperature range and extends the ripening period. The sea brings in enough rain, although very little falls during the summer. Soils are mostly sandy loam with significant patches of alluvial gravels, yellow clays, and lime. This diversity of soils has led to the most detailed terroir mapping of any wine region in the world. Black grape varieties account for over four-fifths of plantings, with Shiraz far in the lead. Compared to the Shiraz of Barossa, that of McLaren Vale tends more towards dark chocolate and savoury spice. McLaren Vale has a proud history of Grenache, with numerous dry-farmed plantings of old vine Grenache. Chapel Hill makes a benchmark example of old vine Grenache. d'Arenberg has been making exceptional Northern and Southern Rhône styles for over a hundred years, including the famed Dead Arm Shiraz.

Clare Valley

At the northern extremity of the Mount Lofty Ranges, the scenic Clare Valley is famed for producing Australia's benchmark style of

Riesling. Yet, the region is also capable of producing red wines of considerable weight. Most vineyards are planted at 400 to 500m (1,312 to 1,640ft) in altitude, and the conditions from one site to the next can vary immensely. Overall, the climate is continental and marked by hot summers. However, afternoon breezes moderate temperatures and extend the ripening period into the dry autumn. Soils are freely draining with significant limestone deposits, especially in the south of the region. Compared to Riesling from Eden Valley, that from Clare Valley is generally more austere in its youth with mouth-puckering acidity and notes of citrus fruits, apples, and minerals. With age, it evolves a more complex toasty character. The Grosset Polish Hill Riesling is one the region's best, with winemaker Jeff Grosset strongly influenced by his early career experience in Germany. Cabernet Sauvignon is also made, either as a varietal wine or blended with Shiraz or Merlot. Varietal Cabernet Sauvignon is inky, rich, and full-bodied with a characteristic eucalyptus note. Jim Barry Wines produce archetypal Clare Valley wine styles.

Coonawarra

Coonawarra ('Honeysuckle'), more than 300km (186mi) southeast of Adelaide and on the border with Victoria, is the main region in the Limestone Coast zone and South Australia's undisputed Cabernet Sauvignon capital. The climate, which has been compared with that of Bordeaux, is significantly cooler than in more northerly regions in South Australia—so much so that spring frosts, harvest rains, and under-ripeness present perennial problems. Coonawarra is famous for its red crumbly topsoil (terra rossa) that sits on top of a limestone ridge. The Coonawarra strip of iron-rich terra rossa is only about 15 by 2km, although similar soils are beginning to be exploited in the neighbouring regions of Padthaway and Wrattonbully. Cabernet Sauvignon accounts for more than half of plantings in Coonawarra. Other important grape varieties—Merlot, Shiraz, and Cabernet Franc—are primarily used for blending. Coonawarra Cabernet Sauvignon is dominated by concentrated blackcurrant and plum notes, verging on prune in hot vintages, coupled with a classic cedar note and eucalyptus. The fashion is for heavily structured tannins extracted in the winemaking.

Western Australia

Western Australia covers the entire western third of the country. The state accounts for 3.5% of the country's output by volume but garners many more trophies and awards than this modest figure might suggest. Winemakers in Western Australia are proud that their state is the only major wine-producing region excluded from the bulk wine South Eastern Australia super-zone. Their focus is almost exclusively on characterful wines that are adapted to, and reflective of, local terroir. Viticulture is only viable around the relatively cool state capital Perth and further south. Vines were first planted in the Swan Valley, northeast of Perth, in the 19th century, but viticulture only really took off in the 1970s, after the state government commissioned a report into the viability of winemaking. The report identified the Margaret River region as most closely matching Bordeaux, and, today, Margaret River is reputed for classic Left Bank-style Cabernet blends and Graves-style dry white wines. More recently, winemaking has expanded south into the cooler Great Southern region.

Margaret River

Margaret River, by far the most important region in Western Australia, occupies a roughly rectangular strip, 90 by 25km (56 by 16mi), on a flat peninsula ~230km (143mi) south of Perth. Cape Leeuwin at the cooler, southern end of the region is the meeting point of the Indian and Southern Oceans. Margaret River receives 1,100mm (43in) annual rainfall, most of which comes in the winter. During the growing season, onshore breezes carry in moisture and exercise a moderating effect on temperatures. Soils are freely draining gravelly loam, ideal for Cabernet Sauvignon. Although the conditions have been compared to those in Bordeaux, the region is some 10° nearer to the Equator and significantly warmer—so perhaps more like Bordeaux in a hot year. Of course, Cabernet Sauvignon is the most planted black grape variety, and, as in France, is more likely to be blended with Merlot than Shiraz. Compared to Cabernet Sauvignon from Coonawarra, that from Margaret River is more herbal and leafy and less eucalyptus—in short, more French. Tannins are usually very firm and the wines reward cellaring. Moss Wood is a benchmark producer. Semillon and Sauvignon Blanc have overtaken Chardonnay as the most planted white grape varieties, and are often blended with each other in homage to the Graves. Vasse Felix, the region's founding wine estate, produces an archetype of the style. The Leeuwin Estate Art Series Chardonnay is considered by many to be the best in Australia.

Great Southern

Great Southern is a young but large region around the coastal town of Albany and extending into rugged inland hills and mountains. Its varied geography is perhaps best described through its five sub-regions. Coastal Denmark and Albany are exposed to the full brunt of the Antarctic currents and onshore breezes. Inland Mount Barker and Frankland have a more continental climate, albeit one that is much cooler than in other Australian regions. In Porongurup—in the lee of striking granite hills and near the dramatic Stirling Ranges—the undulating terrain moderates the southerly breezes. On the whole, soils consist of gravels similar to those in Margaret River or more sandy loams. Great Southern now boasts more than 2,800ha under vine. It is earning a reputation for its Riesling, which has a subtler limey and floral nose than counterparts in the Eden and Clare Valleys, along with a light body and racy acidity. Other white grape varieties, especially Chardonnay, do well, and producers are emulating Margaret River in producing Semillon-Sauvignon Blanc blends. Shiraz is finding its feet as a cool climate style, but other than in select sheltered sites, Cabernet Sauvignon struggles to ripen, yielding wines with herbaceous flavours and tough, angular tannins.

Greater Perth zone

The Swan District to the north of Perth is the most established of the three regions around Perth. First planted in 1829, it was until the 1970s the only notable region in all of Western Australia. The Swan District is reputed for its fortified wines, but Chenin Blanc also thrives in the hot climate and sandy soils. East of Perth, the elevated Perth Hills also produces quality wines. Important grape varieties include Chardonnay, Semillon, Cabernet Sauvignon, and Merlot. Ashley Estate makes an eccentric but lengthy Pinot Noir from vines that are dry-farmed in a cooler valley site. South of Perth, Peel benefits from cooling morning sea breezes, leading to wines with greater acidity and tannic structure than might otherwise be expected for an otherwise hot climate. The Tuart Ridge near the coast is a sand-covered ridge of limestone, and the winery of the same name produces exceptionally refined Merlot. Meanwhile, Peel Estate is famed for its Shiraz, Cabernet Sauvignon, and Chenin Blanc.

Wine styles

Red wines

Black grape varieties account for over three-fifths of Australian plantings. Of these, almost half are Shiraz and over one-quarter Cabernet Sauvignon. In many cases, very hot conditions give rise to baked fruit or dried fruit flavours, high alcohol, and very soft acidity and tannins. Tartaric acid is often added and can elicit a seemingly disconnected or disjointed acidic tingle at the back of the palate. High alcohol is associated with a sweet entry and hot or burning finish. With such wines, it can be difficult to disentangle Shiraz from Cabernet Sauvignon, to say nothing of the ubiquitous Cabernet-Shiraz blends. The classic descriptions that follow only apply to quality wines with discernable varietal and regional characters. But first, a quick note: new American oak has long been favoured in Australia, both for red and white wines, but French oak is increasingly used for Cabernet Sauvignon and old oak or no oak for Shiraz. As there are no regulations to enforce particular practices, there are, at least theoretically, as many wine styles as there are winemakers.

Like the Northern Rhône, Australia produces benchmark expressions of Shiraz. Australian Shiraz has become so important and influential that producers in other New World countries actively decide whether to label their wine 'Syrah' in homage to the Rhône or 'Shiraz' to indicate a more Australian style or influence. But of course, Australian Shiraz is anything but homogeneous. Barossa Shiraz is very dark in colour. On the nose, it typically exudes jammy or stewed black fruit, milk chocolate, sweet spice, black pepper, and eucalyptus. On the palate, it is high in alcohol with soft acidity and velvety tannins. The use of new American oak is traditional but there are also trends towards new French oak and old oak. Shiraz from nearby McLaren Vale is just as powerful, if anything with a propensity to even higher alcohol, with a flavour profile of dark chocolate and spice that is more savoury than sweet. Hunter Valley Shiraz is still more savoury, with notes of jammy (but not stewed) black fruit, cured meat, black pepper, and liquorice. Alcohol is often lower, acidity higher, and tannins more marked and gripping. Heathcote Shiraz is Victoria's most recognized style of Shiraz, with a flavour profile of ripe plum, cherry, black fruits, coffee, leather, anise, and black pepper, fresh acidity, and firm and mouth-coating tannins. Compared to Hunter Valley Shiraz, acidity is not quite as high. There have been some experiments with cool-climate Shiraz in recent years. The emerging style from southwest Western Australia is quite distinct from styles from further east or indeed the Rhône or New Zealand. The wines are lighter in colour and body with only just-ripe plum fruit and herbal green notes; if full phenolic ripeness has not been attained, they can even be sour.

For Cabernet Sauvignon, there are two benchmark styles in Australia: Coonawarra and Margaret River. Coonawarra tends to fairly high levels of alcohol although the grape variety's characteristic acidity is retained. The fruit profile is ripe, with notes of concentrated blackcurrant and plum, verging on prune in hot vintages, coupled with a classic cedar note and eucalyptus rather than green pepper. Tannins are structured and fine-grained but less austere or chalky than in Bordeaux. In some cases, Shiraz is used to round out the wine in the same way that Merlot is used in Bordeaux. Margaret River is more like Left Bank Bordeaux and more likely to be blended with Merlot and Cabernet Franc. Alcohol levels can still be high but the fruit is less likely to be stewed. Fresh green pepper replaces eucalyptus, tannins are firmer, and the use of French oak is much more likely. All said, it is often difficult to distinguish Coonawarra from Margaret River.

The Cabernet-Shiraz blend originated from the impulse to round out Cabernet Sauvignon in climes where Merlot failed to thrive. It is produced thoughout Australia and has become a style in its own right. There are no rules governing the proportion of each grape variety in the blend, except that, if the varieties are stated on the label, the dominant variety must feature first. Cabernet Sauvignon contributes acidity and fine, structured tannins to the blend, while Shiraz contributes generous ripe fruit and, in the best of cases, a subtle meaty pepperiness. Needless to say, Cabernet-Shiraz blends are difficult to pick out in blind tastings, and all the more so if they hail from a hot climate.

Grenache and Mourvèdre (Mataro) are classically cultivated in the Barossa and in McLaren Vale. Grenache in particular thrives in the heat, yielding varietal wines with notes of strawberry jam and ginger or white pepper, very high alcohol, and powdery, mouth-coating tannins. However, in most cases it is blended with Shiraz and Mourvèdre (Mataro) to produce full-bodied wines not unlike their inspirations in the Southern Rhône, with notes of ripe strawberry and plum fruit, game, pepper, cloves, liquorice, and herbs.

Wines made from Pinot Noir are typically very clean and fruit-driven with good acidity. Unfortunately, they are sometimes marred by high alcohol or, at least, alcohol that is too high in relation to their light body. The best examples avoid jammy fruit and tend to more earthy notes, often with marked eucalyptus or herbal mint. Much Australian Pinot Noir hails from the cooler regions of the Port Phillip zone in Victoria.

White wines

In the space of a few decades, Chardonnay has come to account for almost half of Australia's plantings of white grape varieties. The 1980s and 1990s favoured full-bodied wines with tropical fruit flavours and a certain 'sweetness' from the liberal use of new American oak. When markets tired of this big and bolshie style, many winemakers hastily went the other way, seeking out cooler sites and regions and eschewing new oak to make lean, lemony, and characterless wines. Fortunately, some winemakers have settled for a happier middle ground making judiciously oaked Burgundy-inspired wines. Given this variety of styles and the malleability of Chardonnay, it is difficult to provide a generic tasting note for Australian Chardonnay. All that can be said is that it is often made in a very clean style, and that oak, when used, can seem almost clinical in its application. Wines from cooler regions are likely to reveal citrus, fresh apple, and floral aromas, often with ripe stone fruit on the palate, whereas wines from warmer regions tend to be dominated by notes of fig, melon, and tropical fruit. Australian Chardonnay tends to lack the yoghurt or 'dairy' note often found in New Zealand expressions. Less ambitious wines may betray added tartaric acid or the crude use of oak staves or chips. Overall, the best sites for Chardonnay are in the Hunter Valley, the regions around Port Phillip Bay, Tasmania, Adelaide Hills, and Margaret River.

The Hunter Valley produces a unique style of Semillon that is very pale in colour with vaguely floral, citrus, fennel, and fresh grass notes, high acidity, and low alcohol. The wines are dry and often quite textural on the palate and the best examples are extraordinarily lengthy. Though austere and flinty in their youth, with age they develop a complex bouquet of toast, nuts, beeswax, and tarragon. Owing to this toast, aged Semillon can seem to have been oaked, but this is almost never the case. Semillon from the Barossa is entirely different. The hot climate favours the development of rich wines with low acidity, medium-to-high alcohol, and notes of peach jam, mangoes, and coconut or vanilla from new, often American, oak. In Margaret River, Semillon is typically blended with Sauvignon Blanc and aged in new French oak. The wines are full-bodied with medium-to-high alcohol, crisp acidity, and intense flavours of peaches and honey from the Semillon and herbs and gooseberry from the Sauvignon Blanc. Compared to Graves, they are made in a much 'cleaner' style with more intense, finely etched flavours, and may also be fuller in body and higher in alcohol. Unblended varietal Semillon from Margaret River is significantly more herbaceous than that from the Hunter Valley. Riverina produces Australia's best botrytized Semillon. The wine is reminiscent of Sauternes but typically lacks the Sauvignon Blanc and Muscadelle components of Sauternes and is lower in acidity. There is also far less vintage variation than in Sauternes or coastal areas of Australia. The flavour profile is of honeyed peaches overlain with vanilla from, usually, new French oak. Botrytized Semillon is also produced in South Australia, although the botrytis is brought about artificially by covering the vines with netting and spraying water to increase humidity.

Although it is the second most planted white grape variety in the country (just ahead of Semillon), Australian Sauvignon Blanc has yet to achieve anything like the stylistic unity and recognition of Marlborough Sauvignon Blanc. In most places, the climate is simply too hot to achieve the zesty acidity and herbaceous notes favoured by consumers. Growers in cool climate areas are much more interested in higher value Pinot Noir, Chardonnay, and Riesling. The best Australian Sauvignon Blanc arguably comes from Margaret River where it is typically blended with Semillon. Distinct varietal styles of Sauvignon Blanc are emerging from Adelaide Hills and Orange. Orange Sauvignon Blanc is very delicate and floral with a light body, high acidity, and low alcohol. Adelaide Hills Sauvignon Blanc is more conventional with some grassy notes, but remains less characterful or intense than Sancerre and Marlborough Sauvignon Blanc.

Riesling from the elevated sites of the Clare Valley and Eden Valley has become a classic world style. The wines are marked by mineral austerity and searingly high acidity, but unlike, say, Rheingau Riesling, their fruit profile leans very strongly towards lime, whether this be, depending on ripeness, lime zest, fresh lime juice, or lime cordial. Some examples exhibit a mineral pungency derided by critics as 'fly spray'. The best wines are complex enough to overlay the 'limeyness' with floral, appley, and waxy notes, and are further distinguished by a certain talcum or chalky texture from lees ageing and a long, dry, acidic finish. Riesling from Clare Valley is generally considered to be drier and leaner than that from Eden Valley, although the two styles are difficult to tell apart. Spritz in the glass is evidence of fermentation in stainless steel, which is commonly practised in Australia. Off-dry or sweet Riesling is not particularly popular in Australia. Dessert-style wines are made in South Australia using the 'cut cane' method. Once the grapes have arrived at phenolic ripeness, their canes are nicked to prevent sap from flowing to them and they are left to dry on the vine. Riesling is increasingly popular in the Great Southern region of Western Australia. The style is very light, almost water-white in colour with subtle floral and mineral water notes.

Australia has a plethora of other grape varieties reflecting its history of immigration and the untrammelled inventiveness of its winemakers. Pinot Gris is popular as is Muscat and Petit Verdot, and then there is Tempranillo, Nebbiolo, Barbera, Sangiovese, and many others. There are also some rather obscure cult wines such as Marsanne from Nagambie Lakes, Viognier from South Australia, and Verdelho from New South Wales. Merlot, though common enough, is mostly used for blending or bulk wine.

Chapter 24

South Africa

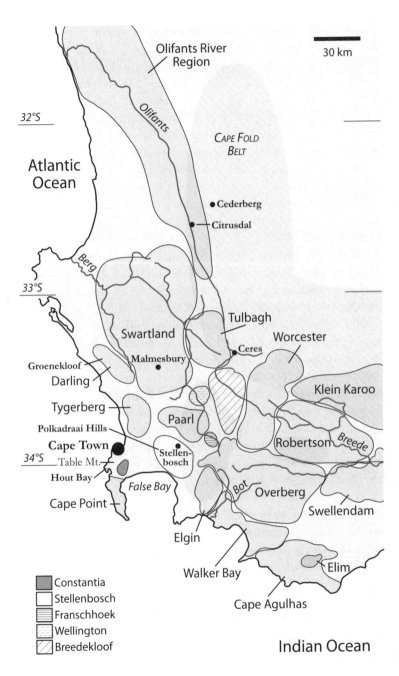

30 km

Olifants River
Region

32°S

Olifants

CAPE FOLD
BELT

Atlantic
Ocean

● Cederberg
●─Citrusdal

Berg

33°S

Tulbagh

Worcester

Swartland

● Ceres

Groenekloof

Malmesbury
●

Klein Karoo

Darling

Tygerberg

Paarl

Polkadraai Hills

Cape Town ●
34°S Table Mt.─
Hout Bay

Stellen-
bosch

Robertson

Breede

False Bay

Cape Point ─

Bot

Overberg

Swellendam

Elgin

Constantia
Stellenbosch
Franschhoek
Wellington
Breedekloof

Walker Bay

Elim

Cape Agulhas

Indian Ocean

South Africa: Western Cape

South Africa has a continuous history of winemaking that stretches back almost four centuries. In 1652, the Dutch East India Company established a farm colony on the Cape of Good Hope to supply fresh produce to sailors en route to the Indies. In 1654, the colony's founder Johan van Riebeeck sent for vine cuttings and, five years later, the Cape produced its first vintage of Muscat of Alexandria. Winemaking remained marginal until Dutch outposts in Batavia (Jakarta) recognized that Cape wine was likely to be more palatable than wine shipped all the way from Europe. In 1679, the colony's new commander Simon van der Stel brought in a French viticulturalist. Van der Stel founded the township of Stellenbosch a few miles from Cape Town and, in 1685, established the Constantia estate in the shadow of Table Mountain. In that same year, Louis XIV of France issued the Edict of Fontainebleau, forcing many Protestant Huguenots to flee for the Dutch colony. The Huguenots established themselves in Franschhoek ('French corner'), and their knowledge and culture of wine came as a boon to the colony's fledgling wine industry. Over the next century, the Cape wine industry catered for the domestic market, trade ships, and other outposts of the Dutch East India Company. In 1778, Stellenbosch landowner Hendrik Cloete purchased the Constantia estate, which had by then fallen into disrepair. Cloete's Vin de Constance, a sweet wine made mostly from Muscat Blanc à Petits Grains, found international acclaim, and is even said to have been Napoleon's last request on his deathbed on Saint Helena. The Napoleonic Wars cut off Britain from her traditional wine suppliers in France, and the Cape, confirmed under British rule in 1814, stepped in to fill this breach for almost fifty years during which wine production grew exponentially.

In 1861, British Chancellor of the Exchequer William Gladstone put an end to preferential tariffs for imperial imports, and, five years later, phylloxera disembarked in the Cape. Growers replanted vineyards with vines grafted onto American rootstocks, but made the mistake of selecting inferior, high-yielding grape varieties. Demand failed to meet supply, and the Cape wine industry fell into long-term decline. 1918 witnessed the foundation of the University of Stellenbosch with its viticulture programme, and also the foundation of the Cooperative Winemakers' Society of South Africa (*Koöperatieve Wijnbouwers Vereniging van Zuid-Afrika*, KWV), which purposed to regulate wine production through enforced quotas and minimum pricing schemes. The KWV can be credited with saving stakeholders from wholesale bankruptcy but, ultimately, privileged quantity over quality. World War, Prohibition in the USA, and the Great Depression damaged exports. The introduction of apartheid in 1948 and subsequent trade tariffs led to quasi invisibility on the international market.

Fortunately, domestic consumption continued unabated, as did innovations emanating from Stellenbosch University. In 1925, the first professor of viticulture Abraham Perold created Pinotage, South Africa's signature grape variety, by crossing Pinot Noir with Cinsault. 1955 saw the establishment of the Viticultural and Oenological Research Institute (now Infruitec-Nietvoorbij), followed, over the next few decades, by other education and trade bodies. Modelled on European wine regulations, the 1973 'Wine of Origin' laws emphasized grape variety and geographical origin. In the 1990s, South Africa transitioned from apartheid to democracy and export bans were lifted. In 1992, the KWV relinquished control over yields, production, and pricing, and, in 1997, became a corporation. The opening of markets and borders fostered an exchange of ideas with winemakers from Europe, America, and the Antipodes, leading to technical and technological improvements and a greater focus on matching grape variety to terroir, a process that continues apace.

The lie of the land

The vast majority of South Africa's ~100,000ha of vineyards are in the Cape Winelands, which extend out from the Cape of Good Hope. About 150km (93mi) southeast of the Cape, Africa's southernmost point Cape Agulhas (34.8°S) marks the dividing point between the Atlantic and Indian Oceans. To the east, the Agulhas (Mozambique) current brings in warm waters from the Indian Ocean, while, to the south, the Benguela current brings in cool waters from the Southern Ocean. On the whole, the climate is Mediterranean, albeit with more sunshine and milder winters than in European Mediterranean regions. The Cape Doctor is an arid, gale-force wind that blows from the southeast during the spring and summer, moderating temperatures and reducing disease pressure from mildew and other fungi—whence its name. However, it can also damage vines and bring heavy rain to the southernmost coastal regions.

A series of mountain ranges, the Cape Fold Belt, run roughly parallel to the coastline. They consist of folded sandstone peaks over granite, with valleys of shale. The highest peak is Seweweekspoortpiek at 2,325m (7,628ft). The mountain foothills and some of the valleys offer prime sites for viticulture, with slope and altitude used to best effect. Soils can be very acidic, and lime is often added to increase pH and calcium content. The mean daily temperature during the harvest (typically February to March) at Cape Town is 22°C (72°F). However, sites on the southern coast and at higher altitudes can be significantly cooler, whereas those in the lee of the mountains are prone to hot summer temperatures of up to 40°C (104°F). Annual precipitation ranges from 1,000mm (39in) in southern coastal areas to less than 200mm (8in) in the Klein Karoo, with most rain falling in the winter months of May to August. Five river systems traverse the region and supply irrigation water to drier areas. The Breede River system in the south is the largest of the five, while the north-flowing Olifants carves out a fertile valley in the west of the region.

Most vines are trained in cordons to facilitate vineyard operations. Some old bush vines can still be found, often producing very high quality fruit. Powdery and downy mildew pose a threat and the use of chemical fungicides is widespread; today, the greatest threat comes from viruses such as leafroll and fanleaf. Overall, the warm Mediterranean climate produces reasonably reliable harvests of fully ripe grapes. Managing phenolic and sugar ripeness can be a challenge. Alcohol levels can rise to unpleasant levels and acidity can be lacking. Alternatively, early-harvested grapes can give rise to unpleasant stalky notes. Cooler sites are being sought at higher altitudes or in the far south, often with an eye for more delicate grape varieties such as Pinot Noir.

Regions

There are five large geographical areas or *units*: Western Cape, Northern Cape, Eastern Cape, Kwazulu-Natal, and Limpopo. Of these, Western Cape, in the southwest, is by far the most important, while Eastern Cape, Kwazulu-Natal, and Limpopo verge on insignificance. Geographical units are divided into large *regions*, which are subdivided into *districts*, which may be further subdivided into *wards* (similar to communes in France).

Costal Region

The Coastal Region is large and diverse, and home to the majority of South Africa's top producers. The Stellenbosch District with its seven wards is centred on the eponymous university town, which lies in a valley surrounded by hills and mountains. The district is open to the cooling influence of the sea from False Bay and benefits considerably from the Cape Doctor. Many producers source fruit from the Helderberg area to the south, which is more exposed to cooling sea breezes. With over 700mm (28in) annual rainfall, producers can grow grapes without resorting to irrigation. Black grape varieties such as Cabernet Sauvignon, Merlot, and Shiraz account for almost two-thirds of the district's plantings. The ward of Polkadraai Hills is making a name for itself with Sauvignon Blanc, which is the most planted white grape variety. Yields are often low: Stellenbosch accounts for 17% of the country's vineyard area but only 9% of its wine production. Notable wineries include Kanonkop, Rustenberg, Jordan Wine Estate, and Kanu.

Paarl District lies north of Stellenbosch, beyond Simonsberg Mountain around the valley of the River Berg. The district is landlocked and sealed off by mountains to the south, east, and west. The climate is warmer than in Stellenbosch, and, despite the landlocked aspect, rainfall is higher. Like Stellenbosch, Paarl is reputed for its quality wines. Many of the best vineyards are found in the ward of Simonsberg-Paarl, on the northern slopes of Simonsberg Mountain. Paarl is home to Nederburg, the district's standout producer, and also to KWV, which has reinvented itself as one of South Africa's largest producers. Varietal Cabernet Sauvignon and Bordeaux blends are favoured, and are typically broader and fuller than their Stellenbosch counterparts. Shiraz, Pinotage, and Chenin Blanc are also important.

The River Berg also flows through two other districts, Franshhoeck Valley, to the southeast of Paarl, and Wellington, to the north of Paarl. Both districts used to be wards of Paarl. Franshhoeck Valley

District is noted for its quality white wines, including Semillon made from old bush vines. Important grape varieties include Chardonnay, Chenin Blanc, and Sauvignon Blanc. Red wines are gaining ground, as is Méthode Cap Classique, South Africa's take on traditional method sparkling wine made from Pinot Noir and Chardonnay. Wellington District is home to the majority of South Africa's vine nurseries. It is associated with Sherry-style fortified wines made from Chenin Blanc, and is also building a reputation for full-bodied red wines.

The Tygerberg District lies to the west of Paarl and reaches into the suburbs of Cape Town. Just as in Pessac-Léognan in Bordeaux, the high quality of the wine produced is helping to hold back urbanization. Sea breezes and afternoon mists exert a cooling influence, as does the altitude (up to 380m or 1,247ft) of some of the vineyards. Tygerberg is noted for its Sauvignon Blanc; other important grape varieties include Chardonnay, Shiraz, Cabernet Sauvignon, and Merlot.

South of Cape Town are Constantia and Hout Bay, two wards that are independent of district association. Constantia is the oldest ward in South Africa, rising up along the south face of Table Mountain. The sweet and ethereal Vin de Constance is still being produced by Klein Constantia, which, together with Groot Constantia and Buitenverwachting, perpetuates the legacy of Simon van der Stel. The climate is relatively cool with plenty of rainfall (>1,000mm or 39in) and a long ripening period. As well as Vin de Constance, Constantia is reputed for high quality Sauvignon Blanc, Chardonnay, and Riesling. The greatest threat to viticulture comes from baboons, which periodically encroach into the higher vineyards. Further south along the peninsula, the new Cape Point District enjoys a similar if slightly cooler maritime climate. Hout Bay is a new ward with a reputation for its Chardonnay, Sauvignon Blanc, and Bordeaux grape varieties

The dry Darling District lies north of Tygerberg. The cooling influence of the nearby Atlantic Ocean preserves fruit flavours and acidity, and the southern ward of Groenekloof ('Green Gap') is reputed for its bush-vine Sauvignon Blanc. Surrounding Darling and extending further north is the hot, dry, and very large Swartland District, of which Darling used to form part. Vineyards are planted along the Atlantic coast, in the foothills of the Cape Fold Belt, and along the fertile valley of the River Berg. The ward of Malmesbury, east of Groenekloof, accounts for most of the district's output. Historically a grain-producing region, Swartland is making a name for its Rhône blends and Pinotage, with Chenin Blanc, Sauvignon Blanc, and Chardonnay thriving in cooler sites.

Nestled between Swartland, Paarl, and the Breede River Valley Region, Tulbagh District in the Klein Berg River valley is surrounded by mountains to the north, east, and west. The best vineyard sites are on stony schistous terraces in the foothills. Tulbagh has long been associated with sparkling and fortified wines, but still red wines, especially Shiraz and Rhône blends, have become very important. Boberg District is an umbrella term for fortified wines from Tulbagh, Paarl, Franschhoek, and Wellington Districts.

Cape South Coast Region

The Cape South Coast Region, which boasts some of the coolest sites in South Africa, lies to the east of False Bay, hugging the coastline to Cape Agulhas and further out to Plettenberg Bay. The vineyards of Walker Bay, between False Bay and Cape Agulhas, are clustered around the seaside town of Hermanus. In 1975, Burgundy lover Tim Hamilton Russell recognized the area's potential for growing Pinot Noir and Chardonnay. He and his then winemaker Peter Finlayson are often thought of as the godfathers of South African Pinot Noir. Hamilton Russell's remarkable success inspired the establishment of other wineries, notably Bouchard Finlayson, a collaboration between Peter Finlayson and Burgundy's Paul Bouchard. Today, Hemel-en-Aarde ('Heaven and Earth') Valley, in the foothills to the north of Hermanus, is the most developed of the district's six wards. Aside from Pinot Noir and Chardonnay, Walker Bay is noted for its outstanding Pinotage and Sauvignon Blanc, and is also acquiring a reputation for Shiraz.

East of the Bot River, the up-and-coming Elgin District reaches inland into hilly terrain. Sauvignon Blanc is the most successful grape variety and there are high hopes for Pinot Noir and Riesling. Top producers include Paul Cluver Estate, Catherine Marshall, and Elgin Vinters. Until recently, Walker Bay and Elgin formed part of the large Overberg District. Today, Overberg's foremost ward is the cool-climate Klein River, around the town of Stanford ~20km (12mi) east of Hermanus.

The Elim Ward accounts for over half of the 250ha of vineyards in the Cape Agulhas District, east of Walker Bay, with production focused on Sauvignon Blanc, Semillon, and Shiraz. Cape South Coast's two other districts are Swellendam and Plettenberg Bay. Swellendam, around the mouth of the Breede River, counts no more than a few dozen hectares of vines; and Plettenberg Bay, over 400km (250mi) east of Cape Agulhas, was only first planted in 2000.

Breede River Valley Region

The River Breede, which takes its source in the mountains near Ceres, carves out a broad, fertile valley through the highlands of the Cape Fold Belt. With the exception of Swellendam District at the mouth of the river, this valley falls under the Breede River Valley Region. The valley floor, which ranges in altitude from 80 to 250m (262 to 820ft), is sheltered from sea breezes by the Cape Fold Belt, with a Mediterranean climate marked by hot and dry summers. The flat, fertile land is suited to bulk wine production: the region boasts over one third of the country's vineyard area and, owing to high yields, an even greater proportion of its wine production. The most important grape varieties include Chenin Blanc, Colombard, Semillon, Chardonnay, Sauvignon Blanc, Muscat, Ruby Cabernet, and Cabernet Sauvignon. The Worcester District and Breedekloof District are responsible for the bulk of the region's output, and are noted for their fortified wines made from red and white Muscat. Robertson District to the east is geographically distinct, with hillier terrain along the banks of the Breede. Though drier than Worcester, this 'Valley of Vines and Roses' with its limestone soils is reputed for its fine Chardonnays as well as its sweet Muscat and off-dry Colombard. Estates such as Graham Beck Wines have been experimenting with Cabernet Sauvignon, Shiraz, and even Sauvignon Blanc, often with excellent results.

Klein Karoo Region

South Africa's driest wine region is situated in a semi-desert area in the far east of the Western Cape. It reputation rests on sweet Muscats and Port-style fortified wines. In recent years, growers have sought out cooler highland sites in which to make crisp, dry whites and rich, full-bodied reds from Port grapes such as Touriga Nacional and Tinta Barroca.

Olifants River Region and Cederberg

The large Olifants River Region is located around the Olifants River system running north of Swartland. The terrain ranges from mountains around Citrusdal in the south to Atlantic coastline in the far north. On the whole, the region is warm and dry, with the Atlantic Ocean exerting a cooling influence in certain parts. The primary focus is on bulk wine, although quality Sauvignon Blanc, Cabernet Sauvignon, Pinotage, and Chenin Blanc is also being made in cooler areas.

To the southeast of the Olifants River Region is the small, district-less ward of Cederberg with just one, eponymous winery. Located at an altitude of 1,100m (3,609ft), Cederberg is reputed for its cool-climate Shiraz, Sauvignon Blanc, and Cabernet Sauvignon.

Northern Cape Unit

The Northern Cape Unit is home to South Africa's most northerly vineyards along the fertile Orange River Valley. The ward of Lower Orange accounts for 5% of the country's vineyards, but is mostly devoted to bulk wine production.

Wine styles

Historically, South Africa has been big on white wine. White grape varieties still make up ~55% of plantings, and white wines ~65% of production by volume. Chenin Blanc accounts for ~18% of plantings, followed by Colombard with ~12%. Each of these grape varieties accounts for 21% of wine production, indicative of strong demand for inexpensive white table wine. Chenin Blanc is also used for quality wines, as is Sauvignon Blanc (which has witnessed something of an explosion in the last decade), Chardonnay, Semillon, and Muscat of Alexandria. The most planted black grape variety is Cabernet Sauvignon, although it has been overtaken by Shiraz in terms of volume of production. Other important black grape varieties are Cabernet Franc, Merlot, and Petit Verdot, which are blended with Cabernet Sauvignon in the Bordeaux-style 'Cape Blend'. There are also significant plantings of Cinsault, Ruby Cabernet, and Pinotage. Plantings of Pinotage and Shiraz have taken off in recent years, often at the expense of Merlot and Cabernet Sauvignon. Reflecting on the origins of its settlers, South Africa is also home to a diversity of cultivars from Italy, Spain, Portugal, Alsace, and Southern France.

Imported from the Loire in the 17th century, Chenin Blanc (Steen) is one of the oldest established grape varieties in South Africa. A lot of South African Chenin is rather generic, but some producers focus on quality expressions similar to those from the Loire, including rich, bone dry wines reminiscent of Savennières and sweet, botrytized wines reminiscent of Coteaux du Layon. Owing to the warmer climate, the emphasis is more on tropical fruits than on apples. Classic notes of honey and nuts can come through in the best examples, but the musty lanolin or 'wet dog' character is mostly absent. In general, acidity, although still high, is lower, and, conversely, alcohol is higher. Most producers focus on regional terroir expressions but some are experimenting with barrel fermentation, making wines not unlike white Bordeaux. The best areas for Chenin Blanc are Stellenbosch, Paarl, Worcester, Wellington, and, in places, Swartland and Lower Orange.

Sauvignon Blanc now accounts for ~10% of all plantings in South Africa. If Marlborough Sauvignon Blanc is ripe and punchy and Loire Sauvignon Blanc is light and lean, then South African Sauvignon Blanc falls somewhere in between. While the gooseberry and nettle is unmistakable, the wine is less overt than Marlborough and fuller in body than Loire. South Africa produces plenty of cheap, sometimes off-dry, Sauvignon Blanc; quality examples with complexity and minerality hail from cooler regions, in particular Walker Bay, Cape Agulhas, and Cape Point. Oaked Sauvignon Blanc, so-called Fumé Blanc or Blanc Fumé, is produced throughout the country, with greater success in slightly warmer areas.

Chardonnay accounts for ~8% of plantings, and, unlike Chenin Blanc and Sauvignon Blanc, is mostly turned into quality wine. Chardonnay production is concentrated in Stellenbosch, Paarl, Worcester, and the chalk soils of Robertson, and, increasingly, in cooler areas such as Walker Bay. Top South African Chardonnay is very difficult to distinguish from that of other countries; pointers may include tropical fruit notes, a full body, and rather heavy oak. On the whole, South African Chardonnay is yet to match the length and finesse of Burgundy or certain parts of Australia, but there are some notable exceptions.

Sweet wines are made from various Muscat varieties, in particular Muscat of Alexandria (Hanepoot). The famous Vin de Constance is made from Muscat Blanc à Petits Grains (Muscat de Frontignan) and develops notes of honey, cloves, marmalade, and chocolate.

South Africa has a large number of other white grape varieties, first among them Semillon and Crouchen Blanc. Semillon has long been in decline. It is typically blended with Sauvignon Blanc in the Bordeaux style or, in cooler parts of the Cape South Coast Region, crafted into a varietal wine. Crouchen Blanc (Cape Riesling) is an unexciting grape variety and also on the decline. There is emerging interest in Viognier, Gewurztraminer, and Rhône varieties such as Roussanne and Marsanne.

Cabernet Sauvignon is the leading black grape variety, accounting for ~12% of plantings. It can be made as a varietal wine, or blended with other Bordeaux grape varieties, or blended with Pinotage and other Bordeaux grape varieties. The traditional homes of Cabernet Sauvignon in South Africa are Stellenbosch and Paarl, and Tygerberg also has some good Cabernet sites. Compared to Bordeaux, the wines are deeper in colour, fuller in body, softer in acidity, and with riper or jammier fruit flavours. On the nose and palate, there are intense notes of blackcurrant, some of the green capsicum character of Bordeaux, and a certain earthy or smoky character particular to South Africa. French oak is commonly used.

Shiraz has come to account for ~11% of plantings. Paarl, Stellenbosch, and Swartland are the most important areas. South African Shiraz is typically rich and ripe, with a sweetness of fruit reminiscent of Barossa Shiraz. Compared to their Australian counterparts, the wines are often smokier, with savoury notes of game, leather, and tar: like Northern Rhône, but 'supercharged'. Both French oak and American oak are commonly used. Owing to higher alcohol and lower acidity, South African Shiraz is not as long-lived as Syrah from the Northern

Rhône. It is often blended with Cabernet Sauvignon or Pinotage. Rhône blends with Grenache and Mourvèdre are increasingly common, as are cool climate expressions from areas such as Walker Bay.

Pinotage is a bit like Marmite: either you love it or you hate it. It has a tendency to retain volatile esters during vinification, which can result in unpleasant paint-like aromas. Critics often deride it as alcoholic and uncouth with coarse tannins, and quite unlike either of its parents, Pinot Noir and Cinsault. However, winemaking techniques such as controlled fermentation times and temperatures and the judicious use of oak can tame the pungent aromas and coarse tannins. Pinotage thrives in South Africa, with high yields of ripe grapes. Plantings have increased over the past five years or so, to ~7%. Winemakers keen to build on Pinotage's unique heritage tend to focus on quality. The best examples bring out the grape's character and complexity, with remarkable notes of banana, coffee bean, clove, and boiled sweet emerging with increasing bottle age. The Coastal Region—especially Paarl, Stellenbosch, and Swartland—and the Breede River Valley are the most important areas for Pinotage. Pinotage can play an important role in 'Cape Blends', which have been envisaged as a readily identifiable wine style for positioning South Africa on the export market. According to some, the blend ought to comprise 30-70% Pinotage, with the balance made up by Bordeaux grape varieties or even Shiraz. According to others, it ought to comprise only Bordeaux grape varieties. The question is still unresolved, and 'Cape Blend' remains a non-specific term.

Pinot Noir, though accounting for only ~1% of plantings, is becoming increasingly important. Walker Bay arguably still makes the country's best Pinot Noir, though plantings now extend throughout the Cape South Coast and Coastal Regions. As in Burgundy, the use of French oak is common, but the fruit is often riper or jammier and the body tends to be fuller.

Merlot, the fourth most planted black grape variety, is mostly blended with Cabernet Sauvignon, as is Cabernet Franc. Grenache and Mourvèdre are used for increasingly popular Southern Rhône GSM blends. Portuguese varieties, particularly Touriga Nacional, are made into Port-style fortified wines as well as varietal or blended light wines. Pockets of old head-trained Carignan vines continue to produce rich, spicy, and elegant wines. Cinsault has a similar heritage, and played an important historical part as one parent of Pinotage. It is often a small component in Cape Blend and other Cabernet-dominated wines. Ruby Cabernet (Cabernet Sauvignon × Cinsault), originally from California, ranks in South Africa's top ten grape varieties by vineyard area. It is mostly used for inexpensive wine or as a blending component.

Chapter 25

Chile

100 km

ANDES

30°S

La Serena ● Elqui

Limarí

Pacific
Ocean

Choapa

Mt Aconcagua

Aconcagua

Mendoza ●

Maipo

Casablanca

San Antonio

Santiago ●

Cachapoal

Rapel

Argentina

Colchagua

Curicó

35°S

Talca ●

Maule

Itata

ANDES

Concepción ●

Bío Bío

Malleco

☐ Coquimbo
☐ Aconcagua
■ Central Valley
■ South

Chile

The Spanish introduced the vine into their South American colonies in the 16th century, principally to provide the blood of Christ with which to bind natives to colonists. In 1524, conquistador Hernán Cortés ordered every landholder in New Spain to grow grapes. After the conquest of the Incas by Francisco Pizarro in 1531, the vine spread south into the newly created Viceroyalty of Peru. In 1554, Diego García de Cáceres planted the first vineyards of Santiago, and, by the end of the century, the vine had reached as far south as the River Bío-Bío. Viticulture developed under the aegis of, among others, Franciscan, Dominican, and Jesuit missionaries. Accordingly, the grape variety that Cortés had imported from Spain came to be called Mission. Under the names of País in Chile and Criolla Grande in Argentina, Mission dominated the continent's wine industry for the next four centuries. Indeed, it is only in recent years that Cabernet Sauvignon displaced País as the most planted grape variety in Chile.

By 1641, Peru was producing so much wine that Spain restricted production in its colonies. This decree all but wiped out the Peruvian wine industry, although in Chile it was largely ignored. Chilean wine could be made much more cheaply than Spanish wine, which served the territory well until consumers became more quality conscious in the 19th century. The arrival in Santiago of the French naturalist Claude Gay in 1828 led to a change in focus to quality wine. Gay petitioned the Chilean government to establish the Quinta Normal, which became a repository for all manner of plant species including *Vitis vinifera*. French winemakers immigrating to Chile in the wake of phylloxera discovered not only a land free of disease but also a rich catalogue of European vine cuttings. This happenstance also ensured the preservation of Carménère, indigenous to Bordeaux but almost entirely killed off by phylloxera. In 1851, the industrialist and oenophile Don Silvestre Ochagavía Echazarreta returned to Chile with some choice cuttings from Bordeaux and established the seminal Viña Ochagavía winery in the Maipo Valley.

Despite increasing taxation, the Chilean wine industry prospered until, in the 1970s, domestic consumption collapsed under the Pinochet regime. A vine pull scheme obliterated half of Chile's vineyards, and the country's wine industry only began to recover in the late 1980s after the restoration of a free market economy. Producers and investors cannily focused on quality wine for the export market; today, Chile exports up to 70% of its wine production, a greater proportion than any other country.

The lie of the land

Chile extends over 4,300km (2,700mi) from north to south, but only, at most, 240km (150mi) from east to west. It is enclosed to the east by the Andes Mountains, to the west by the Pacific Ocean, to the north by the Atacama Desert, and to the south by the Southern Ocean. Its vineyards exist in a state of splendid isolation, untouched by phylloxera and other pests. The cold Humboldt Current exerts a marked effect on the climate, which, overall, is cooler than the latitude range might suggest. High levels of sunshine yield grapes with intense colours and bright fruit flavours. Morning sea mists exert a cooling effect without promoting fungal disease. And the shifting terrain harbours a diversity of mesoclimates. In the absence of phylloxera, *vinifera* rootstocks can be maintained, although some producers prefer to graft their vines onto American rootstocks as an insurance policy or, if drip irrigation is being used, to offer protection from nematodes. The cooler coastal sites are susceptible to frost, but the main threat to the harvest is the El Niño weather system, which, every few years, brings rainfall in the middle of the growing season. La Niña, El Niño's counterpart, poses much less of a threat.

Chile's 120,000ha of vineyards are concentrated in the Central Valley region that extends south from Santiago (33.5°S), although regions to the north are becoming increasingly important. The Central Valley lies between the Andes to the east and the more humble Coastal Range (Cordillera de la Costa) to the west. The Coastal Range shelters the valley from the brunt of the cool sea mists, leading to a Mediterranean climate in the valley. Ocean air that does filter through meets with cold air descending nightly from the Andes, giving rise to large diurnal temperature variations that conserve fruit flavours and acidity. Rainfall is concentrated in the winter, with the growing season largely warm and dry. Irrigation is common, with snowmelt from the Andes channelled into irrigation furrows. Drip irrigation is often preferred for newer sites. Compared to the slopes, the valley floor is warmer and more fertile, yielding fuller wines with riper fruit and softer acidity. To the east, in the foothills of the Andes, poorer volcanic soils and a more continental climate make for crisper and finer wines. To the west, on the slopes of the Coastal Range, the vineyards are generally lower. The Pacific breezes bypass certain sites, creating hot conditions suitable only for the production of full-bodied red wines. Some of Chile's newest and most exciting vineyards are on the windward side of the Coastal Range. The climate here is distinctly cool and maritime, and better suited to Chardonnay, Pinot Noir, and aromatic white grape varieties.

Regions

The most recent revision of Chile's wine regions conserves the traditional names of six regions organized by latitude. These regions are divided into sub-regions or 'valleys', each with one or more of three designations according to whether they are on the coast (*Costa*), in the Coastal Range or valley plateaux (*Cordilleras*), or in the Andes (*Andes*). Sub-regions may be further divided into zones or 'sub-valleys', the most important of which can be found in the historic sub-regions of the Central Valley region and San Antonio Valley in the Aconcagua region. The most northerly region, Atacama, traditionally grows vines for pisco and table grapes; while the most southerly region, Austral, mostly consists of new, experimental vineyards. This leaves four regions to discuss: Coquimbo, Aconcagua, Central Valley, and South.

Coquimbo

The Coquimbo region is roughly centred on La Serena, Chile's second oldest city. Its three disparate valleys are, from north to south, Elqui, Limarí, and Choapa. Elqui and Limarí have both coastal and Andean designations, Choapa only Andean. On the whole, the region is hot and very dry with no more than 100mm (4in) annual rainfall. Quality vineyard sites are planted at altitude in the Andes or facing the Pacific in the coastal area. The 300ha of Elqui Valley are close to the southern border of the Atacama Desert. While the valley floor is best suited to tropical fruits and table grapes, coastal and high altitude (up to 2000m or 6,562ft) vineyards can yield relatively cool climate expressions. The most commonly planted grape varieties are Syrah, Sauvignon Blanc, Carménère, and Cabernet Sauvignon. Only in the 1990s did attention turn to the cool Pacific coast of Limarí Valley, with its significant limestone deposits, as an area for making quality Chardonnay. Today, Chardonnay accounts for more than one third of the ~1,800ha of plantings in Limarí, and Sauvignon Blanc too is on the rise. Sizeable plantings of Syrah and Cabernet Sauvignon are a testament to traditional Limarí red wines. Choapa Valley is at Chile's narrowest point. For now, there are only a few select plantings of Cabernet Sauvignon and Syrah.

Aconcagua

The Aconcagua region counts three valleys: Aconcagua, Casablanca, and San Antonio. Aconcagua Valley sits in the shadow of Mount Aconcagua, the highest mountain in the Americas. The interior has been producing quality red wines for over 150 years. Bordeaux grape varieties, especially Cabernet Sauvignon, have traditionally flourished here, with Syrah and Pinot Noir being much more recent introductions. The family-owned Errázuriz winery, established in 1870, is the area's most recognized producer. Meanwhile, on the coast, Sauvignon Blanc and Chardonnay have been taking off, again with excellent results. White grape varieties currently account for ~20% of Aconcagua's ~1,000ha. Casablanca and San Antonio are exclusively coastal. Casablanca Valley, to the west of Santiago, was planted in the mid 1980s with Cabernet Sauvignon and Carménère. However, the cool Mediterranean climate is better suited to white grape varieties, which, led by Chardonnay and Sauvignon Blanc, have come to dominate the sub-region's ~6,000ha of plantings. Meanwhile, Pinot Noir, also at home in this cool climate, has come to account for the majority of black grape plantings. Unusually, there is no river to tap, and water for irrigation must be supplied from boreholes. Drip irrigation is common, supplemented by dew from the morning mists. Many wineries in Casablanca source fruit for red wine from the nearby Central Valley region. San Antonio Valley, immediately to the south of Casablanca, is newer and smaller, with just over 1,700ha under vine. The climate is similar to that in Casablanca, albeit with less rainfall. Sauvignon Blanc is dominant, and there are also significant plantings of Chardonnay and Pinot Noir. The sub-region's most exciting zone is Leyda Valley, a mere 12km (7mi) from the sea.

Central Valley

Chile's most important wine region consists of four sub-regions, from north to south, Maipo, Rapel, Curicó, and Maule, which alone is responsible for a full half of Chile's export wines. With the exception of Maipo Valley around Santiago, all the sub-regions contain costal, cordilleras, and Andean designations. In the 19th century, under the influence of Don Silvestre Ochagavía Echazarreta, an emerging class of gentlemen industrialists established wineries on their summer estates on the outskirts of Santiago. Today, Santiago is the only capital city with vineyards within the city boundaries, even if most of Maipo's ~12,000ha under vines are in the Andean foothills and on the valley plateau. Cabernet Sauvignon accounts for over half of all plantings. Despite the predominantly clay soils, it thrives on the higher sites in the Andean foothills, the Alto Maipo, benefiting from poorer soils and cooling afternoon breezes. Other black grape varieties include Merlot, Carménère, Cabernet Franc, and Malbec. Bordeaux blends are common, as indeed are varietal wines. There are also sizeable plantings of Syrah, Chardonnay, and Sauvignon Blanc, with the white grape varieties finding favour in the small part of Maipo that is near the coast. Maipo is home to Concha y Toro, founded in 1883 by Don Melchor Concha y Toro and today the largest wine producer in South America.

Further south, the Rapel Valley sub-region contains the large Cachapoal Valley and Colchagua Valley zones. Cachapoal is the smaller, with over one third of the ~10,000ha under vines given over to Cabernet Sauvignon. The best sites are in the Andean foothills. To the west, in the Coastal Range, the climate is warmer and better suited to Carménère and Syrah. Further west, in the coastal regions, there are sizeable plantings of Sauvignon Blanc. Colchagua too is dominated by Cabernet Sauvignon, which makes up more than 10,000ha of the ~25,000ha under vine. As in Cachapoal, Carménère is gaining ground against Merlot. Syrah, Chardonnay, Sauvignon Blanc, Cabernet Franc, and Malbec are also important, and Viognier appears to be on the make.

Colchagua is home to one of Chile's most hallowed terroirs, the Apalta, a group of hills arranged in a natural amphitheatre on the banks of the River Tinguiririca. The Neyen family first planted Cabernet Sauvignon and Carménère on the free-draining stony soils of the Apalta in 1890, and today are still making wine from these vines. Colchagua boasts many long-established wineries and a number of prominent foreign investors, not least Robert Mondavi (Caliterra) and the Lafite branch of the Rothschild family (Los Vascos).

Vines have been cultivated in Curicó Valley since the 19th century. Miguel Torres of Spain began investing in Curicó in 1979, and the sub-region quickly acquired an international standing. Curicó derives from *Kureko*, an indigenous term meaning 'land of black water', and the soils are predominantly alluvial. Summer days can be very hot but the nights are bathed in cool Andean air. Of the 13,500ha under vine, ~4,000ha are given over to Cabernet Sauvignon and ~3,500ha to Sauvignon Blanc. Curicó is still in a state of flux, with old vines, mostly of País, being replaced by higher quality grape varieties.

With ~32,000ha under vine, Maule Valley is Chile's largest wine sub-region by far. Owing to its more southerly latitude, Maule is cooler and cloudier than the rest of the Central Valley. As in Curicó, País is being uprooted in favour of higher quality grape varieties, especially Cabernet Sauvignon, Chardonnay, and Syrah, and there are also significant plantings of Sauvignon Blanc, Merlot, and Carménère. Old and gnarly dry-farmed bush vines, especially of Carignan, attract something of a cult following.

South

In the South region, the Coastal Range is less prominent, allowing in more of the Pacific influence. The climate is cooler and wetter, and irrigation is not required. Annual rainfall averages 1,300mm (51in) in some parts, even if most of this falls in winter. The south region counts three sub-regions, Itata Valley, Bío-Bío Valley, and Malleco Valley. The vine first reached the port of Concepción in Itata Valley in the 16th century. Today, the ~11,000ha under vine are planted with País and Muscat of Alexandria. There are smaller plantings of Cabernet Sauvignon, Semillon, and Carignan, which can make for interesting wines. Like

Itata, Bío-Bío Valley, on the northern banks of the River Renaico, is in a period of transformation, with País, Muscat, and Cabernet Sauvignon being replaced by grape varieties better suited to the cool, wet climate, most notably Pinot Noir, Chardonnay, Riesling, Gewurztraminer, and Sauvignon Blanc. Currently, there are 835ha under vine, which is significantly more than the mere 17ha in Malleco Valley, a full 640km (400mi) south of Santiago.

Wine styles

Chile is South America's second largest wine producer after Argentina, but arguably enjoys the greater reputation on the export market. Black grape varieties account for over three-quarters of the country's plantings. Cabernet Sauvignon makes up ~35% of plantings, followed by Chardonnay and Sauvignon Blanc at ~12% each. In the 1990s, it came to light that much Chilean 'Merlot' was in fact Carménère. Winemakers have since shifted their focus from Merlot to Carménère, which, in Chile, tends to outperform Merlot, and which also has the benefit of being a signature Chilean varietal wine along the lines of Argentina's Malbec and Uruguay's Tannat (see Chapter 26). Bordeaux grape varieties, whether as blends or varietal wines, make up the core of Chile's export wines, although white grape varieties are increasingly popular as are Syrah and Pinot Noir. Chile looks to France not only for its Bordeaux blends, but also for its cool climate Chardonnay and Alsatian-style aromatic wines. For Sauvignon Blanc, it treads a line between the restraint of the Loire and the pungency of Marlborough. At the same time, it is turning increasingly towards the University of California, Davis for expertise, and the USA for its prime export market—which in time may alter the styles of Chilean wine. Although traditional wine-making techniques such as *bâtonnage*, *pigeage*, and maturation in French oak are common, Chile is not hampered by tradition and boasts one of the most modern ensembles of winemaking equipment in the world.

Cabernet Sauvignon is the past, present, and for some time to come, the future of Chilean fine wine. The best examples come from Rapel Valley, Maipo, and Aconcagua. Chilean Cabernet Sauvignon is deep purple with aromas of fresh cassis and, often, a signature smoky, herbaceous note. Legally, a wine need contain only 75% of the grape variety displayed on the label, so a Chilean 'Cab' could well contain other black grape varieties. Top examples are aged in French oak, adding notes of cedar, vanilla, and toast. Cool nights result in crisp acidity, and warm days in high alcohol and riper, softer tannins than Bordeaux.

Carménère is a challenge for the grower. As it is highly vigorous, it requires to be planted on very poor soils. It also ripens late, by which stage acidity in the grapes is dropping. Producers can harvest early to preserve acidity but at the risk of overly herbaceous, medicinal notes. Or they can wait until full ripeness and wind up with a wine that is flabby and jammy. The best producers find the optimal balance, making a wine that is deep ruby in colour with notes of cherry, blueberry, spice, black pepper, bell pepper, and tobacco. On the palate, acidity is low, alcohol high, and tannins soft and silky. Cabernet Sauvignon is often co-opted for extra acidity and tannin structure, and field blends with Merlot are still common. Most plantings of Carménère are in Colchagua.

The valley floors on which most Merlot is planted are often too hot, and Merlot's natural roots do not dig deep enough to sustain the vine through dry spells. Moreover, excess sunshine can burn and shrivel the grapes, leading to a raisined aroma profile and harsh tannins. Solutions include seeking out more suitable vineyard sites and grafting onto deeper-rooting rootstocks. Some of the best examples of Chilean Merlot come from Maipo and Colchagua. Compared to Merlot-dominated Bordeaux blends, Chilean Merlot is deeper in colour with notes of ripe plum, cherry, currants, chocolate, and mint (the latter note similar to the herbaceous quality in Chilean Cabernet Sauvignon and Carménère). On the palate, it is full-bodied with high alcohol, balanced acidity, and soft and silky tannins that are however not without grip.

Introduced as recently as 1993 and accounting for less than 3% of plantings, Syrah has become Chile's most exciting red wine. The most suitable sites for Syrah have turned out to be in the cooler regions, with the high altitude vineyards of Elqui and the coastal vineyards of Casablanca and San Antonio yielding medium-bodied, fragrant, meaty, and peppery Rhône-style wines. Warmer sites such as Maipo and Apalta in Colchagua produce a rounded style with more intense blackberry. Overall, the style is more reminiscent of French Syrah than Australian

Shiraz; yet, the wines are deeper in colour, often with a characteristic smokiness or herbaceousness.

Pinot Noir is still finding its feet in Chile, and already proving successful in certain cool coastal sites. Owing to high levels of sunshine, Chilean Pinot Noir can be deep purple in colour and, sometimes, overly alcoholic. The aroma profile leans towards cherry and black fruit, often with chocolate and herbaceous notes.

The cool climate expression of Chardonnay from Limarí, Casablanca, and San Antonio (especially Leyda) is fast becoming Chile's signature style of Chardonnay. The wines are lean, restrained, and elegant with notes of both citrus and tropical fruits. Ambitious producers employ techniques such as barrique vinification, *batônnage*, and lees ageing, with the current fashion being for less overt oak. The best examples, while not on par with top flight Burgundy, are often hard to distinguish from well-made Mâcon. However, the bulk of Chilean Chardonnay comes from warmer sites in the Central Valley, and is marked by lower acidity, higher alcohol, and more overt tropical fruit.

Much of what used to pass for Chilean Sauvignon Blanc was in fact more humble Sauvignon Vert (Tocai Friulano), and a bottle labelled with just 'Sauvignon' most likely contains Sauvignon Vert. Sauvignon Blanc plantings are disseminated throughout the country, but the best examples hail from Casablanca. Most Chilean Sauvignon Blanc is vinified in stainless steel, and combines gooseberry and tropical fruit with fresh, herbal aromas. It neither matches New Zealand Sauvignon Blanc for punchiness nor Sancerre for restraint, but is instead distinguished by grapefruit and a nettle or smoky herbal note. Wines from warmer sites are often dominated by tropical fruit aromas and can be rather flabby.

Small amounts of quality dessert wine are made from Moscatel de Alejandria. Riesling, Pinot Gris and Gewurztraminer are finding their feet in the Bío-Bío Valley and other cool climate sites, while Viognier is becoming increasingly fashionable along the coast and in the cordilleras.

Chapter 26

Argentina
Uruguay
Brazil

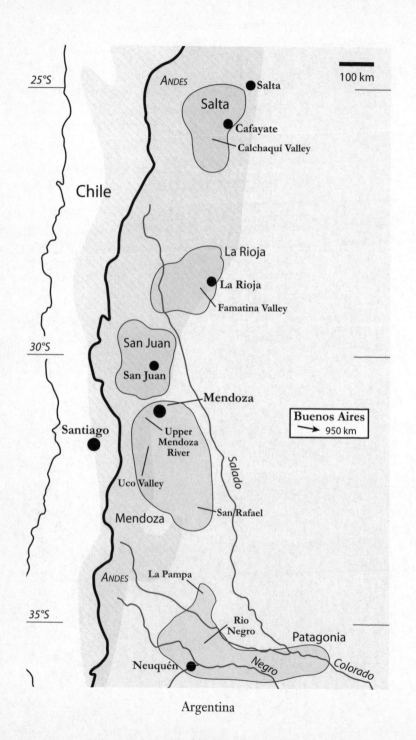

Vines were first brought to Santiago del Estero, the oldest city in what was to become Argentina, in 1557. As the conquistadors and missionaries pushed south into the Mendoza region, they discovered networks of irrigation canals built by the Huarpe under the guidance of the Inca. The purpose of these canals was to distribute snowmelt from the Andes, transforming an arid plateau into a land of plenty. Within ten years of the founding of the city of Mendoza in 1561, vineyards had been firmly established in the region. Most wine was made from Mission (Criolla Chica), which, still today, is cultivated for the production of inexpensive table wine. The 1820s witnessed an influx of European immigrants into a newly independent Argentina. Most came from Spain and Italy and brought with them a huge diversity of grape varieties. From 1853, the French agriculturist Michel Aimé Pouget headed Argentina's first school of agriculture, the Quinta Normal. Pouget introduced vine clippings from France, including Malbec, which, in time, became the country's signature grape variety. Prior to the 1990s, Argentine wine was almost entirely destined for the domestic market. With the backing of international investors, cooler vineyard sites were sought at (even) higher altitudes and more southerly latitudes into Patagonia. The economic crisis at the start of the 21st century curbed investment but not the thirst for quality wine. Today, Argentina's international reputation for wine rests on Malbec and Torrontés. The country is busy expanding its repertoire, exploiting modern winemaking techniques and tapping into its rich library of historic grape varieties.

The lie of the land

Argentina's vineyards span a remarkable 1,600km (1,000mi), from the subtropical Salta at ~24°S to Patagonia at ~40°S. These vineyards are shielded from the cool, moist influence of the Pacific Ocean by the impenetrable curtain of the Andes. The climate in the Argentine Andean foothills is hot, dry, and continental, with viticulture only made possible by high altitude and Andean snowmelt. Indeed, Argentina boasts some of the highest vineyards in the world: the average altitude is 900m (2,953ft) and some sites in Salta are as high as 3000m (9,843ft)! Owing to the dry mountain air, there is little disease pressure on the vines and pesticides are barely needed. Spring frosts pose a risk, and the Zonda, a hot and fierce mountain wind, can play havoc with flowering in the early summer. However, dry air and abundant sunshine ensure that grapes are able to ripen. Overly vigorous vines and excessive alcohol levels are perennial problems, both addressed by restricting irrigation. Flood irrigation is the norm, although drip irrigation is sometimes practised in newer vineyards. The little rain that there is falls mostly in summer, occasionally in the form of destructive hail, and hail nets are common. Owing to the continental geography and high altitudes, the seasons are clearly defined, even in the subtropical north, and the diurnal temperature range can be very high. Cool nights help to preserve acidity in the grapes but, even so, acidification is common. The high sand content in the soils and the practice of flood irrigation may help explain why phylloxera, although present, has not had the same devastating effect as in other countries. Most vines are ungrafted, although grafting is required in newer, drip-irrigated vineyards, which are more prone to nematode infestations. Argentina devotes ~220,000ha to quality wine, with over 70% of this area in Mendoza. There are 25,000 individual vineyards, mostly smallholdings under 5ha. Over one-quarter of the area under vines is controlled by a clutch of big players with estates over 50ha. High trellising, especially the *el parral* system, is commonly used to keep the grapes away from the baking hot ground, although vertical shoot positioning or cordon training are often preferred in newer vineyards.

Regions

Mendoza

As the condor flies, Mendoza is a mere 180km (112mi) from Santiago de Chile, yet the difference in climate could not be more pronounced. Rainfall averages 220mm (9in) per year, a third of that in Napa and considerably less than that in Jerez, one of Europe's driest wine regions. Today, the region consists of five irrigated 'oases' over an area roughly equivalent to the South Island of New Zealand. The soil is composed predominantly of alluvial sand on a subsoil of clay, although the district of Maipú in the Upper Mendoza River sub-region contains an unusually high amount of gravel. About half of plantings are black grape varieties, above all Malbec, Merlot, Cabernet Sauvignon, Bonarda, and Tempranillo. A further quarter of plantings are white grape varieties, particularly Pedro Giménez (not the same as Pedro Ximénez), although Chardonnay is of increasing importance and there are small areas of Semillon, Chenin Blanc, Sauvignon Blanc, and Viognier. The rest are devoted to pink-skinned grape varieties such as Criolla Grande and Cereza used for inexpensive wine and grape concentrate.

The Upper Mendoza River sub-region, around the city of Mendoza itself and rising gently up the Andean foothills, is home to some of the finest vineyards in the country. The district of Luján de Cuyo boasts hundred-year old Malbec vines as well as Argentina's first *Denominación de Origen*, established in 1993 for Malbec only. Other important black grape varieties are Cabernet Sauvignon, Merlot, Pinot Noir, and Syrah. Viticulture is moving higher and higher up the Andean slopes, with Chardonnay and Sauvignon Blanc performing well at ~1,250m (4,101ft). Leading producers include Catena Zapata, Dominio del Plata, and Fabre Montmayou. On account of its gravel deposits, the district of Maipú (which neighbours on Luján de Cuyo) is arguably better suited to Cabernet Sauvignon. Leading producers in Maipú include Benegas and Pascual Toso.

South of the city of Mendoza is the picturesque Uco Valley, which competes with Upper Mendoza River in the quality stakes. Big names such as Lurton, Rothschild, and Rolland have invested in the Uco on account of its excellent climate and free-draining soils. Vineyards range in altitude from 900 to 1,500m (2,953 to 4,921ft), enabling the grapes to retain freshness and acidity. Malbec is dominant (although less so than in other parts of Mendoza) and the sub-region is also the traditional home of Semillon in Argentina. The Uco is fast building a reputation for Chardonnay, Sauvignon Blanc, Riesling, and Pinot Gris. The Cabernet Sauvignon, Merlot, and Tempranillo can also be impressive, and Syrah and Pinot Noir are taking root.

At 560 to 750m (1,837 to 2,461ft), the North Mendoza and East Mendoza sub-regions are relatively flat and low-lying. Traditionally, they have been an important source of inexpensive wines for the domestic market. East Mendoza accounts for 40% of Mendoza's area under vine, and there are moves to boost quality through canopy management and restrictive irrigation.

The final 'oasis' in Mendoza is South Mendoza, an outpost separated from the other four oases and centred upon the Rivers Diamante and Atuel. Vineyards are planted at altitudes of 450 to 800m (1,476 to 2,625ft) on alluvial deposits on a bed of limestone. Unexciting Criolla grape varieties make up around half of plantings, but fine wine is also made, notably from Bonarda, Cabernet Sauvignon, Malbec, and Chenin Blanc. The San Rafael district, home to the notable Goyenechea winery, competes with Luján de Cuyo in laying claim to the title of first Argentine *Denominación de Origen*.

San Juan

San Juan, around the city of San Juan 170km (106mi) north of Mendoza, is Argentina's second most important wine region by volume and also has a tradition of making fortified wine. The climate is hotter and drier than in Mendoza, with over 330 days of sunshine and just ~100mm (4in) of rainfall. There are ~41,000ha under vine, but over a fifth of the crop is turned into raisins and, of the wine produced, half is inexpensive table wine. The vineyards stretch across six valleys irrigated from the River San Juan. Of these, Tulum Valley, with vineyards at around 700m (2,297ft) in altitude, is the most important for quality wine. Further south, the newly established Pedernal Valley, with vineyards up to ~1,300m (4,265ft) in altitude, is building a reputation for fresher, more structured wines. The most planted quality grape variety is Syrah.

Salta and La Rioja

Further north, the climate is hotter and the vineyards higher. Salta, 1,000km (620mi) north of Mendoza and near the Tropic of Capricorn, boasts some of the world's highest vineyards ranging from ~1,650 to 3,000m (5,413 to 9,843ft) in altitude. The climate at these high altitudes is similar to that in Mendoza, with a large diurnal temperature range and annual rainfall of ~200mm (8in). Viticulture is centred on the city of Cafayate in the Calchaquí Valley. Production accounts for a mere 1% of the national total, and much of this is red wine. Yet Salta can boast one of Argentina's most acclaimed and distinctive white wines: an intensely aromatic and floral Torrontés with a rich, full-bodied fruitiness on the palate. Notable producers of Salta Torrontés include El Porvenir and the larger Michel Torino. In La Rioja, Torrontés makes up 35% of the ~8,000ha under vine. Compared to the strain of Torrontés of Salta, that of La Rioja is considered less refined but easier to cultivate. Other important grape varieties in La Rioja include Cabernet Sauvignon, Syrah, and Bonarda. The most reputed district is Famatina Valley, with vineyards at about 800 to 1,400m (2,625 to 4,593ft).

Patagonia

Many people think of Patagonia as a land of tall, jagged mountains spilling glaciers into lakes of frosted glass, but the north of this vast territory lies at latitudes of 37-42°S, roughly equivalent to the northern latitude range of the Mediterranean Sea. The climate is continental, with cold winters and warm, dry, and extended summers marked by sunny days and cool nights. Temperatures are considerably cooler than further north and the vineyards are planted at much lower altitudes. Like most of Argentina, the region lies in the rain shadow of the Andes, but the Rivers Negro and Colorado supply plenty of irrigation water. Patagonia accounts for a mere 1% of Argentine vineyard area, but the focus is firmly on quality wines with pronounced varietal character, crisp acidity, and structured tannins. Most plantings are fairly recent. Malbec and Pinot Noir dominate, and Chardonnay and Sauvignon Blanc also have a strong presence. The region is fast acquiring a reputation for quality sparkling wine, and the Pinot Noir from Rio Negro is held up as the best in the country. Rio Negro is the largest and most southerly of Patagonia's three wine sub-regions, with ~1,700ha of vines extending along the River Negro. The other two sub-regions are Neuquén, named after the regional capital, and La Pampa.

Wine styles

Malbec accounts for ~12% of plantings and the bulk of exports. It is often blended with Cabernet Sauvignon and other Bordeaux grape varieties. Argentine Malbec is very deep in colour, perhaps even inky black. All Malbec is characterized by a plummy fruit profile; however, whereas Malbec from Cahors in France tends to earthy notes of ink and iron, that from Argentina is generally riper (almost jammy) with spicy notes of cinnamon and nutmeg. On the palate, the wine is full-bodied with soft, velvety tannins, high alcohol, and, in many cases, moderate or low acidity. French oak ageing is common, contributing notes of vanilla, coffee, and chocolate. Plantings are widespread, but Mendoza is the most important region, with Luján de Cuyo and the Uco Valley arguably supplying the best fruit.

Bonarda, the second most widely planted grape variety in Argentina, is thought to be related to Bonarda Piemontese and Bonarda Novarese and may be the same as Corbeau. It is turned into inexpensive table wine for the domestic market but there are also some quality varietal expressions. These are deep purple in colour with aromas of raspberry, cherry, and plum (or prune and dried fig in the hottest sites) and a characteristic note of fennel or aniseed. On the palate, the wine is full-bodied with soft and velvety tannins.

Like Argentine Malbec, Argentine Cabernet Sauvignon is fairly visible on export markets. It is cultivated primarily from Salta to Mendoza with the best sites on the gravel soils of Maipú. It ripens so fully in Argentina that it can be turned into a single varietal wine without the 'hole in the middle' that, in Bordeaux, calls for blending with Merlot. Nonetheless, Bordeaux blends are common, especially with Merlot and Malbec. Argentine Cabernet Sauvignon is deep in colour with familiar Cabernet aromas of blackcurrant and capsicum, and vanilla and spice from French oak. With age, higher-end wines develop notes of meat, leather, and tobacco. On the palate, the wine is generally more full-bodied, less acidic, and less tannic than Bordeaux, yet more acidic and structured than Argentine Malbec. In general, Cabernet Sauvignon from the north of the country is jammier, that from the south more earthy and mineral.

On the export market, Argentine Syrah is typically encountered in a blend with Malbec, to which it contributes acidity, fresh fruit flavours, and black pepper spice. Varietal Syrah seeks to emulate either the Barossan 'fruit bomb' style or the more restrained and savoury style of the Northern Rhône.

Merlot thrives in Argentina's cooler sites, especially in the Uco Valley, and, increasingly, Rio Negro. Other red varietal wines include

Tempranillo, Sangiovese, and Pinot Noir. Pinot Noir is yet to find a suitable home in Argentina, although Patagonia does look promising.

The name 'Torrontés' first appears in the 1860s in records from Mendoza. There are in fact three varieties of Torrontés in Argentina: Riojana, Sanjuanino, and Mendocino. Torrontés Riojana, which accounts for 4% of Argentine plantings, is possibly a crossing of Muscat of Alexandria and Criolla Chica and unrelated to the Torrontés of Galicia in Spain or the Terrantez/Torrontés of Madeira. Though more difficult to cultivate than Sanjuanino and Mendocino, it is the more refined of the three and used for the best examples from Salta. The wine is very distinctive, presenting a floral Muscat-like bouquet with notes of rose, jasmine, peach, and citrus fruits. On the palate, it is typically full-bodied and dry to off-dry depending on style. The best examples preserve a fresh acidity. In blind tasting, Torrontés is sometimes confused with Muscat or Gewurztraminer, but is less grapey than Muscat and lacks the distinctive lychee note of Gewurztraminer. The palate is also less oily and more mineral.

Chardonnay is the only other Argentine white wine exported in any sizeable quantity. Most plantings are in Mendoza, yielding full-bodied wines with soft acidity and notes of tropical fruit. Cooler sites at higher altitudes in Mendoza or to the south in Patagonia yield leaner, mineral wines. Oak maturation is common. Almost all Argentine Chardonnay issues from the so-called Mendoza clone, which is also found (often under different names) throughout California, Australia, and New Zealand. The Mendoza clone is prone to *millerandage*, resulting in small berries, a high skin-to-fruit ratio, and a textural mouthfeel.

Chenin Blanc and Sauvignon Blanc are made in small quantities throughout the country. There are also miniscule plantings of Viognier, Riesling, and Pinot Gris.

Uruguay

In the 19th century, Basque settlers introduced Tannat to Uruguay, a small bucolic nation to the northeast of Buenos Aires. The Andes lie more than 1,000km (620mi) to the west and the climate is strongly influenced by the Atlantic Ocean. High humidity and cloud cover put the vines under significant disease pressure. By increasing airflow, Lyre trellising systems reduce the incidence of mildew. Of the ~8,500ha under vine, one-quarter is given over to Tannat. Most vineyards are in the south of the country, in the Canelones region around the capital of Montevideo. Much as Malbec has become Argentina's signature grape variety, so Tannat has become Uruguay's. Styles range from light and fruity rosés to dark, brooding reds. The full-bodied style is deep purple with a heady aroma of plum and dark fruit, tobacco, leather, and petrichor. On the palate, the wine is often quite alcoholic, but with refreshing acidity. As with Madiran, tannins are very high and can be tough or chewy.

Brazil

Brazil is South America's third largest wine producing country by volume, with over 88,000ha under vine. The principal producing region is Rio Grande do Sul, in the far south bordering on Uruguay. This is the only area in this tropical country with sufficiently distinct seasons for the vine to flourish. That said, there are vines in the Vale do São Francisco at 9°S which fruit twice a year! The majority of plantings are American vines or hybrids. Plantings of *vinifera* are increasing and are mostly dedicated to white wine production. Brazil's specialty is sparkling wine, especially sweet Moscato made in the Asti style from one of the many Muscat strains. Dry sparkling wine is becoming more common with increased investment in traditional method sparkling wines made from Pinot Noir and Chardonnay. Plantings of Riesling Italico (Welschriesling) and Malvasia bear witness to the early influence of Italian immigrants. Red wine production is small but growing, with a focus on full-bodied styles made from Cabernet Sauvignon, Merlot, and Cabernet Franc.

Chapter 27

USA
Canada

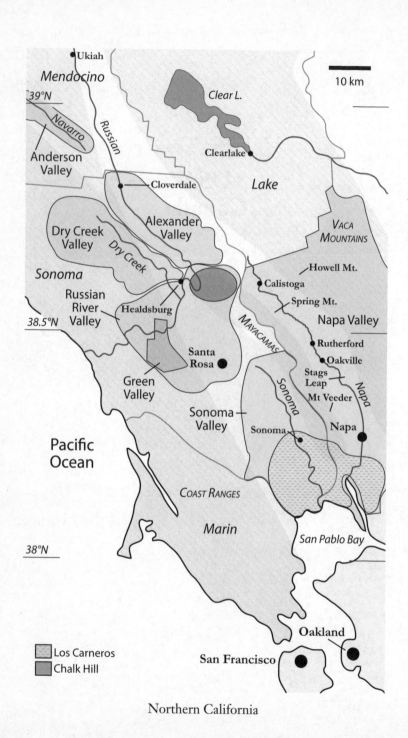

Northern California

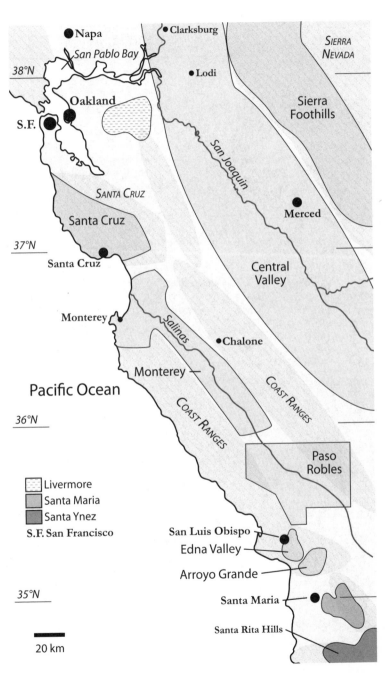

Central California

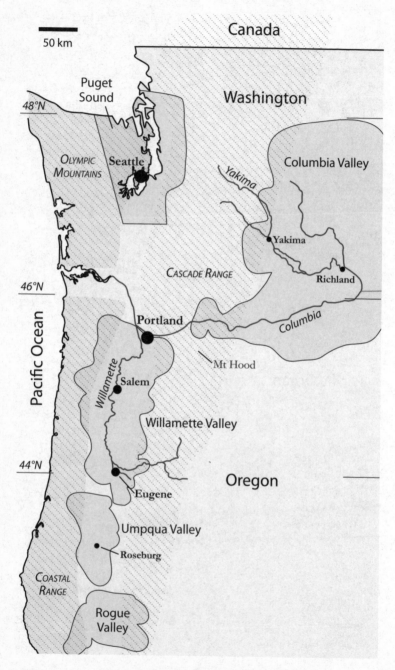

Oregon & Washington

The European discovery of the Americas is attributed to Norse adventurer Leif Ericson (c.970–c.1020). Ericson most probably landed in Newfoundland, where he established a colony he called Vinland—possibly after the grapevines that abounded in the region. In the 1560s, French Huguenot settlers made wine from the large, native Scuppernong grapes in Florida. Over the next 250 years, successive waves of settlers vinified native grapes all along the Eastern Seaboard, but the results, which they described as 'foxy' or 'musky', did not appeal to their European palates. Attempts to establish European vines met with repeated failure as the plants died of a mysterious ailment which, only much later in the mid-19th century, came to be identified as phylloxera. In the early 1800s, on his Monticello estate in Virginia, Thomas Jefferson resigned himself to making wine from native grapes. *Vitis labrusca* proved most promising, and, to this day, *labrusca* varieties and hybrids such as Concord, Catawba, Niagara, and Delaware are still cultivated on the Eastern Seaboard. In the early to mid-19th century, Catawba was the most widely grown grape variety in the United States. It lay behind Nicholas Longworth's acclaimed Ohio sparkling wine, which was exported to Europe and even came to be seen as a threat to Champagne. By the late 1850s, Ohio boasted over one third of the country's vines and earned itself the sobriquet, 'Rhine of America'. In the 1860s, outbreaks of fungal disease, the Civil War, and Longworth's death put an end to Ohio's supremacy, with the centre of viticultural activity moving north to the shores of Lake Erie and east to Pennsylvania and New York.

In the late 1760s, the Spanish developed a renewed interest in Alta California. Franciscan missionaries cultivated the *vinifera* grape variety Mission (País, Criolla Grande) in the phylloxera-free soils of San Diego, Monterey, and San Francisco. In 1821, at the end of the Mexican War of Independence, Alta California entered Mexico; in 1848, at the end of the Mexican-American War, it entered the United States. In that same year, James W. Marshall discovered gold in the American River, drawing population and prosperity to the newly carved out State of California. At last, American growers could cultivate *vinifera* vines on home soil. The classic Bordeaux grape varieties found great success in places such as Napa and Sonoma, where they remain dominant. Italian immigrants introduced Primitivo, which, under the name of Zinfandel, became another important grape variety. In 1880, the University of California (UC) established the precursor to the influential UC Davis Department of Viticulture and Enology. Then disaster struck, first in the form of phylloxera, which arrived in the late 1800s, and later, from 1920 to 1933, in that of Prohibition. The legacy of Prohibition lives on to this day: each state imposes its own alcohol tax with some counties remaining puritanically dry, while exporting wine across state lines can present such a legislative hurdle as to dissuade many small producers from even trying. Mercifully, viticulture perdured during the Prohibition era, if only for the production of table grapes, juice concentrate, raisins, and communion wine for the Church. The revival came about in the 1960s with pioneers such as Robert Mondavi, André Tchelistcheff, and the Gallo brothers shifting the focus from the Port-style fortified wines that had dominated post-Prohibition production to Bordeaux-style Cabernet Sauvignons and Burgundy-influenced Chardonnays. In 1976, British wine merchant Steven Spurrier convened a panel of mostly French wine critics to blind taste the best of California alongside the best of Bordeaux and Burgundy. This so-called Judgement of Paris vindicated the American pioneers, with a Californian wine taking top prize in every category. In volume terms, California has come to account for ~90% of US production: if the Golden State were a country, it would rank fourth after France, Italy, and Spain. Naturally, most of the production is not the hyper-exclusive stuff that wins the prizes, but inexpensive and characterless bulk wine made on an industrial scale.

Wine is produced in all 50 US states including Alaska and Hawaii. However, the standout success of recent years has been in the Pacific Northwest, with Washington and Oregon climbing the ranks to third and fourth by volume after California and New York. In the 1960s, a handful of Californian winemakers sought to cultivate Pinot Noir in the cooler climate of Oregon. In 1979, the Eyrie Vineyards 1975 South Block Reserve Pinot Noir created a stir when it began winning accolades in France. Since then, Oregon has attracted heavy investment, not least from California and Burgundy. Further north, Washington produces considerably more wine than Oregon, but, owing in part to its broad range of styles, does not enjoy the same prestige. Back on the Eastern Seaboard, New York is justifiably proud of its Riesling from the Finger Lakes region and Bordeaux-style wines from Long Island,

and Virginia is finally realizing Thomas Jefferson's dream of crafting elegant, European-style wines.

Classification

US wine regions are divided into American Viticultural Areas (AVAs). In theory, AVAs are, like European appellations, primarily based on geographical features and climatic distinctions; in practice, they are often built around county and state borders. For a wine to qualify for an AVA, at least 85% of the grapes that go into making it must come from within that AVA. Unlike European appellations, AVAs do not place restrictions on such factors as grape varieties, training systems, yields, and winemaking methods, and in that much they have more in common with Italy's *Indicazione Geografica Tipica* (see Chapter 15). The first AVA, Augusta AVA in Missouri, dates back to 1980. Today, there are more than 200 AVAs. These can be very large, sometimes encompassing entire counties, or they can be minute, or nested one inside another.

California

California is about the same size as Germany and the Benelux combined, stretching over 1,600km (1,000mi) from 42°N to 32.6°N. The Pacific Ocean exerts a cooling influence in the Coast Ranges, which extend from the north of the state to Los Angeles in the south. To the east of these mountains lies the Central Valley, 58,000km² of fertile agricultural land irrigated by a series of interconnected rivers and canals that drain into San Francisco Bay. Further east, the land rises once again to form the Sierra Nevada. California is legendary for its sunshine, warmth, and fertility—although, of course, it is hard to generalize over such a large area. Viticulture is concentrated in three broad areas, each one an umbrella AVA: the North Coast, Central Coast, and Central Valley. The North Coast to the north of San Francisco comprises Napa Valley, Sonoma County, Mendocino County, and Lake County. The Central Coast, between San Francisco and Los Angeles, comprises Monterey County, San Luis Obispo County, and Santa Barbara County, as well as the San Francisco Bay area. Within the Central Valley, the southern San Joaquin Valley is a major source of bulk wine, responsible for nearly three-quarters of all Californian wine grapes; and there are also vineyards in the northern Sacramento Valley and Lodi AVA around the San Francisco Bay Delta. In addition, the Sierra Foothills are experiencing a revival in quality winemaking owing in large part to investment from Napa and Sonoma. Small amounts of wine are also made in Southern California, mostly in the Transverse Ranges around Los Angeles and the Peninsular Ranges around San Diego.

Napa Valley

The Napa Valley AVA, which is more or less co-extensive with Napa County, lies to the north of San Francisco and about 50km (31mi) inland. The Napa Valley extends over 55km (34mi) along the Napa River on a NW-SE axis. The ~18,000ha of vines are laid out on the valley floor and foothills of the Mayacamas Mountains and Vaca Mountains. Almost all the land available for viticulture is planted, resulting in high prices for both the land and the wines. Overall, the climate is Mediterranean with long sunlight hours during the growing season. The Mayacamas Mountains block off airstreams from the Pacific Ocean, but the valley remains open to cooling breezes and mists from San Pablo Bay to the south. This creates a rising average temperature gradient from Carneros in the south of the valley to Calistoga in the north. Until they dissipate, the mists shield more southerly vineyards from the morning sun, especially those vineyards closer to the valley floor. Annual rainfall increases from a mere ~500mm (20in) in Carneros to ~1,000mm (39in) in Calistoga. Irrigation is permitted and the use of drip irrigation is increasing. The soils are extremely diverse on account of the seismically active San Andreas Fault that runs through California: in general, the foothills offer stonier, better-draining sites than the alluvial valley floor. Nearby UC Davis supplies Napa producers with state-of-the-art terroir analysis, enabling vineyard sites and grape varieties to be near optimally matched.

Black grape varieties make up the majority of Napa plantings. The most important are the Bordeaux varieties, Pinot Noir, Zinfandel, and Syrah. Cabernet Sauvignon is king, dominating plantings in every sub-region except Carneros. As for white grape varieties, the most important are Chardonnay and Sauvignon Blanc. Napa is comparatively hot and sunny, leading to wines with a darker colour, fuller body, higher alcohol, and lower acidity than their French counterparts. The fashion is for highly concentrated, full-bodied wines with significant French or American oak influence. This even extends to Sauvignon Blanc, which is often made in the 'Fumé Blanc' style pioneered by Robert Mondavi in the 1970s. Inspired by Left Bank Bordeaux, Napa Cabernet Sauvignon aims at structure and elegance. It is typically deep in colour with a flavour profile of concentrated ripe or jammy dark berry fruit overlain by a fresh greenness often manifest as menthol. Merlot can contribute plum and milk chocolate notes, Cabernet Franc flint and herbal notes, and Petit Verdot floral notes. Alcohol can be very high, but, even so, need not be out of balance. Napa Chardonnay typically exhibits notes of baked apple and tropical fruits with added butter, toast, or coconut from the oak.

The most notable sub-regional AVAs in Napa are, from north to south: Calistoga, Howell Mountain, Spring Mountain, Saint Helena, Rutherford, Oakville, Yountville, Stags Leap District, Atlas Peak, Mount Veeder, and Los Carneros.

- Calistoga is home to several notable wineries including Château Montelena and Araujo. It is too far north to benefit from the cooling southern mists, and, despite breezes from the Russian River, the climate is very warm. A 1973 Château Montelena Chardonnay placed first among the white wines in the Judgement of Paris. The Calistoga AVA is very recent and only took effect as of the 2010 vintage.
- In contrast, the Howell Mountain AVA dates back to 1984 and is the oldest Napa sub-regional AVA. Vineyards are planted on volcanic soils on the southwest facing slopes of the Vaca Mountains. High altitudes of up to 670m (2,200ft) lift the vineyards above the mists, but high diurnal temperature variation enables the grapes to preserve acidity and concentrate flavour. The sub-region is reputed for its muscular yet complex and refined red wines.
- Spring Mountain lies opposite Howell Mountain in the Mayacamas and overlooks Saint Helena on the valley floor.

The vineyards are at similar altitudes to those in Howell Mountain, but, as they face east, they are sheltered from the hot afternoon sun. Cabernet Sauvignon has replaced Riesling as the predominant grape variety and the quality of the fruit is very high.

- In 1861, the 'father of Napa wine' Charles Krug established a winery in Saint Helena. The mists, though relatively sparse, exert a cooling effect in the mornings. The alluvial gravels are ideal for Cabernet Sauvignon, which is made in a meaty, luscious style, often with minty notes. Rhodanian grape varieties are increasingly finding favour.

- Rutherford, to the south of Saint Helena and also on the valley floor, boasts a number of historic wineries including Inglenook Winery and Beaulieu Vineyards. Cabernet Sauvignon from the Rutherford Bench, a deposit of alluvial gravels at the foot of the Mayacamas Mountains, is rich, structured, and elegant. Soils closer to the river are more fertile and associated with higher yields.

- In the 1960s, Robert Mondavi built his winery in Oakville in the heart of the Napa Valley. Oakville shares in the same alluvial gravel deposits as Rutherford, but, owing to the mists, the climate is slightly cooler. The Cabernet Sauvignon is just as structured and lengthy as that from Rutherford, but slightly less rich with hints of herbs and spices. The Chardonnay and Sauvignon Blanc are made in a rich, opulent style and often oaked.

- Yountville, also on the valley floor, is cooler still, leading to Cabernet Sauvignon with a more delicate fruit profile and firmer, more structured tannins. Yountville is celebrated both for its wineries (Dominus, Domaine Chandon…) and for its restaurants (French Laundry, Bouchon, Ad Hoc…). It is named after settler George C. Yount, the first person to make wine in Napa. It is reported that, upon seeing the Napa Valley for the first time, Yount said, "In such a place I should love to clear the land and make my home. In such a place I should love to live and die."

- Stags Leap, in the foothills of the Vaca Mountains to the east of Yountville, is a small AVA that almost exclusively specializes in Cabernet Sauvignon. The soils consist of a unique blend of loam and clay sediments and volcanic deposits. The 1973 vintage of Stag's Leap Wine Cellars, not to be confused with Stags' Leap Winery, placed first among the red wines in the Judgement of Paris. Note the different positions of the apostrophes, and the diplomatic lack of an apostrophe in the name of the AVA!

- Above Stags Leap in the Vacas Mountains, Atlas Peak is completely free of mists. Yet, owing to its altitude, it is subject to cooler temperatures and higher diurnal temperature variation, translating into a more European style of Cabernet Sauvignon with a lighter body and higher acidity. Other important grape varieties include Zinfandel, Sangiovese, and Chardonnay. Like the other mountainous sub-regions, Atlas Peak is relatively sparsely planted.

- Mount Veeder lies opposite Atlas Peak in the Mayacamas Mountains and overlooks Yountville on the valley floor. Vineyards are planted at altitude on steep slopes overlain by thin, infertile volcanic soils. The principal grape varieties are the Bordeaux varieties, Zinfandel, and Chardonnay. The overall conditions give rise to robuster tannins in the red wines and exceptional elegance in the white wines.

- Los Carneros ('The Rams'), south of Napa and at the southern extremity of the valley, is the coolest of the sub-regions, with thin and infertile soils, sparse rainfall, and strong winds. Chardonnay and Pinot Noir dominate plantings, and the potential for quality traditional method sparkling wines has attracted significant investment from a number of Champagne and Cava houses. Note that the Carneros AVA sits astride the Napa and Sonoma AVAs.

Sonoma County

At over 400,000ha, Sonoma County is about twice the size of Napa, extending from San Pablo Bay and Carneros in the south to Cloverdale in the north. It is broadly divided into three sections: Sonoma Valley, Northern Sonoma, and Sonoma Coast. Sonoma Valley lies across the

Mayamas Mountains from Napa Valley, and, like Napa Valley, benefits from cooling mists and breezes from San Pablo Bay. Northern Sonoma, north of the agglomeration of Santa Rosa, is much larger, with ten AVAs including Russian River Valley and Alexander Valley. Whereas the rivers of Sonoma Valley drain into San Pablo Bay, those of Northern Sonoma drain into the Pacific Ocean. Sonoma Coast extends along the coastline from the border with Mendocino County in the north to San Pablo Bay in the south, with vineyards scattered in the Outer Coast Ranges. In general, mesoclimates on the valley floor and in the eastern foothills resemble those in Napa, while sites nearer the Pacific are notably cooler and wetter. Soils are extremely varied, more so than in Napa, with, in general, hillside slopes offering stonier, better-draining sites than alluvial valley floors. Boutique producers vie alongside large producers such as E. & J. Gallo and Kendall-Jackson. Although there are, of course, some trophy wines, on the whole Sonoma offers better value than Napa.

Grape varieties are more varied than in Napa. Chardonnay, the most planted grape variety, usually occupies cooler sites and, accordingly, is less 'super-charged' than that from Napa. Just as in Napa, Sauvignon Blanc is made in a fruity, punchy style that is often oaked. Pinot Gris, which is increasingly planted, is the only other significant white grape variety. The most planted black grape variety is Pinot Noir, and Sonoma Pinot Noir is the benchmark style for California. Compared to Burgundy, it is fuller in body and richer in fruit; compared to Oregon Pinot Noir it lacks the crisp green notes; and compared to New Zealand Pinot Noir, it is often lower in acidity. Cabernet Sauvignon tends to be planted on warmer sites on the valley floor, and Sonoma Cabernet blends are difficult to distinguish from their Napa counterparts. The once-fashionable Merlot receives a more even-handed treatment in Sonoma than in Napa, with more producers persisting with varietal Merlot. The best examples exhibit a generous plum-fruit profile with rich, silky tannins, although there is also a vogue for a more generic, soft style with very little tannin. Both the Cabernet Sauvignons and the Merlots tend to be high in alcohol. Zinfandel, California's signature grape variety, achieves one of its finest expressions in Sonoma. The wine is deep ruby in colour with notes of strawberries or rich brambly fruit, fresh cream, black tea, thyme or other herbs, and, sometimes, coconut from new American oak. On the palate, it is full-bodied with high alcohol, moderate acidity, and heavy, fairly coarse tannins. Good examples, such as Ridge Vineyards' Geyserville field blend, are lengthy with a mineral core and savoury finish. Zinfandel is a clonal variation of Primitivo from Puglia in Italy. Compared to Zinfandel, Primitivo typically exhibits a more savoury, dried-fruit profile with, on the palate, a drier entry and more notable tannins. The other significant black grape variety in Sonoma is Syrah, which, like Pinot Gris, is becoming increasingly popular.

The arrangement of sub-appellations in Sonoma County, which is itself an AVA, is more intricate than in Napa, with several overlapping and nested AVAs. The larger AVAs such as Northern Sonoma AVA and Sonoma Coast AVA mostly serve the interests of larger producers with several scattered holdings. From north to south, the most important of the smaller AVAs are Alexander Valley, Dry Creek Valley, Russian River Valley, and Sonoma Valley.

- Alexander Valley, a large AVA in the northeast of Sonoma County, straddles the Russian River as it descends from Cloverdale to Healdsburg. The climate is fairly warm, although the valley does receive a small amount of cooling influence from sea breezes that make it this far north from the Russian River estuary. Alexander Valley is the most fully planted AVA in Sonoma and is especially noted for its Cabernet Sauvignon, which is less earthy than that from Napa. Other important grape varieties include Merlot and Zinfandel.
- Dry Creek is born out of Lake Sonoma in the Ranges and dies in the Russian River just south of Healdsburg. Ocean mists drift into Dry Creek Valley from Russian River Valley to the south, and the valley floor is often cooler than more elevated sites in the foothills. Soils include substantial gravel deposits and a unique soil type made from gravel and red clay. Dry Creek Valley is celebrated for its old-vine Zinfandel. The northern part of the AVA is dominated by black grape varieties including Cabernet Sauvignon, Zinfandel, and Syrah. The southern part, being cooler, is better suited to white grape varieties, with Sauvignon Blanc and Chardonnay commonly planted.

- Russian River Valley, to the south of Dry Creek Valley, is formed around the Russian River in its final stretch from Healdsburg to the Pacific Ocean. The AVA also encompasses the Chalk Hill sub-AVA in the hills southeast of Healdsburg and the Green Valley sub-AVA west of Santa Rosa. Ocean mists exert an important influence, leading to cooler temperatures and a higher diurnal temperature range. Rainfall, at 750mm (30in), is relatively high, and humidity from ocean mists and the area's many rivers increases the risk of rot, especially to susceptible Pinot Noir. The coolest, western part of the valley is mostly planted with Pinot Noir and Chardonnay; further inland, Cabernet Sauvignon and Zinfandel become more important. Some sites are so cool as to enable even Riesling to flourish. Russian River Valley is reputed for its Pinot Noir, which is classically vibrant in colour with cherry and berry fruit flavours and notes of earthy mushroom. The Chardonnay is made in a lean mineral style. Both Pinot Noir and Chardonnay are also employed in traditional method sparkling wines.
- Sonoma Valley AVA, to the south of Santa Rosa, follows the southern course of Sonoma Creek to San Pablo Bay, and encompasses the AVAs of Sonoma Mountain and Bennett Valley. The Sonoma Mountains shelter the area from the cool and wet influence of the Pacific Ocean, although cooling mists do enter through Los Carneros in the south and the Santa Rosa plain in the north. Sonoma Valley is reputed for its rich wines made in particular from Cabernet Sauvignon, Zinfandel, and Chardonnay.

Mendocino County & Lake County

The sparsely populated Mendocino County lies to the north of Sonoma, at the northern limit of California's prime wine producing areas. The Mendocino Range, part of the Pacific Coast Ranges, divides the county into a cooler more maritime area and a warmer inland area. Most vineyards are in the south of the county, and many are organically farmed. There are a number of AVAs, first among which the up-and-coming Anderson Valley, a steep, almost floorless valley carved out of the Coast

Ranges by the Navarro River. Owing to Pacific mists and breezes, the climate is distinctly cool and humid with high diurnal temperature variation. Cooler areas are planted to Pinot Noir, Chardonnay, and Alsatian grape varieties, which are celebrated in an annual Alsatian festival. Warmer areas in the southeast of the valley or on higher slopes above the mists are planted to Cabernet Sauvignon, Zinfandel, and Syrah. The Anderson Valley is especially noted for its traditional method sparkling wines, pioneered in the 1980s by Champagne house Louis Roederer.

Lake County lies across the Mayacamas Mountains to the east of Mendocino and to the north of Napa and Sonoma. Viticulture is centred on Clear Lake, the largest natural lake in California, which exerts a moderating influence on an otherwise warm and dry climate. The volcanic slopes give rise to elegant red wines, especially Cabernet Sauvignon.

San Francisco Bay Area

The area immediately to the south of San Francisco Bay used to be an important wine region until phylloxera hit California in the 19th century. Since then, urban sprawl has pushed most viticulture south into the coastal mountains of Santa Cruz and east into the Livermore Valley. Today, the large San Francisco Bay AVA encompasses a number of smaller AVAs, including Santa Cruz Mountains and Livermore Valley. The Santa Cruz Mountains AVA is defined by its mountain topography, with small, disparate vineyards scattered across a large and diverse area. Altitude and proximity to the Pacific Ocean make for an overall cool climate, with Pinot Noir, Cabernet Sauvignon, and Chardonnay dominating plantings. Paul Draper of Ridge Vineyards masterminded the 1971 Monte Bello Cabernet Sauvignon that placed fifth in the Judgement of Paris. Randall Grahm, who calls himself a 'terroirist' and 'vinarchist', established Bonny Doon Vineyard in 1983 to cultivate Rhodanian grape varieties, and spearheads the 'Rhône Rangers' movement of likeminded American winemakers. The Livermore Valley AVA is relatively shielded from the Pacific Ocean, with a warm albeit windy climate. Plantings of Semillon and Sauvignon Blanc descend from cuttings from Château d'Yquem brought over from Bordeaux by French immigrants. These grape varieties are ideally suited to the stony Graves-like soils of the Livermore Valley, but fashions have led to other grape varieties, most notably Petite Sirah, dominating plantings. Wente Vineyards, founded in 1883, remains a bastion of the white Bordeaux style.

Monterey County

The large and up-and-coming Monterey AVA with its several smaller AVAs lies in eastern Monterey, roughly following the Salinas Valley from Monterey Bay in the north to San Luis Obispo in the south. Vineyards are planted on sandy soils on the valley floor, in the hills of the Santa Lucia Mountains, and in those of the inland Gabilan Mountains. Mists and breezes from Monterey Bay with its deep ocean canyon exert a strong cooling influence with temperatures seldom exceeding 24°C (75°F). The region is very dry, with viticulture only made possible by irrigation from the Salinas River. The principal grape variety is Chardonnay, which, unusually in California, yields wines with high acidity and fresh notes of green apple and citrus fruits. Other important grape varieties include Riesling and Pinot Noir in the north and Bordeaux varieties in the south. Most notable among Monterey's smaller AVAs is the detached Chalone AVA in the Galiban Mountains, originally created for Richard Graff's Chalone Vineyard. Chardonnay and Pinot Noir make the most of Chalone's altitude, cold breezes, very high diurnal temperature range, and thin, free-draining soils. These soils consist of decomposed granite with pockets of limestone, and have been compared to those of Burgundy. A 1974 Chalone Vineyard Chardonnay placed third in the Judgement of Paris.

San Luis Obispo County & Santa Barbara County

South of Monterey, in San Luis Obispo County and Santa Barbara County, the coastal mountain valleys run east to west rather than north to south, exposing vineyards to the full brunt of the Pacific Ocean. Despite their southerly latitudes, the AVAs of Edna Valley and Arroyo Grande Valley in San Luis Obispo and Santa Maria Valley in Santa Barbara are indisputably cool-climate. Plantings in San Luis Obispo are concentrated in the large Paso Robles AVA, which is sheltered from the Pacific Ocean by the Santa Lucia Mountains. The warmer climate of Paso Robles has attracted interest from the Rhône Rangers, among others. Cabernet Sauvignon may be the most planted grape variety, but Rhodanian and Italian grape varieties are stirring greater interest. Merlot and Zinfandel are also important. In general, red wines from Paso Robles are made in a big and brawny style. However, there are also some leaner, more structured styles issuing from cooler sites on the less fertile calcareous slopes of the Santa Lucia Mountains, an area that has attracted heavy investment from the Perrin family of Château Beaucastel. Plantings of Chardonnay in San Luis Obispo are concentrated in the cooler Edna Valley, which is more open to the Pacific Ocean than Paso Robles.

In Santa Barbara, Chardonnay and other white grape varieties account for more than half of plantings. Styles of Chardonnay range from rich and ripe to elegant and restrained. Santa Maria in particular is cooler than either Carneros or Russian River, yielding Chardonnays with higher acidity and greener fruit flavours. The most planted black grape variety is Pinot Noir, and, in the hands of Jim Clendenen of Au Bon Climat, fruit from the Bien Nacido and Le Bon Climat vineyards is crafted into some of the most Burgunian expressions of Pinot Noir in California. Further south, the Santa Ynez Valley AVA is bordered in the north by the Purisima Hills and San Rafael Mountains and in the south by the Santa Ynez Mountains. The Santa Ynez Valley is open to the Pacific Ocean at its narrow western end, and its cooler western section is ideally suited to Pinot Noir, Chardonnay, Sauvignon Blanc, and Riesling. At Solvang, the valley opens out into a broad plain with a much warmer climate better suited to Rhodanian grape varieties.

Central Valley

Enclosed by the California Coast Ranges and the Sierra Nevada, the Central Valley is a vast plain, 700km (435mi) long and 60 to 100km (37 to 62mi) wide. It runs roughly parallel to the Pacific coast, with a northern section drained by the Sacramento River and a larger southern section drained by the San Joaquin River. The rivers form a delta near the agglomerations of Lodi and Clarksburg, which lend their names to the only significant quality AVAs in the valley. Cut off from the Pacific, the Central Valley is hot and sunny. With rich and fertile soils and plenty of water for irrigation, it offers ideal conditions for all types of agriculture. While there are relatively few plantings in the northern Sacramento Valley, the southern San Joaquin Valley contains about three-quarters of all California's vineyards. Needless to say, most of these are devoted to bulk wine production, although the area does turn out some excellent Port-style fortified wines. The Delta Area is the only part of the Central Valley to benefit from cooling sea breezes coming in from San Francisco Bay, not to mention the moderating effect of all that ambient water. The star performer of the Lodi AVA is Zinfandel, made in a riper, jammier style with fleshier tannins than Sonoma Zinfandel. Compared to the Lodi AVA, the Clarksburg AVA is smaller and slightly cooler. Soils are mostly dense clay and loam, which suits Chenin Blanc and Petite Sirah. However, most of the grapes produced are pressed in other parts of California.

Sierra Foothills

First planted during the Gold Rush of the 1850s, the Sierra Foothills have been experiencing something of a revival in recent decades. The AVA is very large and sits astride eight counties, from Yuba County in the north to Mariposa County in the south. On the ground, vineyards are confined to the foothills of the western slopes of the Sierra Nevada. The climate is warm, although moderated by the high altitude and mountain breezes. The soils, which are mostly eroded granite, compel the vines to establish deep roots. The most important grape varieties are Zinfandel, Cabernet Sauvignon, and Syrah. The Zinfandel from Amador County is bold and spicy with unapologetically coarse tannins. Compared to Sonoma Zinfandel, it is more concentrated; compared to Lodi Zinfandel, it is more serious with a darker fruit profile.

Oregon

Oregon has a winemaking tradition that dates back to the mid-19th century. In the 1960s, against the advice of UC Davis, Charles Coury and David Lett established plantings of Pinot Noir, respectively, in Washington County (in Oregon, not Washington State) and the Willamette Valley. Since those early days, Oregon has become inextricably linked to Pinot Noir, which today accounts for about half of the state's production. Although some big players have moved in over the past decade, Oregon remains dominated by small-scale producers bent on quality and individuality of expression. Producers subject themselves to stricter controls than in other parts of the country; for example, for a wine to qualify for an AVA, a full 100% of the grapes that go into making it must come from within the AVA.

Oregon is just over half the size of California. It is sparsely populated with forest-clad mountains, clear lakes, and windswept coastline. Its ~8,000ha of vines are concentrated in north-south valleys between the Coast Range and Cascade Mountains. These valleys are open to the Pacific, with mild winters and cool and cloudy summers. Rainfall is high but the growing season from May to September is relatively dry. The marginal conditions are close to ideal for Pinot Noir, although under-ripeness can sometimes present a problem. Vintage variation can be pronounced. As in Chile and Argentina, the El Niño and La Niña exert a strong influence on weather patterns, with droughts and heat waves seemingly becoming more common.

The most important wine region in Oregon is the Willamette Valley, which traces the path of the Willamette River from Eugene in the south to Portland in the north. This 150km (93mi) stretch is the largest Orgeon AVA with over three-quarters of state plantings and six sub-AVAs that reflect the diversity of terroirs. The vast majority of plantings are in the north of the valley, west of the river in the lee of the Coast Range. To the south of Willamette lies the catchall Southern Oregon AVA, which encompasses the Umpqua Valley AVA and Rogue River Valley AVA along with smaller sub-AVAs. The climate is slightly warmer and drier, enabling more full-bodied black grape varieties to ripen in selected sites.

Oregon Pinot Noir is characterized by purity of fruit, floral aromatics, and, often, an herbaceous pine needle note. Maturation in new French oak is more common than in Burgundy. As with Burgundy, acidity is very high but tannin structure is generally softer. Even so, very fine Oregon Pinot Noir requires several years of cellaring if it is to develop *sous-bois* and other appealing tertiary notes. After Pinot Noir, Pinot Gris is the second most widely planted grape variety. Oregon Pinot Gris is fuller and more interesting than Italian Pinot Grigio, but with crisper acidity than Alsatian Pinot Gris. Other grape varieties include Chardonnay, Riesling, Gewurztraminer, Viognier, Cabernet Sauvignon, Merlot, and Syrah.

Washington

Two Seattle-based corporate giants, Chateau Ste Michelle and Columbia Crest, dominate wine production in Washington State. Yet, small wineries have been popping up with increasing frequency over the past 20 years. Viticulture is concentrated in the southeast of the state, in the rain shadow of the Cascade Mountains. The climate is continental and very dry. Summer temperatures occasionally exceed 40°C (104°F) and winter temperatures can plunge to -26°C (-15°F), with around one in six vintages severely damaged by frost or snow. The Columbia River and its tributaries exert a cooling influence in the summer and mitigate the risk of frost in the spring. With only ~200mm (8in) annual rainfall, these rivers are a vital source of irrigation water. Harsh winters and sandy loam soils seem to have kept phylloxera at bay and many vines are still ungrafted. Washington counts 12 AVAs with all but one, Puget Sound AVA, in Eastern Washington. The largest AVA is Columbia Valley, which extends into northern Oregon and encompasses most of the other Washington AVAs.

In general, the focus is on fresh, clean, expressive varietal wines with deep colour and bright, intense fruit flavours. Chardonnay is the most widely planted white grape variety although much Washington Chardonnay is not especially distinguished. Riesling does much better but is still struggling with its popularity. It is made in a range of styles from dry and austere to sweet and botrytized and even more concentrated ice wine. Other aromatic grape varieties also do well, most notably Pinot Gris and Viognier. Washington has a particular reputation for fine Semillon, made either in a dry or in a sweet botrytized style. L'Ecole is considered one of the best Semillon producers in Washington, indeed, in the world. Other significant white grape varieties include Sauvignon

Blanc and Chenin Blanc. For black grape varieties, Cabernet Sauvignon leads the pack. With restrained notes of blackcurrant, cherry, minty bell pepper, and leather, it is less 'super-charged' than Napa with more finely etched tannins. Merlot, though more sensitive to frost, is better suited to the sand- and clay-based soils. Washington Merlot exhibits a fresh cherry profile with notes of chocolate and mint and hints of sweet spice; compared to Californian Merlot, acidity is higher and tannins are more pronounced, but compared to Right Bank Bordeaux body is fuller and alcohol often higher. Syrah is increasingly popular; although less meaty than Northern Rhône Syrah, the best examples are bold and peppery with notes of blackberry, coffee, and leather. Other important black grape varieties include Cabernet Franc, Malbec, and Petit Verdot, which are produced either as varietals or Bordeaux-style blends, and Grenache, Mourvèdre, Nebbiolo, Sangiovese, and Zinfandel.

New York

American and hybrid grape varieties took off in New York State in the 19th century and still account for the bulk of the state's production. Today, some New York producers occupy a niche market making kosher wine, mostly from American hybrids Concord and Niagara. Concord is also the mainstay of the state's important grape juice and jelly industry. Experiments with *vinifera* vines began in the 1950s with Ukrainian plant scientist Konstantin Frank in the Finger Lakes region. Today, the most notable regions are Finger Lakes with its exceptional Riesling and Long Island with its Bordeaux-style blends. The Finger Lakes AVA encompasses 11 finger-like lakes to the south of the much larger Lake Ontario. Vineyards are established on lakeside slopes, leading to comparisons with the Rhineland in Germany. The climate is continental with cold winters mitigated by the moderating influence of the lakes. Soils are primarily glacial deposits of shale. Riesling is dominant but other grape varieties such as Chardonnay, Pinot Gris, Gewurztraminer, and Pinot Noir are also cultivated. In Long Island, the climate is milder and wetter. Threats to viticulture include autumn rains, hurricanes, salinity from seawater sprays, and hungry birds. Vines are cultivated at the far east of the island on the North Fork and South Fork. The North Fork, with its more free-draining soils, is the more planted AVA. The principal grape varieties are Merlot and Cabernet Franc, which are blended into a Bordeaux-style expression with more restraint than Californian counterparts. Most producers try with Cabernet Sauvignon, which, however, only adequately ripens in good years.

Virginia

Vinifera vines were at last established in Virginia in the 1970s by pioneers such as Gianni Zonin. Today, the state counts ~1,200ha under vine and over 200 mostly small-scale producers. Virginia shares the same latitude lines as southern Spain, but, owing to Atlantic breezes, is subject to a cooler climate. Viticulture is concentrated in the central and northern counties, especially those just east of the Blue Ridge Mountains. The Monticello AVA around Charlottesville is the oldest of the eight Virginia AVAs and encompasses the site of Thomas Jefferson's historic homestead. The increasingly favoured Shenandoah Valley AVA lies across the mountain ridge along the border with West Virginia. Virginia wines are made in an Old World style. So far, the most notable grape varieties are Viognier and Cabernet Franc, although Chardonnay, Cabernet Sauvignon, Merlot, and Vidal are also important. Viognier ripens fully without becoming either flabby or syrupy. The wine is floral with notes of white peach and beeswax and hints of ginger, a full body that is however less oily than Condrieu, medium alcohol, and a long finish. Cabernet Franc is often made as a varietal wine but can also be integrated into a Bordeaux-style blend. Varietal Cabernet Franc exhibits fresh, ripe blackberry fruit without the greenness of Loire expressions such as Chinon, a pencil shaving minerality, and grainy tannins.

Canada

Wine was exempt from Canadian Prohibition, but it was not until the 1970s that the focus shifted from fortified wines made from *labrusca* grape varieties to dry wines made from *vinifera* varieties. Today, plantings are concentrated in southern Ontario and southern British Columbia. The principal area for viticulture in Ontario is the Niagara Peninsula on the southern shores of Lake Ontario, with vineyards extending south to Lake Erie and west towards Lake Huron. The climate is markedly continental although the lakes exercise a moderating influence. Soils are mostly river- or glacier-deposited till and loam. A number of grape varieties are cultivated from Cabernet Sauvignon to Pinot Noir and from Chardonnay to Riesling. Riesling benefits most from the long growing season and can turn out wines of exceptional elegance. Also significant is the hybrid grape variety Vidal, noted for its ability to accumulate high sugar levels in marginal climates. Among the black grape varieties, it is perhaps Cabernet Franc and Gamay that offer the greatest promise. A long growing season followed by a very cold winter makes Canada ideally suited for the production of high quality German-style ice wine, which is by far the most visible style of Canadian wine on the export market. Ontario is especially reputed for its fine ice wine, often made from Riesling or Vidal and distinguished by vibrant fruit and high acidity. In British Columbia, the principal area for viticulture is the glacial Okanagan Valley, which extends 160km (100mi) along Okanagan Lake on a roughly north-south axis. Here, in the lee of the Pacific Ranges, the climate is dry and continental. Many different grape varieties are cultivated including several Germanic varieties. The southern stretch of the valley is warmer, enabling Cabernet Sauvignon, Cabernet Franc, and Merlot to ripen easily. As in Ontario, ice wine is a mainstay of production. Of particular note is that minimum must weight requirements for ice wine are higher in Canada than in either Germany or Austria. And so we end this book, as we should, on an especially sweet note.

Appendices

Appendix A: Setting up a Blind Tasting

Materials

- Six to twelve different wines
- Standardized unmarked bottles or receptacles in which to decant the wines (or bottle sleeves with which to mask the original wine bottles)
- A corkscrew
- A funnel
- Metal foil wine pourers
- ISO wine tasting glasses, one per wine in each flight
- Spittoons
- Tasting sheets
- Crib sheets
- Some spare pens

Note: Tasting sheets and crib sheets can be downloaded from the Oxford Wine Academy website at www.oxfordwineacademy.com.

Process

A typical blind tasting involves six to twelve different wines. The wines ought to be decanted into standardized unmarked bottles or receptacles. This is preferable to using bottle sleeves, which betray the shapes of the original bottles. In the absence of unmarked receptacles and bottle sleeves, the guests need to leave the room while the wine is poured into their glasses, which is quite a palaver.

It is important to pour the right amount of wine into the glass: too little and it is difficult to smell and taste all the components; too much and the wine cannot breathe in the glass. A finger's breadth is a good rule of thumb (no pun intended). At most, a bottle of wine can serve 18-20 portions, which equates to ~40cl per portion. Ideally, white, rosé, and sparkling wines ought to be served at 8-10°C and red wines at 14-18°C, even if the wines will quickly warm up in the glass.

If there are twelve different wines, they may be presented in two flights of six, typically a flight of white wines followed by a flight of red wines. This has a number of advantages, including dividing up the evening and limiting the number of glasses required to just six per person. If there are six wines, they can be presented as a flight of six or two flights of three, and so on. The wines within a flight may or may not have a common theme, for example, grape variety, country or region of origin, or vintage. Remind guests that they need not progress systematically from the first to the last wine in the flight; encourage them instead to start with the lightest wine in the flight and work their way up to the heaviest wine, which, if tasted first, could interfere with their ability to taste the lighter wines.

Each wine calls for five to ten minutes of analysis and ten minutes of discussion. So if there are, for example, six wines presented in two flights of three, allocate thirty minutes for assessing the first flight, thirty minutes for discussing the first flight, thirty minutes for assessing the second flight, and thirty minutes for discussing the second flight. Don't be too rigid about time allocation: if everyone has stopped writing, move on to discussing the wines.

Wine is also about bringing people together, so remember to make time for guests to socialize. If at all possible, sit everyone around a single table: this is more convivial and also facilitates the discussion of the wines. Sit beginners next to more experienced tasters who can encourage and guide them through the tasting process described in Chapter 4. Some people prefer to assess the wines in silence, but complete silence can be intimidating to beginners and restricting to more gregarious or talkative types.

Upon discussing a wine, it is customary to call for one or two tasting notes before taking guesses and opening up the table to a more open-ended discussion of the wine. Once the discussion has been exhausted, the identity of the wine can be revealed. In some cases, particularly if there is a common theme to the flight, it may be more politic to delay the guessing and/or revealing until all the wines in the flight have been discussed. With the tasting at a close, consider asking the guests to dinner with whatever remains of the wines.

Appendix B: Food and Wine Matching

In many European wine regions, the wine styles and culinary traditions developed reciprocally such that the wines naturally pair with the regional fare. Many of these so-called 'food wines' can seem overly tart or tannic if drunk on their own, but come into their own once paired with food, and, in particular, those foods that they co-evolved with. If you respect these time-honored pairings, you are much less likely to go wrong.

Otherwise, you need to choose what to put into focus: the food or the wine. For instance, if it is the wine that you wish to emphasize, pick a dish that is slightly lighter and complements rather than competes with it. Take care not to pick a dish that is too light or it will be overwhelmed by the wine: although you want the wine to lead, you want the dish to follow closely behind. If it is the food that you wish to emphasize, you are effectively using the wine as a sauce or spice. In all instances, your aim is for the wine to bring out the best in the food, and the food the best in the wine. This is certainly the case with such classic pairings as Muscadet and oysters, Claret and lamb, and Sauternes and Roquefort.

Taste, however, is subjective, and there should not and cannot be rigid rules for pairing foods and wines. Indeed, part of the pleasure of the wine lover is in experimenting with combinations and, in so doing, multiplying the flavours, textures, and sensations of everyday life. That having been said, you do need to be versed in the principles that you may or may not decide to break.

First, identify the dominant component of your dish. For example, the dominant component of fish served in a creamy sauce is more likely to be the creamy sauce than the fish itself. Then pick a wine that either complements or contrasts with the dominant component. Examples of complementary pairings are, a citrusy Sauvignon Blanc with sole in a lemon sauce, an earthy Pinot Noir with mushroom vol-au-vents, or a peppery Syrah with a steak in peppercorn sauce.

Four important elements to bear in mind are weight, acidity, tannins, and sweetness. The weight and texture of a wine is determined by such factors as alcohol level, amount of extract and tannin, and the use or non-use of winemaking techniques such as extended maceration, lees ageing, and oaking. In general, lighter wines pair with lighter foods, whereas heavier, more robust wines pair with heavier, more rustic foods. Good examples of pairings by weight are Chardonnay and lobster or Chardonnay and roast chicken.

Acidity stimulates appetite and cuts through oil and fat, explaining the success of such contrasting pairings as Sancerre and goat cheese, Alsatian Riesling and pork belly, and Tokaji and foie gras. In all cases, the wine must be at least as acidic as the dish, and preferably more so: if not, the wine is likely to seem thin or insipid.

Tannins can lend chalkiness or grittiness to a wine, and also bitter astringency. Tannins bind to and react with proteins in food, by which process they are 'softened'. While tannic wines go hand in hand with red meats and some cheeses, they pair poorly with spicy or sweet dishes, which can accentuate their bitterness and astringency, and with fish oils, which can make them seem 'metallic'.

A sweet dish requires a wine that is just as sweet or sweeter, or else the dish will overpower the wine. Sweetness balances heat and spiciness, and also contrasts with saltiness, as, for example, in the case of vintage Port and Stilton. Conversely, alcohol accentuates the heat in spicy food and vice versa. This much explains why Mosel Riesling, which is both high in residual sugar and low in alcohol, is often an excellent choice for spicy food. Unfortunately, very spicy food will overwhelm almost any wine, and ought to be paired with some other beverage such as water, beer, or lassi. Some foods are difficult to pair with wine, most notably chocolate, eggs, fresh tomatoes, and asparagus.

Finally, remember to match your wine also to the occasion, your companions, the season, the weather, the time of day or night, and your mood and tastes. If you are serving more than one wine, think about your line up and make it as varied or interesting or educational as possible.

Appendix C: The European Union and French Classification Systems

The European Union

The French *Appellation d'Origine Contrôlée* (AOC) system, governed by the *Institut national des appellations d'origine* (INAO), dates back to 1935. It has inspired or influenced many other national systems and, ultimately, the European Union (EU) wine laws.

The EU wine laws require that wines produced within the EU be divided into two quality categories, Table Wines (TW) and Quality Wines Produced in Specified Regions (QWpsr), each with different rules for winemaking practices and labelling. The TW and QWpsr categories are adapted into different national classification systems across the EU member states. Some member states have more than two levels of classification, but each level fits into either TW or QWpsr.

Many winemaking practices depend on the classification of the wine as either TW or QWpsr, but some, such as deacidification and chaptalization, depend on where the grapes are grown. Thus, every EU wine growing region belongs to one of six wine growing zones, with Zone A the coolest and Zone C III b the warmest.

As of 2011, the TW and QWpsr quality categories have been replaced with, respectively, Protected Geographical Indication (PGI) and Protected Designation of Origin (PDO).

France

French law divides wine into four categories:

- *Vin de Table*
  - The label only specifies the producer and the fact that the wine is from France.
- *Vin de Pays*
  - The label specifies a particular French region, *département*, or delimited area, for example, *Vin de Pays d'Oc* or *Vin de Pays de Vaucluse*. The wine has to

be made from certain grape varieties or blends and the producer has to submit the wine for analysis and tasting. Maximum or minimum limits are placed on yields, alcohol, pH, and sulphur dioxide. In particular, the designation enables French producers to make non-traditional blends and varietal wines to compete with those from the New World.

- *Vin Délimité de Qualité Supérieure* (VDQS)
  - Abolished in 2011, the VDQS category was mostly interpreted as a stepping-stone to AOC status.
- *Appellation d'Origine Contrôlée* (AOC)
  - Specifies a delimited terroir together with a number of rules and restrictions governing such factors as grape varieties, blends, training systems, yields, and winemaking methods. There are currently over 300 AOC wines. Some, such as Romanée-Conti in Burgundy, are the size of a vineyard; others, such as Alsace AOC, are rather more expansive (and therefore also less restrictive).

In recent years, a new system has been introduced with three rather than four categories. The three categories are:

- Vin de France
  - Essentially replaces *Vin de Table* but enables grape variety or grape varieties and vintage to be indicated on the label. This gives French producers greater flexibility in production, blending, and branding to compete with wines from other countries.
- *Indication Géographique Protégée* (IGP)
  - Essentially replaces *Vin de Pays*.
- *Appellation d'Origine Protégée* (AOP)
  - Essentially replaces AOC.

Vin de France and IGP fit into the EU's PGI category, and AOP into the PDO category.

Blind Tasting Crib Sheets: Red Wines

Gamay

France, Burgundy, Beaujolais

Beaujolais is typically pale in colour with a blue tinge, light in body, high in acidity, and low in tannins. Most Beaujolais is made by semi-carbonic maceration, which contributes estery notes of bananas and bubblegum to the red fruits of the Gamay grape. In contrast, Cru wines tend to be made by traditional vinification and can also be oaked, rendering them more tannic and difficult to recognize as Beaujolais.

Pinot Noir

France, Burgundy, Côte de Nuits

Pinot Noir is typically aromatic with a light to medium body and silky tannins. The wines are often noted for their savoury fleshiness and farm-yard aromas, even if the current vogue is for a lighter, cleaner, and more fruit-driven style. For many people, Côte de Nuits is quintessential Pinot Noir. The character varies from commune to commune although there is a high degree of overlap. For instance, Gevrey-Chambertin is noted for its deep colour, power, and structure: full, rich, but also silky and delicately perfumed. Compared to Gevrey-Chambertin, Chambolle-Musigny is 'feminine', that is, lighter, brighter, more delicate, more elegant, and more seductive. Nuits-Saint-George in contrast is quite masculine, full, firm, and dominated by black rather than red fruits.

France, Burgundy, Côte de Beaune

Compared to Côte de Nuits, Côte de Beaune is lighter, suppler, more fruit-driven, and quicker to mature. That having been said, red Corton (which is the only red wine Grand Cru in the Côte de Beaune) and Pommard tend to be more muscular and tannic, and more akin to Côte de Nuits. While the soils of Pommard are rich in marl, those of nearby Volnay are rich in limestone. As a result, Volnay is especially soft and fragrant, similar to (but lighter than) Chambolle-Musigny in the Côte de Nuits.

New Zealand, Martinborough or Marlborough or Cental Otago

Ultra-clean fruit and high acidity are the hallmarks of New Zealand Pinot Noir. Central Otago Pinot Noir is deep violet in colour with notes of black fruit and cherry and, often, a hint of greenness. On the palate, the wine is full-bodied for Pinot Noir, often with a high alcohol and firm, round tannins. Marlborough Pinot Noir is lighter, both in weight and colour, and dominated by red fruit such as cranberry and raspberry with finely etched, peppery tannins. Martinborough Pinot Noir is often from older vines and most similar to Burgundy. It is weightier than Marlborough Pinot Noir and more complete and complex than Central Otago Pinot Noir. Notes of cherry and plum mingle with game, spice, and chocolate.

Australia, e.g. Victoria, Yarra Valley

Australian Pinot Noir is typically very clean and fruit-driven with good acidity. Unfortunately, it is sometimes marred by high alcohol or, at least, alcohol that is too high in relation to its light body. The best examples avoid jammy fruit and tend to more earthy notes, often with marked eucalyptus or herbal mint. Much Australian Pinot Noir hails from the cooler regions of the Port Phillip zone in Victoria.

USA, Oregon, e.g. Willamette Valley

Oregon Pinot Noir is characterized by purity of fruit, floral aromatics, and, often, an herbaceous pine needle note. Maturation in new French oak is more common than in Burgundy. As with Burgundy, acidity is very high but tannin structure is generally softer. Even so, very fine Oregon Pinot Noir requires several years of cellaring if it is to develop *sous-bois* and other appealing tertiary notes.

USA, California, Sonoma

Sonoma Pinot Noir is the benchmark style for California. In particular, Russian River Valley Pinot Noir is classically vibrant in colour with cherry and berry fruit flavours and notes of earthy mushroom. Compared to Burgundy, Sonoma Pinot Noir is fuller in body and richer in fruit; compared to Oregon Pinot Noir it lacks the crisp green notes; and compared to New Zealand Pinot Noir, it is often lower in acidity.

Cabernet Franc

France, Loire, Chinon or Bourgueil or Saumur

Loire Cabernet Franc is light purple to purple in colour with a nose of raspberries and pencil shavings. With age, it develops earthy, spicy, and animally notes. Unripe vintages may be marked by a certain greenness or herbaceousness. On the palate, the wine is light- to medium-bodied with high acidity, medium alcohol, and fine and powdery tannins. Chinon and Bourgueil tend to be more structured than Saumur.

Cabernet Sauvignon

France, Bordeaux, Left Bank, Pauillac

This Cabernet Sauvignon blend is bluish purple in its childhood, ruby in its adolescence, and further brickens with age. On the nose, it is complex and dominated by notes of cassis, appealing green/bell pepper, cedar, chocolate, cigar box, and vanilla from new French oak. On the palate, it is powerful yet elegant, with a medium body, fairly high acidity, medium alcohol, fine, structured tannins, and a long finish. The other premium Left Bank appellations overlap in style and can be very difficult to distinguish from Pauillac. At its best Margaux is floral and feminine, exuding a refined perfume of acacia and violets. Saint-Julien is a seductive compromise between the power of Pauillac and the magic of Margaux, with a silkier texture and drier finish. Compared to Pauillac, Saint-Julien, and Margaux, Saint-Estèphe tends to be deeper in colour, fuller or coarser in texture, with coarser, more rustic tannins, a touch more acidity, and a touch less perfume. Saint-Estèphe also tends to have a higher proportion of Merlot. Compared to those of the Médoc, the wines of Graves tend to be lighter in colour, body, and tannins, with more fragrance, more Merlot character, and hints of smoke, minerals, and red bricks.

Australia, South Australia, Coonawarra

Coonawarra Cabernet Sauvignon tends to fairly high levels of alcohol although the grape variety's characteristic acidity is retained. The fruit profile is ripe, with notes of concentrated blackcurrant and plum, verging on prune in hot vintages, coupled with a classic cedar note and eucalyptus rather than green pepper. Tannins are structured and fine-grained but less austere or chalky than in Bordeaux. In some cases, Shiraz is used to round out the wine in the same way that Merlot is used in Bordeaux.

Australia, Western Australia, Margaret River

Compared to Coonawarra, Margaret River is more like Left Bank Bordeaux and more likely to be blended with Merlot and Cabernet Franc. Alcohol levels can still be high but the fruit is less likely to be stewed. Fresh green pepper replaces eucalyptus, tannins are firmer, and the use of French oak is much more likely.

USA, California, Napa Valley

Napa is comparatively hot and sunny, leading to wines with a darker colour, fuller body, higher alcohol, and lower acidity than their French counterparts. The fashion is for highly concentrated, full-bodied wines with significant French or American oak influence. Inspired by Left Bank Bordeaux, Napa Cabernet Sauvignon aims at structure and elegance. It is typically deep in colour with a flavour profile of concentrated ripe or jammy dark berry fruit overlaid by a fresh greenness often manifest as menthol. Merlot can contribute plum and milk chocolate notes, Cabernet Franc flint and herbal notes, and Petit Verdot floral notes. Alcohol can be very high, but, even so, need not be out of balance.

Chile, Central Valley or Aconcagua

Chilean Cabernet Sauvignon is deep purple with aromas of fresh cassis and, often, a signature smoky, herbaceous note. Top examples are aged in French oak, adding notes of cedar, vanilla, and toast. Cool nights result in crisp acidity, and warm days in high alcohol and riper, softer tannins than Bordeaux.

South Africa, Western Cape, e.g. Stellenbosch

South African Cabernet Sauvignon can be made as a varietal wine, or blended with other Bordeaux grape varieties, or blended with Pinotage and other Bordeaux grape varieties. Compared to Bordeaux, the wines are deeper in colour, fuller in body, softer in acidity, and with riper or jammier fruit flavours. On the nose and palate, there are intense notes of black-currant, some of the green capsicum character of Bordeaux, and a certain earthy or smoky character particular to South Africa. French oak is commonly used.

Merlot

France, Bordeaux, Right Bank, Pomerol

This Merlot blend is deep ruby in colour with notes of fresh black and red fruit, especially plums, spice, truffles, and vanilla from new French oak. On the palate, it is rich, often opulent, with less acidity and softer tannins than Left Bank Bordeaux. Alcohol ranges from medium to high in hotter years. Compared to Pomerol, Saint-Emilion is drier and more tannic and less obviously from the Right Bank.

Chile, Central Valley

Compared to Merlot-dominated Bordeaux blends, Chilean Merlot is deeper in colour with notes of ripe plum, cherry, currants, chocolate, and mint (the latter note similar to the herbaceous quality in Chilean Cabernet Sauvignon and Carménère). On the palate, it is full-bodied with high alcohol, balanced acidity, and soft and silky tannins that are however not without grip.

Malbec

France, Southwest France, Cahors

Cahors can be reminiscent of Bordeaux, but is darker in colour with more plum, chocolate, and minerals and heavier tannins that can make it austere and unapproachable in its youth. With age, it develops aromas of earth, forest floor, and animal. Acidity is high and body and alcohol only medium. The best examples are aged in oak.

Argentina, Mendoza

Argentine Malbec is very deep in colour, perhaps even inky black. All Malbec is characterized by a plummy fruit profile; however, whereas Malbec from Cahors tends to earthy mineral notes of ink and iron, that from Argentina is generally riper (almost jammy) with spicy notes of cinnamon and nutmeg. On the palate, the wine is full-bodied with soft, velvety tannins, high alcohol, and, in many cases, moderate or low acidity. French oak ageing is common, contributing notes of vanilla, coffee, and chocolate.

Carménère

Chile, Rapel Valley, Colchagua

The best examples of Chilean Carmenère are deep ruby in colour with notes of cherry, blueberry, spice, black pepper, bell pepper, and tobacco. On the palate, acidity is low, alcohol high, and tannins soft and silky. Cabernet Sauvignon is often co-opted for extra acidity and tannin structure, and field blends with Merlot are still common.

Syrah/Shiraz

France, Northern Rhône, Hermitage

Hermitage is dark, full-bodied, and tannic, with intense aromas of soft black fruits accompanied by red fruits, smoke, black pepper and spice, leather, cocoa, and coffee. After about ten years, the wine develops a certain sweetness of fruit and gamey complexity. Significant new oak ageing is more the exception than the rule. Hermitage and other Rhône reds are often confused with Bordeaux, which tends to be higher in acidity with drier and grippier tannins and green or leafy Cabernet notes. Other appellations in the Northern Rhône can be difficult to distinguish from Hermitage and one another. Crozes-Hermitage, though similar to Hermitage, is typically softer and fruitier. Saint-Joseph is lighter than Hermitage and dominated by notes of black fruit and pepper. Traditional Cornas is fuller and richer than Crozes-Hermitage or Saint-Joseph, but more rustic than Hermitage. Cornas can be made in the traditional style or a fresher, more fruit-forward style. Côte-Rôtie marries power and finesse, with a complex nose of raspberry, blueberry, blackberry, plum, bacon, green olives, violets, and leather.

Australia, South Australia, Barossa or McLaren Vale

Barossa Shiraz is very dark in colour. On the nose, it typically exudes jammy or stewed black fruit, milk chocolate, sweet spice, black pepper, and eucalyptus. On the palate, it is high in alcohol with soft acidity and velvety tannins. The use of new American oak is traditional but there are also trends towards new French oak and old oak. Compared to Barossa Shiraz, McLaren Vale Shiraz is just as powerful, with a flavour profile of dark chocolate and spice that is more savoury than sweet.

Australia, New South Wales, Hunter Valley

Compared to McLaren Vale Shiraz, Hunter Valley Shiraz is still more savoury, with notes of jammy (but not stewed) black fruit, cured meat, black pepper, and liquorice. Alcohol is often lower, acidity higher, and tannins more marked and gripping.

South Africa, Western Cape

South African Shiraz is typically rich and ripe, with a sweetness of fruit reminiscent of Barossa Shiraz. Compared to their Australian counterparts, the wines are often smokier, with savoury notes of game, leather, and tar: like Northern Rhône, but 'supercharged'. Both French oak and American oak are commonly used. Owing to higher alcohol and lower acidity, South African Shiraz is not as long-lived as Syrah from the Northern Rhône. It is often blended with Cabernet Sauvignon or Pinotage. Rhône blends with Grenache and Mourvèdre are increasingly common, as are cool climate expressions from areas such as Walker Bay.

Grenache

France, Southern Rhône, Châteauneuf-du-Pape or Gigondas

Red Châteauneuf-du-Pape is typically Grenache blended with other grape varieties, most commonly Syrah, Mourvèdre, and Cinsault. It is medium-to-deep ruby in colour, with notes of red and black fruit, game, tar, leather, and garrigue. On the palate, it is rich and spicy, with dusty or powdery tannins and a higher alcohol and lower acidity than Bordeaux and Northern Rhône. Significant new oak ageing is more the exception than the rule. Red Châteauneuf-du-Pape is rather tight in its youth but softens and opens up after about seven years. Gigondas is a Grenache blend that is typically rich and powerful, and more rustic and animally than Châteauneuf-du-Pape. If Gigondas can be thought of as junior Châteauneuf-du-Pape, then neighbouring Vacqueyras can be thought of as junior Gigondas. Vacqueyras often contains less Grenache than Gigondas.

Spain, Catalonia, Priorat

Priorat is very dark in colour with an intense aroma of ripe but savoury black and red fruits, minerals, earth, spice, liquorice, chocolate, and, in some cases, vanilla from new French oak. On the palate, it is full-bodied with high alcohol, crisp acidity, big and chewy tannins, and a long, dry, and structured finish.

Australia, South Australia, Barossa or McLaren Vale

Grenache thrives in the heat of South Australia, yielding varietal wines with notes of strawberry jam and ginger or white pepper, very high alcohol, and powdery, mouth-coating tannins. However, in most cases it is blended with Shiraz and Mourvèdre to produce full-bodied wines not unlike their inspirations in the Southern Rhône, with notes of ripe strawberry and plum fruit, game, pepper, cloves, liquorice, and herbs.

Mourvèdre

France, Provence, Bandol

Red Bandol consists of at least 50% Mourvèdre, usually completed by Grenache and Cinsault. The wine is dark in colour with notes of black fruit, vanilla, spice, liquorice, leather, and red meat. On the palate, it is full-bodied, intense, and structured, with a high alcohol in the order of 14-15%. It is aged in old oak for at least 18 months prior to release.

Dolcetto

Italy, Piedmont, Dolcetto d'Alba

Dolcetto is deep ruby to purple in colour. It is soft, fruity, and uncomplicated, with notes of black cherry, soft spice, and liquorice, moderate acidity, high alcohol, and a characteristic dry, bitter almond finish. It is often thought of as Italy's best answer to Beaujolais.

Barbera

Italy, Piedmont, Barbera d'Asti

Barbera ranges in style from light and delicate to heavy and powerful. It is typically deep ruby in colour with an intense and mouth-filling fruitiness (often dominated by black cherries), very high acidity, low tannins, and a dry finish. Some modern examples are aged in oak, which imparts tannins and notes of vanilla and spice.

Nebbiolo

Italy, Piedmont, Barolo

Although full-bodied, Barolo is light in colour, typically with a brick or rust red tinge that can make it seem older, sometimes much older, than it really is. The nose is potentially very complex and often shorthanded as 'tar and roses'. Other notes include damsons, mulberries, dried fruit, violets, herbs, dark chocolate, liquorice, and, with increasing age, leather, camphor, tobacco, forest floor, mushrooms, and truffles. The palate is marked by high acidity and alcohol, and, above all, very high tannins, which, in the best of cases, are experienced as a silky or velvety texture. There is also a more modern, earlier drinking style of Barolo that is fruitier and less austere, often with obvious new French oak influence.

Italy, Piedmont, Barbaresco

Barbaresco is similar to Barolo, if often more feminine, that is, more aromatic, elegant, and refined, with softer fruit and suppler, riper tannins. Although tight and tannic in its youth, it requires less cellaring time and is less long-lived.

Corvina

Italy, Veneto, Amarone della Valpolicella

Amarone is deep ruby in colour. The wine is rich, full-bodied, and concentrated with high alcohol, crisp acidity, velvety tannins, and a long, bitter finish. Its complex flavour profile is often compared to that of Port, with notes of raisins, stewed cherries, dark chocolate, and liquorice. If matured in oak, there are accents of vanilla and spice. A more modern style of Amarone is also made, lighter and purer in fruit. Other styles of Valpolicella include Classico, Ripasso, and Recioto.

Sangiovese

Italy, Tuscany, Chianti Classico

Chianti is typically medium ruby in colour with notes of cherries, strawberries, raspberries, plums, soft spice, and herbs—and, with increasing age, tea leaves, tobacco, and leather. Top examples may display additional notes of French oak. On the palate, body is medium, acidity high, alcohol medium to high, and tannins firm. The finish is agreeably dry and accompanied by a note of bitter almonds.

Italy, Tuscany, Brunello di Montalcino

Compared to Chianti, Brunello is darker and richer, more full-bodied, tannic, and alcoholic, and also more complex.

Tempranillo

Spain, Rioja

Rioja is often pale in colour, brick red or garnet with a bronzing rim. On the nose, it is dusty with notes of cooked strawberries and raspberries, tobacco leaf, game, nuts, leather, soft spice, and vanilla and coconut from American oak. On the palate, body is medium, acidity is medium to low, alcohol is medium, and tannins are ripe and silky. Compared to traditional Rioja, international style Rioja generally spends less time in oak and is denser in colour and fruit, with more plum and blackberry.

Spain, Ribera del Duero or Toro

The Tempranillo of Ribera del Duero has thicker, darker skins than that of Rioja, and is also higher in acidity. Compared to most Rioja, the wines are dark and brooding: more full-bodied, concentrated, alcoholic, and tannic, and dominated by black fruits and plums rather than red fruits. Toro is similar in style to Ribera del Duero, but more exuberant and (often) more rustic, with a signature spicy note.

Spain, Navarra

Navarra is often similar to Rioja, if perhaps more New World in style, with a deeper colour, darker blackberry fruit from the use of international grape varieties such as Cabernet Sauvignon and Merlot and, in many cases, French rather than American oak.

Zweigelt

Austria, e.g. Burgenland, Neusiedlersee

Zweigelt is fresh and fruit-driven. It is often deep ruby in colour, with notes of red cherries and soft spice such as cinnamon and nutmeg. On the palate, it is light-to-medium bodied with a supple acidity reminiscent of Barbera, medium alcohol, and soft and subtle tannins. Oak is usually absent.

Blaufränkish

Austria, e.g. Burgenland, Mittelburgenland

Blaufränkish is usually dark purple in colour with notes of red currants or cherries, blackberry, pepper and spice, and liquorice. On the palate, body is medium, acidity high, alcohol medium, and tannins firm and grippy. New French oak may be evident in some examples.

Pinotage

South Africa, Western Cape, e.g. Paarl

Pinotage is deep ruby in colour. The best examples bring out the grape variety's character and complexity, with remarkable notes of banana, coffee bean, clove, and boiled sweet emerging with increasing bottle age. Pinotage has a tendency to retain volatile esters during vinification, which can result in unpleasant paint-like aromas. Critics often deride it as pungent and alcoholic with coarse tannins. However, the pungency and coarse tannins can be tamed by skillful winemaking.

Zinfandel

USA, California, Sonoma

Zinfandel is deep ruby in colour with notes of strawberries or rich brambly fruit, fresh cream, black tea, thyme or other herbs, and, sometimes, coconut from new American oak. On the palate, it is full-bodied with high alcohol, moderate acidity, and heavy, fairly coarse tannins. At its best, it is lengthy with a mineral core and savoury finish. Early-harvested or cool-climate examples are paler and tend to herbal green notes and angular tannins. Zinfandel is a clonal variation of Primitivo from Puglia in Italy. Compared to Zinfandel, Primitivo typically exhibits a more savoury, dried-fruit profile with, on the palate, a drier entry and more notable tannins.

Blind Tasting Crib Sheets: White Wines

Riesling

Germany, Mosel

Riesling is invariably high in acidity and unoaked. Mosel Riesling is pale in colour, sometimes with a touch of effervescence. On the nose, it is intensely fragrant, more floral than fruity with notes of stony rainwater and sherbet. On the palate, it is filigree and delicate, with a mineral or salty finish. Alcohol is very low and acidity very high, but balanced by sugar and extract. Sweeter examples may be botrytized. Rieslings from the Saar and Ruwer valleys are steelier than those from the Middle Mosel.

Germany, Rheingau

Compared to Riesling from the Middle Mosel, Riesling from the Rheingau is more masculine: deeper in colour with a firmer structure and texture, riper fruit, and higher alcohol. It is commonly made in an austere, completely dry style.

France, Alsace

Alsatian Riesling tends to be drier, richer, and higher in alcohol than Riesling from across the Rhine. It is often steely and inexpressive in its youth, with aromas of mineral, apple, citrus fruits, stone fruits, jasmine, and honey. With age, it develops a complex bouquet dominated by pure fruit flavours and appealing petrol or kerosene notes, typically with a long, dry finish that rides home on a backbone of high acidity.

Austria, Wachau or Kremstal or Kamptal

Like Alsatian Riesling, which it resembles most closely, Austrian Riesling is dry with high acidity, medium-to-high alcohol, and pronounced minerality. However, it is typically less austere and dominated by riper stone fruit. 'Hints of lime' is another common tasting note. Riesling from Kremstal and Kamptal is often fuller than that from Wachau.

Australia, South Australia, Clare Valley or Eden Valley

Riesling from Clare Valley or Eden Valley is pale lemon and lime green in colour. Spritz in the glass is evidence of fermentation in stainless steel, which is commonly practised in Australia. The wines are marked by mineral austerity and high acidity, but unlike, say, Rheingau Riesling, their fruit profile leans very strongly towards lime, whether this be, depending on ripeness, lime zest, fresh lime juice, or lime cordial. Some examples exhibit a mineral pungency derided by critics as 'fly spray'. The best wines are complex enough to overlay the 'limeyness' with floral, appley, and waxy notes, and are further distinguished by a certain talcum or chalky texture from lees ageing and a long, dry, acidic finish. Riesling from Clare Valley is generally considered to be drier and leaner than that from Eden Valley, although the two styles are difficult to tell apart.

New Zealand, e.g. South Island, Nelson

When it comes to Riesling, New Zealand looks more to Europe than to Australia, with generally lighter and more delicate styles. The wines are typically crisp and clean with a fresh lime character, as opposed to the pungent lime cordial note of many Australian Rieslings. There are however a range of styles, including delicate, Mosel-like styles and late harvest dessert styles. The climate preserves Riesling's natural searing acidity. With some age, the best examples can develop appealing petrochemical notes.

Gewurztraminer

France, Alsace

Alsatian Gewurztraminer is gold in colour, sometimes with a pink tinge. The nose is intense, with notes of spice, rose petals, lychee, grapefruit, peach kernel, and smoky bacon. On the palate, it is opulent with high alcohol, but, especially in hot vintages, can be flabby and lacking in acidity. It ranges in sweetness from dry to sweet and is never oaked.

Pinot Gris/Pinot Grigio

France, Alsace

Alsatian Pinot Gris is deep lemon in colour, often with a pink tinge. The nose is fairly aromatic, with notes of spice and pear or stone fruit, hints of honey and smoke, and a certain earthy minerality. The palate combines the spiciness and alcohol of Gewurztraminer with some of the structure and acidity of Riesling. The wines often have a distinct oily texture. Sweetness ranges from dry to sweet.

Italy, Friuli-Venezia-Giulia

Compared to Pinot Gris, Pinot Grigio is lighter in colour with less ripe fruit on the nose. On the palate, it is leaner with a tighter structure and higher acidity. It is invariably dry and unoaked, with notes of pear, citrus fruits, white fruits, and flowers, and, often, a mineral finish.

New Zealand, South Island

New Zealand Pinot Gris is much closer to Alsatian Pinot Gris than to Italian Pinot Grigio. It is usually dry or off-dry with notes of fresh pear, apple, honeysuckle, and white pepper. The palate bears the oiliness of an Alsatian Pinot Gris, although often with leaner acidity. There may also be suggestions of lees stirring or barrel ageing.

Melon de Bourgogne

France, Loire, Muscadet

Muscadet is pale, sometimes almost watery, in colour with a slight effervescence that can prickle on the tongue. On the nose, the wine is distinctly unaromatic. On the palate, it is dry and light-bodied with high acidity and a touch of minerality or saltiness. Lees ageing contributes yeasty or nutty aromas and a rounder texture.

Chenin Blanc

France, Loire, Vouvray or Coteaux du Layon

Vouvray is made in a range of styles. In the sweeter styles, the high acidity may be masked by sugar. With increasing age, aromas of green apples, quince, and acacia blossom surrender to complex tertiary aromas dominated by honeysuckle, figs, and lanolin. Botrytis is less common than with Coteaux du Layon, which tends to be fuller in body, sweeter, and lower in acidity. Compared to Sauternes, which is typically associated with peach and honey, the sweet wines of the Loire are more often associated with apple, apricot, and quince, together with a much higher natural acidity and rather less sugar and alcohol.

France, Loire, Savennières

Savennières is golden in colour with intense and concentrated notes of apple, chamomile, warm straw, and beeswax. On the palate, it is dry and unoaked with high acidity and alcohol and a long mineral finish. Compared to dry Vouvray, it is more austere with a fuller body and higher alcohol.

South Africa, Western Cape, e.g. Stellenbosch

A lot of South African Chenin is rather generic, but some producers focus on quality expressions similar to those from the Loire, including rich, bone dry wines reminiscent of Savennières and sweet, botrytized wines reminiscent of Coteaux-du-Layon. Owing to the warmer climate, the emphasis is more on tropical fruits than on apples. Classic notes of honey and nuts can come through in the best examples, but the musty lanolin or 'wet dog' character typical of the Loire is mostly absent. In general, acidity, although still high, is lower, and, conversely, alcohol is higher.

Sauvignon Blanc

France, Loire, Sancerre or Pouilly-Fumé

Sancerre is pale lemon in colour, possibly with a green tinge. Notes of gooseberry and grapefruit are typically accompanied by hints of

blackcurrant leaf, nettles, cut grass, and smoke. The nose is sometimes encapsulated as 'cat's pee on a gooseberry bush'. The wines are
dry, high in acidity, and unoaked, with a mineral finish. In practice, it
is very difficult to distinguish Sancerre from Pouilly-Fumé, although
the latter does tend to be smokier. Compared to, say, Marlborough
Sauvignon Blanc, Sancerre and Pouilly-Fumé are less fruit-driven
with a cooler fruit profile and greater smokiness and minerality.

France, Bordeaux, Graves

White Graves combines the opulence of Sémillon with the verve of
Sauvignon Blanc. The wine can be complex with intense aromas of
citrus fruit, peach, acacia, beeswax, and hazelnut. On the palate, it is
medium in body, acidity, and alcohol, and often oaked. Compared to
Loire Sauvignon Blanc, Sauvignon Blanc from Bordeaux is generally
more expressive of tropical fruits and less so of grass and minerals.

New Zealand, South Island, Marlborough

Compared to Sauvignon Blanc from the Loire, Sauvignon Blanc from
New Zealand is typically riper, higher in alcohol, and less chalky or
mineral. It has a clean, pungent aroma with notes of gooseberry, passion
fruit, asparagus, fresh grass, and blackcurrant leaf. Acidity is high but
somewhat disguised by a smooth texture and, often, a touch of residual sugar that contributes roundness rather than sweetness. The finest
examples can boast a more 'serious' austerity, and, as in Bordeaux, may
be fermented and matured in oak. Sauvignon Blanc from the North
Island is often lighter in style and driven more by tropical fruit.

South Africa, Western Cape, e.g. Walker Bay

If Marlborough Sauvignon Blanc is ripe and punchy and Loire
Sauvignon Blanc is light and lean, then South African Sauvignon Blanc
falls somewhere in between. While the gooseberry and nettle is unmistakeable, the wine is less overt than Marlborough and fuller in body
than Loire. Quality examples with complexity and minerality hail from
cooler regions, in particular Walker Bay, Cape Agulhas, and Cape
Point. Oaked Sauvignon Blanc, so-called Fumé Blanc or Blanc Fumé,
is produced throughout South Africa.

Chile, Aconcagua

Most Chilean Sauvignon Blanc is vinified in stainless steel. It neither matches New Zealand Sauvignon Blanc for punchiness nor Sancerre for restraint, but is instead distinguished by grapefruit and a nettle or smoky herbal note. Wines from warmer sites are often dominated by tropical fruit aromas and can be rather flabby.

USA, California

Californian Sauvignon Blanc is high in alcohol with medium to low acidity. Tropical fruits such as guava, mango, and pineapple overlie the nettle and gooseberry character of Sauvignon Blanc. The oaked 'Fumé Blanc' style is very popular.

Sémillon

France, Bordeaux, Graves

See above.

France, Bordeaux, Sauternes or Barsac

Sauternes is intense, complex, and long, with notes of apricot, peach, passion fruit, orange marmalade, honey, honeysuckle, acacia, hazelnut, and vanilla. In time, the colour transmutes from golden to amber and copper, with notes such as old books, caramel, and crème brulée not uncommon. On the palate, crisp acidity balances the intense sweetness, rich creaminess, and high alcohol. Barsac is difficult to distinguish from Sauternes but is often drier and lighter in body with higher acidity. Note that Sauternes and Barsac are blends of mostly Sémillon with Sauvignon Blanc and sometimes Muscadelle.

Australia, New South Wales, Hunter Valley

The Hunter Valley produces a unique style of Semillon that is very pale in colour with vaguely floral, citrus, fennel, and fresh grass notes, high acidity, and low alcohol. The wines are dry and often quite textural on the palate and the best examples are extraordinarily lengthy. Though austere and flinty in their youth, with age they develop a complex bouquet of toast, nuts, beeswax, and tarragon. Owing to this toast, aged Hunter Valley Semillon can seem to have been oaked, but this is almost never the case.

Australia, South Australia, Barossa

Semillon from the Barossa is entirely different from that from the Hunter Valley. The hot climate favours the development of rich wines with low acidity, medium-to-high alcohol, and notes of peach jam, mangoes, and coconut or vanilla from new, often American, oak.

Australia, Western Australia, Margaret River

In Margaret River, Semillon is typically blended with Sauvignon Blanc and aged in new French oak. The wines are full-bodied with medium-to-high alcohol, crisp acidity, and intense flavours of peaches and honey from the Semillon and herbs and gooseberry from the Sauvignon Blanc. Compared to Graves, they are made in a much 'cleaner' style with more intense, finely etched flavours, and may also be fuller in body and higher in alcohol.

Chardonnay

France, Burgundy, Chablis

Chablis is pale lemon in colour with or without a greenish tinge. On the nose, there are green apples, citrus fruits, honeysuckle, cream, and a characteristic stony or smoky minerality. The palate is lean, dry, and austere with pronounced acidity, which is a key distinguishing feature. New oak is usually absent. Top examples are weightier and can be difficult to distinguish from their counterparts in Beaune.

France, Burgundy, Beaune

Beaune is lemon in colour with a nose dominated by ripe apples and citrus fruit. French oak is common, contributing notes of butter, toast, and vanilla. On the palate, the wine is full-bodied, with crisp acidity and medium-to-high alcohol. It is potentially very intense, complex, and lengthy, evolving notes such as minerals, spice, tropical fruits, lemon tart, and toffee. Puligny-Montrachet is tight and structured, and can be difficult to distinguish from Chassagne-Montrachet, which is often nuttier. In contrast, Meursault is broad and buttery and rather extravagant, although some producers favour leaner styles.

France, Burgundy, Mâcon

As with Chablis, much Mâcon is unoaked. However, Mâcon is much less acidic than Chablis. Compared to Beaune and especially to Chablis, it is deeper in colour, with riper aromas and a fuller and softer or richer body. The Pouilly wines, which are often oaked, tend to be richer and riper on the one hand, and finer and more complex on the other

Australia e.g. New South Wales, Hunter Valley

Australian Chardonnay is often made in a very clean style. Oak, when used, can seem almost clinical in its application. Wines from cooler regions are likely to reveal citrus, fresh apple, and floral aromas, often with ripe stone fruit on the palate, whereas wines from warmer regions tend to be dominated by notes of fig, melon, and tropical fruit. Australian Chardonnay tends to lack the yoghurt or 'dairy' note often found in New Zealand expressions. Less ambitious wines may betray added tartaric acid or the crude use of oak staves or chips. Overall, the best sites for Chardonnay are in the Hunter Valley, the regions around Port Phillip Bay, Tasmania, Adelaide Hills, and Margaret River.

New Zealand, e.g. South Island, Marlborough

New Zealand Chardonnays typically exhibit ripe (although not tropical) fruit and high acidity. Typical notes are ripe apple and stone fruit, sometimes accompanied by a distinct yoghurt note. The finest examples betray Burgundian winemaking techniques, especially oak ageing, with American oak less common than it used to be. Chardonnay from the North Island is often riper, but it is hard to generalize.

USA, California, Napa Valley

Napa is comparatively hot and sunny leading to a darker colour, fuller body, higher alcohol, and lower acidity compared to French counterparts. The fashion is for highly concentrated, glossy wines with significant French or American oak influence. Napa Chardonnay typically exhibits notes of baked apple and tropical fruits with butter, toast, or coconut from oak ageing. Cool climate Chardonnay reminiscent of Chablis is made in certain sites in Sonoma, Mendocino, and Monterey.

Chile, e.g. Coquimbo, Limarí

The cool climate expression of Chardonnay from Limarí, Casablanca, and San Antonio (especially Leyda) is fast becoming Chile's signature style of Chardonnay. The wines are lean, restrained, and elegant with notes of both citrus and tropical fruits. Ambitious producers employ Burgundian techniques, with the current fashion being for less overt oak. The best examples, while not on par with top flight Burgundy, are often hard to distinguish from well-made Mâcon. However, the bulk of Chilean Chardonnay comes from warmer sites in the Central Valley, and is marked by lower acidity, higher alcohol, and more overt tropical fruit.

Viognier

France, Northern Rhône, Condrieu or Château-Grillet

Condrieu is golden in colour. It is characterized by a full, almost oily, body and high alcohol balanced by an intense perfume of peach blossom, apricots, white flowers, and violets. Although dry, the richness and high alcohol can produce an impression of sweetness. Acidity is not as high as for Chardonnay and can be distinctly low. Many examples remain unoaked. Château-Grillet is more Burgundian than Condrieu: drier, lighter, more delicate, less perfumed, and oaked.

Petit Manseng

France, Southwest France, Jurançon

Jurançon is golden in colour, often with a greenish tinge. The nose delivers tropical fruits such as mango, pineapple, and guava together with flowers and sweet spice, and perhaps even beeswax, banana, and coconut. Acidity is high but sweetness can vary quite considerably depending on vintage conditions and time of harvest. Sweet Jurançon is more akin to Vouvray than to nearby Sauternes, both in terms of acid structure and aroma profile. Dry Jurançon is often mistaken for New World Sauvignon Blanc, although Petit Manseng is less herbaceous than Sauvignon Blanc.

Albariño

Spain, Galicia, Rías Baixas

Albariño is pale to medium in colour with hints of gold and green. On the nose, it is aromatic, with notes of white peach, apricot, almonds, honeysuckle, and jasmine. On the palate, it is medium in body with high citrusy acidity, medium alcohol, and a dry or pithy mineral finish. Oak is usually absent. Compared to Riesling, it is fuller in body and lacks the tartness and petrol or fusel oil notes; compared to Pinot Gris, it is drier and higher in acidity; compared to Viognier, it is lighter in body and much higher in acidity; and compared to Grüner Veltliner, it is less acidic and austere and lacks the white pepper note.

Garganega

Italy, Veneto, Soave Classico

Quality Soave is typically straw in colour, with notes of citrus fruits and almonds and hints of flowers and spice, a body ranging from light to fairly full, crisp acidity, medium alcohol, no or little residual sugar, and a mineral or creamy finish with a slightly bitter edge. The best examples can be quite long and complex. Oak is usually absent.

Grüner Veltliner

Austria, Wachau or Kremstal or Kamptal

Grüner Veltliner from Wachau is often pale gold with hints of green. It is typically dry with notes of celery, white pepper, spice, and minerals.

Depending on ripeness, fruit can range across the spectrum from apple and grapefruit to distinctly tropical fruit. Body is medium to full, acidity is high, alcohol is medium-high or high, body is medium to full, and oak is absent. The best examples can develop honeyed and toasty aromas with age. Grüner Veltiner from Kremstal and Kamptal is often fuller than that from Wachau.

Furmint

Hungary, Tokaj-Hegyalja

Compared to Sauternes, with which it is often confused, Tokaji Aszú is a darker, copper colour with higher acidity and notes of apricot, orange zest, barley sugar, spice, and tea.

Hungary, Tokaj-Hegyalja

Dry Furmint is lemony in colour, with notes of smoke, pear, and lime, together with hints of mandarin, apricot, honey, and spice. On the palate, it is light and crisp, with high acidity, medium-high or high alcohol, and a mineral backbone. The finish can be quite long.

Torrontés

Argentina, e.g. Salta

Torrontés is often pale gold in colour. On the nose, the wine presents a floral Muscat-like bouquet with notes of rose, jasmine, peach, and citrus fruits. On the palate, it is typically full-bodied and dry to off-dry depending on style. The best examples preserve a fresh acidity. Torrontés is sometimes confused with Muscat or Gewurztraminer, but is less grapey than Muscat and lacks the distinctive lychee note of Gewurztraminer. The palate is also less oily and more mineral.

Glossary Index of Key Terms and Concepts